The Last Pharaohs

Egypt Under the Ptolemies, 305–30 BC

J. G. Manning

PRINCETON UNIVERSITY PRESS

PRINCETON AND OXFORD

Copyright © 2010 by Princeton University Press
Published by Princeton University Press, 41 William Street,
Princeton, New Jersey 08540
In the United Kingdom: Princeton University Press, 6 Oxford Street,
Woodstock, Oxfordshire OX20 1TW

Library of Congress Cataloging-in-Publication Data

Manning, Joseph Gilbert.
The last pharaohs : Egypt under the Ptolemies, 305-30 BC / J.G. Manning.
    p.   cm.
Includes bibliographical references and index.
ISBN 978-0-691-14262-3 (hbk. : alk. Paper) 1. Ptolemaic dynasty,
305-30 B.C. 2. Pharaohs—History. 3. State, The—History. 4. Egypt—
Politics and government—332 B.C.-30 B.C. 5. Egypt—Economic conditions—
332 B.C.-640 A.D. I. Title.
DT92.M36 2009
932'.021—dc22   2009013223

British Library Cataloging-in-Publication Data is available

This book has been composed in Sabon

Printed on acid-free paper. ∞

press.princeton.edu

Printed in the United States of America

3   5   7   9   10   8   6   4   2

For Naomi

——————————————

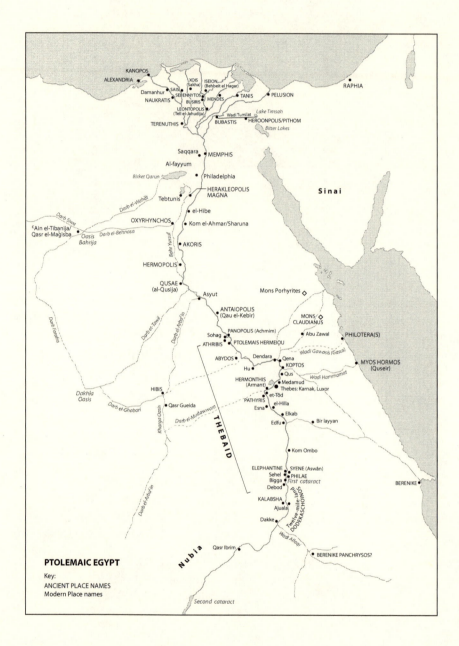

KANOPOS
ALEXANDRIA
Damanhur
SAIS XOIS ISEION
(Sakha) (Behbeit el Hagar)
SEBENNYTOS
NAUKRATIS BUSIRIS MENDES TANIS PELUSION
LEONTOPOLIS
(Tell el-Jahudija)
TERENUTHIS BUBASTIS HEROONPOLIS/PITHOM
Wadi Tumilat Lake Timsah
Bitter Lakes

RAPHIA

Saqqara MEMPHIS
Al-fayyum
Birket Qarun Philadelphia
HERAKLEOPOLIS
Darb el-Wahāt Tebtunis MAGNA

Sinai

el-Hibe
Darb el-Behnasa OXYRHYNCHOS Kom el-Ahmar/Sharuna
ʿAin el-Tibanija/
Qasr el-Maǧisba Oasis
Bahrija
Bahr Yussif AKORIS

Darb Farafra HERMOPOLIS

QUSAE
(al-Qusija) Asyut Mons Porhyrites

ANTAIOPOLIS
(Qau el-Kebir)
MONS
CLAUDIANUS
Darb et-Tawil PANOPOLIS (Achmim)
Sohag Abu Zawal PHILOTERA(S)
Darb el-Arbaʿin ATHRIBIS PTOLEMAIS HERMEIOU
ABYDOS Dendara Qena Wadi Gawasis (Gasus)
Hu KOPTOS MYOS HORMOS
Qus Wadi Hammamat (Quseir)
Dakhla HERMONTHIS Medamud
Oasis HIBIS (Armant) Thebes: Karnak, Luxor
Darb el-Ghabari Qasr Gueida et-Tōd
PATHYRIS el-Hilla
Kharga Oasis Esna Elkab
Darb el-Mudawwara
Edfu Bir Iayyan
THEBAID

Kom Ombo

ELEPHANTINE SYENE (Aswān)
Sehel PHILAE
Bigga First cataract
Debod
Darb el-Arbaʿin BERENIKE
KALABSHA
Ajuala
Nubia
Dakke DODEKASCHOINOS
Twelve-mile-land
Qasr Ibrim Wadi Allaqi
BERENIKE PANCHRYSOS?

Second cataract

PTOLEMAIC EGYPT

Key:
ANCIENT PLACE NAMES
Modern Place names

CONTENTS

ILLUSTRATIONS

PREFACE

THIS BOOK attempts to draw a picture of Ptolemaic state making. My interest in the topic began many years ago when I began trying to understand how we might connect the rich and fascinating documentary material from the period to larger historical issues. Ptolemaic Egypt has for more than a century had a strong presence in academia and elsewhere, but it has often been isolated from other fields of ancient history. That isolation stems from a variety of causes. Ironically, the richness of the source material from the period has been one of the strongest of these. Scholars naturally want to specialize, and the material from Ptolemaic Egypt creates opportunities for many specialties indeed. But in the process the proverbial forest is often lost for the trees. A second, perhaps more vexing reason for Ptolemaic Egypt's isolation from other scholarly fields is the prevailing understanding of Egypt as a place apart, so distinctive that its history has always followed a different course. According to this line of argument, Egypt has produced wonderful documents, but these can only be understood in Egypt's own terms and are useful only for explaining its own history.

On the other hand, Ptolemaic Egypt has always had Kleopatra, and Alexandria, and both have shone in recent years. Kleopatra, the last of the last pharaohs of Egypt, has been the subject of several recent biographies, and a spectacular exhibition of her life and times has been presented in London and in my hometown of Chicago (Walker and Higgs 2001).

As for Alexandria, the great city has been virtually resurrected before our eyes in the last decade. Given the nature of its setting, much of ancient Alexandria will probably remain lost to us forever. But in the last few years, some exciting finds, including the probable discovery of the remains of the great lighthouse itself, have made it possible to match literary descriptions to some parts of the actual Ptolemaic city. The work of two French-led teams in the harbor of Alexandria and its environs has been particularly fruitful. Since the 1990s there has, in fact, been an up tick in archaeological activity throughout Egypt, unlike the other areas of the Hellenistic world. This has been especially true of survey and excavation work in the Fayyum, but there have also been good results in the western and eastern deserts. Roger Bagnall's summary (2001) will provide the reader with an excellent overview of this activity and its important contributions to the understanding of Ptolemaic and Egyptian history in general.

Other areas of research have further enriched our picture of Ptolemaic Egypt. Major studies of Ptolemaic coinage have been published recently (Duyrat 2005; von Reden 2007), and new assessments of Ptolemaic royal portraiture (Ashton 2001; Stanwick 2002) have deepened our understanding of the Ptolemaic period in its longer term historical context, giving us "an Egyptological framework for understanding sculptures that have been predominantly viewed from a classicist perspective" (Stanwick 2002:4). Many of the Egyptian temples of the period, our richest source for understanding ritual and ceremony, have received attention, and an important research project in Germany is overseeing the publication of the Edfu temple corpus. This project has brought us face to face with the world of Egyptian religious thought, and given us in some sense a glimpse of "codified" Egyptian culture as it was being shaped under Ptolemaic rule.

New texts have been published, and demotic Egyptian research tools are beginning, finally, to come up to the high standards set by Greek papyrology. As a result non-specialists now have access to these texts, which offers us fascinating insights into everyday family life, and of the lowest levels of the Ptolemaic administration. Demotic papyrology has in many ways revolutionized our views of Ptolemaic society, and ongoing efforts, especially on bilingual material, such as the superb work of Willy Clarysse and Dorothy Thompson on the Ptolemaic census, will continue to force revisions and refinements in our understanding of the Ptolemaic state. It is an exciting time to be a Ptolemaic historian.

Studies on many aspects of the period continue to appear at breakneck speed. I have not had the opportunity to include all of them in this book. Pfeiffer (2008) and Eckstein (2008) offer important insights into the dynastic cult and into international politics. Both of these studies offer important new ideas that shape our views of the Ptolemaic state, and I have as yet not been able to take full account of them.

Over the past five years I have presented papers in Berkeley, Copenhagen, Stanford, Tokyo, Philadelphia, New Haven, and Paris. The outcome of discussions stemming from these conferences is the basis of this book. I am particularly grateful to Zosia Archibald, Gene Cruz-Uribe, Vincent Gabrielsen, Peter Bang, John Davies, Todd Hickey, Graham Oliver, Bert Van der Spek, Walter Scheidel, Ian Morris, Christophe Chamley, Yoshiyuki Suto, Sugihiko Uchida, François Velde, Joachim Vogt, Josh Ober, Avner Greif, and Steve Haber who offered a good deal of conversation at these meetings, and elsewhere. They have helped to refine my very rough ideas. An earlier version of the section on coinage in chapter five appeared as "Coinage as 'code' in Ptolemaic Egypt" in *The Monetary Systems of the Greeks and Romans*, ed. William Harris (Oxford: Oxford

University Press, 2008), 84–111. I am grateful to Professor Harris for including my work in that volume.

I am fortunate beyond description in having a superb circle of colleagues, many of whom also happen to be my friends. I have received criticism, comments, offprints and suggestions from most of them. Among them, I want to mention Roger Bagnall, Peter Bedford, Bart van Beek, Alan Bowman, Willy Clarysse, Mark Depauw, Steve Haber, Todd Hickey, Jim Keenan, Tomek Markiewicz, Cary Martin, Peter Nadig, Dominic Rathbone, Peter Raulwing, Jane Rowlandson, Dorothy Thompson, Katelijn Vandorpe, Arthur Verhoogt, Terry Wilfong. I also thank Professor Rein Taagepera for, on a moment's notice, sending to me from Estonia a copy of one of his articles that I was having trouble locating. I am grateful to Steve Haber, Andrew Monson, Christelle Fischer, Cary Martin, and Uri Yiftach for reading parts of the manuscript, and for offering suggestions for improvement. Two readers for Princeton University Press offered many important suggestions for improvement and I am grateful to both of them. Great thanks are also due to Professor Todd Hickey and Mr. Geoffrey Metz, Curator of Egyptian antiquities, Uppsala University, for permission to publish the high-quality photographs of texts in this volume.

I take great pleasure in thanking Princeton University Press, especially Rob Tempio for his encouragement and assistance in the final production of the book.

I am thankful as well to other friends near and far. You know who you are. You have sustained me through broken bones, cross-country moves, dark nights of the soul, and other adventures.

This book could not have been completed without Naomi's love and support, and to her it is dedicated.

Guilford, Connecticut
October 2008

ABBREVIATIONS

Abbreviations of classical authors follow those of *The Oxford Classical Dictionary*, 3rd ed., ed. Simon Hornblower and Antony Spawforth (Oxford: Oxford University Press, 1996). For abbreviations of papyri and ostraca I follow John F. Oates, Roger S. Bagnall, Sarah J. Clackson, Alexandra A. O'Brien, Joshua D. Sosin, Terry G. Wilfong, and Klaas A. Worp, *Checklist of Greek, Latin, Demotic and Coptic Papyri, Ostraca and Tablets http://scriptorium.lib.duke.edu/papyrus/texts/clist.html*

AchHist	*Achaemenid History Workshop.* Leiden.
AfP	*Archiv für Papyrusforschung und Verwandte Gebiete*
AHR	*The American Historical Review*
AJA	*American Journal of Archaeology*
BASP	*Bulletin of the American Society of Papyrologists*
BIFAO	*Bulletin de l'Institut français d'archéologie orientale*
CAH	*The Cambridge Ancient History*
Chrest.	*Grundzüge und Chrestomathie der Papyruskunde.* Vol. 1, *Historische Band.* Part 2: *Chrestomathie.* U. Wilcken. Stuttgart: Teubner.
CdE	*Chronique d'Égypte*
CG	*Catalogue General du Musee du Caire*
CP	*Classical Philology*
CQ	*Classical Quarterly*
CRIPEL	*Cahiers de Recherches de l'Institut de Papyrologie et d'Égypt-ologie de Lille*
GM	*Göttinger Miszellen*
EVO	*Egitto e Vicino Oriente*
FGrH	*Die Fragment der griechischen Historiker.* Ed. F. Jacoby. Berlin, 1923–
JARCE	*Journal of the American Research Center in Egypt*
JEA	*Journal of Egyptian Archaeology*
JEH	*Journal of Egyptian History*
JESHO	*Journal of Economic and Social History of the Orient*
JHS	*Journal of Hellenic Studies*
JJP	*The Journal of Juristic Papyrology*
JNES	*Journal of Near Eastern Studies*
JRA	*Journal of Roman Archaeology*
JRS	*Journal of Roman Studies*

LÄ   *Lexikon der Ägyptologie*. Ed. Wolfgang Helck und
                Eberhard Otto. Wiesbaden: Harrassowitz.
MIFAO   *Mémoires publiés par les members de la mission
                archéologique française au Caire*
o   *Ostracon*
p   *Papyrus*
PLBat   *Papyrologica Lugduno-Batava*
RdE   *Revue d'Égyptologie*
s   Stela
SAK   *Studien zur Altägyptischen Kultur*
SAOC   *Studies in Ancient Oriental Civilizations*
SB   *Sammelbuch griechischer Urkunden aus
                Ägypten (1915–)*
SEG   *Supplementum Epigraphicum Graecum*. Leiden,
                Amsterdam.
Select papyri 2 *Select Papyri*. Vol. 2. *Public documents*. Ed.
                A. D. Hunt and C. C. Edgar. Loeb Classical Library,
                Cambridge: Harvard University.
TAPA   *Transactions of the American Philological
                Association*
Urk. II   *Urkunden des ägyptischen Altertums*, Vol. 2.
                K. Sethe, *Hieroglyphische Urkunden der
                griechisch-römischen Zeit*. Leipzig.
WZKM   *Wiener Zeitschrift für die Kunde des Morgenlandes*
YCS   *Yale Classical Studies*
ZÄS   *Zeitschrift für ägyptische sprache und
                altertumskunde*
ZPE   *Zeitschrift für Papyrologie und Epigraphik*
ZSS-RA   *Zeitschrift der Savigny-Stiftung für Rechtsgeschichte.
                Romanistische Abteilung*

The Last Pharaohs

INTRODUCTION

There is "no ruler without men, no men without wealth,
no wealth without prosperity and no prosperity
without justice and good administration."
—*King Ardashir I, cited in Morony (1984:28)*

THIS BOOK is concerned with Ptolemaic institutional reforms in the wake of Ptolemy's founding of Egypt's last ruling dynasty of ancient times, and with the relationship between the Ptolemaic kings and Egyptian society. We will examine the Ptolemies from an Egyptian perspective, with the aim of understanding how, by adopting a pharaonic mode of governance, they fit themselves into long-term Egyptian history, and how, in turn, they shaped Egyptian society and were shaped by it.

I make two claims in this book. First, the Ptolemaic state, far more institutionally heterogeneous than is usually assumed, was initially successful in establishing an equilibrium and in achieving its main aim, namely, revenue capture. This success came in spite of the severe environmental and institutional constraints that the state faced, as well as military threats from competitive regimes, mainly the Seleukids to their East (but there were others). Gradually but inevitably, the rise of aggressive Roman military power in the Mediterranean fundamentally altered the game and shifted the center of politics beginning around 200 BC.[1]

My second claim is that the Ptolemies governed their core territory by exercising power not over society, but rather *through* it. In making this claim I am following Barkey (1994) and Deng (1999) in examining the process of state centralization outside of the European experience, and I adopt Barkey's "bargained incorporation" model of the state centralization process. The state intervened in the internal economy in many ways, for example by monetizing the economy and by means of a closed currency system. But it is the nature of the political economy—the more limited power of the king to control production or the merchant class, and the pre-Ptolemaic institutional continuities—that suggests that a mixed,

---

[1] On states as equilibria, see Aoki (2001), taking a game-theoretic approach; Greif (2006); Deng (1999). For the Ptolemaic state as an equilibrium, see already Préaux (1971:350); (Bingen (1978a). On Roman expansion, see Eckstein (2008).

not a purely statist model is better for the understanding of the economic and legal structure of the state.

My orientation to the Ptolemaic period has been influenced by four trends in Ptolemaic history in the last thirty years. The first is the emphasis that has been placed on Egyptian culture during the Ptolemaic period. That emphasis helps us understand, on the diachronic level, the interplay between the long and short-term, and, on the synchronic level, helps us to see more clearly the society with which the early Ptolemaic kings were interacting. My second source of inspiration has been the work that has come out of a series of volumes and meetings concerned with the details of Persian administrative practices and the interaction of the Greek world with the Near East. The result of this scholarly activity has been to redraw Mediterranean cultural and chronological boundaries, and in some cases to eliminate them altogether. In a sense the many points of contact that existed between Greece and the Near East from the seventh to the third centuries BC have been restored.[2] Above all, Pierre Briant's work on the Persian Empire and on the transition to Hellenistic state formation has shown us the much important institutional continuity between the Persian Empire and its Hellenistic successors. One can also look to the seventh, not the late fourth, century BC for the beginning of Hellenism in Egypt, and that long history certainly shaped the early Ptolemaic state. My third influence has come from those scholars (Claire Préaux and Jean Bingen, among others) who have stressed the fourth century BC Athenian context of Ptolemaic fiscal institutions. Finally, but very important, I would mention the work, particularly in Leuven on bilingual archives, that has given us a picture of the socioeconomic interaction of Greek immigrants with Egyptians and other ethnic groups at the individual and family levels.

The Hellenistic period has often been described as Europe's first invasion of the Middle East, part of a larger process of Greek expansion into the eastern Mediterranean in the wake of the political struggles that followed Alexander the Great's conquest of the Persian Empire and his subsequent death. The impact of this expansion has usually been assessed from the perspective of Greece, and often from an implicitly ideological position that contrasts the evils of state control and central planning characteristic of closed, static, Asian, despotic states with the open, dynamic, Western ideal of a rational, democratic state.

---

[2] Within the vast literature, I would single out the series of volumes of the *Achaemenid History Workshop*, Leiden, and the work by Pierre Briant and Amélie Kuhrt, both of whom have well stressed the institutional continuities between the Persian Empire and the Hellenistic states. For fifth century Athenian-Persian contacts, see the important study by Miller (1997). See also the excellent observations of Davies (2001:13–14), with which I am in complete agreement. On the revolution in Seleukid studies driven by the local Babylonian documents, see Sherwin-White (1987).

But the political situation was more complicated. The Ptolemaic state, within its core territory, was neither an *Egyptian*, nor a *Greek* state.[3] Indeed, it combined the traditions of the Egyptian monarchy—the ancient agricultural system, political control through the division of the country into nomes, and the ancient temples and priesthoods—with Greek fiscal institutions that derive most immediately from the fourth century BC and from "proto-Hellenistic . . . exchange patterns"(Davies 2001:18). It was, to borrow from Runciman (1989:160), a "hybrid," that combined elements of pharaonic, Persian, Macedonian, and Greek practice, with new modes of production and taxation.[4]

That hybridity is now becoming increasingly clear in the archaeology of the capital Alexandria, where a good amount of pharaonic sculpture has been recovered in recent years. Whether this was moved from other sites or is of Ptolemaic date is secondary to the point that the Ptolemaic kings saw pharaonic imagery as an important part of the projection of their power and legitimacy.[5] Their adoption of pharaonic ideology, imagery, and behavior has long been known from the priestly decrees of the period, as well as from other sources. It makes little sense, then, to continue to make a distinction between "modernizing," rational, dynamic Greek institutions on one hand and despotic, irrational, passive Asian ones on the other.

Much of this dichotomy has carried over into modern views of Egypt from the observations of ancient Greeks like Herodotus, who drew contrasts between Greece and Egypt for particular political and social purposes, and later, from the Marxist dichotomy between an "Asiatic" and an "Antique mode of production."[6] Such stark dichotomies are no longer very productive; and in the case of Hellenistic state reformation, for example, we can now see that the institutional framework of the state was far more complex and built on historical connections and institutional compatibilities between "East" and "West." Ideology cannot be a substitute for institutional analysis or for economic history. What remains clear, on the other hand, is that the environment affected economic organization

[3] Cf. Préaux (1939:570): "L'Égypte lagide est grecque." Préaux did, however, acknowledge the real complexities of the Ptolemaic state (see the following note).

[4] Already noted by Préaux (1939:431: "multiplicité des inspirations"), although she concluded (570) that "L'Égypte lagide est grecque." A "hybrid state" is defined by Diamond (2002) as a state that combines aspects of democracy with authoritarian rule. For my purposes, I take the term to mean a state that combines institutional traditions.

[5] Some of this material is probably Roman, and there are debates about the dating of many objects, but it seems certain that at least some of the material is early Ptolemaic. See Yoyotte (1998); Bagnall (2001:229–30); Stanwick (2002:19).

[6] On Hecataeus' and Herodotus' views of Egypt, for example, see the important study by Moyer (2002).

in fundamental ways. In this respect, Egypt, with its ancient flood-recession agriculture, is quite unique.

The concept of "state" in the context of the Hellenistic world is not unproblematic, as Austin's (1986:456) apposite remarks make quite plain. It is certainly true that Hellenistic monarchies were "personal" dynastic regimes. But the reason why the Ptolemies adopted a pharaonic style of governance and many of the ancient institutions that went with it was precisely because this facilitated a claim of political legitimacy over Egyptian territory and was a means by which the new state could penetrate local society.

Ptolemaic governance, then, like the royal portraiture of the period, was a hybrid that combined Greek and Egyptian institutions in a way designed to allocate "free floating" (Eisenstadt 1993) resources in new directions, principally to fighting wars and other state-building activities.[7] The dynasty did not intend a change of course—indeed it went some way to stress continuity—it merely sought to control resources and to survive. There were other forces at work. In a very real sense, and for the first time, the term "globalization," complete with the world's first "big histories" (Diodorus Siculus), is apt (Chaniotis 2005:128). This was a violent, rapidly changing and sometimes dramatic period of Mediterranean history. Splinter states of the Persian Empire became locked in never ending competition, "non-stop border feuding" (Green 1990:188), and predatory behavior that eventually yielded to the one larger state in the west, Rome. The case of the Ptolemies presents the historian with an almost unique instance of political takeover, but also reveals the constraints states faced in development and structural reform.

An analysis of Ptolemaic state reformation and its impact also gives occasion to rethink the use of the terms "Hellenistic" and "hellenization." Both terms have often been ciphers for an historical period that was something less than Hellenic—Greek-like but not fully Greek. This hardly does justice to what was simply a wider world created by Alexander's conquest. That world became a fertile ground for the interaction of cultures and institutions. "Hellenization" was, indeed, a two-way process, involving not merely the spread of Greek culture to the "East," but also cultural and institutional adaptations that produced several kinds of responses, from acceptance to rejection, and many things in between.

Hellenistic history, in which Egypt played a major role, was not merely Greek, although Greek culture played a vital part of it. And it was not only Mediterranean, although it was that as well. Greek institutions, coin-

---

[7] For a new synthesis of the Ptolemaic army, its organization, and its impact on Egyptian society, see Fischer (2008).

age, banks, gymnasia, and language, became part of the state system, joined to the ancient monarchical ideology.

The formation of the Ptolemaic state, as Ma (2003) has recently suggested for the Seleukid empire, involved the careful use of local idiom, of language as well as of image. In the Ptolemaic case, the kings actively adopted ancient modes of governance of Egyptian society that were a part of the existing state system. The Hellenistic world was a culmination of past history, of a complex web of cultural and institutional interactions that produced a relatively unstable interlude between the larger, and more stable imperial frameworks of Persia and Rome.

My arguments in this book represent a synthesis of what is an increasingly dominant paradigm in Ptolemaic studies that attempts to strike a balance between Egyptian and Greek culture and institutions, and between state aims and historical experience. Allow me to give here one brief but well-known example that will illustrate the shift in scholarship. Kornemann (1925), saw two phases in the reign of Ptolemy I, the first from 323 BC to about 312 BC, when Ptolemy sought assimilation and a fusion of Greek and Egyptian cultures in order to consolidate political power in Egypt, and the second after 312 BC, when the court began to occupy the new imperial center in Alexandria. After the court moved to the new capital, the focus turned to creating "a Greco-Macedonian state apparatus for the exploitation of a subject population" (Murray 1970:141).[8]

The nature of the Ptolemaic state "apparatus" consisted of something more than an authoritarian, "Greco-Macedonian" military elite, although they were indeed important, and power relations were not unidirectional. This is clear in the documentation of the Ptolemaic bureaucracy, both at the village level and, higher up, in the picture of kingship projected by synodal decrees of the Egyptian priesthoods at the end of the third and the early second centuries BC. The attempt at establishing a social equilibrium involved continuous bargaining with several different ruling coalitions, including Egyptian priests and the scribal class, as I will describe in chapter 4. The move to Alexandria made the bargaining between the kings and the priesthoods, especially those at the ancient capital of Memphis, only the more important with respect to the kings' political position in Egypt.[9]

While the natural boundaries that traditionally defined Egyptian territory from the Delta to Aswan remained in place, the early Ptolemaic reclamation project in the Fayyum significantly altered the Egyptian landscape. This was a massive project, accomplished essentially by lowering the level

[8] His "nationalist" theories have long since been rejected. See already Westermann (1938).

[9] On the Memphis priesthoods, see Thompson (1988:106–54).

of the Lake of Moeris by radial canalization.[10] It resulted in new land that was settled by *kleruchs* (reservist soldiers given rights to land in exchange for a promise to serve in the army when needed) and others.[11] The organization of labor for the project shows the capacity of the Ptolemies to muster and control the rural workforce, and was both a manifestation of the king's ability to control nature and a statement of royal power. Direct government involvement in the project and the influx of kleruchs to the region resulted in a more homogeneous zone of Ptolemaic dominance. By the end of the reign of Ptolemy II, the region was renamed in honor of his sister/wife Arsinoë with its capital at Krocodilopolis.

SOURCES

There are two great modern cities in Egypt, Cairo and Alexandria. Both were established by foreign imperial regimes that held Egypt at the core of their empires. Cairo was founded by the Fatimids in the tenth century AD. This book tells the story of the second city, Alexandria, and of the Ptolemaic dynasty that ruled from that city over one of the great Hellenistic kingdoms. Each city in its own right may be described as a "monument to the dynasty and a theater for its dramatic representation in the eyes of world" (Brett 2001:334), and both were centers of trade connecting the Mediterranean and the Red Sea to wider trade networks. Sadly, though, very little evidence is left of the hustle and bustle that was Ptolemaic Alexandria.

The most striking historiographic feature of this period of Egyptian history is the large number of primary sources—papyri written in Greek and in demotic Egyptian, Greek and Egyptian (both demotic and hieroglyphic) inscriptions, and ostraca, mainly receipts. Taken together, these sources present us with the first well-documented state in history.[12]

The abundance of documentary material has itself, however, given rise to hermeneutic issues, among which is the difficulty in assessing continuity versus change from earlier periods of Egyptian history. Egypt, of course, had a long bureaucratic and documentary tradition even before the Ptolemaic period, but only fragments of this tradition have survived. We may assume basic continuity in administrative structures under Persian and Ptolemaic rule, but we have precious little in the way of documents to confirm this. (Although late fourth- and early third-century BC demotic

[10] Butzer (1976); Davoli (1998).

[11] Butzer (1976:36–38).

[12] On documentary papyri and historical interpretation, see Bagnall (1995); Bowman (2001); Manning (2003a:13–21).

documents do tend to confirm continuity in scribal practice.) Moreover, although there has been a good deal of new publication in the last twenty years, one additional caveat remains as pertinent as ever: despite the abundance of material, there are still considerable gaps in our knowledge about important places (the two Greek cities of Alexandria and Ptolemaïs, the Egyptian city of Thebes) and regions like Middle Egypt.[13] Needless to say, any broad general conclusions must remain tentative and fragile.

Although the sources, taken as a whole, present both macro- and micro-level views of the society, they tend to be biased toward the point of view of the state and its fiscal needs.[14] The papyri, however, can present us with the ruler's interests in sustaining power and taxing the countryside, but also with a view of individuals who, on the one hand, tended to avoid the state and, on the other, needed it for protection, for enforcement, and so on. Interpretation of the papyri, which up to now have been the main historical source for the period, have very much been "marked by the currents of their times" (Bagnall 2007:1).

Another interpretive problem lies in the nature of language. Ptolemaic documents were written in two languages: Greek, the language of the new administration, and demotic Egyptian, written in a cursive script that was in use from the middle of the seventh century BC until the second century AD.[15] Demotic texts were generally the work of local village scribes and tend to record economic and bureaucratic activity at a very local level. Greek, the language of state administration gradually penetrated local administration. At times it is not clear if certain phrases reflects Greek mentalities, or are translations of Egyptian ones. A famous illustration of the problem was provided by Eric Turner some years ago (1966). A Greek text presented the translator with the possibility that the death penalty was rather unusually imposed on a local official for a seemingly small offense.[16] That colored the understanding of Ptolemaic justice and the nature of the state. But Turner has pointed out that the translation of the Greek term by "hanging by the neck" did not quite capture the semantics, and in fact the Greek phrase was in all likelihood translating the normal, very ancient penalty for official malfeasance, namely, a public flogging.

One reason for the survival of many Ptolemaic documents is that they were discarded and subsequently reused in the process of mummification beginning late in the reign of Ptolemy I or early in the reign of Ptolemy

---

[13] Cf. Préaux (1978/1:358–59).

[14] Similar issues exist in early Chinese sources: Deng (1999:113). The historical debate between micro and macro determinants of history is, of course, an ongoing one (Sewell 2005).

[15] On the rise and decline of demotic Egyptian, see chapter 1, n. 14.

[16] pCair.Zen. II 59202 (254 BC).

II. It is not known exactly why this recycling began; it was perhaps connected to the state monopoly on papyrus, and it may have been a way for local records offices to make money by selling discarded texts to mummifiers. Whatever caused the recycling of documents (known as *cartonnage*), it allowed the preservation of local government records, and even on occasion copies of royal decrees, that might otherwise have been lost to us.[17] The papyri make the Ptolemaic economy the best documented of Hellenistic economies; it is finding both the correct framework and the right scale of analysis that is the major challenge in documentary papyrology.

THE PTOLEMAIC ECONOMY

Finley's influential *The Ancient Economy* excluded Near Eastern (including Egyptian) economies, arguing that they were organized differently from those of the classical world. In the former, the economy was centered around "large palace or temple complexes" which "virtually monopolized anything that can be called 'industrial production' as well as foreign trade . . . and organized the economic, military, political and religious life of the society through a single complicated, bureaucratic, record-keeping operation . . . ."[18] This form of economic organization, centralized and autocratic, was sufficiently different, indeed irrelevant, for Finley until Alexander the Great and the Roman Empire. "At this point," Finley continued, "we shall have to look more closely at this kind of Near Eastern society."

Yet Finley also excluded Hellenistic economies because they did not, to his mind, represent a type of ancient economy different from the Near Eastern model.[19] In terms of historic periodization he was quite right to do so; dividing ancient history into "Archaic," "Classical," and "Hellenistic" is, for economic history, not of much value. But for Finley the point was that "the fundamental social and economic system was not changed by the Macedonian conquerors, or by the Greek migrants who followed behind them" (1999:183).

For Finley, then, Ptolemaic economy was "oriental Greek economy," and neither the Macedonians, nor the Greeks who followed them, nor in fact the Romans later on, wrought any changes. Egypt was in his view a static place, untouched either by Saïte or Persian governance, or by the new post-Persian, multipolar, hyper-competitive reality of Hellenistic states. But, however slow and gradual social or economic change was, it

---

[17] Egyptian *cartonnage* finds a fascinating parallel in eighth-century AD Japanese material known as *Urushi-Gami Monjyo*, lids for lacquer vessels made from recycled government records. See further Furuoya (2005). On *cartonnage*, see Salmenkivi (2002).

[18] Finley (1999:28).

[19] See further Davies (2001); (2006).

was real. The Ptolemaic economy built on institutional trends beginning in the Saïte period (the seventh century BC), carried over important fiscal technology developed particularly in the fourth-century BC Greek world (especially the "increasingly monetised" [Shipton 2000:5] economy at Athens), and then applied it gradually during the first fifty or so years of Ptolemaic rule. There is something more than an "oriental" Greek economy that needs to be explained, and of course, immigration by Greeks and others, and the finances of war surely shaped that economy, just as it shaped the Ptolemaic state as a whole.[20]

Archaeology and numismatics play an increasingly important part in the study of the Ptolemaic economy.[21] While the papyri tend to give us a static picture of the structure of state institutions and how individuals dealt with them, survey and settlement archaeology and numismatic studies are beginning to give us some indication of the economic performance of the state over time. This is of course one destination that we should be "trying to get to" (Davies 2001:14), and we are now at the beginning of the journey.

THE PTOLEMAIC STATE

A detailed study of the Ptolemaic state is important for several reasons. First and foremost among these is the fact that it is the first reasonably

---

[20] On the role of war, see Austin (1986); Davies (2001:36–39); Chaniotis (2005); Fischer (2008).

[21] The archaeology of Ptolemaic Egypt was long dominated by the search for papyri. In more recent years, archaeological exploration has been invaluable in documenting the expansion of trade routes in the eastern desert, the founding of settlements on the Red Sea coast, and the increased use of coinage, among other things. For the eastern desert and Red Sea coast in the Ptolemaic period, see Sidebotham and Wendrich (1996); Gates-Foster (2006). A brief overview of past archaeological work is given by McClellan (1997); Bagnall (2001). Important survey work has been done, but the focus has been on the Fayyum (Rathbone (1996, 1997). An excellent summary of the archaeology of the Fayyum is provided by Davoli (1998). Archaeological activity in the western desert and oases has been extensive. Among the most important potential finds has been the so-called "Valley of the Golden Mummies" in the Bahariya oasis, reported by Hawass (2000), which promises extensive human burials from late Ptolemaic and Roman times. More information on ongoing work at the oasis is on Hawass' website: *http://www.guardians.net/hawass/mummy-main.htm*. Underwater exploration at Alexandria has yielded spectacular finds in recent years: see Goddio (1998, 2006); Empereur (1998); McKenzie (2003). The early Roman papyri from the city are being published by Peter van Minnen, for which see http://classics.uc.edu/~vanminnen/Alexandria/Ancient_Alexandria.html.Outside of epigraphic work on temples, very little survey has been done in the Nile valley itself. The most important town in Upper Egypt under the Ptolemies, Ptolemaïs, which served as the regional capital, has not yet been properly surveyed or excavated. On Ptolemaïs, see further below, p. 107–13. Ptolemaic coinage is discussed below, p. 130–38.

well-documented state in history. Papyri and inscriptions from the period document the full range of state activity, from administrative orders to private contracts and local tax receipts, providing important evidence for understanding what has come to be called *Fiscal Sociology*—how the state collects and spends revenue and what the impact of this activity is on society—and for understanding the role of the state in the economy and in law, both key research areas in Economic Sociology (Swedberg 2003). I discuss these issues in chapters 5 and 6. Study of the Ptolemaic state also raises the question of why authoritarian regimes remain in power. How are we to explain the Ptolemaic revival of pharaonic, authoritarian (or "nondemocratic" to use Acemoglu and Robinson's 2006 preferred term) governance? This form of rule, a feature of Asian states especially but not exclusively, contrasts with the democracies of the west from Athens on. This East/West distinction has existed since Aristotle. More recently, the debate has continued in "modernization theory." Authoritarian, or "despotic," states, are usually regarded as a primitive form of governance yet they persist (in fact are now reemergent), particularly on the Asian continent, and this despite the belief that they can only experience growth through "modernization" and democratization. The Ptolemaic case invites us to consider other factors that shape governance strategies, namely the political economy of the state and the nature of hybrid state forms, and to examine anew the validity of the sharp contrast that has been drawn between Asian despotism and democratic development.

Study of the Ptolemaic state also presents us with an ancient tradition, deeply rooted in the Asian past, that can still be observed in many modern Asian states from Singapore and China, to Vietnam and Malaysia. "Even in the most coercive of states," Sim (2005:176) suggests, "authoritarian governments have always attempted to justify their policies and to acquire legitimacy for their governance." The efforts of the Ptolemies to legitimize their rule through Egyptian institutions had consequences that will be explored in the second half of this book.

Ptolemaic state development can also contribute material to the debate between the "geographical" and the "institutional" hypotheses (Acemoglu, Johnson, and Robinson 2002). This debate turns on whether differences in the economic performance of different countries can be attributed primarily to differences in geography or in the institutional organization of the societies. Will a country rich in resources stay rich under European colonization, or do the incentive structures in the society make a difference? Turning to the case at hand, did the Ptolemaic takeover of Egypt negatively or positively effect economic outcomes? I shall argue below that the combination of new fiscal structures with ancient extractive institutions (despite expansion in the form of new settlements and new building projects) coupled with the cost of enforcement, combined to depress economic performance over the course of the three centuries of Ptolemaic rule. This would provide some a counter-example, *mutatis mutandis*, for the thesis developed by Acemoglu et al. Institutions do matter, but the Nile regime is very difficult to change. If the Ptolemies "reversed the fortune of Egypt," this effect was only temporary.

PTOLEMAIC EGYPT: BEYOND PRÉAUX AND ROSTOVTZEFF?

The Ptolemaic regime in Egypt belongs to an era known commonly as the Hellenistic period.[22] The use of the term Hellenistic carries with it negative connotations of dissolution with classicists who view the period as the time of the decline of classical culture. Egyptologists, too, treat the period as a stepchild, seeing Ptolemaic Egypt as no longer a part of "pharaonic Egypt" but rather of the "late period," *la basse époque*, low in terms of both date *and* culture. It does not help that the rise of the Roman Empire overlaps almost entirely with the creation of the Hellenistic states. The study of Ptolemaic Egypt has thus become the preserve of the specialist papyrologist and epigrapher rather than the ancient historian, who often demurs because of the vast amount of material and the now impressively large body of secondary literature. As a result, a separate field of ancient history, papyrological history, has emerged.[23]

Two scholars have laid the foundations for our understanding of the Ptolemaic economy. Claire Préaux wrote two major synthetic monographs on Ptolemaic Egypt. The first, *L'Économie royale des Lagides*, was published (remarkably) in 1939 when she was thirty-five. It is a masterful summary of the complex papyrological documentation, but marred somewhat by her treatment of state revenues. Préaux adopted a statist model although she acknowledged, both in this work and even more in her synthesis of Hellenistic history (1978), that a statist or planned economy model for the economy was too rigid.[24] The field of demotic studies was too immature in the 1930s and 1940s to take account of the implications of this material for understanding the relationships between local, traditional village and temple economies and the new Ptolemaic royal econ-

[22] The term, only roughly translated from the German "Hellenismus," derives from a famous passage in Droysen's 1836 study and was used to describe the state of mixed culture in the east that gave rise to Christianity in the period from Alexander's campaigns at the end of the fourth century BC to the Roman conquest of the East. See the remarks of Bowersock (1990:xi); Cartledge (1997:2–3).

[23] On the methodologies and approaches of papyrological history, as well as the problems involved, see Frier (1989); Bagnall (1995).

[24] Préaux (1978/1:376, n.1).

omy, a circumstance that also affected the work of Préaux's contemporary, Michael Rostovtzeff.[25]

Rostovtzeff wrote two books that are still widely read today: *A large estate in Egypt in the third century* B.C.: *A study in economic history* (Madison, WI, 1922), and *The social and economic history of the hellenistic world* (Oxford, 1941).[26] They were both synthetic works but, in their use of large amounts of documentary evidence, they were more descriptive than explicitly model driven. Rostovtzeff argued that the Hellenistic world was in fact a distinctive historical phase, marked by several key factors: "a single, interdependent economic system characterized by sustained economic growth that was driven above all by long-distance inter-regional trade conducted by agents of a rising urban bourgeoisie."[27] For Ptolemaic Egypt specifically, Rostovtzeff's "model" was based on dominant state power, marked by economic planning and coercive force.[28] This is an issue that I will treat at greater length in chapter 3.

Rostovtzeff used all of the evidence available to him in creating his picture of the Hellenistic world as an age of experiment, experiments with a new articulation of political institutions, nascent capitalism, a rising bourgeoisie, and economic development and growth. Rostovtzeff's first study focused on what is known as the Zenon archive.[29] This collection of documents, something on the order of 1,700 usable texts, were the records kept by a man from Caria (SW Turkey) who immigrated to Egypt, along with thousands of others from the Greek world, in search of opportunity. He served as estate manager for Apollonios, the *dioikêtês*, or finance minister of Ptolemy II Philadelphos (282–246 BC). The bulk of the texts comprise official correspondence and other documents used in the management of the estate. They range in date from 261 to 229 BC. There are other documents within the archive, however, which are the private papers of Zenon acting on his own behalf.[30]

---

[25] Cf. the remarks of Davies (2001:21).

[26] For the University of Wisconsin background of the first book, see Bowersock (1986, esp. p. 396). The later book was written during Rostovtzeff's tenure at Yale University that began in 1925. I do not include a discussion here of Rostovtzeff's chapter on Ptolemaic Egypt for the *Cambridge Ancient History*, vol. 7, 1928, which is a more general discussion of the period. For Rostovtzeff as an historian, see Momigliano (1966); Wes (1990); Shaw (1992); Archibald (2001); Rowlandson (2003).

[27] This is an important contrast with Finley's thesis, which is well summarized by Cartledge (1997:11–12). The differences between Finley and Rostovtzeff are perhaps to some degree exaggerated, on which see Saller (2002). On the unity of the Hellenistic world, see Davies (1984).

[28] Still the standard view. See Rathbone (2000).

[29] The literature on this estate is massive. For an orientation, see Pestman (1981); and the surveys of Orrieux (1983); (1985); Clarysse and Vandorpe (1995).

[30] For recent attempts to isolate the private papers of Zenon, which counted 450 texts, see Orrieux (1983, 1985). For the criticism of isolating documents based on an assumption of two systems of accounts, see Franko (1988).

As Rostovtzeff stressed in his introductory chapter, this archive is among the most important collections of papyri from the early Ptolemaic period, a time when the Fayyum region was put under intensive cultivation. Along with what is known as the "Revenue Laws" papyrus (*pRev.*), the Zenon archive has formed the core documentation for our understanding of the workings of the economy. It is not valuable for local history alone. Indeed Rostovtzeff keenly felt that the documents recovered from this large estate offered insights into the "conception of the ancient world in general."[31] Above all, he stressed the close relationship of the king and the finance minister to the estate and its management as revealed by the texts. But for our purposes, locating the texts within the specific geographical and socioeconomic context of third-century BC Fayyum is crucial to their interpretation.

Rostovtzeff's second work is a synthetic study of the entire Hellenistic world, based in large part on extensive and complex evidence obtained from inscriptions and papyri. Underlying his treatment was a belief in the unity of the Hellenistic world and in the efficiency and rationality of the Ptolemaic system, run by a large and professional bureaucracy. Rostovtzeff, to be sure, focused on the reign of Ptolemy II, and thus the height of the Ptolemaic system, but there are other ways to read the evidence, and we are today better able to distinguish rural Egyptian reality from Ptolemaic goals.

Since Rostovtzeff there has been no comparable synthesis of the Hellenistic period, either in the scope of material used or in the historical vision. Most scholars today work below the level of large-scale narrative, studying archives and other groups of related texts and, given the large numbers of demotic papyri of which Rostovtzeff had only limited knowledge (although he did acknowledge their importance, 1941:257), it would be impossible for one person to command a perspective as broad as Rostovtzeff's. From his comprehensive viewpoint he read in the papyri evidence that a fundamental shift occurred in the Hellenistic period, a shift from the classical Greek world to a more modern kind of state-planned economy that above all was interested in economic growth. His understanding of the economic operations on the large estate was constantly reinforced by other evidence from the third century, in particular the "Revenue Laws" papyrus (*pRev.*),[32] and *pTebt.* III 703,[33] a text that Rostovtzeff himself edited with detailed commentary in 1933.

---

[31] Rostovtzeff (1922:15).

[32] Text edition by Grenfell and Mahaffy (1896); extensive comments by Préaux (1939). An important new text edition was published by Bingen (1952) and should be read in conjunction with his new interpretation of the entire document, Bingen (1978a).

[33] Published in the third volume of the Tebtunis Papyri. See the comments by Samuel (1971).

Since the 1950s, our understanding of the Ptolemaic state has been reshaped by a kind of "post-colonial" thinking that questions the extent of the state's ability to control the economy, and by a broader concern for culture and the underlying Egyptian society.[34] Eric Turner's (1984) chapter in the *Cambridge Ancient History* is a "flat rejection of Rostovtzeff" (Austin 1986:452) and his planned economic model, seeing Ptolemy II as the villain, not the hero. Although Rostovtzeff and Turner agreed in viewing the Ptolemaic economy as fundamentally modern, Turner's assessment is essentially a negative one: the state failed to achieve growth and ended in a "sterile stalemate" (1984:167) between Egyptians and Greeks.

Turner developed two models of the obligations of individuals to the royal economic structure (i.e., the taxation structure). Model I, based on late second-century documents from the Fayyum but presumed to apply to the whole of Egypt throughout the regime, centers on royal land and the peasants who farmed it. The king provided a seed loan and equipment to the farmer, and the farmer agreed at the time of the loan to pay a fixed rent at the harvest.[35] There was no written lease and, while force was occasionally used, the king was required to negotiate and, after the harvest, to carefully monitor grain shipments each step of the way to the royal granaries. A good part of this system was informal and traditional in Egypt, state needs being joined to production and distribution through the use of labor contracts and private capital in the form of contractors, shipowners, and boat captains. Moreover, royal land was only part of the agricultural system in Egypt; social relationships may have differed substantially in Upper Egypt where temples and landed estates were still functioning throughout the period.[36]

Private capital is even more in evidence in Turner's Model II. Here the tax on agricultural production (other than grain) and on raw materials was calculated in money. The king controlled production in key monopolized industries (oil, linen, and banking, among others) in licensed factories. The right to sell goods in these industries was also regulated by the public tender of licenses. In this system, we see more of the new, Greek-inspired plan to stabilize economic production, but we are still a long way from the old notion of a planned economy.[37] Rather, the system envisaged by *pRev.* was a mixed one, formed by the king in collaboration with private parties who bid for the right to sell manufactured goods and collect

---

[34] Bagnall's (2007) summary of trends in Ptolemaic scholarship gives an excellent overview. See also Samuel (1989).

[35] The rent was established on the basis of the quality of the land.

[36] For the royal/temple land distinctions, see Manning (2003a), and chapter 5.

[37] See the remarks of Turner (1984:151–53).

particular taxes, and who ran the royal banks used to deposit tax receipts. The primary concern of the king seems to have been to reduce risk caused by fluctuations in production and tax revenue. Turner has stressed that the aim was fiscal, intended to increase production and collect rents, rather than to control the entire economy.[38] The taxes collected under Model II were collected in coin. The silver standard remained, but most taxes were probably paid in bronze coinage for which a conversion charge, or *agio*, was collected. I shall argue below that there may well have been political motivations for the new fiscal organizations that have nothing to do with increasing revenue or reducing risk.

In recent years it has been the work of Jean Bingen that has been per-haps the most influential in revising our views of the Ptolemaic state.[39] Although his work focused on the immigrant Greek population and how they coped with their new Egyptian environment, Bingen's close reading of *pRev.* revealed that the text is in fact a compilation of seven separate texts and should be regarded as an ad hoc document written to produce immediate results rather than as evidence of long-term central planning.[40] That there exists this gap between intentions, about which we know much, and evolving rural realities over the three centuries of Ptolemaic rule has now become the accepted view. For Bingen, the Ptolemaic state was a failure not so much for what it did but for what it did not do.

The gap between Ptolemaic economic policy in the third century BC and its actual implementation in Egypt is well illustrated by the other key text, the famous *pTebt.* III 703. A "policy manual" written by the *di-oikêtês* for the *oikonomos* in charge of royal revenues in the nome, the text is detailed, but far from being a comprehensive guide to the office, and it contains no specific references to time or place.[41] It stands, however, in a long pharaonic lineage of written instructions for officials. We have on the one hand then the traditional Tebtunis papyrus, and on the other hand *pRev.*, which shows an attempt to adapt Greek economic thought on tax farming to the very different conditions of Egypt. Both documents provide detailed descriptions of the operation of monopoly industries, and give evidence of close supervision by nome officials of agriculture, irrigation, and animal husbandry. It is important to note, however, that both were written from the central government's point of view.

Comprehensive state control over the economy is the principal distinc-tion between Ptolemaic Egyptian and classical Greek economies. Ptole-maic Egypt was for Rostovtzeff a "strong and well organized state," dom-

---

[38] Turner (1984:152).

[39] See his translated collected essays in Bingen (2007).

[40] Bingen (1978a).

[41] Bagnall and Derow (2005:165).

Figure 1. *pTebt*. III 703.

inated by a minority Greek population. It was organized rationally and planned efficiently, but at the same time it preserved ancient Egyptian institutions (local economic organization around temple estates controlled by priests) centered on the ancient administrative structure of the nomes.[42] The Ptolemies followed pharaonic theology by claiming ownership of all the land, and thus all sources of production in Egypt. This was certainly the ideology of the Egyptian state, and the strongly centralized, autocratic (or hydraulic) model of Ptolemaic Egypt had in its origins this reading of the ancient Egyptian state. Any "right" claimed by the Ptolemies, however, must have been backed up by coercive power, or at least by a threat of coercive power. And coercion there certainly was, as we know from specific incidents and can infer from the size of the rural police force.[43] There is as well much good evidence to suggest that the *structure* of the economy (taxation administration and the flow of information from village to nome capital to Alexandria) was planned. But the massive revolt in the Thebaid (the southern Nile valley), which effectively expelled Greek presence there for twenty years (205–186 BC), is enough to suggest that there were enforcement problems and practical limits on state building. A new manifestation of this old conception was the royal monopoly of key industries that regulated production and fixed prices of raw materials.

The power of the Ptolemaic state itself and its ability to directly intervene at the local level were key components of Rostovtzeff's model. The legacy of his work is this "statist," "dirigiste," or command economy model in which orders were issued from the king and transmitted down the chain of administrative command.[44] Throughout his work, Rostovtzeff stressed the ideals of the Ptolemaic "administrative machine" as against the realities: the king, as the pharaohs before him, was the embodiment of the state, and he controlled the population absolutely.[45]

For Turner (1984), it was not only the state's ability to intervene in the economy so heavily as to cause its collapse, but more significantly the institutional structure established by Ptolemy II to fund war that was to blame for Ptolemaic failure.

---

[42] Rostovtzeff (1922:3–4). Cf. ibid. p. 126 stressing continuity with ancient Egypt. Something of a contradiction between the "rational" organization stressed by the Greek papyri and the fact that the Ptolemies added a new layer of control on top of ancient institutions.

[43] Clarysse and Thompson (2006).

[44] This centralized conception of the Ptolemaic economy derived ultimately from Mahaffy and Grenfell's *editio princeps* of the Revenue Laws papyrus (1896). See the remarks of Turner (1984:148).

[45] Rostovtzeff (1922:126). He offered as specific parallels the kings of Dynasty 4, 11, and 18, i.e. the height of centralized power in pharaonic Egypt, for some reason leaving out Dynasty 19, a much more effective period of coerced labor.

The Methodology of this Study

My methodology differs from earlier approaches to Ptolemaic history in two principal areas. First, I write from the point of view of long-term Egyptian history and focus on how the Ptolemies established themselves within the existing institutional framework of Egyptian society, a society that was neither moribund nor static at the time of their arrival. Secondly, I situate Ptolemaic state making in the history of premodern states, and I broaden the analysis by including a chapter on law, which I argue was fundamentally important in the state-making project.

I begin with a summary of the history of Egypt during the first millennium BC. It is that history—and in particular the formation of the Saïte state in 664 BC and Egypt's subsequent annexation into the Persian Empire in 525 BC—that directly shaped the Ptolemaic state and Egyptian society. In chapter 2 I discuss the various ways in which the Ptolemaic state has been understood, and then in the following chapter, I set the Ptolemaic state into the historical context of premodern states and the issues that confronted their rulers. Those issues, which I treat in some detail in chapter 4, required the rulers to bargain continually with key constituencies. Finally, in the last two substantive chapters, I examine the role and the impact of the Ptolemaic state in shaping economic and legal institutions. I attempt to strike a careful balance between the power of the rulers to act unilaterally in trying to achieve their goals and the bargains that they struck with constituent groups. In taking over a state that had socioeconomic institutions extending back three thousand years before their arrival, the Ptolemies faced an unusual situation, paralleled only by the Seleukids. It is important to examine the economic and legal institutions together because they show, in a sense, the "topography" of the core of the Ptolemaic state. On one hand the aim of the new rulers was to extract resources. Toward this end the Ptolemies utilized new economic institutions such as banks and coinage within what was essentially an ancient bureaucratic framework. On the other hand, when it came to the law, the Ptolemies incorporated the various legal traditions within the bureaucratic framework they inherited. The economic and legal reforms went hand in hand. And in both cases, Ptolemaic action was informed by the Egyptian past.

Chapter 1

EGYPT IN THE FIRST MILLENNIUM BC

> When Egypt was reached in 332 BC, the Persian
> satrap surrendered without striking a blow. Alexander
> hastened upstream to Memphis, sacrificed to the
> Apis bull, was accepted as pharaoh, and then returned
> to the coast. Here on the shore of the Mediterranean
> near a village named Rhacotis he traced out the
> lines of the future great city of Alexandria before
> starting out on his famous visit to the oracle of
> Amun in the oasis of Siwa.
> —*Gardiner (1961:381)*

IN THIS BOOK I examine Ptolemaic rule of its core territory, Egypt, and explore the ways in which the Ptolemies shaped a government that would serve their own ends. The Ptolemaic kingdom, like most ancient states, was authoritarian. But unlike some modern authoritarian states, it was constrained by history, by an ancient institutional structure that gave little wiggle room for maneuver. Engaging with that ancient institutional structure was a deliberate policy decision taken by Ptolemy, the founder of the dynasty. Before moving ahead to discuss the Ptolemaic state and its institutions, it may therefore be useful to take a glance backward to first-millennium BC Egypt in order to situate ourselves in the historical experience that was to have so profound an influence on Ptolemaic policy.[1]

FROM THE END OF THE NEW KINGDOM TO THE ASSYRIAN INVASION

The New Kingdom and its Near Eastern and Nubian empire collapsed in 1069 BC with the death of Ramses XI. The last century of its history was wracked with political turmoil, some of it no doubt exacerbated by environmental stresses that may be inferred from the grain prices of the period (Janssen 1975b), evidence of the silting up of the Pelusiac branch of the Nile, and references in these years to "the year of the hyenas, when

---

[1] Those who are familiar with the history of the period may wish to skip to the next chapter. I follow here the chronology of Shaw (2000).

there was hunger." There were also disruptive and worrisome incursions by Libyans into the Theban area. Earlier, under the reign of Ramses III, Egypt had lost its imperial territory under the pressure of another problematic migratory movement of groups of people whom the Egyptians called the "Sea Peoples" (Dothan 1992). The power of the central state declined significantly in these years, as royal prerogative yielded ground to hereditary elites. The Theban area was under the charge of one Panehsy, who had rebelled against royal influence in the south. He appears to have led at least one failed attempt at conquering the north. Eventually Ramses XI established a kind of federal power throughout Egypt, appointing Herihor, a general of very likely Libyan descent to control the south, and another general Smendes, to control the north. In governing the Thebaid, Herihor also took the title "high priest of Amun," which tied him into the Amun temple, the dominant political, economic, and religious center in the Nile valley.

The search for political legitimacy through religious institutions, and the strategy of using these institutions to achieve centralized control of Egypt, are major themes of post–New Kingdom times. It is no accident that so many of the official and literary texts produced during the first millennium BC are concerned with the selection and behavior of legitimate kings and with connections to a glorious royal past (Gozzoli 2006). Egyptian scribes and priests perhaps found their influence underscored because it was they who were the transmitters of (theological) history that lay at the foundation of political stability.

After the demise of the New Kingdom state, the political ideal of an Upper and Lower Egypt united under one king became a distant memory. Egypt split into as many as eleven political units, although a basic north-south divide continued, with a border between the regions established at el-Hibe. The chief northern center was at Tanis, in the eastern Delta, which had replaced the late New Kingdom royal city at Piramesse on the Pelusiac branch of the Nile. In the south, the dominant city was the ancient religious center at Thebes, which was under the control of warlords who carried priestly titles associated with the city's great Amun temple, a continuation of the practice seen earlier in Herihor's governorship (Kitchen 1986:16–23).

Libyans, probably in the main from Cyrenaica, increasingly dominated politics, and the army, in the north.[2] Their political and cultural institutions differed substantially from Egyptian ones, yet they held sway over the north of Egypt for nearly four centuries. Three concurrent dynasties, Manetho's twenty-second, twenty-third, and twenty-fourth, were estab-

---

[2] For an overview of the Libyans in Egypt, see Leahy (1985).

lished in three separate urban centers in the Delta. Political events in the north are, thus, complex to reconstruct (Kitchen 1986).

The southern stretches of the Egyptian Nile valley were controlled by both the traditional authority of priesthoods centered on the Amun temple at Thebes, and by soldiers. Both institutions were effectively combined in the "great army commanders," descendants of the warlord Herihor, who ruled in the south. Eventually control of the Nile valley was divided into two polities, one centered at Thebes and the other at Herakleopolis.

The involvements of the New Kingdom in Syria-Palestine and Nubia also shaped events in the first centuries of the first millennium BC. Egypt was invaded from both. The Kushite (Nubian) king Piye (747–716 BC), having already gained nominal control of the Theban region through his sister's installation as "God's wife of Amun" in Thebes, invaded Egypt to check the halt of the northern ruler Tefnakhte's advances southward. The result was dynasty 25 in Manetho's chronicle.[3] The 25th dynasty was characterized by halting Nubian control of Egypt and the resurrection of some very ancient features of Egyptian civilization as the Nubians attempted to take political control over the whole of Egypt. Nubian expansion northward met the Neo-Assyrian imperial expansion against the Babylonians in 701 BC, northwest of Jerusalem. The Assyrians eventually invaded Egypt briefly, and established an accord with local rulers in the Delta.[4] It is from that agreement that the important Saïte dynasty sprang.

THE SAÏTE RESTORATION

Psammetichus (Psamtek) was a ruler of the city of Saïs and an Assyrian client. He successfully established a new dynasty, Dynasty 26, and had consolidated his control of a reunited Egypt by 656 BC. The Saïte dynasty would become, especially during the reign of Amasis (570–526 BC), one of the great periods in Egyptian history.[5] The details of political consolidation remain largely a mystery, but it is certain that both an iron fist and an acceptance of strong political and cultural traditions played a role; in today's parlance, Psammetichus deployed both "hard" and "soft" power.[6] Interestingly, the formation of the Saïte state coincided with major

---

[3] Manetho was a Ptolemaic-period priest whose division of Egyptian history into ruling dynastic families is, in the main, still followed by modern scholars.

[4] On the Assyrian invasions of Egypt, see Onasch (1994).

[5] Hdt. 2.161–63, 169–74, 177–79, 181–82. Cf. Diod. Sic. 1.79; 94–95. For Herodotus on the Saïte dynasty, see Lloyd (1988b:174–241).

[6] Summaries of Saïte history in Kienitz (1953:11–34); Kitchen (1986:403–08); Lloyd (2003).

adjustments to climate change during the early first millennium BC, seen throughout the Mediterranean and beyond (Bokovenko 2004).[7]

Several trends of the seventh century BC are especially important in understanding the later Ptolemaic state reformation. The use of Ionian and Carian mercenaries was key for the consolidation of political power, especially in the Delta, and the (gradual) imposition of the demotic Egyptian script throughout Egypt was crucial in establishing greater administrative uniformity. We know from the discovery of some archaic Greek art at Memphis that Greek culture was not unknown in Egypt, and although Egyptian artists seem to have resisted Greek stylistic influence (Smith 1998:239), the Greek presence cannot have been without impact. Herodotus' treatment of Egypt served as an important Greek bridge between the Saïte kings and the Ptolemies, and we know from Necho II's exploration of the African coast with Phoenician sailors that the Saïte kings were engaged in trade and had an interest in the wider world.

Rather than conquering Upper Egypt by military force, Psammetichus I (664–610 BC) used diplomacy toward the important temple of Amun at Thebes. His daughter Nitocris was adopted by Shepenwepet II, who held the important priestly title "the God's Wife of Amun," in the temple, the priestly institution by which pharaohs, and Piye, had controlled the Theban temple, its priesthoods, and their resources.[8] The text that documents this political solution, erected within a temple context and therefore overtly pious in its tone, shows how carefully the king couched the move in religious terms, acknowledging the tradition of the Theban theocratic state that arose out of the ashes of the collapse of political authority at the end of the New Kingdom. The adoption of Psammetichus' daughter into the family of the powerful, effective rulers of the Theban region must have involved more than their simple acceptance of the girl, but we are ignorant of details. Psammetichus also reached an accord with the powerbroker Montuemhat, whose family had fostered strong ties with both the Theban priesthoods and the Kushite (i.e., Dynasty 25, 747–656 BC) kings. These delicate political maneuvers by Psammetichus show the continuing economic and political power of both the temple of Amun and the civil authority, the majordomo Montuemhat. The administration of the south of the country appears, indeed, not to have been much disturbed by Saïte recentralization.

---

[7] Between 650 BC and the Hellenistic period there was a significant shift to wetter conditions in the eastern Mediterranean (Issar 2003:24; cf. Hdt. 3.10).

[8] Egyptian Museum, Cairo, *JdE* 36327. Caminos (1964) remains the essential study. See also Manuelian (1994). The most recent treatment of the *Nitocris Adoption Stela* is Gozzoli (2006:87–92).

The Saïte kings quite intentionally stressed, through the use of image and language, their deep connection to Egypt's ancient history and their Egyptian origins (Lloyd 1983:289). But the political and economic power of the Saïtes was established on a new foundation. Both the employment of Greek advisors and pro-Greek policies are notable features of the age.[9] The founding of the trading colony (*emporion*) at Naukratis in the western Delta by Psammetichus I was a major opening up of Egypt to Greek trade; and Amasis' alliance with Polykrates of Samos reveals the extent of Egyptian connections with the Aegean.

The projection of Saïte power in the Mediterranean into the Red Sea and Syria-Palestine, was supported by a navy.[10] The Saïte kings were also involved in military campaigns into Nubia, notably under Psammetichus II in 595 BC. The use of iron, although it was not widespread apparently, was introduced.[11]

Within a couple of generations, that is by the death of Psammetichus in 610 BC, Egypt was once again a unified state from the Delta to Aswan and a strong force in the eastern Mediterranean. How exactly this was accomplished we do not know, but we can make some educated guesses. Without doubt this period, and the following Persian period, were characterized by an extensive military presence throughout the country, as witness the fascinating Carian and Greek graffiti recorded in 591 BC on the famous monument of Ramses II at Abu Simbel.[12]

Memphis was established again as the political center of the country; and foreigners settled there (and throughout Egypt) in large numbers. They included Greeks and Easterners—Carians and Phoenicians and Jews (Thompson 1988:82–105). Many in these diverse communities of immigrants assimilated to Egyptian culture to a remarkable extent during the Late Period.[13]

In large part this interest in matters outside Egypt, especially to the East, was the result of Persian expansion, but it was also a continuation of second millennium interstate competition for the control of trade flows through Syria-Palestine. Trade is not easily measured in exact terms but it clearly increased in volume under the Saïtes and created new wealth among the capital's elite, a wealth that we see displayed in their tombs. It was also during the Saïte period that the use of coinage began.

Much has been made of the increase in private documentary records in Egypt beginning with the reign of Shabako (ca. 700 BC) and continuing

[9] On Saïte naval intentions, see Hdt. 2.159, and further in Lloyd (2000).

[10] Hdt. 2.159; Lloyd (1977, 2000).

[11] Lloyd (1983:329). On the town itself, see Bresson (2005a); Möller (2000); and the series of articles in *Topoi* 12–13/1 (2005).

[12] See Bernand and Masson (1957); Peden (2001:28).

[13] Ray (1994:54–59).

through the Saïte period. Whether the increase signals real reforms or merely major economic adjustments, there can be no doubt that that Egypt's opening up to the Mediterranean and to the Red Sea brought about an increase of economic activity. The introduction and the diffusion of demotic Egyptian, carrying with it its distinct legal traditions, was no doubt one of the most important and long-lasting changes began by Psammetichus I. Demotic was a cursive script tradition, native to the Delta that was used by the new kings to assert central authority throughout Egypt. The script and its use reached southern Egypt, at Thebes, where it replaced the hieratic writing tradition there in the sixth century BC.[14]

Saïte administrative structures appear to have been traditional (Lloyd 1983:332–33 provides a brief summary). "Governors" (nomarchs) were appointed over districts (nomes) and were responsible to the king primarily for fiscal and to a lesser extent judicial matters. Upper Egypt remained a distinctive region, with caution applied because of the sensitivities, and the great influence of the Theban temples.[15]

Saïte reforms are crucial to an understanding of Persian and Ptolemaic governance. Strong Greek presence throughout the country, a quasi-independent Upper Egypt dominated by Thebes, the use of demotic, and a turn backward to the glorious past of ancient times would characterize the remainder of the first millennium BC.

PERSIAN RULE

Persian plans and preparations for the invasion of Egypt came to fruition in 525 BC, perhaps aided by some defectors from Amasis' army (Hdt. 3.4).[16] This marked the first time in history that Egypt became part of an imperial state system—the Assyrian and Nubian invasions were short-lived and unhappy precursors. The Persian King Cambyses, despite the nasty personal reputation attributed to him by Herodotus, seems to have respected the Egyptians' royal and religious traditions.[17] Where possible, the Persians attempted a synthesis between Persian and Egyptian tradi-

[14] On the introduction of demotic to the south of Egypt, see Vleeming (1981) and most recently Martin (2007). See also Ray (1994); Manning (2003a), Houston et al. (2003), and for Roman period demotic, Muhs (2005b). On the establishment of demotic at Thebes, see Donker van Heel (1994).

[15] The chart of Gyles (1959:76) illustrates the bifurcation of Upper and Lower Egyptian administrative structure.

[16] On the notable absence of the Saïte navy during the Persian invasion, see the remarks of Lloyd (2000).

[17] Bresciani (1985:503). On Cambyses' actual (pious) behavior toward Egyptian animal cults, see Depuydt (1995).

tions of kingship, but in fact the two systems were largely incompatible (Gozzoli 2006:111–25). The Persians were not especially interested in governing Egypt. They saw it, in the main, as territory through which valuable trade flowed to the oases and across North Africa.

Egypt's Persian imperial rulers maintained her well-developed state and local administrative structures and practices.[18] "In general," Ray (1987:79) concludes, "the Persians seem to have governed the country with as light a hand as possible, relying on strategically placed garrisons and a good network of intelligence." Given the size of the Persian Empire, a basic continuity of local institutions and traditions would be unsurprising. Memphis served as the seat of the satrap and of the state treasury, the overseer of which was at least at times an Egyptian (Lloyd 1983:334). The Persian tributary system relied on the local elite to raise the required tribute. Darius seems to have centralized the system to great effect (Briant 2002:413–15).

One of the texts recorded on the verso of the *Demotic Chronicle*, an important historical source for the period, reports Cambyses' attempt at limited restructuring of some temples' finances, a move paralleled later by Xerxes and widely unpopular among the priesthoods.[19] It may have been little more than an attempt at centralizing revenue, but the reaction to it, at least the reaction that the written record preserves, was harsh. Cambyses, deservedly or not, had a bad press, which was no doubt at least in part due to how bitterly the Persian invasion was viewed by some elements of the Egyptian priesthood.[20] Throughout their history, the Egyptians disdained Asiatic rulers who attempted to control the Nile valley, and the Persians were no doubt seen as merely the latest in a line that begun with the Hyksos invasion in the eighteenth century BC and continued with the brief Assyrian incursion in the seventh century BC and, finally, the invasions of Cambyses and Artaxerxes. The Ptolemies, surely aware of this anti-Persian feeling and knowing the value of a good press, used pharaonic imagery and practices to minimize their own foreignness.

Persian rule relied on the Saïte fiscal structure, and Memphis remained the seat of governance.[21] Donations to the temples continued, and Darius'

---

[18] Johnson (1994). A review of Persian administration in Egypt is provided by Briant (2002:413–21). On Persian administrative practice in general, see Tuplin (1987). For current research on the Persian period, including new archaeological discoveries, see http://www.achemenet.com/

[19] For the *Demotic Chronicle* (*pBib. Nat.* 215, dated to the third century BC), see Spiegelberg (1914); Johnson (1974); Felber (2002).

[20] Lloyd (1988a); Devauchelle (1995); Briant (2002:55–61). Later traditions are presered in the *Coptic Cambyses Romance*: Jansen (1950), and the *Chronicle of John of Nikiu* 51.20ff. (Charles 1916); Carrié (2003).

[21] On the Persian administration's adoption of the Saïte taxation system, see Briant and Descat (1998).

respect for Egyptian kingship and the Egyptian gods is demonstrated in the famous biography of the Egyptian official Udjahorresnet[22] inscribed on the Tell el-Maskhuteh stela that records Darius' construction of a canal,[23] and by Darius' pious donation of land to the Horus temple at Edfu.[24] In other respects as well, Persian rule left Egyptian institutions intact. The Persian king did however grant land to soldiers and administrators throughout Egypt, another ancient practice that would be continued by the Ptolemies.[25]

Persian rule may have been broadly accepted, but there were revolts throughout the period. Some were probably the result of Greek involvement with certain elite families in Egypt, who made for good bedfellows in opposition to Persian rule. Others may have merely been opportunistic. The Persians were expelled by force of arms upon the death of Darius II in the revolt of Amyrtaios in 404 BC.

THE FOURTH CENTURY BC

The fourth century BC was an unstable period, that saw Egypt caught in the middle between Greece and Persia, the latter always keeping its eye out for opportunities to retake it (which they in fact did, briefly, in 343BC. Our direct sources for the period are few and far between. Serious disturbances led to the rise of the Egypt's last dynasty (Dynasty 30) of native pharaohs, Nectanebo I (380–362 BC) and II (360–343 BC). The period was dominated by the military, with Greek mercenaries and advisors playing important roles; the two kings were little more than a "junta," to use Ray's term (1987:85). Despite the need for a heavy hand, however, Nectanebo II, perhaps somewhat unexpectedly, became one of the greatest Egyptian kings of the first millennium BC, sponsoring building projects throughout the country. Although the total figure would be difficult to estimate, the number of private demotic contracts from this period that have been preserved might well stand as an indication of overall prosper-

[22] Vatican Museum 158 [113], 17–20. The hieroglyphic text is given in Posener (1936:1–26). For an English translation, see Lichtheim (1980:38). Additional insights are provided by Ray (1988:258–59); Verner (1989).

[23] Most recently discussed by Bresciani (1998); Lloyd (2007:99–104).

[24] For the Hibis temple, see most recently the study by Klotz (2006). On the land donation to the Edfu temple by Darius, see Meeks (1972); Manning (2003a:74–79). Darius' building program was treated recently by Lloyd (2007), who raised doubts about his involvement in building activity at the Hibis temple in the Khargeh oasis, traditionally seen as at least partially built by the king. For Darius' activity at the Ghueita temple south of Hibis, see Darnell (2007).

[25] On these land grants, see Briant (2002:417–18). Cf. Xen., *Oec.*, IV.5.

ity (Ray 1987:87).[26] In 343 BC the Persians invaded Egypt and briefly placed it once more under Persian control. This second Persian occupation (343–332 BC) was unsuccessful and spawned yet more unrest (the revolt of Khabbabash probably occurred at this time, ca. 338–336 BC[27]) as well as anti-Persian feeling that Alexander and Ptolemy were soon able to exploit.

The eastern Mediterranean world was rapidly changing in the quarter century after 338 BC in ways important to an understanding of many Hellenistic institutions. Scholars are divided on whether we can analyze or isolate a distinctive "Hellenistic" economy, but whichever side of the debate one chooses, it seems clear that the fiscal institutions and trading patterns that would define the post-Alexandrian world were already emerging during the fourth century BC.[28] The controversy, then, should not really turn on the term "Hellenistic," which simply refers to the period after Alexander, but rather on the extent to which the Hellenistic kingdoms represented a rupture with the past. My brief survey of first millennium BC Egyptian history suggests that we must see the formation of the Hellenistic kingdoms and their economies as continuing trends already in place by the fourth century BC from the point of view of the Greek world, and with a lineage much older still from the point of view of Egypt.

ALEXANDER AND PTOLEMY

Histories of the Hellenistic world usually begin either with Alexander's invasion of the Persian Empire or with his death (Austin 2006:18). But the Macedonian takeover of Egypt, and the subsequent formation of the Ptolemaic dynasty, was only the culmination of past centuries of direct and sustained Greek engagement with Egypt (and other parts of the Persian Empire). Egypt's engagement with the Greek world is reflected in the influx of Greeks in the early Saïte period, in the founding of the Greek trading city of Naukratis, in the writings of Herodotus, and in much fourth century Greek political thought as well. While it is possible to view the Ptolemaic reformation as the beginning of the "Greek millennium" (Clarysse 2000) in Egypt, it was, in my view, the *consummation* and not the *beginning* of a long process of understanding and accommodation between two cultures that had been in direct and sustained contact with

[26] It was Nectanebo II who was later identified as Alexander's father in the *Alexander Romance*: Stoneman (1991); Merkelbach (1977).

[27] Burstein (2000).

[28] On the debate, see Finley (1999); and the recent overview by Davies (2001).

each other since the seventh century BC. The "Greek millennium" in Egypt was indeed a long millennium.

Alexander and Ptolemy, who knew each other from childhood, had observed the Persian Empire firsthand. They knew that the best way to govern an empire of that size was to honor local customs and practices in so far as possible. The tale of Cambyses in Egypt as reported by Herodotus, however polemical, and the incident recorded by Udjahorresnet of Persian soldiers' disregard for temple precincts, provide vivid counterexamples of respecting the religion of subject peoples. Such respect is explicitly demanded of soldiers in a small Ptolemaic papyrus found at Saqqara known as the Peukestas papyrus. It records an order of Alexander's commander in Memphis Peukestas to the effect that soldiers in Egypt (as indeed elsewhere in the Hellenistic world) should respect sacred space.[29] The Ptolemaic state in Egypt, as the other Hellenistic states in the third century BC, had roots planted firmly in the soil of Persian provincial rule.

[29] For the *Udjahorresnet* inscription, see Lloyd (1982) and Baines (1996) and this chapter n. 22. For the Peukestas text, see Turner (1974), and the general treatment of Ptolemaic policy toward Egyptian temples by Thompson (1988:106–54). For another example from the Hellenistc world: Ma (2000:304–05, text 15, from Labraunda, 203 BC [reign of Antiochus III]).

Chapter 2

THE HISTORICAL UNDERSTANDING
OF THE PTOLEMAIC STATE

. . . classicists should be prepared to insist on the
importance of the fact that Egypt was effectively
dominated by a Greek-speaking culture for a
millennium, without complete obliteration of other
cultural elements. If we fail to do this we run the
risk of underplaying, for example, the decisive effect
which Alexandria had on the cultural, social and
economic history of the Mediterranean world and its
role as a link between Egypt and that wider world;
or of creating a deeply damaging rift between its
history before the Arab conquest and after it (when,
after all, both Greek and Coptic language and
culture did survive, now in a subordinate rather
than a dominant role).
—*Bowman (2006)*

Oh, East is East, and West is West, and never the
twain shall meet, Till Earth and Sky stand presently
at God's great Judgment Seat; But there is neither
East nor West, Border, nor Breed, nor Birth, When
two strong men stand face to face, though they come
from the ends of the earth!
—*Kipling*

THIS CHAPTER surveys previous views of the Ptolemaic state. I shift the
emphasis away from the perspective of the Greek world by examining the
Egyptian core of the empire and the conscious continuation of a pharaonic style of governance. The Ptolemies' active accommodation to Egyptian kingship and to the legitimizing authority of the priesthoods puts
them in sharp contrast to both the Persians who came before and the
Romans who came after them. But the nature of royal power must be set
into its historical context and measured against real power. The usual

claim by historians, for example, that the kings "owned" the state by virtue of divine office must be tempered by the more limited actual "patrimonial" power that most kings in Egypt historically wielded.[1]

THE NATURE OF PTOLEMAIC RULE

As with assessments of nineteenth-century French and British interventions in Egypt, and assessments of the Hellenistic world broadly speaking, there are two prevailing views of the Ptolemaic state.[2] On the one hand are the optimists who stress, for example, the output of literature, new temple building, state expansion, and the achievements of Alexandrian scholars. On the other hand is the dominant "brief Summer and endless Autumn" (Davidson 1998:380) school, already the majority view by the 1930s, which sees ultimate failure either because of structural weaknesses or because of the over-extractive fiscal policies of the king.[3] Tarn and Griffith (1952:208–09) sum up the pessimistic school this way:

> Doubtless the early Ptolemies desired to acquire money as an aid to the construction of a strong state; their condemnation is that the money they acquired was in no sense used for the benefit of those who made it. They improved the land; they did not improve the condition of the people. There was no desire to oppress the Egyptians; but there was no desire to help them, beyond keeping them fit to work, a thing done by every business-like slave owner.[4]

It is true that the early Ptolemaic state privileged those who could function within the new state—soldiers, scribes, even priests, as well as others. But to focus exclusively on those who were in a position to increase the revenues of the ruler is to judge the Ptolemaic state by the wrong standard and misses out on much of the state system, its development, and its wider impact on society.

Scholarship has tended to paint Ptolemaic Egypt as a Manichean world—Greek/Egyptian, a success/a failure, efficient/irrational, a land of opportunity/a land of exploitation—but that is the result of over- or underweighting very particular kinds of documentary evidence, and of confusing intention with end results. And it tends very much to come from a

---

[1] Cf. Hölbl (2001:61).

[2] See Welles (1949), summarizing the opposing views of Préaux, who argued for strong continuity in the traditional economy of Egypt, and Rostovtzeff, who stressed new Greek features. On the views of the nineteenth-century state, see Owen (1972).

[3] The two opposing historical schools of thought are well summarized in Cartledge (1997). Cf. Westermann (1938).

[4] Cf. Rostovtzeff (1920).

one-track view of Ptolemaic aims: to take a specific case, from the at times brutal realities of tax collection. Those without power or influence were always and everywhere in the ancient world exploited, as much under the earlier pharaohs as under the Ptolemies.

I shall argue below that an analysis of state aims presents only one side of a rather complicated story. When it comes to the treatment of farmers, the role of tax collectors, and so on, the longer-term view would suggest that there was not much new under the Ptolemies. The "concrete structures," as Davidson (1998:382) calls them, of tax collection and policing were not part of an "ethnic" policy of the Ptolemies. They were quite ancient features of Egyptian administration. What was different from earlier regimes, however, was the introduction by the Ptolemies of new political realities, and new fiscal institutions, which altered bureaucratic and economic relations in such a way as to sometimes pit Greek against Egyptian, but at other times Greek against Greek, or Egyptian against Egyptian. The use of ethnic designations as the basis of tax collection (see chapter 5), for example was a matter of convenience to identify particular groups. It was not a racist policy for the sake of racism.

I will argue the case for (relative) Ptolemaic success, a case that has generally been lost in the court of academic opinion. In order to win the case, and to rehabilitate the Ptolemaic age as one of the most successful periods in Egypt's long history, I shall set the Ptolemies within the context of premodern states, before examining in detail how the Ptolemies came into Egypt and how they established a new political and economic order. Moreover, I am arguing for success not on the basis of "fortune," as did Polybius, the great historian of the age (i.e., the Ptolemies were simply lucky), although Ptolemy's seizure of Egypt was indeed fortunate, but because of the specific policies of the Ptolemaic kings and the way those policies dealt with the constraints imposed on the kings in the political, economic, and legal spheres.[5]

The Ptolemaic state was the longest lasting of the Hellenistic "successor" states. Indeed, the Ptolemies were the longest lasting dynasty in Egyptian history. In earlier analyses of Ptolemaic royal behavior and socioeconomic development, the existence of a strong, highly centralized state has been one of the main underlying assumptions: as heirs of the pharaohs, the kings sat atop a strong state and were therefore the only source of power worth analyzing.[6] But while the Ptolemies were certainly heirs to

---

[5] On Polybius' attributing Ptolemaic success to Fortune, see Walbank (1979 [2002]: 68–69).

[6] Such a "strong state" scheme is implicitly present in much of the literature. Bevan ([1927] 1968); Rostovtzeff (1941). Préaux (1939:533–57) emphasizes in particular the "superior right of the state" in legal conflicts with individuals.

a core territory long used to centralized authority, the third century BC was a time of state reformation, and both internal and external events (warfare being a prime example), were engines of change and adjustment.

State history in Egypt has typically been viewed as dynastic history; the state was the king and his court, and vice versa.[7] There is a long tradition of such a view in the Islamic period as well. And there are good reasons for it: among the most obvious, the fact that the evidence tends to be generated by the dynasty itself.[8] Ancient states, however, were far more complicated, and assessing the constraints that rulers faced are equally as important as assessing the actions they took. In Egypt, the supreme ruler was one actor in a complex world that grew increasingly more complex in the New Kingdom with the rise of powerful temple estates and a standing army that often combined forces to push back against the ruler and his aims. The revenue of the state, therefore, should be distinguished from that of the king.[9]

Rather than emphasizing "culture," I take a balanced view of the state in terms of its institutions, and I set the Ptolemies in the context of Egyptian history.[10] Throughout the book, I will stress that the dynasty was a reasonably successful one by premodern standards.[11] That success requires explanation. I do not see the Ptolemies as "an entirely new departure in Middle Eastern history," but, rather, as a state built on the strong institutional foundations of Saïte and Persian centralized governance. And this even though Persian rule was in some ways a serious rupture with earlier pharaonic history.[12]

Ptolemaic state making operated on many different levels and within a complex web of institutions and social networks. Brent Shaw recently described the Ptolemaic period as "one of the greatest 'take-overs' in all of antiquity."[13] But Ptolemy's taking of Egypt in 323 BC was more than a land grab. Ptolemaic governance had profound, long-term consequences for Egyptian history. It also resulted in the formation of ancient Egypt's legacy to the West.

Egyptology, as Bowman has recently emphasized, has typically been a field closed off from, and unengaged with, other disciplines, including the historical social sciences, despite much work in those disciplines that

---

[7] This is also the attitude of Polybius, on whom see Walbank (1979).

[8] See the apt comments of Brett (2001:5).

[9] Assuming here that state revenue included that generated by temples. See chapter 5 on revenues.

[10] Cf. Bin Wong (1997) on writing Chinese history from a Chinese perspective.

[11] Cf. the excellent remarks of Erskine (2003:3).

[12] I take an approach in line with an important recent study of the Seleukids, Sherwin-White and Kuhrt (1993:1).

[13] Shaw (1992:281); cf. Austin (1986:454–55).

bears directly on questions concerning Egyptian economy and society. The study of the Ptolemaic period, moreover, has for a long time been hampered by an odd division of labor based on linguistic training: classicists studying the Greek documentation, Egyptologists the Egyptian. The Ptolemaic historian is thus faced with the arduous task of bringing together disparate types of evidence scattered across the technical publications of several disciplines. This is further complicated by the fact that the historian must keep multiple viewpoints in his or her head at the same time. Turner (1984:132) summarized the problem well:

> Usually attention is focused on what the Greeks had to give and the Egyptian contribution is under-rated. Undeniably the Greeks brought with them initiative, energy, intelligence, new technology, an outsider's experience and institutions; but they deployed these gifts in a land of high culture with a respect for craftsmanship and philosophical thinking (imaginative rather than logical), and a tradition of social and political stability.

Egyptian institutions and culture were supported and invigorated by Ptolemaic rule, and this part of the story had profound effects on Egypt's (hellenized) legacy. Ptolemaic Egypt, then, was not simply a world in which Egyptians were pitted against Greeks. It is the ways in which both cultures viewed, interpreted, and engaged with the other that is the real story (Bowersock 1986).

The debate about the nature and the quality of the Ptolemaic state has been charged with modern anxiety over issues of racism, imperialism and colonialism, which has over the years spawned something of a cultural war between Classicists and Egyptologists, and has led to untenable characterizations of the period that are based on nineteenth- and twentieth-century concepts. Indeed, parallels with the Fatimid state are, in my view, far more instructive. It may be, however, that no one approach, no single model, could accurately capture the totality of the Ptolemaic state. Boundaries between "polity" and "political system," or the line between state and trade networks, or that between social networks and commodity flows, are difficult to draw.[14] As with earlier Egyptian state formations, that of the Ptolemies was loose and flexible. Within Egypt, they adapted regional strategies of control as they were needed, and they did not change ancient institutional structures rapidly, realizing that this would have been a rallying cry for resistance. Their external holdings, protected by a closed currency system that among other things kept the circulation of silver within a single trading zone, was both defensive and exploitative.[15] Rather

---

[14] See the illuminating study by Finley (1976).
[15] Polyb. V.34.2–9. Cf. Walbank (1982:217).

than seeing Greek rule in Egypt as a rupture with the past, I am treating the Ptolemaic period as part of Egyptian history. The "cultural war" that divides into Greek and Egyptian factions obscures many issues on the nature of premodern states.

UNDERSTANDING THE PTOLEMAIC STATE

This book draws on two distinct bodies of research and attempts to bring them together in a new understanding of the Ptolemaic state, its relationship to the Egyptian past, and its unique qualities. First, I rely heavily on the empirical work of many other scholars who have published the primary historical sources of the period. These range from demotic Egyptian and Greek documentary papyri and ostraca, to Greek and Egyptian (demotic and hieroglyphic) inscriptions, coinage, and archaeological material. Writing history using these sources, scattered across time and space, randomly preserved, and very often difficult to interpret, is fraught with problems, not the least of which is that in a world of increasing urbanization, the papyri and ostraca, which comprise the main corpus of sources, tend to give a rural perspective.[16] Second, I bring into this study some political science and economics literature that analyzes how states work and what makes them successful.

Egypt is among the earliest territorial states in the world.[17] While we can observe considerable fluctuations in the size and capacity of the state over the millennia, a few basic facts emerge from an examination of Egyptian history that show that Egypt basically conformed to the preindustrial model with unique institutional arrangements generated by its environmental setting.[18] The Nile River did make a difference in preventing political fragmentation over the short term to a greater degree than might otherwise be typical of a preindustrial state. To be sure, compared to the Seleukids' lands, Egypt was a far more homogenous territory, and therefore far easier to govern.[19]

The king, supported by well-developed state mythology, guaranteed stability and the social order and collected surplus production through taxation. This activity was mediated by the hierarchical, bureaucratic control of territory through regional and local elites. The territorial boundaries of the state had been established by Old Kingdom times, and

---

[16] For an introduction to using papyrological sources, see Bagnall (1995).

[17] The earliest Egyptian state formation is well treated by Wilkinson (2000).

[18] The best treatment of the pharaonic state and its evolution is Kemp (2006). On the premodern pattern see chapter 3.

[19] See Gellner (1983) for the basic agrarian state model, and Manning (2003a:130–33).

this basic core of the Nile River valley from Aswan to Memphis, the Delta and the Fayyum, was, in periods of centralized political control, dominated by a single ruler.

The elites were tied to the central court, and their loyalty was theoretically maintained through the granting of elaborate court titles and land. Temples and cult practice played a key role in further embedding the ruler within local social networks. With their landed estates and literate priesthoods, the temples also provided important infrastructural capacity that integrated local production and distribution and tied regions to the center through elaborate public ritual.

The basic patterns of governance continued from the Saïte period through the Ptolemaic. Earlier analysis of the Ptolemaic state, especially analyses that were concerned with the economy, emphasized the strong role of the state in economic development.[20] I shall have more to say on this topic in chapter 4. Here it suffices to mention that a link has often been noted between Ptolemaic royal ideology and the direct management of the economy by the extensive bureaucratic structure that the Ptolemies inherited directly from pharaonic practice. "The monarchy," Samuel concluded in his discussion of Ptolemaic royal ideology, "existed alongside the bureaucracy, in a sense, rather than being part of it" (Samuel 1993:192). This separation is an exaggeration, since the bureaucracy could never be totally removed from royal power. But it does also suggest, rightly, that we must consider bureaucratic *behavior* as something only loosely connected to actual royal *control*. The kings must have had some connection to the administration, and certainly attempted to control and regulate bureaucratic behavior. At least some of the administrative structure, particularly with respect to military operations, must have been under royal control. The interests of the king and the bureaucracy could indeed align and act as one (Eisenstadt 1993:118). Over time, however, the Ptolemaic kings had less room to maneuver. Yet even as the monarchy grew weaker, the bureaucracy continued to develop.[21]

The limits placed on royal power by the existence of a strong bureaucracy raise an important issue. Most approaches to the Egyptian state have emphasized a top down model. In such a model the king is absolute owner of everything within Egypt, and he can shape the entire state system by his own decree. This has been true of interpretations of the pharaonic as well as the Ptolemaic period, and has been heavily influenced by despotic and dirigiste models (below). A very different approach is advocated by Lehner (2000), Eyre (2004) and in my own work on Ptolemaic land

---

[20] A basic summary of the arguments may be found in Rathbone (2000).

[21] In my view this explains the role of local bureaucrats in legal affairs in the second century BC as represented by the Hermias trial, further discussed below.

tenure (Manning 2003a), which emphasizes local institutions, including legal ones, and household economies that were only very loosely, if at all, connected to the central state. This approach is consonant with a good deal of work on premodern states.[22] This "bottom up" approach, as Eyre calls it (2004:158), stresses the gaps between both local and central elites, and between rule by consensus in villages and authority imposed from the top.

In step with changing academic fashions, the nature of the Ptolemaic state has been variously understood by historians over the last century. The three most important models have been despotism, dirigisme, and colonialism. All have been shaped by the contemporary historical experience of course, and all have tended to underplay the role of political negotiations between the ruler and constituent groups (below, chapter 5).[23] I do not argue that these concepts are completely irrelevant in understanding the premodern Egyptian state, but, rather, that the ancient experience is sufficiently different to warrant caution in analyzing Ptolemaic state formation through the lens of either the nineteenth-century nation state colonial experience or twentieth century postcolonial reactions to colonization.

EGYPT AND ORIENTAL DESPOTISM

Although Greek and Egyptian civilization had had frequent and sustained contact with each other for many centuries before the formation of the Ptolemaic state, Ptolemy's kingship was the first direct encounter of Greek governance with Egypt.[24] It is almost natural that the reign of Muhammed Ali (1805–1848), of Albanian-Macedonian parentage, has been frequently used as an historic parallel.[25] But that comparison won't do. The historical analogy is particularly misleading when it comes to understanding agriculture and the irrigation system. It was not until the nineteenth century that large-scale deep canal dredging allowed the chain of irrigation basins to be connected, thereby swallowing up many of the earlier, smaller-scale units of production for which Girard's work in the *Description de l'Égypte* is a most valuable historical source.[26] The anachronistic projection of nineteenth-century state power and European colonialism

---

[22] Geller (1983); Feinman and Marcus (1998); Eyre (2004); Kemp (2006).
[23] The process of "Ptolemaicizing" Egypt is also treated well by Falivene (1991).
[24] On the Greek literary encounter with Egypt, see Vasunia (2001); Stephens (2003).
[25] For the reign of Muhammed Ali in Egypt, see Marsot 1984; Fahmy 1998.
[26] On this point, see Eyre (2004:160), citing the important study of Alleaume (1992).

back onto Hellenistic state formation has led to an overestimation of state power and a concomitant lack of attention to local social organization.[27]

One of the main challenges in understanding the Ptolemies is to grasp the way in which the new state functioned in its dealings with Egyptian institutions. Seen from this perspective the period has been viewed as a crucial one in many current debates about "East-West" encounters in general. Almost unavoidably, it has been Edward Said's *Orientalism* that has served as a kind of touchstone for these debates, although Said's concern was primarily with the "West's" depiction of the Near East over the last two centuries. [28]

The notion that Asian states, both ancient and modern, are despotic has been one of the central tenets in European political thought from Herodotus and Aristotle to Montesquieu, Voltaire, Marx, and Weber, and their related concept of the "Asiatic mode of production," down to the influential study of Karl Wittfogel (1957).[29] Even if the academic debate is now "closed" on this subject (Briant 2006:344), it is useful to see where we have been, if only to get a sense of what is still carried over from earlier scholarship. Typically, the notion of Asiatic despotism stood as a kind of shorthand for the (assumed) political economy of Asian states, and the concept fit well with many scholars' views, even the views of "Orientalists," about the differences between East and West.[30] Beginning with the contrast between Greece and Persia that is the central thesis of Herodotus' *Histories* and Aristotle's critique of Asian states (*Politics* I.1255b), through the influential writing of Max Weber, it was calculated to highlight the difference between Asian *monarchies* and the *democratic* states of the West.[31] The former were characterized by an absolute ruler, a labor force tied to the land, an absence of private property, and a static society, and the latter by a democratic government and individual freedom. A coercive system of labor organization and property relations explained the large public works projects in the ancient river valley states of China, India, Mesopotamia, and Egypt. The ruler was without opposition, and was supported by a dependent bureaucratic elite (O'Leary 1989:41). The association of despotism with Egyptian pharaohs has been in particular a theme of German scholars examining the role of the New Kingdom

[27] Alleaume (1992:301–02).

[28] The response to *Orientalism* is enormous. For an overview, see Irwin (2006). For the ancient historical context, see Millar (1998).

[29] O'Leary (1989:40–81) offers an excellent summary of the history of the concept of oriental despotism and its connection to the Marxist "Asiatic mode of production." See also the overview by Reich (2004). I thank Andrew Monson for pointing me to this latter piece.

[30] See for example Morris (1994:20–21).

[31] As Van de Mieroop (1997:4–5).

pharaoh Akhenaten in the light of the totalitarian regimes that emerged after World War II.[32] The rhetoric and the basic contrast are still with us, and they represent a serious misreading of ancient Egyptian politics.[33] *Monarchy*, despite the etymology of the word, was not one-man rule.

Mann (1986) distinguished two types of political power: "despotic" vs. "infrastructural" (cf. Blanton 1998:151). Despotic power is character-ized by the absence of any "constitutional constraint on a ruler to take a specific action." Infrastructural power is measured by the degree to which the ruler can effect political action throughout the state. Pyramid build-ing, as Goldstone (2006:265) rightly stresses, was a matter of the infra-structural power of Old Kingdom pharaohs, requiring their ability to command and coordinate labor and materials over a long period of time. The challenge for the ancient historian is not merely to define the position of the king, since kings always act despotically and all states (and econo-mies) are, to some degree, coercive by their nature, but to determine to what extent the Ptolemaic regime had control *over* or control *through* Egyptian society.[34]

The concept of oriental despotism as a state type, Asian or otherwise, has been criticized heavily in many quarters.[35] The only reason to summa-rize the arguments once again before moving on to discuss other theories of the Ptolemaic state is that some of the assumptions of despotic theory are still used to explain Ptolemaic development; i.e., that the kings in Alexandria had the ability to effect change when and where they wanted, because they had total power to do so. It is from this assumption of total control, and then the loss of it—the loss of land tenure rules for example—that the subsequent decline of the state has often been viewed.[36]

The rhetoric of Medieval European political philosophy invoked the concept of oriental despotism to attack the power of the popes (O'Leary 1989:46–47). The concept was further refined in the context of European disdain for Asian states. This was in essence a "revival" of Aristotle for the purpose of specific political analyses, and it led to an "unhappy confusion

---

[32] Breger (2005). Cf. Assmann's (2000) critique of Oriental despotism as a (poor) model for ancient Egyptian governance.

[33] Springborg (1992). Today it is most often, but not exclusively (Hodges and Gandy 2002), used to refer to Asian states (China, Iraq, North Korea) and certainly to nondemo-cratic ones, in which there are no legal or constitutional constraints on executive power. The term, indeed, is most often used rhetorically, having become popular in current debates in some political circles. See for example Hannity (2005).

[34] This distinction is clarified by Schroeder (2006) in his critique of Mann.

[35] The literature is vast. See briefly, for ancient Egypt, the classic study by Butzer (1976). Broader issues are discussed by Mann (1986); O'Leary (1989). With respect to Weber, see the critique by Blaut (2000:21–30).

[36] Manning (2003a). Cf. Rostovtzeff (1941:1081).

between despotic government and oriental monarchies."[37] In seventeenth- and eighteenth-century political debates, "oriental despotism" replaced "tyranny" as the term used to denote total political domination by a ruler.[38] Montesquieu is the classic source. In his *The Spirit of the Laws* (1746) he identified three forms of government: republican, monarchic, and despotic. The latter two are distinguished by the fact that in monarchies the ruler governs by "fixed and established laws" (Part I, Book 2, Chapter 1), whereas the despot rules "alone, without law and without rule, drawing everything along by his will and his caprices" (Part I, Book 2, Chapter 1). "Such are the principles of the three governments: this does not mean ... that in a particular despotic state, there is fear, but that unless it is there, the government is imperfect" (Part I, Book 3, Chapter 11). The size of the state (large states produce despotic forms of rule) and the environment (hot climates produce a servile population) combine to explain the form taken by the state. Irrigation and the bureaucracy that was required to supervise it led to the concentration of political power and rural misery. Montesquieu's theories were put into operation with the Napoleonic invasion of Egypt (Laurens 1987) *despite* Volney's analysis, not *because of* it as Said has claimed (Irwin 2006:136).

Wittfogel's monumental treatise (1957) summarized much nineteenth-century historical thinking about the political economy of early states, particularly those Asian states that practiced irrigation agriculture. His argument is complex, and his attempt to link water management to levels of technology, property rights, the structure of the state, and social power is impressive. At its most basic level, Wittfogel's despotic model for Egypt was a "linear causality model" that linked environmental stress to irrigation: the need to control irrigation networks led to the formation of a hydraulic bureaucracy to centralize control of economic resources (Butzer 1976:111). "Hydraulic" agriculture led to "total power" within the state. While there is still much of interest in Wittfogel's book, most assessments have soundly rejected the basic theory as being "overextended" and "undifferentiated," and as lacking, among the most important things, an awareness of the intricate social networks and landholding patterns created above all by the social interconnections between temples.[39] Irrigation in Egypt was generally on a small scale, coordinated locally without much

<hr />

[37] Stelling-Michaud (1960:1, 329) translated by O'Leary (1989:47).

[38] Nicolet (2003) on the French historical experience coloring Roman history.

[39] Mann (1986); Butzer (1996). For a critique of Wittfogel with respect to China: Deng (1999:103–05), downplaying the amount of irrigated land; with respect to Bali: Lansing (1991). Although an early Roman text, the close economic connections between Akhmim, Ptolemaïs, and Elephantine that are documented in a house sale contract of a priest at Elephantine (*pBerl.* 13534 =Martin 1996, text C34, 2 BC) would not have been uncommon.

state interference. As in China, the state played a minimal role in the agricultural sector, never achieving total control over any area (cf. Deng 1999:105–06).

The Egyptian irrigation system, its extensive canal network, and in particular the model of large scale agricultural production in irrigation basins, led Wittfogel to conclude that the entire economy was managed and controlled by a strongly centralized state apparatus on analogy with socialist state planning.[40] Control of the key assets for production led to total power residing in the central authority. A ready supply of labor through the use of the corvée was a distinctive feature of the system, and abundant manpower enabled other characteristic state activities, such as the construction of enormous palaces, temples, and pyramids, as well as other enterprises that required a monopoly of power, such as calendar-making and record-keeping, maintaining weak inheritance laws, and periodic redistributions of land. Law codes were imposed from above (see chapter 7), there was a unified elite bureaucratic class, and there was no institutional resistance to the ruler's power, although state power was naturally checked by its difficulty in penetrating into the level of village and family structures.

Despite long, sustained and rigorous criticism of Wittfogel from the time of the book's appearance, from such figures as Arnold Toynbee, who claimed it was "resuscitating a Greek myth" (O'Leary 1989:236), and O'Leary's own forceful "critical obituary" (1989), oriental despotism as a political concept dies hard, and many of the assumptions that underlie the theory percolate down into writings that seek to define the difference between Europe and Asian states.[41]

The theory, indeed, has been very much a part of the larger problem of the Greek filter through which Egypt is seen in the writings of Herodotus and many other classical writers, and perhaps more strongly in the Greek/barbarian polarity that emerged with the Persian wars. The Greeks' self-identification, combined with their ignorance of language, did much to perpetuate a stereotype of Egyptian civilization.[42] Only after Champollion's 1822 decipherment of Egyptian, when the work of translating texts began in earnest, could Egypt begin to be understood in its own terms.

---

[40] For Weber, (1978 2:973), irrigation canals were analogous to roads, and in nineteenth-century Germany it was the railroads that enhanced state power. In Wittfogel's analysis (1957:38) Rome was a "Hellenistically despotic state" because of its control of roads. I rely here on O'Leary's (1989:235–61) excellent treatment of Wittfogel's theory.

[41] Cf. Mann (1986).

[42] On the limits of even what Hellenistic Greeks knew of Near Eastern civilizations, see the classic account of Momigliano (1976). Direct knowledge of Egypt, however, is a slightly different story. I cannot agree that there "was . . . no dramatic change in the Greek evaluation of Egypt during the Hellenistic period" per Momigliano (1976:3).

But even then social theory and the specialized publication of Egyptian texts did not often cross paths. It has indeed not been easy, even with extensive scholarly publication of Egyptian texts, to "detach" from a "classical or Western perspective" (Millar 1998:508).

If most European analyses were at best superficial and used to promote particular political agendas, there were other scholars who produced firsthand accounts of Asian states that directly contradicted Montesquieu and others. One such important account was that of Abraham-Hyacinthe Anquetil-du Perron (1731–1805).[43] A student of Indian and Semitic languages and Asian history, who lived in India between 1755 and 1761, Anquetil-du Perron wrote a serious critique of Montesquieu's use of the concept of oriental despotism to characterize Near Eastern empires (1778).[44] This was a landmark, full-blooded attack of the concept, and while he is mentioned by Said (1978), it is, oddly, not for his specific, and important, critique of oriental despotism. Anquetil-du Perron's criticism of Montesquieu turned on two key points: (1) the existence of private property in some Asian states (namely, Turkey, Persia, and India), and (2) the fact that kings were constrained by legal codes. Many subsequent commentaries have overlooked the subtleties of Asian states emphasized by Anquetil's careful analysis.[45]

From Political and Economic Theory to Ptolemaic History

Assumptions about the image and the power of the despotic ruler have long been a part of Ptolemaic history, bound up as it is within a dialectic of difference emphasized by two competing academic disciplines, Classics and Ancient Near Eastern Studies.[46] Despotism, whether specifically acknowledged as such or not, has underpinned analyses of Ptolemaic development, and also has been used widely in ancient and contemporary commentary on the Ptolemaic dynasty itself.[47]

[43] Whelan (2001).

[44] Cf. Voltaire's remarks with respect to the Mughal empire in his *Essai sur les moeurs et l'esprit des nations* 2 (1754:782), treated briefly by Bang (2007:11).

[45] Cf. briefly O'Leary (1989:66–67). See Lansing (1991) on the subtleties of social organization in Bali missed by the Dutch.

[46] Bevan (1927:132): "In so far as Egypt is governed by *foreigners* of Hellenistic culture, Ptolemaic rule is the first chapter of a new epoch, an epoch in which the old Egyptian people has finally lost its freedom—if freedom means that men are governed despotically by rulers of their own race . . . ." Cf. Eyre (2004:159).

[47] For a critical account of the use of despotic theories to understand the Ptolemies, see Helmis (1990). Cf. Van de Mieroop (1997:4–5).

The image of the unrestrained ruler who could act on a whim has been a staple of Egyptian history since ancient times. From stories like the Middle Kingdom *Tale of King Cheops and His Court*, to the Joseph story in the Old Testament (Genesis 37–50), to Herodotus, Aristotle, and later European travelers, the trope of royal wealth in imperial centers, monumental buildings, and rapacious tax collectors who impoverish the rural population is well known.[48]

It has been this literary image of Egyptian kingship that has driven much of our understanding of the ancient political economy in Egypt. The institution of kingship in Egypt is arguably the best documented and therefore the most studied. At the same time, it is extremely difficult to pierce the veil created by the pervasiveness of these royal images and of the theology created to define and (usually) defend the king's position in the state. Scholars were long ago familiar with doctrines of the "king's two bodies," earthly and divine (Bell 1985), and of his divine birth and succession. The ritual primacy of the king throughout the state was assumed to be the normal state of affairs. He was the guarantor of order and stability in the world, but this, it was believed, was the theological expression of a political need to maintain a semblance of unity within what was a dynamic and highly diverse territory. Divine kingship was required.

The real world of the kings was unavoidably different. Kings were recognized as human beings, even explicitly stressed as such from the Middle Kingdom (2055–1650 BC) onward. The distinction between the institution of kingship and the person who occupied the throne may well have already been made during the Old Kingdom.[49] What most Egyptians never saw, ironically, was reported by the Roman mystic Publius Nigidius Figulus, a friend of Cicero's and an eyewitness in the first century BC, to the coronation ceremony itself.[50] In this most sacred of rituals, which took place in the temple of Ptah in Memphis, the king, having been initiated in sacred learning and having taken the Apis bull in a circuit around the city, is led into the inner sanctum of the temple where he takes an oath that he will, among other things, protect the land and the water of Egypt.

All monarchs wish to act despotically, and in some cases they do in fact act in an arbitrary manner. That is an inherent possibility in a monarchy without constitutional restraints. The issue is how and to what the degree

---

[48] For good treatments of the Joseph story, see Vergote (1959); Redford (1970).

[49] The literature on Egyptian kingship is enormous of course. On the discounting of the Egyptian ideology and the human nature of kings, see Posener (1960). A good general introduction is provided by O'Connor and Silverman (1995). See further the literature cited by Delia (1993:199, n. 33).

[50] See briefly Thompson (1988:146–47).

Ptolemaic royal power could be arbitrarily exercised and in what ways it was limited (see chapter 4). Without any doubt some kings were more effective than others (one thinks immediately of Ramses II), but all kings required loyal bureaucrats and a ruling coalition to pull off their divinity. As Kemp (1995:41) summarized the issue: "For long periods, kings seem to have shared power with other leading families, even though decorum made royal power appear to be absolute." There were many constraints on royal power, including those embodied in literary conceptions of the "good king." This vast theoretical literature, existing in many different forms—in stories, in the great myths, and in art—is a major reason pharaonic government lasted for three thousand years.[51] Much later, the Arab writers on Egyptian kingship preserve, it seems, at least an authentic version of the pharaonic *ideal* of the efficiency and kindness of the kings, "dedicated to the well-being of their subjects" (El-Daly 2005:123).[52]

Despite the recognized constraints, the theory of the absolute power of the pharaohs has been an important element in the political analysis of Ptolemaic rulers for much of the twentieth century.[53] For Rostovtzeff despotism was a "fundamental theme" (Shaw 1992:226) of his main work despite the cautious remarks of Westermann (1938:276, n. 19):

> Future investigation . . . must determine what is meant by "the theoretical absolutism" of the Ptolemies. The constant emphasis upon the "theory" implies that their sovereignty was, in practice, limited by so many recognized institutions that, even in its treatment of the native Egyptians, it was not an absolutism, much less a despotism.

Even when Oriental despotism was not explicitly invoked, Rostovtzeff surely had the basic contrast in political economy between the Greek world and Egypt on his mind. "Greek genius" contrasted with "oriental stagnation."[54] The Ptolemies continued to exploit the "twin pillars of an oriental monarchy": ownership of the land and a compulsory labor system (Rostovtzeff 1941:271).

More recent historical work follows the same lines. Peter Green's (1990) understanding of the Ptolemaic state, for example, echoes the earlier viewpoint of Wilcken (1912), Rostovtzeff, Tarn and Griffith (1952),

---

[51] Bonhême and Forgeau (1988).

[52] The realities of premodern kings' attitudes toward their subjects was different of course. Cf. Westermann (1938).

[53] See e.g., Wilcken (1912:3:"*Als absoluter Herrscher war der König ursprünglich alleiniger Eigentümer von Grund und Boden.*" Also, Green (1990:188): "Ptolemaic rule did not in any sense depend on a willing consent, much less active choice, by the governed. . . ."

[54] (1941:1081ff.). Cf. his *A social and economic history of the Roman Empire*, 502–41. It is instructive to read Hegel's views on India in this regard, on which see the comments of O'Leary (1989:70–71).

and others. Egypt was changeless; the king of Egypt personally owned the country; Egyptians were treated as a single group; a "cavalier" treatment of private property prevailed (Green 1990:191), as did a "powerful centralized bureaucracy," "strangling royal interference in every area," and "systematic exploitation."[55]

If the political relationships were subtler and more complex than these early understandings suggest, one overriding factor that created major differences in rural production and social structure between the classical world and Egypt remains. That factor is the Nile itself. But irrigation did not lead to authoritarian rule, as Wittfogel suggests. Rather, the environmental constraint imposed on Egypt by a river corridor flowing through a desert held the population captive and thereby created conditions ripe for centralized political control. In the final analysis, it was the Nile flood regime that was the real despot, wielding the power of a kind of "social cage" created by the rich soil of the flood plain bounded by harsh desert to either side. The state, its institutions, and individual farmers had to respond and to adjust to the basic forces of the annual inundation and its recession. The flood could not be prevented, only contained; and the population was quite effectively "caged" in the river corridor (Mann 1986). The rural population itself was organized around village hierarchies—complex social networks built around land tenure and tax obligations, and a cohesive group solidarity focused on production in an irrigated environment.[56] The need to control an irrigated landscape in which production was locally organized, led not to despotic kings who claimed ownership of the entire state and its apparatus, but to the development of bureaucracy and a "centralizing principal" (Chaudhuri 1990:261). There never was any connection between irrigation and centralized state power outside of the concern for revenue.[57] The king could be a director, but it was the actors—the local elites and the growing bureaucracy—who were the players on the stage of a dynamic and variable ecosystem. The outcome could be rather different from the script. We come to a subtler understanding of political power in Egypt.[58]

There was no despotic centralized state power as a consequence of irrigation. There was no state bureaucracy in charge of managing the irrigation system, either in ancient Egypt or under the Ptolemies. The environment evoked a flexible state response, not centralized planning of the economy (or centralized planning of anything else for that matter). The

---

[55] Bingen (2007) offers a subtler picture of the politics.

[56] For ancient Egypt, see Eyre (2004). Lansing's study (1991) of social organization around irrigation in Bali is instructive.

[57] O'Leary (1989:252). Cf. Butzer (1976:110).

[58] Eyre (forthcoming).

king could set the tone, send signals about expectations, make a display of his divinity, and so on, but the bureaucracy functioned in a sphere apart. As we shall see, the king did play an important role in reshaping the economic and legal systems, in founding new cities and towns, and in establishing a new language of government. But how far his reach could extend, and how effective it was, depended not just on the king's will but also on the political relationships he had established.

DIRIGISME

The term *dirigisme* in its original use referred to the strong role of the state in the regulation of the French economy. It has come to be applied in rather more pejorative ways to states that have centrally planned, highly administered economies. The degree of administration of the economy is usually not specified, but that is the key factor. All modern economies contain a mixture of state and private sector activity. The term, then, is not useful unless we can be more specific. In the case of Ptolemaic Egypt, the term has been historically used as a cipher for a centralized, planned royal economy, with Ptolemy II's reforms anticipating Colbert by some two millennia.[59] In this sense the dirigisme of the Ptolemies derived from their despotism. Total power combined effectively with a desire to reshape the economy. The classic discussion, as with so much else that concerns the Ptolemaic economy, is Rostovtzeff's (1941:267–316). The king owned everything within the state. All resources, material and human (including their "unrestricted obedience"), were at his disposal to do with as he pleased. A "stricter, more efficient, and more logical system" (1941:272) was designed to enrich the king and his circle. State control (*étatisme*) was applied to agricultural production and other industries to increase output, even to the founding of new towns. [60] State control, in fact, extended so far as the establishment of new cults, such as that of Serapis.[61]

As with despotism, the origins of the concept of Ptolemaic dirigisme and centralized bureaucratic control were believed to lie deep in the ancient Egyptian past. The Ptolemies merely continued, and probably expanded, the tradition. The basis of the economy was the production of grain and its redistribution through state and temple granaries. Distribu-

---

[59] Cf. Davies (2001:42–43). As Walbank (1991–1992) reminds us, Ptolemy II's career has excited both a negative and a positive press over the years. Rostovtzeff and Préaux were generally positive; Turner (1984) accuses him of being both the inventor of the new fiscal system and the bankrupter of the dynasty. On Ptolemy II's activity, see Thompson (2008), and chapters 4 and 5.

[60] See chapter 4.

[61] Samuel (1983: 93–94). Thompson (1988).

tion was along a "complex network of quasi-autonomous pious foundations or religious institutions where the focus of attention was the cult of
statues of gods and kings . . . ." (Kemp 2006:305). This network of temple foundations, of varying sizes and degrees of importance, supported a
large staff, many of whom served part-time in service rotations (the so-
called *phyle* system). As Kemp has pointed out, the ancient economy
from a certain perspective looks both well organized and "systematic."
In fact, however, there were "channels of authority" (Kemp 2006:305)
that were compartmentalized around particular tasks. There was no
intellectual rationale to the economic system, merely particular responses
by the state to particular needs. It was, in other words, reactive rather
than planned, and managerial skill resided in the temples rather than with
the king.[62]

No one should doubt that the early Ptolemies, beginning with the first
Ptolemy while he was still functioning technically as a satrap, had a plan.
That is evident, for example, in the new settlement patterns, in the founding of Ptolemaïs in the Thebaid, in the division of the Fayyum into nom-
archies, in the introduction of new fiscal institutions, and so on. But a
plan is not the same thing as a planned economy, and a "centralizing
principal" is not the same as a fully integrated economy.

Direction from the king traditionally came in the form of royal decrees,
the standard method of laying down rules and responding to problems
prompted by petitions or by the reports of officials. Kemp (2006:308)
summarizes:

> Government in ancient Egypt was by royal decree, the system of ad-
> ministration was the sum of these decrees, and the resulting overlaps
> and confusions of responsibility were tackled by fresh decrees in re-
> sponse to specific complaints.

The king could establish a rule or clarify a procedure. Enforcing these
was another matter entirely. For example, the king's direction coupled
with the temples' redistribution network was not the whole of the economy. The important Hekanakhte letters dating to the Middle Kingdom
(Dynasty 12) reveal a world in which an individual farmer constructed
rational household budgets and had an economic strategy to buy and rent
land to grow particular crops, and he did so without any state interference.[63] Indeed without any mention of the state at all. Although we cannot
make too much of one group of texts, the social standing of the writer

---

[62] On the important role of temples in the Egyptian economy, mainly in the New Kingdom state, see also Janssen (1975a, 1979); and Haring (1997) on royal memorial temple
estates in Thebes during the New Kingdom.

[63] Allen (2002).

suggests that these letters provide a window onto what may well have been typical of small-scale farming activity in villages.

Rathbone (2000:45) has argued that we should retain dirigisme as a concept because recent work on the Ptolemaic economy has "underestimated the ability of governments to affect production," and the king had the "ultimate right to administer tenure on most land." The three administrative categories of land—royal, sacred, and kleruchic (land given to soldiers)—"were all essentially state land . . . the king could create them *ex novo*, he could reallocate tenure of particular plots, [and] intervene in the conditions of tenure." Priests and kleruchs were, Rathbone argued, part of the royal administration of the land. "Summaries, if not the full details, had to be sent to Alexandria." Other items marshaled to show state power were the ability of the state, "by royal coercion," (Rathbone 2000:47; *SB* XX 14699) to move people around; the demand by the kings for priests and royal scribes to meet in Alexandria; new experimentation in crop species; the demand for double cropping; the imposition of payment by coinage in the taxation system; the use of corvée labor; and the development of the Fayyum.

The assumption of state control has also been at the foundation of much work on the extensive documentary papyri of the period. The Revenue Laws papyrus, for example, and the Zenon archive, documenting the large estate of the *dioikêtês* Apollonios, both dating to the mid-third century BC, were treated as confirmation of the theory of strong state direction and penetration into local economic organization. The corpus of demotic texts known as "land allotment receipts," believed to show the state's ability to compel farmers to bring derelict land under production (*Zwangspacht*), and the notable absence of animal sales in Ptolemaic papyri have both been explained by Ptolemaic state dirigisme. But recent, careful analysis of these texts has substantially altered the picture. Bingen's study of the Revenue Laws papyrus (1978a), for example, has shown that this document (indeed the single most important surviving document of the Ptolemaic economy) was in no way a comprehensive attempt to organize the economy. The series of rules set out in it were, rather, more reactive to the realities of Egypt than they were directives from the center. In like wise, Vandorpe's study (2000a) of land allotment receipts suggests that, rather than documenting state compulsion to farm, these texts are in fact receipts generated by the survey of crops that fixed the harvest tax on an individual holding.

The movement of people, whether for immigration and new settlement or, on a local level, a mobilization labor for canal work or other projects, has also been viewed through a dirigiste lens. New immigration into Egypt and the relocation of people within the country were both important in Ptolemaic state building. It is difficult to know the scale of these movements, and we normally remain ignorant of the rationale for moving (in part because we have only official records and not the personal accounts of those who moved). But the view that movement was "solicited and directed by the Ptolemies" (Rathbone 1990:47) should be qualified (cf. Mueller 2006:165–80).The theory of corvée labor has been a standard feature of most descriptions of the Ptolemaic economy, but it has largely been assumed.[64] Scholars have often asserted that rural labor could be coerced for long- and short-term projects at the whim of the ruler or his agents. Eyre (2004) is right to point out that the labor system in ancient Egypt was more complex, organized around service obligations within local social hierarchies. "Institutionalized" (Eyre 2004:181) demand for labor service should be distinguished from regular short-term work, such as canal clearance. Royal demands to mobilize labor should also be distinguished from local community needs. At least some of the aspects of the corvée system were a response to the work that needed to be done each year by the farmers to guarantee a proper flooding of the fields. The farmers themselves had at least as much a stake in the matter as the king. Typically it is a combination of the carrot and the stick that characterizes state/farmer relations.

While there is reason to accept some aspects of the dirigiste model in terms of the theoretical structure of the state and the aims of royal action, the power of the ruler must be qualified. A major assumption of the dirigiste model is the state's access to information or "knowledge." "The central government had, in theory, access to abundant information about the productive resources, especially the agricultural and human resources, of its kingdom" (Rathbone 2000:46). Information came in the form of land surveys, a census of inhabitants taken annually, and a biennial census of livestock. For Tarn and Griffith (1952:195) this meant that "Ptolemy knew each day what each of his subjects was worth and what most of them were doing." The centralized collection of information, while theoretically possible as Rathbone has argued, was hardly perfect, and we must remain cautious in assuming good information flow on the basis of state bureaucratic structure alone.[65] Centralized and accurate, detailed information is constantly stressed in ancient texts, but the information, for example on the number of persons available for corvée labor, is really only required at the local level where it enables village elites to organize.[66]

---

[64] On the corvée: Préaux (1939:395–400); Rostovtzeff (1941:275).

[65] Rathbone (2000:46). The flow of information from villages to the capital is also stressed by Clarysse and Thompson (2006, esp. 2:65).

[66] See e.g., *The Instructions of Rekhmire*, a New Kingdom "vizier" responsible for the administration of justice. For a study of the text, see Van den Boorn (1988). On the instructions to the vizier, see chapter 5.

The king, therefore, needed only to keep track of his local officials, not of the entire population.

All of this assumes both the accuracy of the information and that a firm link had been established and was maintained between the village and the capital in Alexandria, conditions that may not always have been met. The rulers certainly desired good, centralized information, and many fiscal structures such as the census of people and animals were designed specifically to this end (chapter 4). The accuracy and the frequency of these institutional controls, however, remain uncertain.

COLONIALISM

From the point of view of social relationships, Ptolemaic Egypt and the Hellenistic Near East have frequently been viewed, unconsciously or not, through the lens of the European nation-state colonial experience.[67] The British Raj has often been invoked, and it is natural that this was the dominant paradigm in pre–World War II Europe, particularly in England.[68] While there has been occasional criticism of the over broad use of colonialism as a model for understanding the Hellenistic state in its totality, it remains a common reference point.[69] Davies (2002:6) is unequivocal in his judgment: Hellenistic states were "predatory, exploitative, monopolist, racist, and colonialist." The first three items on his list, as we will see in the next chapter, could describe every premodern state in history, differences being only in the relative degree of predation, exploitation, and monopolization achieved by the individual state. In the Hellenistic state, racism, as opposed to cultural prejudice, is hardly in evidence at all (though of course there would have been attitudes of cultural superiority on all sides), and so we are left with the last feature, colonialism.[70]

The use of colonialism as a model of the Ptolemaic (and Seleukid) state is built upon on two premises. First, a "Hellenocentric" perspective that sees a unilateral diffusion of Greek language and culture; and second, assumptions about power relationships between Greeks and Egyptians.[71]

[67] Will (1985); Austin (1986:455); Lewis (1986:135); Samuel (1983); cf. Heinen (1987:118); Samuel (1989:1–12); Bagnall (1997).

[68] Green (1990, 1993); Alcock (1994:171). So too for the Seleukids: Sherwin-White and Kuhrt (1993:155).

[69] Ritner (1999) attacked the colonialist model on many fronts, but principally on the basis of the status of Egyptian culture under the Ptolemies.

[70] On the absence of racism: Bagnall (1997:230, n. 14). Cf. Ritner (1999:289).

[71] I have found Sherwin-White and Kuhrt (1993:141–87) very stimulating and suggestive. See reactions to the book and the response of the authors in *Topoi* 4 (1994).

Tarn and many others of his time, following Plutarch (*Moralia* 328c-f), viewed the spread of Greek culture much like the spread of British institutions in the nineteenth century. Hellenistic kings were understood as having "an almost missionary role as disseminators of hellenism" (Sherwin-White and Kuhrt 1993:186); in general Greeks held privileged social position, and Greek culture "triumphed" (Peters 1970). For the most part, that view of hellenization has now been dropped in favor of a more complex model of cultural interaction (Hornblower 1996).

The idea that Hellenistic states had an intentional state *policy* to hellenize local populations, as opposed to the notion that Hellenism spread because the Egyptians chose to adopt the culture of their Greek rulers, has rightly been questioned (Sherwin-White and Kuhrt 1993:145). It remains true, however, that both "imperialist dreams and ambitions" and "actual conquest" had become a Greek reality by the fourth centuries BC. The key question, and one not easily answered, is what degree of coercion was employed in the promulgation of Greek culture, however that is defined. It seems more likely that individuals were drawn to the new imperial culture by various means, including by incentives.[72] There are some aspects of hellenization, at least the ideology of it, that were in fact state policy under the Ptolemies. Clarysse and Thompson (2006/2:52–53), for example, see the salt tax exemption for teachers of Greek, athletes, and actors as supporting the "cultural aims" of the dynasty. The extensive adoption of the Greek language and of Greek loan words, and the amount of Greek later preserved in Coptic, are impressive measures of the effects of Ptolemaic governance and the acceptance of Greek culture in Egypt. It is important to note in this regard that the imposition of Greek was slow and was not compulsory. The state provided incentives to switch.

The Ptolemaic administrative papyri constitute the first historical corpus that provides details on a micro level of social relationships centered on production. They indeed give evidence of the rise of a new elite, but not to the exclusion of older, entrenched social groups, such as the priests. The Ptolemies did not knock out older structures and elite ideologies but in fact supported them. Some old elites generated their own "legitimating discourses" (Haldon 1993:34), while others seem to have accepted the new power structure readily. Those with citizenship status in Alexandria or in Ptolemaïs certainly had precedence over Egyptians and over other Greeks, but their status was not based merely on ethnicity. The new ruling class was certainly Greek, but it was neither homogeneous nor completely Greek. It was above all the use of the Greek language that had profound and long-lasting effects on Egypt, however much a Greek ruling class

---

[72] I follow here Austin's (2003) excellent analysis in regard to the Seleukid state. For state incentives, see e.g., Clarysse and Thompson (2006 2:7).

dominated local social structures. Nevertheless, demotic Egyptian persisted at the local levels of administration. The range of the surviving documentation gives the impression (and it can be no more than an impression) that the extent to which Greek was adopted and demotic continued in use varied widely.[73]

Edouard Will (1985) published an extended analysis of the Hellenistic world using modern colonial analogies that has been particularly influential. Will insisted that Préaux and Rostovtzeff had overemphasized the role of the state and underemphasized social relations between Greeks and Egyptians, and that they were too fixed on the Greek point of view of the "colonial" enterprise. Bagnall's (1997) "decolonizing" critique of Will has rightly criticized the use of the colonial analogy, basically on the grounds that it can only describe a part of the very complex social relationships of the period (1997:228).[74] It matters a great deal whether we are concerned with social relationships between the Ptolemaic kings and Egyptian priests or, on a more local level, between villagers and tax collectors, and whether we are talking about social power in a hierarchy or in "politico-religious culture" (Haldon 1993:9).

The movement of Greeks around the Mediterranean began in the eighth century BC. By the middle of the seventh century, they were well known in Egypt and living in established communities—notably in Naukratis and Memphis, but elsewhere as well.[75] Greek communities were founded around the eastern Mediterranean for a variety of reasons, and they served many purposes. No single modern theory adequately addresses the rather complex typology of Greek colonization (Tsetskhladze 2006).[76]

There were certainly aspects of colonialism in some social relationships in Ptolemaic Egypt (e.g., kleruchs leasing land to Egyptians), in the founding of new towns, in the movement of people, in the fact that Greeks (or at least Greek-speaking persons) served in administrative capacities, even in the temples. And there were certainly social tensions brought about by the Ptolemaic takeover, the creation of a new fiscal system, and the practice of billeting soldiers in rural areas. The Ptolemies were sensitive to the problems thus created. It is indeed true that Greeks were the ruling power in the period, established new communities, and were in certain cases in

---

[73] See for example the demotic legal texts that survive into the Roman period at Tebtunis and Dîme, now being actively published by the Würzburg project. See Lippert and Schentuleit (2006). The use of demotic in tax receipts appears, for the moment anyway, to have been in part regional, and the use of demotic may have been more persistent in southern villages; e.g., demotic used in the census text *pCount* 53–54 (Asyut, second century BC).

[74] Decolonization is also called for by Falivene (1991:226).

[75] On Naukratis, see Möller (2000). The *Hellenomemphite* and *Karomemphite* communities in Memphis are treated by Thompson (1988). See most recently Boardman (2006).

[76] See also Finley (1976)

an advantageous position because Greek became the language of the new government. Ptolemaic fiscal divisions of the country may also have had, on occasion, deleterious effects on traditional occupations.[77]

But Ptolemaic Egypt lacks certain important features of a colonial state, and it is important to keep in mind that Greeks from many places in the Mediterranean had settled in Egypt centuries before the Ptolemies arrived. One recent survey of ancient colonial states suggests that the Ptolemaic state was a case of "colonialism without colonies."[78] For that matter, it would be a case of a colony without a *metropole*.[79] As one reviewer noted, this stretches any reasonable definition of the term "colonialism" and makes clear the limits of the model.[80] Power relationships on the land were hardly ever "colonial" if we mean by that that Greeks always had the advantage over Egyptians. As Bingen has shown, Greeks were often excluded from gaining access to land.[81]

It was, however the colonial model of society that directed much interpretation of the documents. Shaw (1992:281) invoked Will's argument for Ptolemaic Egypt being an example of "classic colonialism," stressing "new networks of power" that excluded Egyptians "from almost every level of formal state power, and from almost every ancillary area of life in which the settler government controlled access to resources." Social separation was further aggravated by a "country/town" divide, as well as divisions along cultural, linguistic, and religious lines, all exacerbated by state demands that official documents be written in Greek. Economic exploitation was so thorough that "all known holders of the most extensive properties and richest lands were now Greeks." Egyptians were reduced to being "tied peasants" on state or temple land or "holders of small or marginal pieces of land." State power was so extensive that it even restricted naming practices on pain of death.

That this picture exaggerates the situation is in part due to the nature of the surviving documentary evidence, which tends to present us with a viewpoint from the perspective of new settlements and from state aims. Moreover, scholars have concentrated on Greek documents and on the study of Greek settlements in preference to Egyptian documents and settlements, and this has of course produced an overemphasis on colonial relationships.[82] Greek settlers showed a preference for living in the towns.

---

[77] Bingen (1978b), on the requirements of mobility in apiculture that was in conflict with rigid Ptolemaic fiscal geography.

[78] Gosden (2004).

[79] Cf. the remarks of Bagnall (1997:231–32).

[80] Dawdy (2005).

[81] Cf. Anagnostou-Canas (1994), and Shaw (1992:281) with Bingen (1984); Manning (2003a), and the comments by Bagnall (1997:236, n. 34).

[82] Cf. Alcock (1994:174–75). On the Fayyum bias, Manning (2003a:101–03).

Some of these towns, like Krokodilopolis in the Fayyum, were new. Towns in the Delta or the Nile valley, however, were hardly "false *poleis*" as Shaw calls them, or "Greek-type town settlements." They were old and important cult centers in which some Greeks, as well as others, had settled. Other places like Alexandria and Ptolemaïs, which were certainly Greek-style *poleis*, did have heavy Greek populations. The exclusion of Egyptians from formal state power is also not strictly true, although for the Greek institutions that Shaw lists—athletics, eponymous priesthoods, and the Greek law courts— this is indeed the case. But the point is that there were parallel Egyptian institutions that were incorporated into the state apparatus and not eliminated. Moreover, Egyptian elites were not only well aware of Greek culture but absorbed it and in some cases transformed it for their own political ends.[83]

In recent years, the use of Egyptian documentary sources has clarified our understanding of the forces and traditions that underlie local economic and social conditions, especially in the south (Manning 2003a). Better survey archaeology has also given us a richer evidentiary base from which to view settlement patterns and the interaction of local with Greek culture. The archaeology of settlements has, however, so far tended to proceed from a colonialist perspective.[84] It has been the standard view that new settlements, and in particular the new cities of Alexandria and Ptolemaïs, were "purely Greek." Increasingly, however, it can be shown that such new settlements were heterogeneous, and that this is probably true even of places like Ptolemaïs (discussed in chapter 3).

There is no doubt that the Ptolemaic taxation system was more extensive and more thorough than anything seen before in Egypt. The tax farming system and the rent-seeking behavior of agents certainly led to abuse.[85] None of this, though, can be specifically ascribed to colonial state behavior. To be sure, there were abuses and the potential for the abuse of agricultural producers, and this was recognized by the ancient Egyptian state and treated in literary texts.[86] Tax collection caused at all times in Egyptian history tension between taxpayers and tax collectors. The major difference, I would suggest, between these relationships in the Ptolemaic period and in earlier times is simply that they are so much better documented in the Ptolemaic period. Colonial models of the Ptolemaic state, in the final analysis, capture some, but not all, of the social dynamics of

[83] Cf. Bagnall (1993:323).

[84] Alcock (1994:174). As Alcock's piece admits, archaeological survey of Hellenistic Egyptian sites lags behind other parts of the Hellenistic world.

[85] See chapter 5 on tax farming.

[86] See inter alia the Middle Kingdom story *The Tale of the Eloquent Peasant* (Parkinson 1991); and on coercion, the *Late Egyptian Miscellanies* published by Gardiner (1937).

the period (many elite Egyptians would have been familiar with Greek and Greek culture long before Alexander arrived on the scene), and hardly at all elucidate the differences between nation-state colonialism and premodern state colonialism.

In order to set the Ptolemies in historical context, I now move on to a general treatment of premodern states and the ways in which the Ptolemies fit into the general pattern of such states. Having situated the Ptolemies in that broad framework, and having established some metrics by which the Ptolemaic state may be judged in a positive light, I will shift in chapters 4 and 5 to a detailed analysis of the economic and legal developments that shaped governance during the three centuries of Ptolemaic rule and beyond, and will explain why the Ptolemaic state ranks as one of the most successful in antiquity.

Chapter 3

MOVING BEYOND DESPOTISM, ECONOMIC PLANNING, AND STATE BANDITRY

PTOLEMAIC EGYPT AS A PREMODERN STATE

> An immense conquest presupposes despotism. In
> this case, the army that is spread out in the provinces
> is insufficient. There must always be a specially
> trustworthy body around the prince, always ready
> to assail the part of the empire that may waiver. This
> guard should constrain the others and make trem-
> ble all those to whom one has been obliged to leave
> some authority in the empire.
> —*Montesquieu,* The spirit of the laws
> *(1748: Book 10.16)*

> *Oriental Despotism* was the consequence of
> hydrophobia and hydrocephalus in
> a Cold War warrior.
> —*O'Leary (1989:261)*

IN THE LAST CHAPTER, I reviewed the historiographic understanding of the Ptolemaic state. I argued against previous attempts at characterizing the Ptolemaic reforms through models of despotism, dirigisme, and colonialism. All three of these concepts were, to be sure, operative in Ptolemaic Egypt. But I suggested that were more factors in the equation than the king, that there were limits on his ability to direct the economy, and that the colonial model was inadequate to explain the dynamics of social power. We can avoid some of the problems with the typology of the Ptolemaic state by simply stating that it was a premodern "bureaucratic empire" (Eisenstadt 1993), a Mediterranean empire with an Egyptian core, established by conquest, with its main metropole at Alexandria, and a secondary center at Ptolemaïs in Upper Egypt.[1] That it was a takeover

---

[1] On the problems of ancient state typology, see Finley (1976). The "stable" core of the empire was comprised of Egypt, Cyrenaica, Cyprus, amd much of the Red Sea coast. On the Ptolemaic empire, see Bagnall (1976); Hölbl (2001), poetically expressed by Theoc. *Id.*

by an outside military power is important in understanding the dynasty's concern for the search for political legitimacy through traditional Egyptian institutions (chapter 5). At the height of their power in the early third century BC, the Ptolemies controlled a "maximum stable territory" (Taagepera 1979) slightly under one quarter the size of the Seleukid empire, with a population of, perhaps, a little more than one quarter that of the Seleukid kingdom at its height.[2]

Most studies of state formation have been based on studies of European states, especially those that have arisen in the last two centuries. I follow Barkey (1994:1) who argued that the "western model does not exhaust all possible forms of state centralization." Having said that, the basic issues that the Ptolemaic kings faced were, in broad outlines, similar to those summarized by Barkey for the Ottoman Empire, who suggests one more variant on state making (1994:1–23). The "capturing" of society by the state generated both bargaining and opposition; practices like revoking the privileges of local elites and the billeting of soldiers at private expense were resented, and bureaucratic development was often resisted, passively or actively.

When it comes to defining a state, a "formal consensus" hardly exists (Haldon 1993:32). There are, in fact, as many definitions as scholars who have worked on the issue. On the other hand, most would agree on a few basic features of the premodern state: a state is a territorially bounded entity that attempts to enforce rules and to "mobilize *enough* means of violence to retain its position as ultimate arbiter" (Crone 2003:7). This already is a slightly more nuanced, and better, definition than the classic Weberian one, which viewed states as the legitimate *monopolizers* of violence. That is what states wanted to claim, but that is not what states could actually accomplish. Our basic definition presents certain problems, however, when it comes to boundaries, and perhaps even typologies, because in Egypt the reach of the state was hardly uniform from Alexandria to Philae over the three centuries of Ptolemaic rule.[3] Nor was the state static, in its structure or its institutions. The Ptolemies attempted to solve the problem of penetrating local society by several strategies. The most of important of these, as we shall later see, were the establishment loyal

17.86–90. On the concept of empire applied to the Ptolemies, see the remarks of Mueller (2006:42–47).

[2] Measuring territory, in my view, is less important than measuring the control of trade flows, which is what the Ptolemies were after. On calculating the Seleukid population, see Aperghis (2004:35–58). For the population of Ptolemaic Egypt, see chapter 5.

[3] On the problem of political boundaries of states not always being clear-cut, see Haldon(1993:5). On the issue of "typologies" in the historical analysis of the ancient world, see the critical remarks by Horden and Purcell (2000:101).

Greek communities, the use of religion, the monetizing of the economy, and the reshaping of the legal system.

All rulers, and the elites who surround them, share the desire to remain in power and to accomplish two important goals. First, to fend off rivals and defend their territory; and second, to raise revenue. The institutional structure of the state determines whether rulers succeed or fail in these aims. States vary in size and in their ability to enforce rules.[4] The main reason why the historical experience of premodern states was not in line with their rulers' aims is that they were usually weak with respect to their control of territory, given difficulties of communication and transportation, and they suffered from an inherent shortage of administrative manpower and cash. [5]

The prevalent premodern form of rule was authoritarian. In Egypt's case, this took the form of divine kingship. The ruler claimed absolute authority and that authority was usually grounded in religious ideology and cult practice. There was no constitutional opposition to this authority. The ruler was, however, hampered by a lack of the information required to govern a complex territory, and his reach restricted by the spheres of influence of other important power holders, mainly the priesthoods, soldiers, and the literate class.[6] The ruler, in other words, was bounded by constraints inherent in asymmetric information flow and by social groups whose loyalty he required. Constraints in the latter case can be measured by the "cost of exit" from the state of these groups and by the cost of replacing one ruler with another (Furubotn and Richter 2000:414). Given the inherent "information problem," the ruler might devise different strategies to gain control over regions and villages far from the political center. In terms of comparative history, these institutional expedients are of interest. But, as Crone (2003:45) concludes, "genuine control over provincial affairs simply could not be achieved."

An historical analysis of the functions of states shows a wide range of solutions to problems that arose from the constraints that I have just mentioned. However, a few broad patterns emerge. Successful states are those that defend their territory, guarantee social order, and collect taxes in some form. A consensus on the proper behavior of the king usually develops. Whatever the ideological claims about the sources of his power, a good king supports political stability by dispensing justice and ensuring order. Most of the economic activities of rulers relate to fiscal or revenue

[4] Cf. Mann (1986:26–27); Levi (1988); Haldon (1993:32–33); Barkey (1994:10); Furubotn and Richter (2000:413–17, 430–33).

[5] I rely here on the summary of Crone (2003).

[6] On the basic issues involved, from a European point of view but still an excellent treatment of royal power applicable to an ancient context as well, see Bendix (1978).

issues; i.e., their activities are overwhelmingly concerned with the state itself and not with the welfare of the population. Among the most common activities of kings are the founding of new towns, the expansion of arable land, the creation of government monopolies, the building of roads, and the introduction of currencies and uniform systems of weights and measures. Overall though, the preindustrial state is weaker and more limited in its activity than its modern successor.[7]

Measuring the strength of a state is of course fraught with problems, particularly when we are dealing with an ancient state. One particularly important distinction should be kept in mind, and that is the difference between *extensive* and *intensive* power.[8] These two concepts have often been conflated, but it is crucial to keep them separate. The ruler of an empire had the ability to mobilize a large number of people across considerable distances for "minimal co-operation" (Crone 2003:57), but did not have the same ability to organize the state internally to solve particular problems. Penetrating village structures proved difficult. It is not hard to see where some historians have simply ascribed total power to the state by looking at certain phenomena and assuming that the power of the ruler, theoretically absolute, could be applied to any issue at any time. While premodern states could be effective at mobilizing their population for war, and were often brutal in extracting resources from their population, they were weak in terms of their ability to control and coordinate that population. Viewing the premodern state from the perspective of the modern world, it is easy to forget how much more fragmented ancient societies were, how much more localized was their history, and to how great a degree "social action" happened within "limited and tightly bounded spatial contexts."[9] Recognizing these factors provides a context for the behavior of premodern rulers in general, at the same time as it will explain the particular behavior of the Ptolemies in Egypt.

The links between rulers, the elite, and the rest of the population were always complex. Rulers did need to serve elite interests, but they could also act autonomously; i.e., outside of the organizational structure in which the elites functioned. A focus on the behavior of rulers in bureaucratic empires and their desire for autonomous power, rather than setting them in the more complex network of social groups and organizations within an imperial state, is perhaps a better starting point for understanding the ruler as the embodiment of the state (cf. Levi 1988:2; Eisenstadt 1993:18–19; Barkey 1994:10). The ruler's policy or aims were shaped both by the new

---

[7] For the relationship between the state and the economy in modern economies, see Block and Evans (2005).

[8] On the concept, see Mann (1986:7–10); Crone (2003:57).

[9] O'Brian (1998:13) summarizing the work of the sociologist Anthony Giddens.

institutions that were introduced and the relationship between these and ancient, established institutional structures and organizations.

In such a mode, following Olson, we can view rulers as bandits who establish themselves within a territory.[10] On analogy with the economics of Mafia families, the state is seen as having a monopoly of the crime on its turf, which produces an incentive not to predate because doing so would affect the state's long-term interests. The Mafia family prefers instead to sell protection. The banditry model ties together autocracy, economic performance, and the durability of a state. The state itself is viewed as a kind of protection racket. Coercive power and protection coincides with self-interest of the community to foster production and trade.[11] The nexus between coercion and development is an important one. Taxation and the provision of public goods go hand in hand. A ruler who controls territory—what Olson refers to as a "stationary bandit"—is "not like a wolf that preys on the elk, but more like the rancher who makes sure that his cattle are protected and given water" (Olson 2000:11). This image of the "rancher," or "shepherd" is exactly the ideology fostered by Egyptian kings. It is interesting to note here that Turner, in his treatment of Ptolemaic history (1984:133), said in passing that there were no protection rackets documented in pharaonic Egypt, although he does not exclude the possibility of their existence. Viewing the state as the protection racket par excellence would suggest that the phenomenon was hiding in plain view.

There has been criticism of Olson's model, not least because the "stationary bandit" is actually quite rare historically, and because a singular focus on the ruler ignores the role and loyalty or disloyalty of organizations and social groups. "The case study literature on long-lived dictatorships," Haber (2006) argues, "indicates, in fact, that they are highly predatory." The state requires revenue to protect its territory and to collect a surplus over and above the cost of this protection. Indeed, if there were a single "self-interested" ruler, he would tend to maximize tribute at whatever costs and "be indifferent to the level of protection rent," (i.e., the income merchants might receive gained from the protection from piracy that was traded for loyalty to the state) (Tilly 1985:176, following the arguments of Lane).

In some ways, Hellenistic rulers were similar to bandits in their desire for revenue. Indeed, even in ancient times, the behavior of rulers was sometimes couched in terms of thievery, the major difference between kings and mere bandits being the scale of their activity, as Saint Augustine famously pointed out (*De Civ. D.* 4.4):

[10] I follow Olson's (1982, 2000) analysis here.
[11] Cf. Mann (1986:100).

Justice being taken away, then, what are kingdoms but great robberies? For what are robberies themselves, but little kingdoms? The
band itself is made up of men; it is ruled by the authority of a prince,
it is knit together by the pact of the confederacy; the booty is divided
by the law agreed on. If, by the admittance of abandoned men, this
evil increases to such a degree that it holds places, fixes abodes,
takes possession of cities, and subdues peoples, it assumes the more
plainly the name of a kingdom, because the reality is now manifestly
conferred on it, not by the removal of covetousness, but by the addition of impunity. Indeed, that was an apt and true reply which was
given to Alexander the Great by a pirate who had been seized. For
when that king had asked the man what he meant by keeping hostile
possession of the sea, he answered with bold pride, "What thou
meanest by seizing the whole earth; but because I do it with a petty
ship, I am called a robber, whilst thou who dost it with a great fleet
art styled emperor.

Predatory behavior was a major feature of the Hellenistic world, a natural
extension of the collapse of the Athenian and then the Persian imperial
regimes (Shaw 1984). Warfare was a productive part of the economy and
it was endemic.[12] Banditry was a popular subject in contemporary literature, and not only outlaws but also legitimate rulers acted the part of
bandits throughout the Hellenistic world (Fowler 2007; cf. 3 Maccabees
on the treatment of Jews in Egypt by Ptolemy IV). There is, however, an
important behavioral difference between rulers and ordinary bandits. The
ruler is both stationary and visible; the common bandit, on the other
hand, roams from place to place and, ideally, remains invisible.[13] The
Hellenistic kings were interested in gaining advantage against rival kingdoms, in economic gain, and in exploitation, as were other imperial states
that were restrained only by conventions rather than by a constitution.
In order to accomplish these goals a ruler needed to co-opt a much
broader section of a territory's population than would an ordinary bandit.[14] Coercion and extortion were the flip side of the protection rackets
that states offered.[15]

To place ancient Egypt within a premodern state framework as a pre-
text for understanding the Ptolemaic state, we should emphasize both
royal ideology and the constraint of royal power dictated by local agricultural production, which was controlled by village and temple elites and

---

[12] Cf. Ma (2000:110). On Hellenistic warfare, see Austin (1986); Chaniotis (2005).
[13] Cf. Fowler (2007:156).
[14] See chapter 5.
[15] On states as protection rackets: Tilly (1985); Mann (1986:100). Cf. Ma (2000:121).

by the Nile itself. One of the hallmarks of the Egyptian state throughout its history is its flexibility. Considerable political adjustments in the position of the ruler within the state ideological system came in response to central state collapse and reformation (Kemp 2006:334; Butzer 1980). State intervention in local structures, in village governance for example, was probably minimal (Trigger 2003; Lehner 2000), and the pharaonic state had to be ever ready to confront the environmental challenges posed by a variable water supply (Butzer 1980). A large degree of local autonomy, as Trigger (2003:208) correctly stresses, was cheaper in terms of enforcement costs than a highly centralized system, but it came at the price of potential political fragmentation, and it left the ruler dependant on the flow of accurate information from a bureaucratic elite that was not always loyal. Religion was a two-edged sword, providing the ruler "access to local society" (Crone 2003:79), but also creating "horizontal linkages" (Crone 2003:71) that could potentially undermine state authority. The division of the state into administrative districts called nomes was an important link between villages and the royal court.

Trigger (2003) distinguished two types of control in territorial states: delegational and bureaucratic. Delegational (or "segmentary") systems were those that placed an official representative and his associates in charge of a region. In bureaucratic systems, of which Egypt is an example, a hierarchy of officials was put in charge of specific portfolios. Recruiting and controlling these officials and maintaining their loyalty were problematic in ancient bureaucracies. It is interesting to note that, as far as we know, Egypt never developed a civil service examination system, with its complex hierarchy of positions, as was done in China or in British India; nor, apparently, did Egypt develop an ideological "code of conduct" (Deng 1999:121) equivalent to Confucianism's by which the scribal elite were bound together.[16]

Such a system in the Chinese case "endowed it [the Chinese state] with something close to a monopoly on the distribution of prestige (a situation which countless rulers must have dreamed of, but which few achieved)" (Crone 2003:173). In Egypt, which was a much smaller state system than China (at its ancient height in the Ptolemaic period it was about one-tenth the size of Han-controlled China), such prestige was generated by personal ties between the elites and the king. Ruler cults and others, such as the cult of Serapis, may have played an important role. Unlike the Chinese with their examination system, the Ptolemies relied on the loyalty

---

[16] For the imperial Chinese examination system, see the account by Chaffee (1995). Many literary texts from pharaonic as well as Ptolemaic times, lay out the basic advantages of being loyal to the state. Among these was the promise of promotion for a job well done. See Crawford (1978). On the nominations of scribes, see chapter 4.

of a close circle. Administrative instructions passed down the bureaucratic chain by the circulation of letters from high-ranking officials to
lower-ranking ones that stressed expectations, and by means of personal
visits by higher-ranking officials (Crawford 1978). Only later, in the early
second century BC, were a series of honorific, hierarchical court titles
given to those who had specific functions, and then only to the highest
level of officials (Mooren 1975; Rowlandson 2007).

Many Ptolemaic reforms of the ancient Egyptian system, an increased
articulation of the bureaucracy established in the New Kingdom, and the
theoretical ability of the king to replace disloyal officials, allowed him a
modicum of control, but it was hardly absolute, and the heights of centralized bureaucratic power of the much smaller Old Kingdom were never
reached again.[17] This is an issue to which I shall return later.

Ptolemaic Egypt, marking the beginning a new cycle of centralization,
fits well into the general patterns of the requirements of premodern states.
The kings had an immediate need to eliminate rivals both outside of Egypt
(and there were many) and within. They needed to form a ruling coalition
(discussed in chapter 5) and to collect revenue. The early Ptolemaic kings
found sophisticated institutions and a deeply embedded social structure
created by a complex web of social relationships and land tenure patterns.
Egypt was a comparatively large polity with a unique natural feature at
its core: the Nile, which produced some of the potentially most productive
soil on Earth and was the best communication corridor in the ancient
world. The Ptolemies faced as well the usual problems of any new foreign
ruling class: a limited supply of loyal bureaucrats, the strong natural resistance of tightly organized communities not predisposed to trusting the
state and its tax collection mechanisms, information problems, and an
entrenched local elite. But given these constraints, and as I have argued
elsewhere in my treatment of Ptolemaic land tenure patterns (Manning
2003a), the Ptolemaic state found solutions that, at least in part, assuaged
the state's natural fragility. The caging effects of the Nile river were always
a powerful unifying force, but the political adjustments necessitated
by the Nile flood, as also the need to import grain in 245 BC because
of a severe drought, make it abundantly clear that the river was a
mixed blessing.

Thus Ptolemy confronted a range of historical and contemporary com-
plications when he began to build his new state, a state that was neither
wholly Greek nor wholly Egyptian, but bound up with the political path
dependence of state institutions and an irrigation regime that was not
easily altered. Assumptions about the nature of royal power have led some

[17] Strudwick (1985).

scholars to downplay the constraints inherent in any state system, but it is clear that the king was one actor in a complex system, however theoretically unlimited the power of his office might be.

The Ptolemaic solution to the problem that Haber lays out—the tendency to over extract because of the "short time horizon" of an ageing dictator—stands in sharp contrast to the tactics of most modern dictators. The Ptolemies successfully used Egypt's own dynastic mechanism and its ideology to legitimize their rule. Once, that is, an equilibrium had been reached with the other generals of Alexander, who were carving out their own turf in the Mediterranean, a process which effectively lasted until 281 BC. The normal tendency of states to over extract, or to act in a purely "predatory" manner was of course tempered by political constraints generated by ruling coalitions embedded in ancient institutions (Levi 1988:12). Establishing a dynastic mechanism created a long-term time horizon; for this and other reasons it was crucial for political stability. The Ptolemies found an excellent historical precedent in Egypt, backed by thousands of years of literary production, myth, and image designed to support legitimate rule by a family that precluded usurpers.

Moreover, the experience in the first millennium BC had dislodged legitimacy as a criterion for native kingship (although there was some conservative priestly reaction to this development). The full impact of the dynastic solution, a common one in the premodern world of course, was to lower costs, increase political stability, and furnish a concession to other power holders ("clients" or the "ruling coalition," for which see chapter 4) in the state. Others were tempted to try the same thing within Egypt, to carve out territory and claim kingship. That is what happened, for example, in the great Theban revolt (205–186 BC, when two successive "kings" claimed Upper Egypt.[18] These Theban "usurpers" of Ptolemaic territory were considered "impious" by the state. Who they were in reality we do not know, but they were something other than Hobsbawm's (1969) "social bandits." The revolt may have been purely a grab for power at a time of central weakness.

But Olson's "stationary bandit" model suggests something about Ptolemaic success. The Ptolemies were in it for the long term, hence the monarchic, pharaonic ideal was readily adapted with respect to the Egyptian core of their empire. They wanted to protect their turf, hence their interest in securing justice, order, and other aspects of public well being, and in bargaining with elites. It is well worth remembering that Ptolemaic kingship was not territorial; i.e., that the Egyptian pharaonic model was only part of what they were. There is a logical nexus between tax collection

[18] The extent of their control in not known. On the revolts, see McGing (1997); Veïsse (2004).

and the incentive for the state to provide public goods that can be missed in an analysis that sees the state as either predatory or contractual. The Ptolemaic kings, even the queens (!), certainly, and regularly, dressed the part of bandits in Greek contexts by wearing military clothing, reminding us too that the real power of royalty can be quite different from royal power in theory (Walbank 1984:67; Austin 1986).[19] That fashion statement reveals much about who they were and what their organizational framework was. Military dress was a deliberate use of an authoritarian symbol to reinforce the political authority of the kings. The "gangster look," as Buruma (2007) recently described it in a piece in the *Financial Times* on modern avatars of bandit political leaders, that serves to mobilize socially and politically diverse groups, can be found in real historical examples, and much further back in time than the myth of Robin Hood.

It is the central argument of this book that the Ptolemaic state was a reasonably successful premodern state. It was a new synthesis of politics, religion, and economic institutions. The size of the Roman Empire to come was of course on an entirely different scale, as even a quick glance of Taagepera's growth-decline curves shows. In some descriptions, Ptolemaic Egypt would seem to be the ancient cousin of Honaker's East Germany, or the predecessor of Botha's South Africa (Bathish and Löwstedt 1999).[20] Such hyperboles aside, even in many sober assessments, the Ptolemaic dynasty is often regarded, to use a term much in vogue at the moment, as a "failed state." In Bagnall's summary of Bingen's work (Bagnall 2007:11):

> Bingen presents to us a largely unsuccessful state and society, one without enough imagination or inner strength to get beyond the crippling constraints put on it from the start by its dual Greco-Macedonian and Egyptian antecedents, with their largely incompatible ways of operation.

Much evidence of this "failure" has allegedly been found in the documents, and the view has become a common one.[21] Tarn and Griffith (1952) considered Egypt "Ptolemy's estate;" the new economic structure

---

[19] The most famous example of a Ptolemaic queen wearing military clothing is the mosaic from Thmuis, dated ca. 200 BC, depicting Berenike II. See further Koenen (1993:27) with the literature cited therein.

[20] The authors' definition of apartheid (p. 3) as "a society where an oppressive, economically exploitative and ideologically racist minority is in power, with or without the rule of law," would already exclude the Ptolemaic case, because there was no "ideological racism." The authors stress "cultural genocide" rather than "physical genocide" by the Ptolemaic state, arguing, wrongly, that the Egyptian language was "gone by the end of the Roman period." Cf. Walbank (1991/1992:102), who uses the phrase "cultural and religious apartheid," to mean the *de facto* separation of cultures.

[21] Préaux (1939:426–35) in a famous assessment of Ptolemaic revenue.

was a "thorough-going system of nationalization," and "efficient," which led directly to "brutality and decay." A similar attitude prevails in Turner's (1984:159) conclusions about the royal economy:

> ... the screw is tightened progressively and the pressures of an already oppressive exploitation directly cause the explosion of the 240s BC. . . . It was Philadelphus, not Philopator, who bankrupted Egypt.

Instances of "failure" have been seen in the development or in the redistribution of royal wealth. For Wilcken (1921), who compared the Ptolemies to seventeenth- and eighteenth-century European states (!), they failed to "conceive of the idea of increasing salaries in order to increase the purchasing power of the population."[22] That is perhaps too high a standard by which to judge the Ptolemies. We should not expect from an ancient kingship a progressive policy of economic development or of per capita improvement (Eisenstadt 1993:126). Another shortcoming long ago noted was the failure to apply technological improvements to production.[23]

Rathbone (1990) suggested another "lost opportunity;" namely, that the Ptolemies could have but didn't develop more perennially irrigated land. He (2000:51) asks why the state did not do more in the way of economic development, given the impressive capabilities displayed in the mid-third-century Fayyum reclamation project. "A psychological factor," he says, "may have been at work. To begin with, there was the exciting challenge of the new. The fun then faded as the Greeks realized that they were facing an endless cycle of degradation of the land and its reclamation." But Rathbone concludes (1990:51): "The Ptolemaic state was, in my view, broadly successful in its aim of maintaining both surplus production and a largely free population."

Indeed the Ptolemies were successful by other standards as well. Take, for example, dynastic survival. From the point of view Hellenistic or ancient Egyptian history, or indeed from the point of view of the history of premodern states in general, the Ptolemaic dynasty fared very well indeed. Could a contrast be any clearer than that between most of the Ptolemaic kings and Seleucus VI Epiphanes, burned alive in 94–93 BC by a mob after less than one year's rule? For an outside regime to come into Egypt and hold onto it for any length of time was no mean feat, as the Assyrian and Persian occupations attest. The Ptolemaic dynasty was the longest lasting of the Hellenistic "successor states" (275 years; 300 total years if we count from Alexander's invasion, when there was technically no dy-

---

[22] As summarized by Préaux (1939:432): "*Cette negligence est grosse de conséquences.*"

[23] On the problem of technological improvements, see inter alia Finley (1965:148); Préaux (1971); Samuel (1983:48–61); Schneider (2007).

nasty yet established) and indeed the longest lasting (and final) dynasty in Egyptian history.[24] The durability and stability of its territory would place the Ptolemies at the top of the league tables of Egyptian pharaohs along with the two other dynasties considered by Egyptologists to have reigned over the greatest periods of culture, Dynasty 12 of the Middle Kingdom and Dynasty 18 of the New Kingdom. To these measures of Ptolemaic success we would add the important cultural output of Alexandria, the new temples built throughout the country, and literary works in both Greek and demotic Egyptian. These achievements do not of course explain success, but they are signs that the Ptolemaic state was reasonably stable and durable despite the political problems of the dynasty, despite revolts, and despite the invasion of Antiochus IV. Above all else, perhaps the most significant accomplishment of the Ptolemies lies in the fact that those living within Egypt did not experience the impact of external wars as did all other Hellenistic states.[25]

When we consider politics on the ground, we observe a slightly different picture, and it becomes clear that Wittfogel's theory of despotic states was written purely from an ideological perspective. In Wittfogel's "total power" model, despotic states were defined as having four key components (O'Leary 1989:254–56): (1) stability and continuity of the dynasty and the bureaucracy supporting it; (2) ownership of more than half of the land by the state; (3) state use of more than half of surplus production; and (4) the display of subordination by all subjects. Some of these traits were characteristic at least for much of Ptolemaic history, although there were serious challenges both to the dynasty itself and to its territory. To borrow from O'Leary, the Ptolemaic state, like all premodern empires, was a "dual polity."[26] The central court controlled the military and foreign relations and farmed out taxes. Agricultural production, religious practices, tax collection, and the legal system were, on the other hand, by and large in the hands of local elites. The ruler and his court were constrained by a variety of factors, including the environment that dictated local organized production, an entrenched elite usually tied to the temple hierarchy, and the usual problems of agency and asymmetric information

---

[24] There is of course some artificiality in dividing the phases of centralized power in pharaonic Egypt into dynastic families rather than whole periods, (Old, Middle, and New Kingdoms), especially when there are clearly established family links across Manetho's dynasties; e.g., family connections between dynasty 2 and 3 are well established (Gozzoli [2006:200]), but nevertheless there are good reasons to maintain the dynastic structure as unique ruling family cycles and to thus regard the Ptolemies as the single most durable dynasty.

[25] Hölbl (2001:67). The invasion of Antiochus IV, temporary as it was, did not have longer-term deleterious effects. Internal revolts, on the other hand, were another matter.

[26] See O'Leary (1989:256–58) for a good summary of the issues involved.

Dynasty	Dates (BC)	Length
Dynasty 4	2613–2494	119 years
Dynasty 5	2494–2345	149 years
Dynasty 6	2345–2181	164 years
Dynasty 12	1985–1773	212 years
Dynasty 18	1550–1295	255 years
Dynasty 19	1295–1186	109 years
Dynasty 20	1186–1069	117 years
Dynasty 26 (The Saïtes)	656–525	131 years
Dynasty 27 (First Persian Period)	525–404	121 years
Dynasty 31 (The Ptolemies)	305–30	275 years

Figure 2. Length of important dynasties in Egyptian history

Note: Year dates taken from Shaw (2000). All dates are BC. The dynasty numbering follows the traditional numbering in Manetho, with the exception of dynasty 31, a later Hellenistic addition to Manetho. So Redford (1986:331).

flow with respect to taxation. It is in the nature of monarchy that the king acted despotically despite the fact that, like most premodern states, Egypt had limited ability to control and reform local structures.

This basic duality of the state was not new with the Ptolemies, although their new fiscal institutions and new administrative language certainly had profound effects. As O'Leary rightly points out, the power relations between the ruler and the rest of society did not amount to a zero sum game. It is the negotiations between ruler and society, and the equilibrium established between the extractive power of the ruler and the benefits gained by the ruled that ultimately determine a state's success and longevity; as well as the amount of support that the regime enjoys.[27] Such equilibrium may be observed, for example, in the Tokugawa shogunate (whose rule was almost identical in length to the Ptolemies' at 268 years [1600–1868]), which effectively balanced central and local power by means of its own unique political solutions (Bendix 1978:431–90).

[27] Cf. Ibn Khaldun, *Muqaddimah* 3.8. Cf. the remarks by Turchin (2003:38–40) on Ibn Khaldun's political theory.

There were other factors. As long as the Nile flooded at regular levels, Egypt was the most stable territory in the Hellenistic world. Indeed state success is correlated to Nile flooding throughout Egyptian history (Butzer 1980). Above and beyond that environmental stability (in normal years), the Ptolemies built a new social infrastructure. Perhaps the most intense activity of the new state was the planting of new settlements, not just in the Fayyum but throughout Egypt (as discussed in chapter 4). It has in fact been proposed that a major difference between Seleukid and Ptolemaic policy was in their new foundations. The Seleukids were well known for their new coastal "polis-style" cities, but the Ptolemies were, *mutatis mutandis*, equally interested in founding new towns in Egyptian contexts, as well as in places much further afield (Mueller 2006). Mueller has suggested that unlike the Seleukids' new foundations, the Ptolemies' "were pursued outside the framework of urban settlement" (2006:3). Establishing loyal, and controllable, communities was a major goal of Ptolemaic state formation. City foundation, the establishment of new administrative centers, and the movement of populations were important factors throughout Egyptian history, and the Ptolemies remained true to the pattern.

Most important of all was the correlation between state size and durability.[28] In his study of Chinese history, Elvin (1973:17–22) advanced a model that connected the size of states to their level of technology relative to that of neighboring states. He identified three variables that determined the size of a state and its ability to sustain its power: (1) the size of the "political unit," (2) the productivity of the economy, and (3) the proportion of output spent on the administration and the military. I do not have the leisure here to consider Peter Turchin's (2003) stimulating "cliodynamic" model that links a state's success to its underlying demographics. I will leave that to others.

It is no coincidence that the three most durable Egyptian dynasties—Manetho's Dynasties 12 and 18 and the Ptolemies—coincided with the periods of greatest state expansion and greatest central control in terms of royal ideology, the development of new revenue bases, and a strong military capacity. All three dynasties expanded settlements within Egypt (the Fayyum was an important region to all three), established new administrative centers, expanded infrastructure (new land, roads, and irrigation works) and controlled imperial territory, including trade routes and commodity flows outside of the Nile valley core. All three dynasties were periods of intense state building, political reforms, and imperial expansion into the Near East, the eastern Mediterranean, and Nubia (although

[28] Greek political theory was aware of the association between durability of the state and the size of its territory and population. See e.g., Aristot., *Politics* VII. 1326.

unlike the New Kingdom pharaohs, the Ptolemies faced a strong opponent in the Meroitic Kingdom).[29]

If productivity and state finance are the main drivers of state success, there are other factors to consider as well. Westermann (1938:285, n. 55) has suggested that the Ptolemies' success compared to that of the other Hellenistic states was the result of the "acuteness and realism of Ptolemaic diplomacy, its constant subservience to the demands of the Roman senate, the internal and external policies of Rome, the military and political weakness of Egypt which did not arouse the active fears of Roman leadership and the *Tyche*, the goddess of chance, to which Polybius ascribes such importance in the conduct of human relations." In other words, the Ptolemaic kings were shrewd politicians.[30] Alexander's conquest of the Persian Empire is a classic example of a takeover, but it was not long-lived. The Ptolemaic dynasty, on the other hand, was not merely a takeover, but an attempt to create a new state—"the last major empire formation with an Egyptian core before the rise of [the] Fatimids a thousand years later" (Taagepera 1979:123).

The Ptolemaic state, with a loosely held external empire mainly focused Coele-Syria, Cyprus, Cyrenaica, and on the Red Sea coast but with strong connections with coastal Asia Minor and the Aegean during the third century BC, was small by comparison with Rome; but in an overall assessment of imperial duration and size, it ranks among the largest states of antiquity (Taagepera 1979:133).

The connection to the Greek world was important for many reasons, among the most critical being the defense of Egyptian territory and the supply of manpower. The Ptolemies' core territory, however, was always the Nile valley. By looking at the Ptolemies from the broad perspective of Egyptian history, and making use of the many new studies that have provided valuable information by which to judge the Ptolemaic state, we may begin to build a more complex and therefore richer picture of the lived human experience in Egypt during the last the centuries BC.

In this chapter I have discussed the various ways in which the Ptolemaic state has been viewed. The "despotic" model overestimates the ruler's ability to act autocratically, and it misunderstands the relationship between the ruler and the locally organized irrigation system in Egypt. The "dirigiste" model does a better job of explaining the aims of the Ptolemies.

---

[29] The text of the *Annals of Amenemhat II* discovered in Memphis in 1974 suggests an even wider Middle Kingdom expansion than was previously known, perhaps even into Cyprus. On Middle Kingdom Nubia, see Smith (1995). For the New Kingdom empire, see Kemp (1978); Frandsen (1979).

[30] Rowlandson (2007:30) adds that internal court rivalries kept Egypt from directly confronting Rome militarily, which paradoxically enhanced Egypt's ability to survive.

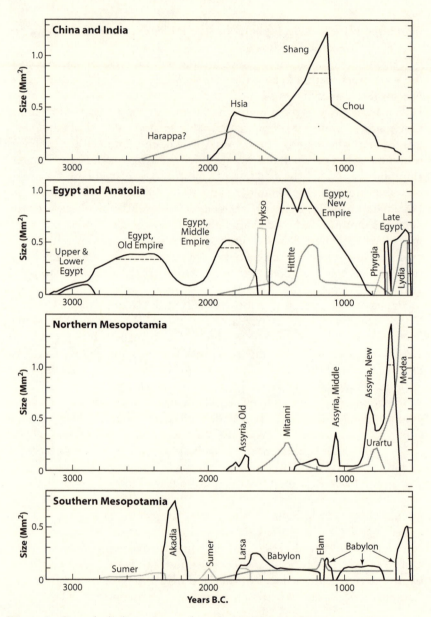

Figure 3. Growth-decline curves of empires, 3000 to 500 BC. From Taagepera (1978).

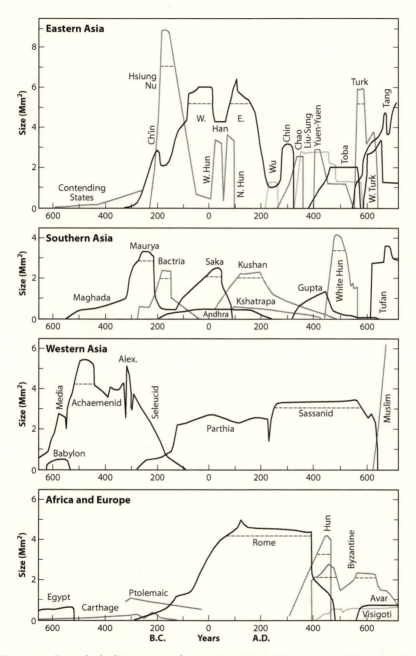

Figure 4. Growth-decline curves of ancient empires 650 BC to AD 700. Note the scale of the Ptolemaic compared to the Achaemenid and Roman Empires. From Taagepera (1979).

Colonial models used to understand social relationships, like despotic or dirigiste models of economic development, miss the subtleties of the complex social relationships through which the Ptolemies controlled Egypt. I have also argued here that the Ptolemies were among the most successful rulers in Egyptian history, and that their rule had profound effects on Egypt. The question raised by this discussion is: What kept Ptolemaic Egypt together for so long? In order to answer that, we must examine the political economy, and so it is to that subject that I will now turn.

Chapter 4

SHAPING A NEW STATE

The Political Economy of the Ptolemies

Early bureaucratic states failed to provide the
basis for peaceful evolution towards a rational
harmonious society.
—*Kemp (1989:183)*

The Ptolemaic splinter of the Iranian empire . . .
was the last major empire formation with an
Egyptian core before the rise of [the] Fatimids
a thousand years later.
—*Taagepera (1979:123)*

IN THIS CHAPTER, I will bring Egyptian society back into the picture and
examine the relationships established between the Ptolemies and the coalitions that were necessary to create a new political and social equilibrium.
By definition, then, I move beyond the model of despotic "one man rule"
("mon-archy", Ps. Aristot., *Oec.* 1), into the real world in which the
kings, in forming a new, centralized state, had to incorporate and bargain
with social groups.[1]

As a result of their need to interact with a broad range of social entities,
the Ptolemaic kings, like their counterparts elsewhere, formed a multidi-
mensional kingship that was informed both by past royal experience
(Achaemenid, Macedonian, ancient Egyptian) and, especially in the cities,
by more current Greek conventions. But in Egypt, Achaemenid kingship
was not the Ptolemies' immediate inspiration, although they were following Achaemenid imperial practice in adopting the pharaonic model, and
indeed they did so more thoroughly than the Persians.[2] Instead, the Ptolemies found models in the last "good" Egyptian pharaohs, Nectanebo I
(380–362 BC) and Nectanebo II (360–343 BC) of Dynasty 30, a period of

---

[1] For the basic issues involved, see Barkey (1994).
[2] On Hellenistic patterns of kingship, see Ma (2003).

great building activity and a revival of Egyptian culture that was consciously, and energetically, pursued in many forms.[3]

My understanding of Ptolemaic state formation is informed by Barkey's (1994) "bargained incorporation" model. I argue here that it was the political economy, the bargaining between ruler and constituent groups, that formed the basis of the Ptolemaic economic and legal systems. While the external Ptolemaic empire is fascinating in many respects, and without question influenced internal Egyptian developments—immigration, trade income, silver importation, and warfare—political relationships within the Ptolemaic core territory were more important in the long term, particularly after ca. 250 BC.

Most historical analyses have not distinguished carefully enough, in my view, between the early and later phases of the Ptolemaic state, and the political processes that were involved in gaining control of Egyptian institutions. Absolute control, obviously, was unattainable in practice, although that has not prevented the idea from being part of the analysis of the new political and economic order that the Ptolemies imposed. That this concept of total power does not hold in ancient monarchies has been well established by Briant (1982) and Mileta (2002) and need not detain us. But it is important to keep in mind that kingship, now more broadly conceived, formed the crucial link that joined together not only all populations within Egypt, but those living in the greater Ptolemaic empire as well.

There is something else to consider here. Ptolemaic governance was a complex game between two main ethnic groups, the Greeks, who as we have seen were not an entirely new population in third-century BC Egypt, and the Egyptians. On the one hand, the Hellenistic king, heir to Alexander's legacy, embodied the state in his person (and gradually so did members of the dynastic family as represented in the dynastic cult). On the other hand, Egyptian kingship, which the Ptolemies tried very hard to emulate, embodied a rich history and implied a series of relationships.[4]

In the last chapter I suggested that the despotic, dirigiste, and colonial models explain only part of the process of state centralization, top-down from the point of view of the ruler and the minority Greek population. In this chapter, I explore in more detail the political relationships between the ruler and the key social groups, whom we might perhaps understand as "first adaptors" of the new state rules.

---

[3] On Ptolemaic artistic inspiration, see Ashton (2003). On the fourth century BC in Egypt, see the excellent summary by Ray (1987). The Ptolemaic continuation of Nectanebid temple building is summarized by Arnold (1999:137–41). For early Ptolemaic royal portraiture inspired by Dynasty 30 style, see Stanwick (2002:66–68).

[4] The contrast between the Hellenistic king and the Egyptian pharaoh is very well analyzed by Hölbl (2001).

It must first be said that the Ptolemies ruled over a very complex state, with interests that stretched from the Aegean into Asia Minor and south into Nubia, modern- day Sudan. The rulers had to manage a variety of social groups with different interests and different degrees of loyalty, living in a dynamic and to some extent unpredictable environment. They also had to make almost daily calculations in positioning themselves somewhere between a pharaonic mode of governance, with its supporting religious ideology (and the necessity therefore of priestly support), and the Greek communities' very different expectations of kingship.

The king should not be "de-centered" from the political economy, because that institution remained central to the conception of the state, both in theory and in reality, and it was pivotal in creating an equilibrium. By the time Ptolemy I was forming his new state, Egyptian society had three millennia of political institutional history. The role of pharaoh in providing a framework, what Greif (2006) has called a "cognitive model," in which organizations and individuals acted, was ready made. But the almost constant political instability of the dynasty after the third century BC, and the evolution of the bureaucracy, shows that kingship cannot be analyzed in isolation. Aside from the important shift to the use of the Greek language, the bureaucracy that was established in the third century BC built on ancient administrative practices. It was not simply a framework imposed from above in a single moment, but, rather, evolved over the course of that century out of the specific aims of the new Ptolemaic kings sitting in Alexandria. This was not a state "built to last," although it did. It was instead a state built to control.[5] This stems from the basic fact that premodern states were what Crone (2003:57) has called "capstone governments," sitting on top of large populations, policing rather than organizing. Importantly, there was no movement toward the development of either an autonomous aristocratic land-owning class or an independent merchant class. The institutional framework of the state was, thus, more or less stable, despite serious challenges from many quarters.[6]

I see four overlapping phases in the Ptolemaic takeover of Egypt. These are contained within two broader historical cycles of equilibrium formation: Greek institutional adaptation to Egypt (items 1–3) and the bureaucratic evolution of the state (item 4):

(1) *Continuation of Persian state structure" (323–305* BC). The previous state structure is maintained unchanged. Unlike transfers of power other parts of the Hellenistic world, there is little violence in the Macedonian takeover.

---

[5] See chapter 5, on the economic structure of control.

[6] Eisenstadt (1993:323–28) treats well the historical tendencies that could alter social structure.

(2) *Equilibrium formation, and the building of a new, bureaucratic empire (305–220 BC.* Greek cities are founded: Alexandria as capital, Ptolemaïs in the south. Reforms begin under Ptolemy II: monetization of the economy, control of temples and priesthoods by the 230s, reshaping of the legal system.[7] There is a gradual loss of imperial territory.

(3) *Institutional consolidation in Egypt (250–180 BC.* The new fiscal institutions of coinage and banking spread; a tax farming system is established.

(4) *Rupture, reconsolidation, and the Roman takeover (217–30 BC.* Political instability increases with dynastic struggles in the royal family and revolts, particularly in Upper Egypt; local bureaucratized economic and legal systems evolve; Rome annexes Egypt. The number of priestly decrees are notable at the beginning of this phase.

The generally accepted view of the Ptolemaic dynasty has been that it was initially successful, or "cohesive," and then all hell broke loose in spasms of murders, court intrigues, and open revolt at the death of Ptolemy III in 222 BC.[8] An internal dynastic crisis spilled over into a "power transition crisis" (Eckstein 2008:124–29) throughout the Hellenistic world. Scholars usually refer to the revolt of soldiers returning from the Battle of Raphia, an event reported by Polybius, as the beginning of internal discord. The rioting of soldiers suggests both problems the state faced when soldiers were demobilized and, perhaps, wider social issues. There were other issues. The dynastic problems after Ptolemy III, the loss of the Aegean empire by the end of the third century, and the loss of internal political control as evidenced by resistance and revolts are all put forward as symptoms of decline. Interestingly, this model corresponds almost perfectly with Ibn Khaldun's historical model (which in turn bears some similarity to those of Aristotle and Polybius) that predicts that dynasties do

---

[7] Welles (1949:22) notes Wilcken's (1912:3) observation that the first two Ptolemaic kings constituted a "royalty" (Gr. *basilea*), not a state.

[8] This is what I (Manning 2003a) have termed the "Polybius model," and it is focused on political history and the political power of the kings themselves. Essentially Hölbl (2001:304–11) follows this model: (1) Golden Age: Alexander through Ptolemy III. Formation of kingdom; (2) Transition and decline. Political crisis, the fiscal drain of the battle of Raphia after 217 BC, the increased power of the Seleukids, the rise of Roman military power; (3) 168–30 BC Roman authority in the Mediterranean. For a major new assessment of Hellenistic history, including the discounting of a third-century "balance of power" between the major states, see Heinen (2003). See also the important study of Eckstein (2008), stressing the lack of international law leading to an anarchic situation and the "power transition crisis" that led to Roman intervention.

not typically survive longer than three generations; i.e., about 120 years (*The Muqaddimah* 3.12). By the third generation, he says:

> Group feeling disappears completely. People forget to protect and defend themselves and press their claims. . . . The ruler, then, has need of other, brave people to support him. He takes clients and followers. They help the dynasty to some degree, until God permits it to be destroyed, and it goes with everything it stands for.

It is certainly true that there were signs of troubles after the third generation. And not just in Egypt. The years between 223 and 221 BC were without a doubt a "turning point" in Hellenistic history (Chamoux 2001:99). Very young rulers held sway in three important kingdoms: Philip V of Macedon, aged seventeen; Antiochus III, aged about twenty; and Ptolemy IV, aged about twenty-two. Power struggles within the royal court became increasingly problematic. If we factor in growing Roman power in the eastern Mediterranean, we can simplify things even further, dividing Ptolemaic history into two halves lying on either side of 168 BC, the year that Gaius Popillius Laenas drew his "line in the sand" in a suburb of Alexandria, demanding that the Seleukid king Antiochus IV (whose invasion of Egypt was a serious threat to Ptolemaic rule) withdraw from Egypt.[9] That same year, Rome put an end to the Macedonian kingdom at the Battle at Pydna. The Hellenistic world as we know it could well have come to an end that year; but it did not.[10]

I want to broaden the analysis by suggesting that a study of the Ptolemaic state as a whole, of the king and his circle, and of the key constituent groups with which they interacted, shows a far more complex series of developments that can ultimately be traced back to the relationship between the rulers' aim (staying in power) and these key groups. In order to govern Egypt, the early Ptolemies utilized existing institutional frameworks and social groups to establish political legitimacy. They were thus never in a particularly strong position vis-à-vis the major constituent groups, which in turn made it difficult to create a more generalized power framework (Eisenstadt 1993). By deciding to hold Egypt as the core territory in a pharaonic model, the kings were constrained by history and therefore in the choices they could make.

The takeover of Egypt and the subsequent development of the state rests on two historical foundations: first, the political recentralization of the early Saïte kings (664–525 BC); and secondly, the first (525–404 BC) and second (341–323 BC) incorporations of Egypt into the Persian Em-

[9] Livy XLIV.29.1; XLV.2–3; 12; Polyb. XXIX.27; Diod. XXXI.2.

[10] For the historian Polybius, that year saw the recovery of Egypt, which may be viewed as an exaggeration, per Walbank (1979 [2002:69])

pire.[11] Like the Fatimid takeover of Egypt in the tenth century AD, or the Ottoman takeover of Crete in the seventeenth century AD (Greene 2000), Ptolemaic state capacity built on the continuity of institutional arrangements, in Egypt's case those established in these two periods and in the independent years of the fourth century BC.[12] In order to build a new state, the Ptolemaic kings relied both on traditional priestly support and on the formation of a new bureaucratic elite. In a sense, their reach into the past went back even further. Just as the Nubian kings of dynasty 25, the Saïtes in the seventh century BC, and the Nectanebids in the fourth century BC drew on artistic representations and on religious and cultural features from the Old Kingdom to legitimize their rule, the Ptolemies looked to the New Kingdom pharaohs, the great military conquerors, for inspiration. Egyptian history was used to justify, and to broadcast, Ptolemaic rule.[13]

From the beginning, Ptolemaic Egypt was a Mediterraneanized Egypt (Heinen 1987; Hölbl 2001:28), with frameworks of Greek culture and Greek ideas already in place well ahead of the Ptolemies' arrival.[14] In fact, Egyptian elites had been absorbing other cultures for centuries even before Alexander came on the scene. Greek culture found especially fertile ground in Egypt, and the engagement of the two cultures was mutual, as Greek interest in Egyptian culture reflects.[15] The Saïte kings brought Egypt firmly and fully *into* the eastern Mediterranean world and made it an important part *of* that world, but this trend was already underway when the *Tale of Wenamun* was written at the end of the New Kingdom.[16] The Ptolemies built on fourth-century developments, some of which were due in part at least to Greek influence: recentralization of the state by political alliances, standardization of weights and measures, military mobilization, fiscal institutions, the introduction of coinage and the beginnings of a monetized economy, the promotion of long distance trade and trade routes, increased influence in the Mediterranean, temple building, and

[11] Briant (1982, 2002) stressing Persian/Hellenistic continuities. Cf. Hölbl (2001:4).

[12] Continuity between the fourth and the third centuries in the Ptolemaic overseas possessions is also noted. See inter alia Bagnall (1976), Gygax (2005).

[13] General considerations in Murray (1970).

[14] Naval strength, for example, was an important feature of both Saïte and early Ptolemaic military and economic power in the Mediterranean. On the Saïte navy, see Lloyd (2000); and for the Ptolemies, Van t'-Dack and Hauben (1978); Hauben (1987).

[15] *pOxy*. 1381 (second century AD), for example, an aretology to the god Imouthes (eg., Imhotep), is a translation from Egyptian to Greek ordered by Nectenebo I. See the comments by Quack (2004).

[16] On the "in/of" distinction, see Horden and Purcell (2000:9–10). For a translation of *Wenamun* (= *pMoscow* 120), composed in the eleventh century BC, see Lichtheim (1976:224–30); and the analysis of de Spens (1998); Schipper (2005). On Greco-Roman Egypt within the Mediterranean context, see Bagnall (2005).

the greater importance of mercenaries (Ray 1987; Davies 2006).[17] It is worth underscoring that the extensive Greek-Egyptian interaction was not just between literary elites, but occurred in the economic, military, and political spheres as well. The Perseus myth is enough to show strong convergence between Greece, Egypt and Persia, but the relationship between the Persepolis fortification tablets, showing us firsthand the Persian imperial taxation system at work, and Pseudo-Aristotle's *Oikonomika*, is even more instructive in explaining the basic, broader continuities in the eastern Mediterranean between the fourth and third centuries BC.[18] Our understanding of Ptolemaic political economy must, then, rest on the three and a half centuries of experience before Alexander arrived on Egypt's shores.[19]

Ptolemaic strategy was similar to that of other "bureaucratic empires." It sought to decrease independent power, and thus to reduce the percentage of "committed resources" that were embedded within traditional social structures (Eisenstadt 1993:118). At the same time, it sought to increase the surplus that the king could control, to create, in other words, what Eisenstadt has called "free-floating resources." Such diversion of resources to the central state was not of course without social cost. Drawing resources away from local needs to supply those of the central state, among which the making of war was paramount in the third century BC, sparked resistance and rebellion that at least on one occasion posed a major threat to Ptolemaic sovereignty within Egypt.[20]

The military contributed in important ways to the internal organizational capacity of the state by offering a "built in" command structure. Its role was dominant, or "promiscuous" to use Mann's term (1986), and was an important "motor of financial change."[21] The need to finance the military was an important incentive for monetizing the economy, and the

---

[17] Persian standardization in Egypt: the grain measure known as the *artaba* in the Egyptian text was a Persian-imposed standard used throughout Egypt The Persians also used a standard silver weight administered through the temple of Ptah in Memphis for money.

[18] Hdt. 2.91; Gruen (1996); Lloyd (1969). On the fortification tablets: Briant (2002:451–52 with the "research note" pp. 938–39 for bibliography).

[19] See Kienitz (1953) for an historical outline.

[20] For theoretical concerns, but from a European historical perspective, see Tilly (1981, 1990); for the Ottoman experience, Barkey (1994).

[21] Ferguson (2001:23). For a detailed analysis of the role of the military in Ptolemaic society, see Fischer (2008). I do not have the space here to explore some of the interesting parallels with the Fatimid state (969–1171 AD) in terms of state structure, military power, and the ability of the military to generate independent power bases that threatened central rule caused by the assigning of revenue from land to soldiers. There are other parallels as well, including in the development of the bureaucracy and the use of elaborate urban parades to project political power. For an overview of the Fatimid period in Egypt, see Sanders (1998); Lev (1991); Brett (2001).

state's role as "employer" in general was crucial. The arena for the creation of such "free-floating resources" was not only inside Egypt, but also within the imperial sphere beyond Egypt's borders. The successful creation of these resources must have been one of the keys to Ptolemaic longevity, as I argued in chapter 2.

The mid-third-century land reclamation project in the Fayyum is a good example of the policy. For various reasons, the possibility of expanding arable land was limited, as far as the evidence permits us to know, to the Fayyum, and perhaps to the area around the new city of Ptolemaïs Hermeiou (below).[22] The Ptolemaic empire faced serious issues already in the mid-third century, and the kings continually made guarantees of revenue streams to traditional groups (e.g., the *apomoira* [traditional first fruits tax on vineyards] for the temples), to their own cost.[23] Concessions made to soldiers and to the temples limited free-floating resources. These constraints in turn limited the ruler's power, and the competition between the ruler and other stakeholders constituted the major cause of political struggle throughout the period.[24] Many of the socioeconomic problems that the papyri detail can be laid at the doorstep of this struggle.

POLITICAL ORGANIZATIONS IN EGYPT

The formation of the Ptolemaic state marked the return to a pharaonic dynastic model. The king once again united territory and cult practice in what was a major shift from the political ideology underpinning Persian rule.[25] The Ptolemies were in this regard like the Seleukids, who also insisted on a definitive break with Persian ways of governing, at least in terms of ideology.[26] The Ptolemaic state was a "centralized bureaucratic empire" whose core was an ancient bureaucratic empire, the effects of Persian rule not withstanding (Eisenstadt 1993). Many scholars have understood Ptolemaic governance as "a continuation of pharaonic practice," although caution is in order since the term "pharaonic" is over-

---

[22] On technology, Butzer (1976); Eyre (1994); Wilson (2002).

[23] On the royal decrees, see below. For Ptolemaic revenue, see chapter 5.

[24] This is in essence Mann's (1986) distinction between "despotic" and "infrastructural power," mentioned in chapter 2.

[25] We might contrast Ptolemaic attitudes to kingship with the Persian in noting here that a copy of the famous Behistun inscription, the classic statement by Darius I of Persian royal ideology, was ordered to be sent to each province of the empire and displayed in a prominent location. An Aramaic copy survives from Elephantine island perhaps, like the biography of Darius found at Elephantine, merely reflecting "curiosity" (Ray 1994:57) about the Persians in this Jewish colony. See Briant (2002:123); Greenfield and Porten (1982).

[26] Austin (2003:128).

broad (Préaux 1939; Delia 1993:194). The decision to keep a pharaoh at
the center of the state was, primarily, a practical one aimed at institutional
stability. To be sure the institutional basis of Ptolemaic society was different from than of New Kingdom times. And we are, of course in any case
on thin ice trying to measure institutional change based on the notoriously
meager evidence available for the first millennium. Still, many basic features appear to be continued at least from Saïte times and, of course, some
institutions—kingship, the economic and religious role of temples and
their estates, the scribal tradition of bureaucratic record-keeping and document making for examples—were much older than that.

Bagnall (1976:10) summarizes the basic issue well:

> We find diversity in Ptolemaic Egypt because it already existed,
> because it was easier to cope with it than to change it, and be-
> cause government policy encouraged a lack of uniformity in new
> development.[27]

There were, thus, several channels of Ptolemaic political power. Governance was both traditional and personal. Claims to political legitimacy,
therefore, were couched in terms of pharaonic institutions, above all in
the king as the "centralizing principal" of the state. But legitimacy also
had to be negotiated with stakeholders, which included military communities, the Egyptian priest, and citizens in the two Ptolemaic *poleis*, Alexandria and Ptolemaïs.[28] The latter were essentially a new feature in Egypt
since the Persians did not found new cities, and they did not truly support
pharaonic governance. The causes of some of the resistance observed later
in the third century may be found in such inherent "ancien régime" resistance to Ptolemaic centralization and revenue collection. As Eisenstadt
stressed, "the endemic coexistence of these different types of limitation on
generalized power is characteristic of the political systems of the historical
bureaucratic polities, and is also a fundamental prerequisite of their
continuity" (1993:305–06).

As in other instances of political takeover, the Ptolemies wanted to establish a stable political order, an equilibrium, and they wanted to shift
resources away from ancient, traditional power structures to more "generalized" ones (Eisenstadt 1993:14). We can see the Ptolemies' efforts at
state building in several areas, above all in their use of imagery. The royal
portraits of the kings tend Royal images tend to offer the modern observer
a picture of either an Egyptian pharaoh or of a Macedonian king in Alexandria, but this captures neither the political dynamics nor the aims of

[27] Cf. Gellner (1983) on the lack of incentive to impose a uniform culture.
[28] The privileged groups benefited from taxation policy. See Clarysse and Thompson
(2006).

the regime. Part of this ambiguity is the result of Ptolemaic practicality in using and adopting symbols of both Greek and Egyptian political power to their own ends. The image of Ptolemy IV on the stele recording the Raphia decree shows him in Macedonian military costume on a horse rearing up in front of his enemy Antiochus III, but we see that he is also wearing the Egyptian double crown. This is an excellent example of the Ptolemaic state's hybrid nature, reflected so extensively in the literature and art of the period.[29]

If the Ptolemies followed ancient practice in using image as a means to project political stability, they were still subject to the dictates of the Nile. The Egyptian state always had to be flexible enough to adjust to a variable flood regime. In most years the flood was relatively predictable, as Park stressed, "chaotic flood distribution" over time "has no intrinsic implications for frequent catastrophe" (1992:101). This interannual variability of the flooding did, however, have serious implications for the state in terms of structure, revenue capture, and development. Political stability was directly linked as much to long-term flood trends as it was to the dynastic mechanism and to external threats.[30]

Kingship was authoritarian in form, but the king could not be indifferent to the loyalty required from constituent groups or to the historic traditions of legitimacy. The Ptolemies also required loyalty of course, but now attention was paid to Greek groups as well as Egyptian ones. A different political dynamic obtained within the Ptolemaic state, driven by (1) a new bureaucratic structure, administered in Greek, (2) a professional army installed on the land throughout Egypt, and (3) the growth of Greek urban centers. These processes cut across, and to some extent undermined, traditional Egyptian power structures. Ptolemy faced no large land-owning aristocracy, although the priesthoods attached to the larger temple estates came close to being an "aristocratized bureaucracy" (Eisenstadt 1993:332). Because of the amount of land these temples owned,[31] some of the priesthoods were able to exert great influence on the regime in a manner not unlike that of a "'classic' aristocracy" (Rowlandson 2007:45).

Temples remained in nominal control of their temple estates, and private landholding within these estates was not disrupted (Manning 2003a). These conciliatory gestures ensured that the temples continued

---

[29] See the comments by Thompson (1988:118, with plate vi). On the decree, see Thissen (1966); Simpson (1996), Winnicki (2001). Ma (2003: 189–90) stresses the hybrid nature of the image as well.

[30] On Nile trends and the political consequences for dynastic Egypt, see Bell (1971, 1975); Butzer (1980); Seidlmayer (2001); and Bonneau (1993) for Greco-Roman times.

[31] On the problem of identifying an aristocratic class, see further Rowlandson (2007).

to be important institutions, actively supported by the new regime throughout the state. The priesthood and temple of Ptah at Memphis remained the main center of state religious life, even after the court moved to the new capital at Alexandria. For this reason, it was the location of a number of Egypt-wide synods (Thompson 1988). In Upper Egypt, several important temples were completely rebuilt, beginning with that of Horus of Edfu in 237.

Temples were not only ritual centers but were also the coordinators of economic land management, record keeping, and storage.[32] Above all else, the Egyptian priests bestowed legitimacy on the pharaohs, including of course the Ptolemaic pharaohs. Each temple estate was a system unto itself; a coordinating mechanism for land portfolios, manufacturing (inter alia, textiles), and the distribution of grain. Although the Ptolemies did not challenge the ownership of the temple estates, they were successful at penetrating this system and taking over some of its important functions: storage (royal granaries), tax collection (royal banks), and, eventually, even dispute resolution. Ptolemaic penetration of Egyptian society in the south of the country can be clearly seen in the documentation from Edfu at the end of the third century, and was perhaps associated with the re-building of the temple there.[33]

The relationship between the kings and the new Greek cities was another major arena of power conflicts in Ptolemaic Egypt, as elsewhere in the Hellenistic world.[34] In the cities were key allies of the kings, but as semi-independent entities, with legally defined rights, and in Alexandria's case, a large population many of whom did not have citizenship rights, the cities were also potential adversaries. There can be no question but that Alexandria, Ptolemaïs, and to a lesser extent perhaps the Saïte-period treaty port of Naukratis, added new dynamics in the political relationship between ruler and society.[35] The kings were "protectors" of the Greek cities, committed to close and loyal relations with the citizen body. The later problem of mob action, particularly reported in Alexandria and caused in large part by the family intrigues within the dynasty, reveals another side of the relationship between the ruler and the city. The "mob" was frequently a factor in determining dynastic succession during the second and first centuries.[36] We might, then, suggest a simple model of the Ptolemaic state as follows:

[32] A very good introduction to a temple economy is Haring (1997).

[33] The so-called Milon archive, most recently treated by Clarysse (2003).

[34] Shipley (2000:59–107). For Alexandria, and the constitutional relationship between the king and the citizen body, see Fraser (1972:106–31).

[35] On the royal circle in Alexandria, see Fraser (1972:101–05).

[36] Fraser (1972:119–31); Barry (1993).

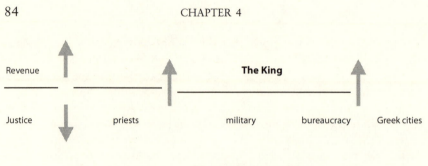

Figure 5. A model of the Ptolemaic state showing the relationship between the king and Ptolemaic society.

Some scholars have emphasized the distinctive character of, and separation between, Greek and Egyptian institutions. Rostovtzeff, for example, suggested that the Ptolemaic bureaucracy was distinctive, something newly created by the Ptolemaic kings and their agents, combining old and new methods that grew out of the immediate experience and needs of those filling new functions that the state required. It was "more refined, more logical and more coherent" than bureaucracies in earlier Egyptian history (1941:1079). Bingen (1978a:188) has stressed the role of Greek individuals, with "initiative, experience and aptitude for handling risk." But there were Egyptians at many social levels, and others as well, who played important parts in the shaping of the new state. The traditional literate class, priests and professional scribes, played a similar role in the new Ptolemaic state to that of the Copts and the Coptic Church under the Fatimids.[37] To what degree were older groups "dislocated" from the new groups needed to administer the state? This question has been at the core of much debate about the period, and while it is usually couched in ethnic terms, the political situation was subtler, and over time, more Egyptians and other social groups became important actors.

FORMING A COALITION

The early Ptolemaic kings (and their queens, who played no small role throughout the period) had two primary aims (in addition to fending off rivals): (1) mobilizing support for the new politically centralized state, and (2) mobilizing resources.[38] A bureaucracy in control of resources and a military were the two organizations necessary for the stable extraction

[37] On the importance of Copts in the Fatimid bureaucracy, see Wilfong (1998).
[38] Cf. Seleucus' actions in Babylon to gain local support: Sherwin-White (1987:15).

of surplus.[39] The kings needed to recruit a new bureaucratic elite and maintain an army, while creating a monopoly of prestige. The end result of the early kings' promotion of this new elite was mixed. By the late Ptolemaic/early Roman period, an entrenched former (?) military elite, often associated with temples, was clearly well established in local administration, as is especially well documented in the Thebaid.[40] What is altogether less clear from the evidence we possess is the extent to which this reflects a social evolution (as it clearly did under the Fatimids when the military grew in strength because of the *iqta* system [stipendiary grants of revenue from the land]), and to what extent our fragmentary evidence for the early Ptolemaic bureaucracy hides a similar picture of the role of the military in society. In a sense, Ptolemaic Egypt was as much a "soldier state" (Brett 2001:342) as the Fatimid Caliphate.[41] The military was certainly a key component of the Ptolemies' ruling coalition formation, which was a complex process in premodern states.

In Haber's analysis of authoritarian governments (2006), a political takeover is analyzed as a game played between the ruler and key constituent groups:

> Neither side in this game plays from a state of nature:they inherit a preexisting set of political institutions and organizations, along with an economy and society. This means that the game has multiple outcomes. A close reading of the case study literature indicates, however, that the set of the dictator's winning strategies is small. He may terrorize the launching organization's leadership, co-opt them by providing them with private goods, or raise their costs of collective action by proliferating yet more organizations. Each of these strategies generates quite different property rights systems, and each of those property rights systems have consequences for economic growth and distribution.

The fourteenth century Arab historian Ibn Khaldun, in his analysis of the Abbasid Caliphate, was well aware of the phenomenon:

---

[39] Chaudhuri (1990:90).

[40] See for example, the Dendera *strategoi*, for which Farid (1993); Vleeming (2001 [texts 39–55]); the Monkores family, who held the office of *stratêgos* in several nomes, on whom see Thissen (1977); Kallimachos also a *stratêgos* ca. 74 BC and his son until 29 BC. On Kallimachos, whose honors rivaled those traditionally associated with pharaoh, see further Ricketts (1982–83); Hölbl (2001:239–40). Cf. Vleeming (2001 [text 140= *sBerlin* 19369]), a dedicatory inscription of a "general" at a temple in Philadelphia dated to 129 BC. In this text, the man's title is ambiguous. The demotic title can mean "general" or be taken as a local priestly title.

[41] Details in Fischer (forthcoming).

[The rulers] maintain their hold over the government and their own
dynasty with the help, then, either of clients and followers who grew
up in the shadow and power of group feeling, or of tribal groups of
a different descent who have become their clients.
(*The Muqaddimah* 3.2)

The launching organization that Haber refers to was the military, already clearly established in the army's declaration of Ptolemy as king in
306 BC, and at least some of the key priesthoods. All three strategies—
terror, cooptation, and raising the cost of collective action— may have
been in play. To be sure, Ptolemy co-opted elites and created organizations
that competed against each other, thus making coordination at the local
level difficult.[42] Such a strategy is evident across the gamut of Ptolemaic
society, in the military sphere, in warfare and military privilege, in the
support of temples, and, as we will see in the next two chapters, also
in the economic and legal spheres.[43] Such a system, created, at least to
the modern observer, "structural tensions" in Ptolemaic society and the
conflicts between:

> the interests of the agricultural administration, the financial adminis-
> tration, the controllers who supervised this financial administration,
> the more or less independent businessmen who farmed the royal reve-
> nues, the small local contractors, and all the guarantors who were
> involved in the tax-farming system of the third century.[44]

A new Greek bureaucratic order was established to realign the loyalties
of the key constituent groups of the ruling classes.[45] There was the inner
circle of the court, the "friends" of the king as they were called, the Greco-
Macedonian bodyguard and the military class generally, and high officials
in charge of diplomatic matters, correspondence, and military and civil
administration.[46] This Greco-Macedonian "ethno-class," to borrow the
term Briant applied to the Achaemenid ruling elite, was clearly the power

---

[42] Again Fatimid parallels suggest themselves. See for example the comments by Goitein
(1967:33) on rival military factions. It is possible to see in the increasing exemptions from
the salt tax that some collective bargaining between groups and the state was at work here.
Cf. Clarysse and Thompson (2006/1:56–59).

[43] Soldiers received a kind of diplomatic immunity from lawsuits in Alexandria, a law
preserved in *pHal.* 1:124–65 (mid-third century BC).

[44] Bingen (1984:191).

[45] For a general comparative analysis, see Eisenstadt (1993:13–32). For state formation
in the Hellenistic context, see Mileta (2002).

[46] On the king's inner circle in the Hellenistic kingdoms, see Habicht (1958); Herman
(1980–81); McKechnie (1989:204–15). Cf. Theoc., *Id.* 17.93–94, with brief comments by
Hunter (2003:168–69).

surrounding the throne initially.[47] We know little about this inner circle beyond the literary representations of some of the more notorious figures (Rowlandson 2007). Ma (2003), following Briant's analysis of Hellenistic kings extending the traditions of the Persian kings in ruling over diverse local populations, makes much use of the images of ruling elite power, even in local Egyptian contexts, such as the depiction of Ptolemy IV in the Raphia stela. But how much impact these really had on local populations is difficult to judge. The crucial point is that the Ptolemies, as other Hellenistic kings, created a uniform ideology that inserted their new kingship into ancient traditions. Thus Ptolemy IV depicted in Macedonian military dress on a rearing horse on the Raphia stela is the visual equivalent of Manetho's Egyptian history, which inserted the Ptolemies into the long line of legitimate Egyptian pharaohs, and to the kings' actions in building new entrance gates at ancient temples.

Much of this new structure stood on the base of very ancient institutions, among them village organization, family traditions, and the nome, or provincial administrative structure, which was driven by the need for local monitoring and control of the irrigation system.[48] The Egyptian elite consisting of the ancient priestly classes was also crucial to the new bureaucratic structure. This new order, however, did not displace demotic as the language of the villages or of the local bureaucracy. As in the New Kingdom state, local bureaucracy was normally rather independent of the king and his circle.[49] Land was generally held communally in family or "lineage" groups. "Shares" of real property were handed on through a partible inheritance system, but real divisions of land could be achieved. Land was also frequently leased. This "flood recession" system that tied households to "land portfolios" is already observable in Middle Kingdom (ca. 1900 BC) private documents.[50]

A locally dictated village structure centered on agricultural production was deeply rooted historically, as were the temples and priestly organizations. Herein lay the cause of a good amount of what Bingen (1984) has called the "structural tensions" of the Ptolemaic state. The limited economic restructuring that was possible (chapter 6) created a kind of arena of social conflict between a new mentality and an ancient system, between Greeks, Egyptians, and other social groups competing for resources, autonomy, and control over and the cooperation of important constituencies.

[47] Briant (2002) with Ma (2003).

[48] On local elite control of water, Bonneau (1993); Allam (2002); Eyre (1994).

[49] On the New Kingdom bureaucracy and the extent of central control over local structures, see van den Boorn (1988:317–31).

[50] The Hekanakhte papers (Dynasty 12, ca. 1900 BC), for which see Allen (2002). On ancient Egyptian village structure, see Lehner (2000).

We do not know much about the mechanisms by which bureaucratic elites were recruited. On the village level, and in the realm of private contract making, scribes almost certainly came from old scribal families based in temples and trained in demotic scribal traditions and local customs.[51] Scribal offices were traditionally inherited, in some cases even shared by brothers. The state made some attempt to control these office holders and their fees.[52] A text from the second century BC shows something of the process by which candidates could be nominated for the office of temple scribe (the official who wrote demotic legal contracts) by temple officials in cooperation with Ptolemaic officials. Fees for drawing up such contracts were regulated.[53] Those who served in the state administration often took on Greek names. Others did not, leaving the modern scholar on occasion baffled in trying to ascribe ethnicity to a particular person. The Ptolemaic state encouraged persons to become "Hellenes"; i.e., to learn Greek in order to function in the new bureaucracy. Such "Hellenes," the majority of whom (but not all) were of Greek origin, were given a more favorable salt tax rate.[54] Specific ethnicity, then, was subordinated to official function in the state, with an obvious emphasis on "Greek" functions.[55] Here, quite clearly, is the "ethnic policy" of the Ptolemies. In other contexts, the regulation of social status, as well as the name and personal origin of a person, were taken quite seriously for reasons that we must ascribe to the state's concern for social stability and legal order.[56]

It is the usual view that the highest levels of the bureaucracy in Alexandria were Greek. While we cannot be completely certain, in the main this cannot be in doubt. Hecataeus's study of Egypt, written early in the reign of the first Ptolemy, suggests that there was some contact by the ruling Greek elite with Egyptians; the king surely required an intermediary between himself and the body of priesthoods on whom the monarchy relied.[57] The separation between Greeks and Egyptians that the simple for-

---

[51] Zauzich (1968).

[52] That state regulation was not always successful is well illustrated in the second-century BC Menches archive: Verhoogt (1998).

[53] pRyl. IV 572, 30–64.

[54] See Clarysse and Thompson (2006/2:123–205) for "privileged" ethnic groups. BGU XIV 2367; pHamb. II 168.

[55] There was probably an evolution in the period, so that by the second century BC, there were "hellenized Egyptians" functioning in various capacities, including as state bankers.

[56] See, for example, pEleph.Wagner 1 (241/40 BC, Elephantine) that records the punishment of a man being "sent to the rocks," i.e., hard labor in a quarry, for misrepresenting himself as the legal guardian of a woman. For an English translation, see Bagnall and Derow (2004, text 128). The text provides the first known occurrence of the royal courts, the chrêmatistai. On the regulation of names and origins in the legal context, see BGU VI.1213.3 (third century BC); Hübsch (1968); Thompson (2001a).

[57] On Hecataeus: Murray (1970); Burstein (1992).

mula "Egyptians in the villages, Greeks in the cities" implies was, on the one hand, the normal division between central state elites and local social groups, and, on the other hand, certainly an inaccurate portrayal of the local situation. At the village level, social integration and interaction were a function of social networks and personal variables, such as knowledge of Greek, marriage choice, preference of contract language in the legal sphere, and so on. Military settlers in the countryside had a different experience of Ptolemaic Egypt than did Greeks who lived in Alexandria. The Ptolemies had good reasons to be wary of giving Egyptians power, but there was little alternative, given the state's manpower shortage and the ebbing of Greek immigration into Egypt.

There were similar issues of bureaucratic alienation from the ruler in earlier Egyptian history.[58] For example, during the later New Kingdom, in an environment in which the kings were politically weak, there was a marked tendency for a few powerful families to control key high-level positions within the state through marriage and inheritance, with one family sometimes holding several such positions simultaneously.[59] More than likely the Ptolemies would have had the same difficulties altering these village- and temple-based structures as the earlier kings experienced. Their aim was to achieve stability and unity within the territory, to maintain their position within the state, fend off rivals, and mobilize resources "independent of the fixed ascriptive rights and duties" of traditional social groups (Eisenstadt 1993:117).

POLITICAL PROCESS OF THE TAKEOVER

Details of the first fifty years of Ptolemaic rule are few and far between, but a general outline can be established. Between the years 321 and 305, Egypt grew from a "splinter" of the Persian Empire to a nascent independent state with two new political centers. Hints at a traditional Egyptian economic structure continued despite the political disturbances that rocked Egypt in these heady days between revolts, the Persian retreat from Egypt, Alexander's invasion, and the formation of the new state by Ptolemy.[60]

Ptolemy quickly removed Kleomenes, a governor appointed by Alexander, and operated as satrap. It was Ptolemy, therefore, not Alexander or

---

[58] See the general remarks on the tendency by Eisenstadt (1993:286–87).

[59] See Lloyd (1983:229–30, and fig. 3.11); Bierbrier (1975).

[60] On Kleomenes, see Vogt (1971); Seibert (1972); Huß (2001:76–78 with bibliography p. 76, n. 1); Pseudo-Aristotle, *Oec.* II.2.33.; Dem., *Against Dionysodorus*. Nomarchs were

even Darius III's son, who was "the last of the Achaemenids."[61] There
were certainly Egyptians in the inner circle (the "launching organization")
at the capital, just as there had been Greeks, like the Athenian Chabrias,
who served as advisors to Egyptian kings in the fourth century BC (Falivene 1991). There were men of action, too, who must have helped Ptolemy, not the least among them being the military commander Nectanebo,
a relative of king Nectanebo I (380–362 BC).[62] Greek culture was not
unfamiliar to the highest level of Egyptian priests in the early Ptolemaic
period (Derchain 2000).[63]

Historically, priests and soldiers were the two principal landholding
classes (the king being in a class by himself, cf. Diodorus 1.73). Egyptian
priests, many of whom were literate, were the mediators between the ruler
and his circle on the one hand and temples and agricultural production
on the other. They were, at least a certain percentage of them, actively
involved in the formation of the dynasty, in the acceptance of the ruler
cult within the temples, in meeting to celebrate the dynasty, and even in
collecting revenues.

The priests were probably not a unified political body, though Ptolemaic policy may have promoted the possibility of this, but they were very
important players in the first millennium BC, when politics was so fragmented and uncertain, acting as guardians of an authentic historical tradition and of political legitimacy. They were also the conservators of literary
texts and traditions, such as the *Chaosbeschreibung*, which may have fo-
mented sentiments against foreign rule (Dillery 2005).[64] Later on, in the
synods or statewide meetings of priests, the politics between ruler and the
body of priests shows itself in the clear light of day. The priests of Ptah
at Memphis played a very important role in state politics throughout the
period, and it is likely that other priesthoods did as well.[65] We can hope
to know more about this elite, and its relationships to the rulers, when
more of the biographical inscriptions have been studied.[66] But we shall

---

still left in charge of collecting taxes in their districts. See also the treatment of Egypt in
Pseudo-Aristotle, *Oec.* 25a, 25b, 37.

[61] Briant (1982:330, 2002:876). Cf. the remarks of Fox (2007). On Ptolemy and his background, see Bingen (2007).

[62] On the Egyptian elite in the early Ptolemaic period, see Peremans (1977); Lloyd (2002).
More broadly, Baines (2004).

[63] See further Falivene (1991:205) on the pre-Ptolemaic Greek involvement with the
Egyptian economy.

[64] The literary tradition originates in New Kingdom literature, and has a long history
well beyond Ptolemaic times. See further Venticinque (2006) and the literature cited therein.
On the ambiguous role of religious groups, see Eisenstadt (1993:189–93).

[65] On the Memphite priests, see Crawford (1980); Thompson (1988).

[66] Lloyd (2002); Baines (2004).

perhaps never know the extent of Egyptian (and others') involvement at the highest level of state administration.

The reign of Ptolemy II has provided the most plentiful evidence of how broad a sweep Ptolemaic attempts at consolidation were. This has led to the view, now nearly universal, that it was this Ptolemy who was responsible for the "Ptolemaic" reorganization of Egypt. Perhaps the most important account of political consolidation and legitimization came in the form of an Egyptian history, written in Greek during his reign, by Manetho of Sebennytus.[67] At the same time, many important fiscal reforms were introduced, among them the use of coinage and receipts in the taxation system (chapter 5), the use of the list of dynastic cult priests in the dating protocol of Egyptian contracts (chapter 6), and the insertion of the royal cult into Egyptian temple ritual (below).

THE CAPTURE OF KINGSHIP

In order for the Ptolemaic kings to achieve their aims, for which the control of Egypt was a sine qua non, they needed to legitimize their rule. A major channel of this legitimacy would be found in the ancient Egyptian royal tradition (Samuel 1993; Hölbl 2001). Ptolemy's coronation in the ancient capital of Memphis sent the first important signal:the Ptolemies would follow the Persian imperial model, subsuming local traditions within their imperial, Greek framework (Ma 2005:191). We have just seen examples of how the Ptolemies embedded themselves within Egypt's traditions and within what Bowman (2007:166) has recently called its "institutional iconography." They were "culturally oriented" in this respect (and with respect to the elite international Greek world as well, as attested by the creation of the *museion* and library at Alexandria), seeing themselves as the bearers of a vast dual tradition of kingship, bringing together the Egyptian and the "Greco-Macedonian cultural background" (Davies 2001:39; Eisenstadt 1993:227–38). Egyptian kingship was a major component, then, of the "cognitive framework" of the state, enabling it to penetrate local structures and to claim resources. Egyptians, and Egyptian priesthoods, believed in the system already, while the Greeks held onto their own expectations of kingship. The kings played well to both audiences in their use of language as well as image, and in their beneficence toward cult and, in times of crisis, toward the country as a whole.[68] Ptolemaic kingship, therefore, was the crucial unifying

---

[67] Verbrugghe and Wickersham (1996); Dillery (1999); Gozzoli (2006).

[68] On the subtlety of royal imagery, see e.g., Ashton (2001). One famous example of Ptolemaic munificence toward Egypt occurred when Ptolemy III imported grain to save Egypt from famine. The event is recorded in the Kanopos decree, on which pp. 97–98.

force that brought together the different ethnic groups under the umbrella of the new state.

Ptolemaic strategy, wherever possible, was to satisfy both Greek and Egyptian expectations of kingship, binding together diverse ethnic groups within one imperial framework in which local populations, led by priests, played an active role (cf. Hölbl 2001:112). The penetration of that framework into local levels is seen in the use of phrases such as "the king's canal" in boundary descriptions of land conveyances and "for the king" in the context of tax payments, and in the adjudication of disputes (discussed in chapter 6). In these cases, however, I view such phrases as having more the sense of "public," and indicating the successful use of kingship in binding local areas to the central state ideology.[69] Legitimized kingship and the key Egyptian concept of *Ma'at* were the unifying ideologies of governance.

Part of the Ptolemaic style of kingship, then, was "orientalized" from the very beginning, a blend of legitimacy secured through Egyptian religion and through military power. It was for no other reason that Alexander the Great rebuilt the bark shrine in the Luxor temple, a temple dedicated specifically to the cult of the royal *Ka* that linked together through cult all legitimate kings. In order for Alexander to be accepted as the rightful king of Egypt, he had, in theory, to be confirmed by the god Amun-Re at the all-important *Opet* festival where legitimacy was transferred through elaborate ritual.[70]

The political relationship between the Ptolemaic kings and the family of priests at the temple of Ptah in the ancient capital of Memphis was particularly close and important.[71] There was in fact no *degeneration* into an "oriental monarchy" by later kings.[72] The path was laid down many years before by Alexander's visit to the Siwa oasis, by his coronation in Memphis, and by Ptolemy's decree recorded in the so-called Satrap Stela (below). The reliance on legitimacy expressed and granted through traditional institutions was at once a strength and, ultimately, a weakness of the regime. The acceptance of the Ptolemies as legitimate pharaohs may be counted as one of the greatest successes of Ptolemaic strategy.[73] But it was the priesthoods who were the guarantors of political legitimacy, the conduit through which Egyptian culture was understood, and indeed

[69] Cf. Clarysse and Thompson (2206/2:8).
[70] Bell (1985:270).
[71] Thompson (1988:138–46); Hölbl (2001).
[72] As expressed, for example, in Polybius' contempt of Ptolemy IV. On the reasons for the particular hostility toward Ptolemy IV, see Walbank (1979 [2002]:63–64).
[73] See Thompson (1988:125–38).

the creators of the renewed image of kingship.[74] Therefore it was the bargain between the king and the priests that grew to become increasingly important in the course of Ptolemaic history. Conversely, emphasis on the Greek conception of kingship appears to have declined, perhaps a development related to the loss of parts of the Ptolemaic empire and of general prestige in the Mediterranean. Thus the political importance of the role of pharaoh, originally meant for internal consumption within Egypt, increased not because of a political struggle between the king and the priesthoods in which the king lost, but out of a need to preserve the core of the empire.[75]

Ptolemaic interest in Egyptian culture can be seen in many arenas, including perhaps in the outpouring of Egyptian literary production during this period. The important demotic literary corpus known as the *Cycle of Pedubastis*, although set in the past, with historical echoes from the Third Intermediate and the Nubian and Saïte/Persian periods, was written in Ptolemaic and early Roman times.[76] It has been suggested that the motivation to record the stories came from Ptolemy II's interest in Egyptian culture (Kitchen 1986:461). This probably assigns too much credit to Ptolemy II; such literary production was more likely the result of the pride of Egyptian scribes in a heroic Egyptian past. Nevertheless, it is clear that the early Ptolemies were keenly interested in the Egypt's history, and, like their Saïte predecessors, used the past to create a new, unified state. As we have already seen, the presence of Egyptian statuary in Alexandria demonstrates their reverence for the pharaonic past. The extent of the relationship between Egypt's past and the new Ptolemaic state is not known, nor are the modes of interaction. The library at Alexandria may well be one locus, but it does not take great imagination to suggest that it happened often in more informal circles.

Egyptian kingship (and queenship), with its powerful and ancient symbolism, was personal and performative.[77] It was also mobile and visible. And there was a major element of theater in it. The grand procession recorded by Kallixeinos of Rhodes that took place in Alexandria during the reign of Ptolemy II gives contemporary witness to the fact that political power was *performed*. The ritualized public display, or "theater," of power would continue to be a major component of Egypt's politics well

---

[74] Murray (1970, especially pp. 155–56).

[75] See the remarks of Hölbl (2001:106).

[76] Stories of Egypt's past were certainly circulating widely. Posener (1953:107) noted, for example, Diodorus' (1.89.3) probable citation of the New Kingdom story known as *The Doomed Prince* (P. Harris 500, verso). An English translation of this story is available in Lichtheim (1976:200–203).

[77] On the depiction of Ptolemaic queens, see Minas (2005).

into the future.[78] The king was *de jure* the chief priest in every cult throughout Egypt, and the guarantor of justice and harmony.[79] Kingship and mythic/cult practice bound the ruler to claims of territory and people. Territorial control through ritual in addition to bureaucratic routine, an ancient feature of kingship, was enhanced by dynastic festivals (Koenen 1993:70–81), visits to temples, etc.[80] It offered an effective cognitive framework, political stability (theoretically), and a means by which to mobilize resources. Monarchy, and the performance of monarchy, meant a significant expenditure of resources that the ruler could in turn use to reinforce his legitimacy and political authority. For the Ptolemies, this aspect of kingship was reinforced by Hellenistic tradition.[81] Of course local traditions mattered as well; the Ptolemaic kings were aware of, and sensitive to, Egyptian pharaonic customs. The Greek king, conceptually different and tied more to Alexander's vision, was increasingly joined to the Egyptian tradition via the dynastic cult in Alexandria and the Egyptian Ptolemaic cult in the temples.

Indeed, Ptolemaic rule in Egypt represents something of a revival in Egyptian kingship, and there can be little doubt that it was the active participation of the Egyptian priesthoods that was largely responsible.[82] As for Ptolemaic attitudes, they certainly reflect Darius' example, but they were also a product of an intense Hellenistic interest with Egypt.[83] This was the last period when at least the image of the pharaoh held real currency, because Egypt was the core of the Ptolemaic empire, whereas for the Persians, Egypt was a province.[84] We might say in evoking Ptolemaic kingship: big state, big king. It seems highly likely that the first five Ptolemaic kings participated in traditional coronation ceremonies at Mem-

---

[78] On this procession, preserved by Athenaeus, see Thompson (2000b). For ritualized public display of political power under the Fatimids, see Sanders (1994:87–98). For the state as "theater" see Geertz (1980); Lansing (1991); Brett (2001:327).

[79] Heinen (1987); Koenen (1985, 1993).

[80] On Ptolemaic visits to Egyptian temples, see Clarysse (2000a).

[81] On Hellenistic kingship, perhaps the largest single subject of study in Hellenistic history, see inter alia: Préaux (1978/1:181–294); Mooren (1983); Walbank (1984); Samuel (1993); Rajak et al. (2007).

[82] For a good general introduction to Egyptian kingship, see the volume edited by O'Connor and Silverman (1995).

[83] The Pithom Stela (*CG* 22183, = *Urk* II. 81–105, newly translated in Mueller [2006:192–99)] and Thiers (2007), cf. Roeder [1959]), and the Mendes Stela (*CG* 22181, = *Urk*. II, 28–54), and the priestly synodal decrees discussed below, show how keen the kings were on projecting the image of legitimate pharaohs. On the visiting temples to perform public rituals, see Winnicki (1994). Initial Persian attitudes toward Egyptian kingship: Lloyd (1983:293–99). For Greek scholarly interest in Egypt, see among others the surveys of Froidefond (1971), and Burstein (1996b).

[84] On the Ptolemaic royal portraiture, see Ashton (2001); Stanwick (2002).

phis.[85] The young Ptolemy V Epiphanes made preparations for his coronation ceremony by defeating rebels in the Delta and later murdering them at the ceremony itself. The entire scene, described on the Rosetta Stone, invoked the mythic victories of the gods Re and Horus (Greek text, 1.26). Like Alexander, here Ptolemy V reenacted a scene from Egyptian myth, the same scene of the king executing enemies that had been a part of the visual and literary myth of Egyptian kingship since the First Dynasty (Schulman 1988).

The conception of the ideal king—divine descent, warrior prowess, reverence towards the gods, and wealth coupled with generosity toward his subjects—fits well into both Egyptian and Hellenistic ideology (Samuel 1993:181). Ptolemaic kingship was complex, because the kings had to play to two primary audiences, Greek and Egyptian, to obtain the same goal, namely the loyalty of the population (Koenen 1993). This loyalty was secured through a variety of bargains. From the Egyptian population's viewpoint, this bargaining is well documented in the royal decrees that depict the ruler as a legitimate pharaoh acting piously and beneficently toward Egyptian gods and their temples.[86]

The Satrap Stela, erected in regnal year 7 of Alexander IV (311 BC), the first royal decree of the Ptolemaic period, provides important evidence for the early relationship between key priesthoods and Ptolemy.[87] The text is written in the form of a royal donation restoring traditional endowments of land and animals to the temple of Edjo at Buto in the Delta, which was reestablished by Khababash after Xerxes' sequestration. In the offering scene at the top of the stela, a pharaoh is depicted making offerings to two gods, Uto and Harendotes. The cartouches are blank, but it is likely that the "pharaoh" depicted is Ptolemy rather than Alexander as Alexander's cartouches are regularly inscribed in hieroglyphic.[88]

---

[85] I follow Hölbl (2001:32, n. 47) here in accepting that the first four kings probably celebrated the coronation ceremony. The actual evidence is equivocal. It is the Rosetta decree announcing the coronation of Ptolemy V that is the first actual evidence of a Ptolemy being crowned king in (pseudo?) Egyptian fashion. Cf. Koenen (1993:71). The coronation of Ptolemy XII by Psherenptah, the high priest of Ptah of Memphis, was recorded in the latter's autobiographical text British Museum EA 886, a brief treatment of which is provided by Baines (2004:56–61).

[86] *Euergesia*, one of the key points of convergence in Greek and Egyptian political thought on kingship. Cf. Murray (1970:159–60).

[87] For the text (=CG 22182), see the literature cited in Manning (2003a:42, n. 98) and Gozzoli (2006). The restoration of temple property by the Ptolemaic kings is discussed by Winnicki (1994); Devauchelle (1995); Briant (2003). Summaries of the historical context of the text may be found in Gozzoli (2006), who cites earlier studies of same.

[88] I agree with Ritner (2003:393) that there was intentional ambiguity here, Ptolemy already in 311 BC having every intention of ruling Egypt, while his claims in the Greek world were more tenuous and thus, by necessity, restrained.

Acting on behalf of Alexander IV, who was king in name only, Ptolemy is portrayed in the text as a legitimate pharaoh by his behavior toward temples, although he is referred to explicitly as "satrap." Long before he publicly took the title of king (in 305 BC), Ptolemy appears here as a traditional pharaoh (just as Cambyses did in the Udjahorresnet text), showing piety toward traditional Egyptian cults and divine law, respect for the population, especially toward the priests, and bound to Egyptian territory. The text also mentions military campaigns in the Near East and into lower Nubia. However "traditional" or pseudo-epigraphic the events described on the stela may be, it illustrates very well that Ptolemy intended to legitimize his rule, and to be constrained by priestly expectations, within a traditional royal context.

As I mentioned in the last chapter, religion gave rulers access to local society, but the organizational power of religion at local levels could also be a potent source of resistance against the state. Egyptian temples and their priesthoods were the main source of political legitimacy inside the Egyptian territory. They were the storehouses of cultural memory, educational and bureaucratic power, and political legitimacy, and they exercised economic control over considerable territories. Perhaps most important of all—and this is often forgotten— the temples represented religious authority for a deeply religious people. Charged with the maintenance of cosmic order through daily temple ritual, the priests also represented to the king the traditions of justice and rural order. The Ptolemies, therefore, needed Egyptian temples and the organizational capacity they represented in order to control Egypt and to legitimize their rule, but they were required to walk a fine line between embedding their rule within the tradition and becoming captives of the priesthoods.

Ptolemy I with his wife Berenike I received cultic honors as "savior gods," and he was also honored as the founder of Ptolemaïs. Deification of the royal family, begun by Ptolemy II, and the installation of the ruler cult within Egyptian temples reinforced the royal family's legitimacy through religion, although the nature of Ptolemaic royal deification probably owed more to fourth-century Greek tradition than to Egyptian (Walbank 1991–92:109). The royal cult, including the worship of the living monarch, was nevertheless accepted by both Greeks and Egyptians, in part because the kings carefully selected cult names that resonated with both populations (Thompson 1988:125–38; Koenen 1993; Hölbl 2001). This was a largely a successful strategy.[89]

---

[89] On the complexities of the dynastic cult, see Koenen (1993) and the earlier literature cited therein. The wine jars used for libation offerings in the royal cult, known as *oinochoai*, are of particular importance for showing the subtleties of Greek and Egyptian iconography. On them, see Thompson (1973). For a good treatment of the historical background to the decrees, see Thompson (1988:117–22).

PRIESTLY ACCEPTANCE

Acceptance by the only political group among the Egyptians, the priests, is well documented in the priestly decrees that emanated from the synods of the priesthoods and were issued in bilingual or trilingual (depending on whether one is counting languages or scripts) texts.[90] The multilingual aspect of these decrees is unique in the Hellenistic world. Synod meetings of representatives of all of the priesthoods, and the subsequent copies of the decrees that were set up in all of the temples, are also unique in Egyptian history, and they appear to have been a new feature of the Ptolemaic state.[91] At least fifteen such assemblies took place during the later third and second centuries, and they reflect the continual two-way bargaining process between the king and the priesthoods.[92]

The concentration of synodal decrees in these years might reflect the loss of empire abroad and the urgency felt by the kings to control the core of their territory. The political potency of the texts, which were erected in prominent places in the temples, bridged new and ancient political and ideological orthodoxies on the nature of royal power. This was discovered by the first Roman prefect of Egypt, Cornelius Gallus, who was forced to commit suicide after celebrating a military victory by erecting a trilingual text at Philae.[93] Such texts were the exclusive preserve of the ruler, and Gallus no doubt came too close to Ptolemaic practice for the comfort of Augustus.[94] The Roman attitude toward priests was founded on an entirely different principle.

The most famous of these texts, the Memphis decree (preserved on the Rosetta Stone) records the requirement that Egyptian priests meet yearly in Alexandria, and states that it was remitted, presumably as a concession to the priesthoods:

> . . . and he released the members of the priestly class from the annual obligation to sail down the river to Alexandria . . . (Greek text. Trans. Austin [2006])

The first preserved (not the first) of these texts, the Kanopos Decree (7 March 238) states that priests had assembled to celebrate the king's birth-

---

[90] For the demotic version of the most important decrees, see Simpson (1996). Cf. Tietze et al. (2005).

[91] Huß (1991); Clarysse (2000b); Hölbl (2001:162–69); Gozzoli (2006:126–52).

[92] Cf. Ma (2000:108–11) on the process in Seleukid Asia Minor.

[93] For Gallus' stela, see Lyons and Borchardt (1896) and the announced forthcoming study by Minas-Nerpel and Pfeiffer.

[94] Hdt. (4.166) tells us that the Persian satrap Aryandes, ca. 518 BC, met his end because of a desire to mint silver coinage, another royal perogative. Cf. Briant (2002:409–10).

day and to create honors for the recently deceased princess Berenike.[95] These decrees provide our best evidence for a crucial aspect of the "ruling coalition" (discussed above), and they imply at least the potential for "proto-national" sentiment and a willingness to preserve the memory of good kings on the part of the priestly elite. Sentiments of this nature later found expressions in such texts as *The Oracle of the Potter* and the *Papyrus Jumilhac*, which so fervently foretells the doom of Egypt if proper rituals are not observed.[96] By encouraging the loyalty of the priests through the creation of what Crone (2003:71) calls "horizontal linkages," the Ptolemies may have in fact strengthened their sense of empowerment and identity, especially against a weak regime, just as the recording of the population in the census reinforced group identities.[97] Be that as it may, a reading of the language of synodal decrees, the active involvement of the priesthoods in establishing the royal cult in the temples, and the creation of royal images, are all signs that instilling loyalty and cooperation was a royal goal.[98] That loyalty was expressed most in the Kanopos decree with the requirement that priests wear rings engraved with the words "priesthood of the beneficent gods" (i.e., Ptolemy III and Berenike II). The most recent assessment of the synodal decrees has suggested that the texts were originally drafted by Egyptian priests, probably in Greek.[99] As we have seen, the synods appear to have been a creation of the Ptolemies, although there were historical precedents for priests meeting at particularly important royal celebrations like the *Sed* festival. It has been observed that many of the later synodal decrees came out of Memphis and not from the Ptolemaic capital, which very likely indicates only that Memphis was the recognized religious center of Egypt (Thompson 1988) and does not signal a shift in power between the king and the priesthoods as Clarysse (2000b) contends.[100] The *Sed* festival, a very ancient ritual

[95] For the Kanopos decree, see the recent study by Pfeiffer (2004). New copies of the text were discovered in 2001 at Naga ed-Deir in southern Egypt, and at 2004 at Bubastis in the Delta. See Tietze et al. (2005). On the celebration of the royal birthday, see Perpillou-Thomas (1993). For the important site of Kanopos (mod. Abu Qir), about 15 km east of Alexandria, see Goddio (1995), and the summary by Stanwick (2002:20). Goddio's ongoing work is well presented online at http://www.franckgoddio.org/

[96] Koenen (1968). Hecataeus' work on Egyptian kingship, written while Ptolemy was still functioning as a satrap, offers critical insight into the attitudes toward kingship. Cf. Murray (1970:153).

[97] See chapter 5.

[98] On the royal images, see Stanwick (2002:7–12).

[99] For the debate on which language was first, and whether it matters, see Bingen (1989:263–64). The format of the texts is Greek. On this point, see Clarysse (2000b); Gozzoli (2006:148). Derchain (1987) reaches a different conclusion, arguing that the demotic and Greek texts were composed simultaneously.

[100] For one decree that originated from Alexandria, see *Philae II* (= *Urk*. II.214–30), a decree from a synod meeting at Alexandria after the great Theban revolt was put down in the Thebaid in 186 BC.

that celebrated kingship, brought together statues of the gods and their priests from throughout Egypt, and there are other recorded instances of ad hoc gatherings of priests.[101] Some festivals, the rise of the Nile flood for example (Bonneau 1993), would have been widely celebrated, though most occurred within a particular temple estate or, like the marriage festival of Hathor of Dendera and Horus of Edfu, were celebrated at a regional level.[102] As far as we know, there had never been a requirement in the past for Egyptian priests from across Egypt to meet in one place annually. There were, however, officials charged with administering the priesthoods of particular deities across Egypt, so it is possible that the Ptolemies were reinforcing earlier trends toward centralized control as they sought acceptance by, and kept control over, a powerful and influential part of their coalition.[103] But there is something distinctly Ptolemaic about these deliberative bodies of priests.

The deliberative character of the assemblies may have been modeled on Greek assembly practice, although admittedly on a different scale than in other Greek cities, and perhaps under the influence of the Greek citizen bodies at Alexandria and Ptolemaïs. Earlier Ptolemaic evidence suggests that the king's birthday was widely celebrated in Alexandria, and also in the countryside. One famous inscription lists victorious kleruchs assembled at an athletic competition in honor of Ptolemy II's birthday.[104] The synodal decrees do in fact function in a similar manner to decrees of Greek poleis of the period (Ma 2000:228–35), and the language of texts such as the Kanopos decree demonstrate that it "is a thoroughly Greek *psephisma*" (van Minnen 2007:710).

Whether we view these assemblies as harking back to Egyptian or Greek practice or, much less likely, to Persian inspiration, such gatherings of elites and the making of decrees show us how elite behavior functioned in an imperial culture, in the wider Hellenistic context of royal euergetism, and in the specific Ptolemaic context of royal state building. The decrees also confirm for us that Egyptian priests, and Egyptian religion, could accommodate new features of kingship and could innovate by establishing new festivals within their own cultural tradition while expressing it in Greek terms.[105]

---

[101] See Briant (2002:173–200). See also the mention of priests gathered at the request of Psammetichus II in *pRyl*.dem 9. 3.16ff. and 14.16–22.

[102] On festivals, Bleeker (1967); for the Ptolemaic period, Perpillou-Thomas (1993).

[103] The priest Somtutefnakht, an eyewitness to some of Alexander the Great's campaigns in Asia, was "chief priest of Sekhmet in the entire land" in the fourth century BC. For his titles, see *sNaples* 1035, *Urk*. II.1–6, translated in Lichtheim (1980:41–44).

[104] Cairo JdE 90702 (267 BC, probably from the Fayyum). See Koenen (1977). A photograph and translation is provided in Walker and Higgs (2001:115–16).

[105] On these decrees showing us the ability of Egyptian priests to innovate and adapt, see the recent analysis by Pfeiffer (2004).

The Ptolemaic decrees show us, moreover, the extent of Ptolemaic involvement with priesthoods and temples—in stark contrast to the Persian and Roman attitude—which became especially intense in the 180s.[106] Their bilingual nature confirms that the resolution of the priests on behalf of the king was intended to reach both Greek and Egyptian audiences.[107]

The concentration of these decrees in the wake of major disturbances throughout Egypt appears to have been at least an attempt by the king to reestablish state equilibrium by offering concessions to the priesthoods and thereby using them as a means to regain political control of the countryside. These priestly decrees, therefore, are the local Egyptian equivalent of the widely documented Hellenistic phenomenon of kings preserving the local customs and traditions of diverse populations while incorporating them within the larger framework of state building.[108] The bilingual nature of the Egyptian decrees highlights only more powerfully the tensions between royal and local power, and between the historic traditions of Egyptian kingship on the one hand and the ideology of Hellenistic kingship on the other. The distribution of these decrees throughout Egypt is a measure of Ptolemaic success in connecting to the various priesthoods, and the extension of the number of priestly phyles from four to five by the Kanopos decree marks serious attempt at broadening the political base.

While the kings certainly relied on the loyalty of the priests, the priests were also controlled by the state in various ways. Here the famous Rosetta Stone has much to teach us. In this decree, which reaffirms the close political and religious relationship between the king and the priesthoods of all of the temples throughout Egypt, the young Ptolemy V (or, more likely, his advisors accepting terms offered by the priests) offered a remission of several practices, including, as we have seen, the requirement that the priests must meet annually in Alexandria. The text also remitted the "consecration tax" that priests had to pay upon assuming office.

Bingen (1989) has pointed out that while a comparison of the language of the dating protocols in the Kanopos decree of 238 BC and the Rosetta decree of 196 BC has tempted some scholars to see a decline of royal influence in such meetings and a concomitant increase in the power of the priesthoods, the actual political situation reflected in these decrees is too

---

[106] On this point, see Thompson (1988:121).

[107] In theory the setting up of these decrees in the outer courtyards of temples through Egypt made the priestly decisions recorded on them available to "everyone" (Hölbl 2001:106). The literacy rate would have limited firsthand consumption of the text, but the visual aspects of the stelae and their prominent location in the temples may have widely and successfully disseminated the basic message.

[108] On this basic point, see Ma (2000, esp. pp. 235–42).

complex to suggest such a zero sum game. The mechanisms behind the issuance of each decree, perhaps even the location of the two synods (Alexandria for the Kanopos decree, Memphis for the Rosetta decree) as Bingen suggests, may have influenced the "tone" of the two texts. Both decrees express the legitimacy of royal action and the pious munificence of the king, and it is the acceptance by the priesthoods of the king's legitimacy and piety that is the key to their relationship (Hölbl 2001:265).

Whatever the process by which the Ptolemies adopted the traditions, actions, and images of Egyptian kingship, they used them well. The texts suggest a special connection to New Kingdom royal ideology, the last imperial age of Egypt, and no doubt a conscious borrowing of the language and imagery of the imperial pharaohs. The Ptolemies wrote their own history in an Egyptian medium in the same way as the Nubian pharaohs had done before them. In both cases, it was the royal actions of the New Kingdom pharaohs that were copied. It is no accident that the early Ptolemaic kings took New Kingdom pharaonic royal names as their throne names. The behavior of Ptolemy IV in the Raphia decree (217 BC) reads like the much earlier description of Ramses II's battle of Kadesh. In a similar fashion, reading Polybius (V.85.8) one almost has the feeling that he was looking at the Abu Simbel reliefs of Ramses II while he was writing his description of the battle of Raphia. Perhaps those soldiers who had visited the monument and left graffiti had been similarly inspired by the beautiful Kadesh battle scenes inside. In Kallimachos' *Hymn to Delos* the Ptolemaic king "conquers what the sun encircles." At the opposite end of the social spectrum, a religious recluse living in the Serapeum at Saqqara ends his petition to the king by saying:

> Therefore I ask you, O Sun King!, not to overlook me, who am in seclusion, but, if it seems right to you, write to Poseidonius the bodyguard and *stratêgos*, to free him [the petitioner's brother] from his duties of service so he can be with me. May Isis and Serapis, the greatest of the gods, give to you and to your children the domain of every land on which the sun shines forever. [*UPZ* I 15].[109]

This solar imagery of the Egyptian king ruling over every land on which the sun shines occurs in a variety of texts and contexts, from priestly decrees to the historical account of Polybius. It clearly goes back to New Kingdom imperial ideology, and it must have been part of the Zeitgeist under the Ptolemies, as indeed it was in the Persian period, a fascinating reminder of the strong currents of culture that are not always present in our documentation, but which were certainly part of the political land-

---

[109] For the background to this text, see Thompson (1988).

scape.[110] Whether it was a New Kingdom, a Saïte, a Persian, or a Ptolemaic king, it was above all the important role of the priesthoods in legitimizing the pharaoh, and thus the state, that was paramount.

Building New Settlements

The founding of new cities and towns was a major source of royal legitimacy and authority in the ancient Near East. Cities indeed were "like electric transformers" as Braudel (1981:479) once famously concluded. And so they were in the Hellenistic world, and nothing better illustrates how important the process was than the founding of the new Ptolemaic capital at Alexandria and of Greek cities throughout the imperial territory.[111] Traditionally settlements in the Nile valley were located on higher lying land at key trade junctions, and they were managed locally (Eyre forthcoming). It was understandably important for the Ptolemies to alter this locally-based political organization of the state by founding new towns that would be not local but imperial centers. It was a matter of extending the reach of their political power into the countryside, but equally it was a method of recruiting responsible officials. The building of two new capital *poleis* at Alexandria and Ptolemaïs, and the founding of new settlements elsewhere, played an important role in establishing sovereignty throughout Egypt and the empire. Moreover, by founding two imperial centers, the Ptolemies were following the ancient custom of the pharaohs in having two centers of power, one in the north and the other in Upper Egypt. As in Hellenistic Asia Minor, and indeed elsewhere, the expansion of a "royal area" was a key strategy for extending the king's influence (Mileta 2002) and for monetizing the economy (Aperghis 2005). Here the traditional royal claim to territory is contrasted with the new territorial claims (i.e., the expansion of Greek presence) of the new Ptolemaic state. Egypt before the Ptolemies already had many towns and villages, and several cities of notable size. It also had a regional adminis-

[110] On the New Kingdom ideology, see e.g., the *Horemheb Coronation Inscription* (Turin 1379 = *Urk.* IV.2119, 8–2120, 17) treated by Gardiner (1953). The famous Adulis inscription (*OGIS* 54), a sixth-century copy by Cosmas Indicopleustes (*Christian topography* 2.58–59) of a supposed Ptolemaic original at Massawa, is not without historic echoes of New Kingdom military glory. The text records the extensive conquests by Ptolemy III during the Third Syrian War, which reached as far east as Bactria. Recent English translations may be found in Burstein (1985, text 99); Bagnall and Derow (2004, text 26); Austin (2006, text 268). A good Persian period example may be found in the Tell el-Maskhuteh stela of Darius I, on which see most recently Lloyd (2007).

[111] The basic history of Alexandria is still that of Fraser (1972). For major archaeological activity in recent years, see Goddio (1998) and Empereur (1998) for overviews.

trative system that linked agricultural production to administrative district capitals.

Ptolemaic strategy involved two main processes with respect to settlement. It established soldiers on plots of land throughout Egypt, and it built new settlements. Building new towns and the concomitant need to quarry stone were major hallmarks of Egyptian kingship and a major source of power and prestige. Just so, the power and prestige of the Ptolemies was surely projected by its newly-founded capital, Alexandria, and by the southern capital, Ptolemaïs. It is something of a shame that we know so little about the construction of these cities, although work in the Alexandrian harbor in recent years is revealing something of the actual character of this great city.

The Ptolemies' political strategy with respect to the traditional villages and towns of Egypt appears to have been much the same as in earlier periods. Traditional village structure was left unaltered, a condition paralleled in other premodern states, which are characterized by a limited ability to penetrate local village structure (chapter 2). Each village was autonomous, run by a headman who was responsible to the bureaucratic chain of command.[112] Land was worked in small plots, which were family-owned, though usually also subject to institutional claims (i.e. taxes, to the king and a temple) on a portion of the production. As in China, social solidarity was based more on the local irrigation networks than on social differentiation, and this probably served the interests of the ruler in preventing the development of independent "centers of power" (Eisenstadt 1993:235–36). The taxation system (see chapter 5) also promoted, or maintained, social divisions that effectively precluded "collective action."

A notable feature of Egyptian agriculture in all periods is its flexible nature. This is reflected in the access to land by individuals (through annual lease contracts, for example), in labor mobilizations, and in the ways the state dealt with regional variability in social customs, annual variability in flood conditions, and the perennial problem of loyal agents. It is important to stress that there was no attempt by the Ptolemies to displace entrenched local elites or ancient institutional structures. This was a powerful limiting factor on the formation of a landed aristocratic class (Rowlandson 2007), and it had an effect on settlement patterns as well as on land grants.

The Ptolemaic state affected the landscape in other ways. Greek town planning in Hippodamian grids has been viewed generally as good evidence for state direction in the Hellenistic period (Rostovtzeff 1941:1051;

---

[112] I rely here on the studies of Lehner (2000), and Eyre (2004).

Winter 1984; Mueller 2006:109–21). Since very few towns in Egypt have
been excavated or surveyed, a grid plan is only really proven at Philadelphia and in a few other places in the Fayyum (Rowlandson 2005:256),
but both Alexandria and Ptolemaïs in the south would certainly have been
laid out on a Hippodamian plan. "Rectilinear planned" towns were, of
course, well known in ancient Egypt, but it does not appear that all new
towns built by the Ptolemies conformed to the grid plan.[113]

Indeed "Egyptian" style towns seem to be the norm even in the Fayyum,
arguably the area with the most new building activity in the period
(Mueller 2006:121). Rostovtzeff's case for Hellenistic unity through town
planning (1941:1051) was, indeed, overstated. The founding of a new
town involved state direction and private initiative.[114]

In contrast to the Fayyum, which was a region of low institutional resistance and as a result the region with the most state activity directed at
land reclamation and new settlement, Upper Egypt shows a very different
pattern of Ptolemaic state formation and resistance. There, the state had
to capture ancient institutional structures and the rights and privileges of
the elite, as well as the authority they wielded, and incorporate them
into the greater state framework. Part of this process entailed sending
"representatives of the center" (Barkey 1994:3) to assert central authority
over a large, densely populated territory dominated by temples and religious authority. The new temples in the south, whatever the sources of
their funding, also effectively projected the desired image of a legitimate,
powerful pharaoh.

The Capture of the Thebaid

The ancient temple city of Thebes, prominent in Egyptian history since
the Middle Kingdom, was the center of an important region known in
Greek sources as the Thebaid. It was dominated since the New Kingdom
by the vast temple estate of Amun. This entire stretch of the Egyptian Nile
valley from roughly Asyut up to Aswan was governed as a single territory,
called in Egyptian *P3-ts-n-Niw.t*, "the district of Thebes." The boundaries
of the Thebaid and its institutions of governance seem to have varied over
time. The Persian administration, for example, divided the southern Nile
valley into two districts, with centers at Thebes and Elephantine (Briant
2002:472). The Egyptian name of Thebes was, in fact, the word for
"city," Thebes being considered *the* city par excellence by Egyptian reck-

---

[113] Rowlandson (2005:250) citing Kemp (2006:241–44).
[114] Cf. Mueller (2006:121–31).

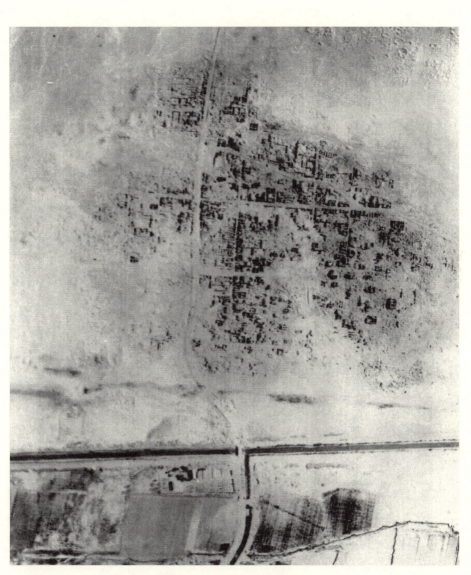

Figure 6. An aerial photograph of Philadelphia showing the basic plan of the town. Viereck (1928, plate1).

oning. On the west side of the river was an entire district of temples and tombs dedicated to the memory of New Kingdom pharaohs. On the east bank, the settlement side of Thebes, lay the mighty temple of Amun-Re, "king of the gods." Throughout much of its history, the temple and the priests who administered it controlled a significant percentage of the natural resources of the southern Nile valley. The extent of their control reached its height in the late New Kingdom. The Ptolemies continued the practice of administering the Thebaid as a region, although now using Ptolemaïs as the administrative center.[115]

Rostovtzeff rightly stressed the economic and social differences that prevailed in Upper Egypt.[116] He believed, however, that Upper Egypt was never a permanent part of the state (1941:1053).[117] One possible reason behind this theory may lie in the nature of the sources themselves. The Egyptian material that is so abundant from the south does tend to present a different world, documenting in the main the business transactions of traditional Egyptian families, primarily members of priesthoods. These family archives do offer a different perspective on the lived human experience of Ptolemaic Egypt, as well as on Egyptian family structure, inheritance patterns, contractual relationships, and the like.[118]

The founding of Ptolemaïs by Ptolemy I was an important first step in establishing political authority in Upper Egypt. To establish this authority, the Ptolemies needed to "overcome the rule of regional institutions and elites" (Barkey 1994:3). Ptolemy II's expansion into the western and eastern deserts and to Red Sea coast also shows that southern Egypt and the roads leading to the coast and through the oases to the west were vital to the early Ptolemaic state's interests. In both cases, it was the trade routes that the rulers wanted to secure, just as it was control of the caravan trade that motivated Ptolemy I's expansion west of Cyrenaica (Hölbl 2001:18).[119] The building of road networks in the deserts (not entirely new with the Ptolemies, but certainly an extensive Ptolemaic activity, par-

---

[115] The administrative control of the Thebaid as one political unit is attested by the existence of the Ptolemaic official known as the *stratêgos* of the Thebaid, whereas in other cases the *stratêgos* was placed in charge of a single nome. See further Thomas (1975). The Thebaid continued to be a separate province under Roman rule, on which see most recently Derda (2006).

[116] I have previously emphasized the structural differences in the land tenure regimes of the Thebaid and the Fayyum in Manning (2003a).

[117] " . . . the upper course of the Nile retained its pre-Ptolemaic social structure and cultural features. These regions [he also refers in the previous sentence to Arabia and Iran] however, were never, or only for short periods, constituent parts of the Hellenistic monarchies. I assume that by "upper course of the Nile" Rostovtzeff meant the Thebaid, and not the Nubian Nile valley.

[118] For an orientation to these archives, see Depauw 1997:155–59.

[119] On the troops used to secure the desert roads, see Hennig (2003).

ticularly under Ptolemy II; e.g., the very important Edfu-Berenike high-way [Strabo 17.1.45]) and the founding of towns on the Red Sea coast, show just how important the southern Nile valley and the eastern desert was to Ptolemaic trade traffic, especially in gold and elephants (and of course ivory).[120] To aid in controlling these areas, tribal peoples such as the Blemmyes, well known in the eastern desert, were incorporated into the state in various capacities. All of this enhanced the "connectivity" of southern Egypt to the Red Sea and the Mediterranean.[121]

New foundations and settlements of soldiers throughout the Nile valley were fundamentally important for Ptolemaic control of the region, and for expansion into the eastern desert to secure Red Sea trade routes. Greek soldiers were certainly established at the key military town of Ele-phantine/Aswan, but probably elsewhere as well, although early documentation is lacking. The entire process of gaining control of the region seems to have been gradual and, where possible, targeted and minimally disruptive. Wherever they faced with serious resistance, I think in part a response to the political process of gaining control, the Ptolemies responded by installing more officials to monitor the area, and by establishing more military settlements.[122] Thebes, the site of the great Amun temple, seems to have received only a small number of Greeks and little new building activity, except for gates at several important temples.[123] The early kings in essence built a new state around Thebes. Of course, Thebes itself, from an economic (and even from a religious) point of view, was less important to the Ptolemies than were sites such as Edfu, an important terminus for eastern desert traffic, and of course the Ptah temple at Memphis, which had been a vital nexus between Egyptian priests and the Persian provincial government.

An early and important step in the takeover of the Thebaid was the foundation by Ptolemy I of the new city of Ptolemaïs Hermeiou (demotic *P3-Sy*, modern el-Manshah).[124] Akhmim (Panopolis), a large and im-

---

[120] Murray (1967); Scullard (1974:123–37); Burstein (1996a); Mueller (2006:151–57). On the road network, see Sidebotham and Wendrich (1996); Sidebotham (2000); Alcock et al. (2005); Gates-Foster (2006).

[121] On the issue of connectivity to the Mediterranean, see Bresson (2005b).

[122] The founding of camps at Pathyris and Krocodilopolis are good examples of the new military foundations.

[123] See for example *pGrenf.* I 21 (second century BC, = *Select papyri* 1, 83, = *pDryton* 4. A second copy of the text is *PLBat*, vol. 19.4.ii 1–25; = *pDryton* 3), which mentions very few Greeks available to write Greek. On Ptolemaic building activity, see Arnold (1999:154–224); for Karnak specifically, see Aufrère (2000).

[124] Mueller (2006:166–67) on the founding of Ptolemaïs Hermeiou. See also Cohen (2006:350–52) A Cyrenaean city of the same name was also founded by Ptolemy (Kraeling 1962; Mueller 2006:143–46; Laronde 1987. On Ptolemy and Cyrenaica, see Mørkholm (1980).

portant Egyptian city with a mixed Greek and Egyptian population
(Lloyd 1969:85) was nearby, but we do not know much about the connections between the two.[125] Panopolis was the site of major unrest in the
second century and was apparently forbidden from rebuilding its houses
and temples by the amnesty decree of Ptolemy VIII and Kleopatra II and
III in 118 BC (pTebt. 5 136–38).

Whether we follow Leo Africanus (Descr. Africae I.734) in believing
that Akhmim was the oldest of Egyptian cities, it was certainly in this
region that Egyptian civilization originated, as the important and very
ancient town of Thinis (modern Girga) and the Abydos necropolis on the
west bank of the river confirm. Limestone quarries that furnished the
stone to build Ptolemaïs are located across the river on the east bank,
especially in the vicinity of Gebel Tukh.[126] Hints of a pre-Ptolemaic Greek
settlement on the site might be found in a famous passage in Herodotus
(2.91), which mentions a "new city (Neapolis)" situated very near Akhmim. The name suggests a Greek foundation, and Lloyd has cogently
argued (1969:80) that the reference to a Greek city located near Akhmim
must indicate that a pre-Ptolemaic settlement was located on the future
site of Ptolemaïs. If this thesis is correct, and we have no way of confirm-
ing it at present, it would be another example of the Ptolemies continuing
cultural and economic patterns established as early as the seventh to
fifth centuries BC.

An administrative center at a site where there had already been a Greek
settlement would be both logical and the path of least resistance in establishing a Ptolemaic presence in the south. The fact that Greeks were settled
earlier in the millennium, perhaps under the Saïtes, at the future site of
Ptolemaïs points to an early and important Ptolemaic strategy. Because
Ptolemaïs sat at an important terminus for trade routes from the western
oases chain, which led west and north out to Cyrenaica, and from Nubia
to the south, its presence served as a kind of gate, controlling trade along
the southern Nile. Such "gating" is clearly seen at Therenuthis in the western Delta, which stood at the head of a major trade route into the Wadi
Natrun; at Edfu, with its new temple begun in 237 BC; and at Philae, the
latter two being important termini of key trade routes from the east and

---

[125] For Akhmim and its environs, see the very general survey by Kanawati (1990, 1999);
Kuhlmann (1983); Egberts et al. (2002). It was a center of textile production and quarrying.
On Ptolemaïs: Plaumann (1910); Vandorpe (1995:210); Abd el-Ghani (2001). For one example of real socioeconomic connections between the two cities, see the text cited above in
this chapter.

[126] de Morgan et al. (1894). Demotic, Greek, and Latin graffiti are documented in
the quarries.

south. This method of control is also observable in the archaeology of the eastern desert roads (Gates-Foster 2006).

Rostovtzeff (1941:156) believed that Ptolemaïs was intended as a second Alexandria. It never became quite that. Whether it was built on a Hippodamian grid plan or not we do not know, but it would seem likely that it was. Its institutional "Greekness" and status as a *polis* is certain (Plaumann 1910; Fraser 1972). Ptolemaïs had tax-free land, a theater and a guild of actors, a cult of the founder Ptolemy I, and it was a seat, from the time of Ptolemy IV, of dynastic priests in whose names both Greek and demotic legal instruments were usually dated. The lost history of Ptolemaïs by Istrus was perhaps written to lend moral support to the Greek community there, just as the new dynastic priesthood did (Fraser 1972:512). Although much about the early years of this city remains shrouded in darkness, the Ptolemies' intentions are clear: to establish control of the south. The city became the seat not only of a garrison but also of all of the Ptolemaic regional administrators, including an important branch of the *chrêmatistai*, royal courts that received petitions from throughout the Thebaid. From Strabo's (17.1.42) description of the city in the first century BC, we know that the foundation, at least in his day, was sizeable:

> Then one comes to the city of Ptolemaïs, which is the largest of the cities in the Thebaid, is no smaller than Memphis, and also has a form of government modeled on that of the Greeks.

There are hints of the origins of the Greeks who settled the city, but it seems increasingly unlikely that it had a "purely Greek character" (Fraser 1972:512).[127] Rather, Ptolemaïs appears similar to Naukratis and Alexandria in the north: a Greek city and trade center, but with an Egyptian temple precinct and a mixed population. There were, from a legal point of view, clearly defined social lines drawn between citizens of the new city and non-citizens, but the purpose of the foundation (or refoundation) was to facilitate interaction between government representatives of the state and local populations in the region.

The founding, or refounding, of the city is sufficient to show that Ptolemy understood that to govern Egypt as a whole he required a separate administrative center in the Thebaid. Just as Thebes counterbalanced Memphis in antiquity, so too Ptolemaïs served (theoretically) as a stabilizing counterweight to Alexandria in the north. The massive and ugly re-

---

[127] The location of the Isis temple outside of the city walls remains to be proven. Plaumann (1910:58) made the suggestion on the basis of St. Petersburg inscription Golenischeff, a granite stela found at the site and dated 76/5 BC.

volt, and the formation of an independent state in the Thebaid between 205 and 186 BC, is sufficient evidence to show that there were natural fault lines between the Upper Egyptian Nile valley and the north. Ptolemaïs probably was not intended to counterbalance Thebes itself (not a particularly important place in the Ptolemaic period, in contrast to the other ancient city, Memphis, which remained a focus of dynastic legitimacy via the family of high priests of Ptah), and it is unlikely that its primary purpose was to "hellenize" (if we mean by the term the specific policy of spreading Greek culture) the Thebaid (Abd el-Ghani 2001), although Greek cultural influence in the region was obviously reinforced as a result.[128] The founding of this new royal city in the south mirrors in many ways the history of Hellenistic Asia Minor where "colonies had often been founded on, or adjacent to, the site of a preexisting indigenous village or city" (Mileta 2002:166), with the main purpose of establishing a "royal area" in strategic locations. Control was the main issue, not hellenization. Ptolemaïs would appear to be yet another case of this Hellenistic practice.

We do not know as much as we would like about the original settlement of the city. Where did the original settlers come from and who were they? Rostovtzeff (1941:149) thought, surely rightly, that "a large proportion of the first settlers of Ptolemaïs . . . were soldiers." It certainly became the site of an important Ptolemaic garrison (Winnicki 1978). The following excerpt from the well-known "Constitution of Cyrene" recording a political settlement for the city by Ptolemy may offer us more intriguing details of its early population:[129]

> Shall be citizens [the men] from [a Cyrenaean father] and a Cyrenaean mother, and [those born from] the Libyan women between Catabathmos and Authamalax, and those born from the *[settlers] from the cities beyond Thinis*, whom the Cyrenaeans sent as colonists [and/those] Ptolemy designates, and those admitted by the body of citizens, in conformity with the following laws. [Trans. Austin (2006:69)]

The text concerns the formation of a citizen body at Cyrene at a very early stage of Ptolemaic influence there. The date of the text has been fairly certainly established as 321 BC, a time when Ptolemy had incorporated the region as the first Ptolemaic external territory. It is tempting to suggest that the phrase "the [settlers] from the cities beyond Thinis" refers to

---

[128] On the important administrative role of Ptolemaïs, see also chapter 5.

[129] *SEG* IX 1 (322/1 BC), with extensive bibliography. Bagnall (1976:28–29); Austin (2006:69–71). Important notes on the text are in Fraser (1958:120–27).

settlements where Cyrenaean soldiers were established in the Thebaid, including, perhaps, Ptolemaïs, which was situated in the Thinite nome.[130] The text would also suggest a very early date for the city's foundation. There would have been good reasons for Cyrenaeans to flee to Egypt in the 320s BC given the social unrest in Cyrene at the time. Cyrenaeans moreover are well known as soldiers in Egypt.[131] The "troops from Libya" mentioned by Polybius (V.65.5), were Cyrenaean cavalry stationed at Oxyrhynchus,[132] and it is beyond question that Cyrenaeans were settled throughout the Nile valley. "Their domination in terms of both land and household size is a feature of Ptolemaic Egypt in the third century BC" (Clarysse and Thompson 2006/2:246; cf. Mueller 2006:170).[133] The Greek dialect of Cyrene, Doric, may also have connected the population in an intimate way with the early Ptolemaic court.[134] It is, in fact, not much of a leap to suggest that Cyrenaeans were among the earliest settlers of this southern capital.[135] The region, and the chain of oases in the western desert, important already in the Persian period, became increasingly so under the Ptolemies.

Important new information about the ethnic composition of Ptolemaïs is provided by two demotic texts recently published by Ray (2005).[136]

---

[130] Cf. Austin (2006:71), who suggests "location unknown." Cf. remarks of Oliveri, *Revista di Filologia* NS 6/2–3 (1928), who thought it referred to the Khargeh oasis. The inscription also refers to "exiles who fled to Egypt."

[131] One of the witnesses, certainly a soldier, to the first dated Greek contract from the Ptolemaic period (*pEleph*. 1, 310 BC) is a Cyrenean.

[132] See La'da (2002). The connections between Cyrene and Egypt in fact go much further back in time than this. There were certainly connections, not all of them peaceful, between the Libyan coast and New Kingdom Egypt. The "homeland" of the Libyan dynasts of Dynasty 21–24 during the "Third Intermediate Period" was probably in the Cyrenaica. Under the Saites, see Hdt. 2.181. Amasis married a Cyrenaean woman to seal the connection between Egypt and Cyrenaica. For an overview, see Leahy (1985), stressing Libyan impact on Egyptian society. Cyrene was considered a part of the Egyptian satrapy by the Persian administration, Hdt. 3.91. The Greek colony there was founded, from Thera, in the seventh century BC, Hdt. 2.161, 4.150–59. For a general description of Cyrenaica, see Horden and Purcell (2000:65–74.)

[133] On Cyrenaeans in Ptolemaic Egypt generally, see Hens (1979).

[134] On the Doric dialect and its connection to the Ptolemaic court, see Buck (1946); Clarysse (1998); Dobias-Lalou (2000).

[135] There were Greeks from elsewhere settled there as well, at least later. See *SEG* XX.665, a second-century AD copy of an early Ptolemaic text, mentioning Greeks from Argos, Sparta, and Thessaly(?). On the text, see Fraser (1960); and the comments of Mueller (2006:166–68).

[136] The papyri were found by excavators at Qasr Ibrim in 1980. They are now housed in the Egyptian Museum, Cairo, where they have the inventory numbers *pCairo* JdE 95205 and *pCairo* JdE 95206. They were treated prior to Ray's edition by Zaghloul (1994) and Zauzich (1999). Precise dating of the texts is not possible. The only basis of the dates is

The two papyri, found at Qasr Ibrim but written "somewhere in or near Ptolemaïs" (Ray 2005:1), mention Nubians in such a way as to suggest that they may have been living in or near the city. Another possible interpretation is that the Nubians had come to Ptolemaïs to visit an important oracle there (Ray 2005:27). Various Nubian tribes were present throughout the Thebaid, assimilated into Egyptian culture and language, and they functioned in many capacities.[137] Text 2 furnishes us with more information about the cults of the city and suggests that Nubians might have formed "part of the earliest stratum of the population of Ptolemaïs" (Ray 2005:25).

More work needs to be done,[138] but if this is eventually proven it will be striking evidence of cultures living side by side and of the "multiethnic" character of Ptolemaic foundations in Egypt.[139] Ptolemaïs had strong connections to Nubia in the Roman period and indeed, given the caravan route that connected Ptolemaïs to Qasr Ibrim, it would not be surprising to find earlier connections between the two locations. A reevaluation of previous views of Ptolemaïs—that it was a "stronghold of Hellenism" (Rostovtzeff 1941:1055), or that "it was not as universal and mingling as Alexandria" (Abd el-Ghani 2001:33)—is certainly in order.[140] If we mean by the latter description that Ptolemaïs was a kind of Greek "island community" set off from the surrounding territory, this is certainly not correct, for the reasons I have just laid out. It seems to have been a city more analogous to Seleukid Babylonia, and indeed to other Seleukid foundations as well, a multiethnic settlement with ancient institutions existing side by side with Greek ones.[141] Ptolemaïs was founded at a key trade junction, and it served to foster a core area loyal to the state, from which people sometimes moved out. There is ample documentation of citizens of Ptolemaïs living elsewhere, and visiting Egyptian temples, leaving their names scratched on their walls.[142] The city was the seat not only of a garrison but also, as we have noted, of all of the Ptolemaic regional admin-

---

the archaeolgical context, which establishes a date ante quem, and paleography, a highly unreliable criterion. The excavation level of the texts suggests that the texts must be prior to 23 BC, when the site was destroyed by the Meroitic invasion. Ray favors a date in the late Ptolemaic or early Roman period; Depauw (2006:34), suggests a date in the third or second century BC.

[137] Blemmyes and Megabarians in the third century BC (*pHausw.* 6; *pHausw.* 15); at Gebelein (*pRyl.*dem.16). Blemmyes as mercenaries: Meeks (1972:122).

[138] See the fascinating analysis by Ray (2005:26–31).

[139] Mueller (2006:136–38). Cf. the case of Hellenistic Susa, Sherwin-White and Kuhrt (1993:148).

[140] Cf. Lewis (1986:88–103) on the Greek "purity" of the city.

[141] On Seleukid foundations, see Aperghis (2005).

[142] Demetrios the son of Theon, for example, visited the *Memnonion* at Abydos on at least three occasions: Lajtar (2006:85, n. 320). On pilgrimage, see Rutherford (2005).

istrators. "Egyptian" towns like Edfu should likewise be viewed not as a "purely Egyptian" places, but, rather, as Hellenistic towns connected to the wider economic and social currents of the Ptolemaic world.

These observations place new light on the interesting case of Rhodon son of Lysimachus, whom I mentioned in chapter 1. If I am right in suggesting that Rhodon was Greek and a "citizen of Ptolemaïs" (as he is called in the Bir 'Iayyan inscription), who functioned as a Ptolemaic official and, later in life, appeared as a witness to an Egyptian legal agreement in Edfu, this would be remarkable testimony to the fact that Ptolemaic elites could function quite normally in at least some Egyptian social contexts.[143] Here we observe, at ground level, the process of "hellenization," but the phenomenon is of a different nature, and subtler than the en bloc cultural competition that has usually been posited. Like his fellow second-century Ptolemian Dryton, a Cretan cavalry officer later stationed in Gebelein/Pathyris, whose second wife may have been a descendant of a Cyrenaean soldier, Rhodon may well have settled into the Egyptian milieu of Edfu later in life.[144]

Acting as a witness to an Egyptian agreement shows that he likely knew Egyptian, at least the spoken language, though he could have known demotic script as well. It also demonstrates mobility, across both geography and culture. The case of Rhodon points in the same direction as the more famous (and fascinating) example of the military and priestly family in second/first century Edfu (Yoyotte 1969). Several stelae survive of this family, in two copies in fact. In one case, a Greek text with an epigram highlights the military nature of the family. Parallel stelae, carved in Egyptian hieroglyphics, and with the honoree having priestly titles, recount a more traditional Egyptian biography. This may well signal the inroads that the army had made in Egypt by the second century.

Edfu appears to have been the focus of exceptional royal attention in the third century BC. Unlike the rest of the Thebaid before the massive revolt that disrupted economic life there for twenty years and left many villages devastated, Edfu received a new temple, begun in 237 BC (one year after the political accommodation of the Kanopos decree), a settlement of kleruchs, and other royal institutions, including, importantly, a royal bank. One would guess that all of this royal attention bestowed on Edfu was the result, mainly, of the need to control the routes out to the eastern (and perhaps the western) desert.[145] But Edfu was also an important religious center, and it had strong links to other places like Dendera through public festivals and private social connections. The

---

[143] A Greek loaning money in Edfu appears in *pHausw*. 18 (Edfu. 212 BC).

[144] On Dryton and his important bilingual family archive, see Vandorpe (2002).

[145] On Ptolemaic Edfu, see Vandorpe and Clarysse (2003); Manning (2003a).

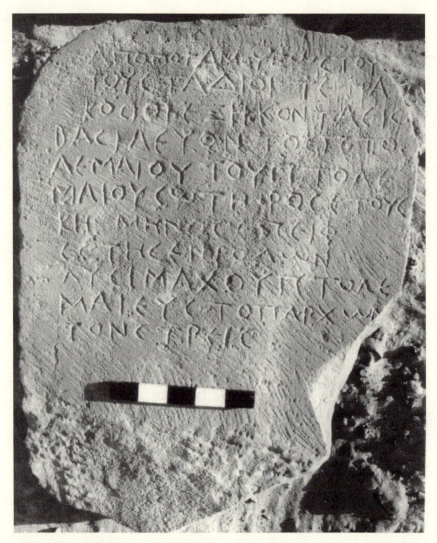

Figure 7. A recently discovered inscription from Bir 'Iayyan in the eastern desert. The text is a milestone along the Edfu-Berenike road, issued on behalf of "Rhodon, son of Lysimachus, citizen of Ptolemaïs and toparch of the three." The text was published by Bagnall et al. (1996). Photo by Steven Sidebotham.

building of the new temple, whatever its sources of funding, must count as a real Ptolemaic success story, and a part of a statewide strategy to build coalitions.[146]

We have seen in this chapter that the Ptolemies ruled over a very complex state, with interests that stretched from the Aegean to Asia Minor and the Sudan. The rulers had to manage a variety of social groups with different interests and different degrees of loyalty, living in a dynamic and to some extent unpredictable environment, dependant not only on the annual flood of the Nile, but also on external political machinations, and ever-cognizant of the growing power of Rome. They also had to make almost daily calculations of their position between pharaonic governance and its supporting religious ideology, and the Greek (and other) communities and their contrasting expectations.

Historians have tended to view the Ptolemaic political economy through the lens of Polybius' observations that divided Ptolemaic history into two parts, with a tipping point in the reign of the "corrupt" Ptolemy IV and his ironic victory over the Seleukid king at Raphia in 217. Ironic because while the Ptolemaic army was victorious in that battle, the aftermath of Raphia saw Egyptian troops return to Egypt where they rioted, setting off a series of unhappy consequences. Part of the struggles that ensued stemmed, it was believed, from the fact that there were severe tensions between the Egyptian majority and the ruling Greek minority. While social tension was real, of course, it was also a calculated result of Ptolemaic policies aimed at curbing collective action.

Claire Préaux, the great historian of the period, concluded (1939:530) that there was no overlap between political power and landholding, probably as the result of a labor shortage. This environment indeed, as Préaux concluded, "saved the crown for a long time." No formidable power base was established on the basis of land ownership; in fact, there are no known large landholders in the late Ptolemaic period. But individuals and groups did evolve. The elites accommodated and engaged with some aspects of Egyptian culture. For example, the sarcophagus of the *dioikêtês* Dioskourides, now in the Louvre, has an Egyptian funerary form, but the intimate portrayal of the deceased on the lid reveals his important Greek status as a *syngenes* (Baines 2004:42–43). He moved comfortably between the Ptolemaic administrative world in Alexandria and the cultural world of the Egypt with as much apparent ease as did Rhodon son of Lysimachus, who lived in the new southern capital of Ptolemaïs but could also witness an Egyptian contract.

---

[146] The sources are equivocal on the sources of funds for temple building. See Quaegebeur 1979.

As I have just outlined, the world of the temples and religious practice was a powerful draw for those who wanted to assimilate into Egyptian culture. In the economic and legal spheres, to which we next turn, the Ptolemies went to great lengths to accommodate Egyptian institutions in their new state structure. The degree of their success in this endeavor was intimately linked to the political relationships between them and key Greek and Egyptian constituencies. In both the economic and the legal arenas, the same pattern will be observed: the complexity of the organizational structure that was reinforced by Ptolemaic policy made it difficult to form sustainable opposition to royal authority. At the same time, the adoption of new institutional structures was fostered not by command of the king alone, but by accommodation to existing structures and by gradual adaptation, probably at first by key groups at important population centers.

Chapter 5

CREATING A NEW ECONOMIC ORDER

ECONOMIC LIFE AND ECONOMIC POLICY
UNDER THE PTOLEMIES

> Government seems to have been primarily interested
> in agriculture as a tax base—i.e., as an end-
> product—contributing little to its direct organization
> or maintenance. Agricultural productivity,
> although influenced by public order and security
> and responsive to new technologies, was primarily a
> response to the Nile floods. The health of the overall
> economic system, overwhelmingly dependent on
> agriculture, was consequently controlled as much by
> environmental as by human variables. Ultimately,
> the central government was weak when the national
> economy was weak, although a weak government
> could equally well lead to a weak economy.
> —*Butzer (1980)*

IN 225 BC, some twelve years after the inauguration of the great building
project of the new temple of Horus, a prominent priestly family in Edfu
found themselves in severe financial difficulty.[1] A state official had been
appointed to investigate. Three brothers in the family were late with payments for family land that they had mortgaged to securitize payments to
the state for the cloth tax, and they had mortgaged family land to secure
the payments. Private and public finance were entwined. The arrears had
apparently been a long-standing problem, going back to at least the year
246. Each of the brothers at various times, and their father as well, had
served as the lesonis, (dem. *mr-šn*) a temple official who was responsible

---

[1] The documentation of these events is to be found in a group of bilingual texts (thirty-
two in all, ten of them written in demotic Egyptian) known as the Milon archive. The Greek
texts were first published by Rubensohn (1907); the demotic ones were treated initially by
Spiegelberg (1908); and later by Sethe and Partsch (1920) with some dubious new readings.
For a good summary of events and of the texts in the archive, see now Clarysse (2003).

for payments to the state.[2] The manufacture and sale of cloth had been an ancient temple industry, Egypt producing from its flax crop some of the finest linen ever made. In the Ptolemaic system, cloth was one of the "monopoly" industries that the state attempted to regulate. In return for allowing the temples to continue manufacturing cloth and to receive income from it, the state required the temples had to pay a percentage of production as tax.

The family of priests had apparently gotten behind in these payments. From the Rosetta stone, we learn that the tax was remitted, and so it appears that this problem had become widespread. As a result, the land that had been pledged by the priest as security for making the payments, as well as a house, a share of another house in Edfu, and a small shrine in Dendera were put up for public auction, one of the new fiscal institutions introduced to Egypt from the Greek world in this period (further below). We learn in some detail about the structure of this auction from the official archive that preserves the affairs of the priestly family.

We do not know the subsequent history of the family, but we learn several other things from this archive that tell us a good amount about the new Ptolemaic economy and how it worked both in theory and in practice. The archive of documents derives from an official's papers, mostly those of a man named Milon, a *praktor*, or "special commissioner" of the temples in Edfu.[3] It was his job, apparently, to resolve the financial problems of the priests and of the temple. In one letter, he was told to compile a kind of financial statement about funds raised to build the new temple of Horus and to send a report to the "city," which most scholars assume is a reference to Alexandria.[4] Even though the monies and grain used to pay for the building appear to have been raised locally, and there are hints in the archive that this was the case, it is remarkable that officials, perhaps the king himself, showed an interest in the building finances of the temple.[5] This is worthy of note, but not surprising given how important Edfu was to the Ptolemies.

Another fact, astonishing at first sight but perhaps absolutely typical in such a system, is the behavior of Milon himself. One of his jobs was to auction off the seized property of the priests to settle their tax debt. The

---

[2] On the *lesonis*: Redford (2001:156 n. 160).

[3] A few of the texts derive from Milon's predecessor in office and were subsequently handed over to Milon.

[4] Interestingly, on 15 August 222 BC, Milon's superior, Euphronios, wrote from Thebes, which in Egyptian was called "the city" (dem. *Ne*). One wonders if "the city" referred to in *pEleph.Gr.* 10, dated 7 August 222 BC, is also Thebes, where Euphronios may already have been, rather than Alexandria.

[5] On the building of the temple: Dietze (2000), stressing the "strategic influence" of the Ptolemies.

rules and regulations of the state auction process were spelled out in detail, and in fact they are preserved in the archive.[6] Milon apparently had exact directions as to what he had to do. And yet he did not follow them. Several bids were posted, and the land was given to a low bidder.[7] However ordered the Ptolemaic economy was, we can see in this the fact that, despite personal liability, officials did not always behave with the interests of the state uppermost in their minds. Milon was at one point scolded by his superior by letter on account of a delayed report:

> Euphronios to Milon, greetings. When we arrived in Edfu, I looked for you . . . in the (usual?) places, but they said that you were in Aswan. Therefore you are acting improperly by putting off the matter. When you read this letter, having come to me . . . bringing with you all documents, and if you have done anything else, bring also the copies of the receipts which you have made. We want to talk to you about these matters you sent. Farewell.[8]

These stern words may have frightened Milon. In his response, he claimed that he had been beaten up and had had to flee. We do not know the reason for his dilemma, and no doubt we will never know. We do know that he fled to the island of Elephantine at the Egyptian border, where his papers were eventually placed in a jar for safekeeping and forgotten until 1906, when a German archaeologist was fortunate enough to find them still in their (badly damaged) jar.

The Milon archive, as we now call it, dating to the final years in the reign of Ptolemy III Euergetes, is a good case study of what we might call the mature Ptolemaic economy.[9] We learn several things from the priestly family problems, and along the way some other basic facts about the local economy of Edfu. First, we learn that state income was guaranteed by individual office holders. Second, that the auction process, while theoretically yielding property to the highest bidder, did not always do so. The state ran up against the problem of enforcement costs and of information, suggesting that in many matters the use of local elites was as problematic as it was practical. We also learn something about the financing of temple building in the period, although the details are not completely clear. It seems that other temples in the area contributed to the project. We also learn something about the bureaucracy and the flow of information. It also seems that the central state was greatly concerned about the use of

---

[6] *pEleph.Gr.* 14.

[7] A petition by one of the higher bidders is preserved in *pEleph.Gr.* 19 (= *pBerl.* 13508).

[8] *pEleph.Gr.* 11 (= *pBerl.* 13520, 16 November 223 BC).

[9] Previous surveys of the Ptolemaic economy: Préaux (1939); Rostovtzeff (1941, rev. 1955); Habermann and Tenger (2004); von Reden (2006); Manning (2007).

the funds for building and demanded an accounting. We learn also about the income of the priests in the temple, which continued to be important economic centers for the production of cloth and other commodities.

The Milon archive tells us much about the Ptolemaic economy. In the last chapter, we have seen that the Ptolemaic kings were actively involved in political relationships with key constituencies. They took on the role of the pharaoh, and all of the theater that went with it. The economic and legal systems, which I will examine in the next two chapters, were the results of the political economy and its evolving nature.

In chapter 3, I argued that a despotic or dirigiste model of the economy does not adequately capture the political and economic realities of Egypt. I argued further that understanding the organization of the economy in top down terms does not sufficiently elucidate the dynamics between the state and local groups. More subtlety is called for, and a greater attention to what is called Fiscal Sociology (*Finanzsoziologie*), defined as the study of:

> How the generation of income and its expenditure by the state and other political authorities affect the political authorities themselves, the economy, and the rest of society.[10]

Despite the lure of the documents, which makes the economy appear on paper as a rigid, hierarchical and planned system, Ptolemaic economic institutions were flexible, and utilized existing structure and social networks in so far as possible. That is to say, the structures of the Ptolemaic economy were in large part responses to the "new" society, which was in part an ancient one, and in part a world of Greeks, soldiers, and profit seekers, who came to Egypt for all the reasons modern immigrants leave their homeland. This is the context in which we must understand the introduction of new fiscal institutions. This state flexibility was indeed a tried and true recipe for success in Egypt, both before and after the Ptolemies. It was flexibility attributable in part, as I have already explained, to a dynamic river system, flood recession agriculture, and the ancient social structure that had adapted to these physical conditions of life along the Nile River for millennia.[11]

The Royal Economy

The economy of the king and the Ptolemaic economy as a whole have usually been conflated into one entity, which, following Claire Préaux, is known as the "royal economy," i.e., the fiscal system created to finance

---

[10] Swedberg (2003:174).
[11] Cf. the later Fatimid policy in Sanders (1998:161–65).

the "household" of the king and the administration.[12] In that broad sense, it is an ancient notion.[13] It has been common to distinguish between a private and a royal sector, or even to posit a tripartite division into private, public, and royal (Briant 2006). But the lines between these categories are unclear, and suggest distinctions that, in my view, are not significant. More importantly, though, such a conception tends to ignore economic activity that was beyond the reach of the king: private exchange, production on temple estates, and so on.

The traditional view developed by Préaux and Rostovtzeff is that Ptolemaic policy was mercantilist, promoting exports, restricting imports, and tightly controlling the economy through monopolies and exchange regulations, a veritable predecessor by some two millennia to Louis XIV and Colbert's France. This goes too far.[14] It should be stressed that any single model of the Ptolemaic, or any Hellenistic economy, is apt to describe or emphasize merely one part of a very complex situation that is only incompletely documented.

There were some similarities to mercantilist behavior, but in terms of scale and in the ability of the kings to exercise effective control, the Ptolemies could not have managed a true mercantilist policy over any length of time. It is the important contrast between the nature of the Ptolemaic state and the modern nation-state that arose in the sixteenth century that precludes such a model of the Ptolemaic economy.[15] While trading grain for silver (unavailable in Egypt) was certainly an important part of the Ptolemaic economy, the economy in grain by itself remained vital. The "form" of the royal economy appears in some of its aspects mercantilist (Davies 2001:44), especially in the third century at the height of the Ptolemaic empire, but the actualities reveal a large gap between intentions and reality.

This is not to say that the kings did not experience gains from trade or attempt to control the economy. Rather, at its heart, we can say simply that they were concerned with revenue purely and opportunistically, and that individual entrepreneurs played a major role. It is surely true that

[12] Préaux (1939:569); Descat (2003:156). The same working definition is adopted by Aperghis in his study of the Seleukid royal economy (2004).

[13] Not only from Pseudo-Aristotle's *Oikonomika*, as Descat (2003:153) points out, but even in much earlier Egyptian thinking. For the similar ancient Egyptian conception, the state as a large household (king = *pr-c3*, lit. "big house) among other households, see Goelet (2004). It is in fact a common conception in the ancient Near East: Old Persian *vith*, Aramaic *beyt*.

[14] Cf. Davies (2001:42). The organization of merchants in Alexandria appears on the whole to have been rather "loose," (Fraser 1972:186), especially in the third century BC.

[15] On the nation state as a recent phenomenon, see Gellner (1983) and Crone (2003). Several Egyptologists have in recent years argued for ancient Egypt as a "nation." See Kemp (2006:19–25), and Wilkinson (2001:28–59).

that "capitalism has been *potentially* visible since the dawn of history."[16] State ideology and the rulers' efforts, even if we can see the beginnings of the mercantilist mentality, which was surely carried over from the fourth-century Greek world, could only extend so far. The environmental and social constraints the Ptolemies faced in their core territory could only be altered so much.

The Hellenistic economy as a particular phase of ancient economy has been largely ignored by scholars, with the notable exception of Rostovtzeff who, with Weber, viewed the Hellenistic world and its economy as modernizing.[17] Moses Finley never treated Ptolemaic Egypt, for example, because he did not isolate a "Hellenistic" economy. Rather, even in this period, the economy was for Finley bifurcated into an "ancient" and an "oriental" sector, without any attempt at integrating the two.[18] But Ptolemaic state formation did not merely join two economic sectors. Rather it attempted to accommodate ancient institutional structures within a new fiscal system.[19] From the point of view of Egyptian history, even if many of the institutions were not entirely new, the formation of the Ptolemaic economy can be seen as "modernizing," i.e., bringing a new institutional basis of economic behavior into Egypt, connecting it to the Mediterranean, and intensifying market activity across a wide range of the economic spectrum.

The state as taxer and as consumer certainly had a profound impact on overall demand in the economy, both in its structure and in its scale. Public events, such as the famous *pompe* at Alexandria under Ptolemy II that Kallixeinos describes, provide a rich background and perhaps, if we believe the numbers, a sense of the scale of state consumption.[20] We may assume that along with festivals, the finance of the military was the major component of state expenditure.[21] It is its taxing power, however, that has been perhaps the most commented upon aspect of the Ptolemaic state. Did the Ptolemies extract more revenue from the existing economy (cf. Samuel 1983:32), or did the tax stimulus drive overall demand and thus improve economic life as Rostovtzeff understood (1941:351)?

[16] Braudel (1981:620).

[17] Well summarized by Descat (2003).

[18] Finley (1999:183). The "oriental" sector, the economics of Ptolemaic Egypt and Seleucid Syria predominantly, were in Finley's opinion unchanged by the new political regimes. They were merely extentions of the older system of exploitation, with large state sectors and little private enterprise or private production. Saller (2002) is probably right to deemphasize the differences between Finley and Rostovtzeff when it comes to the "primitive-modernist" debate on the ancient economy, but on the issue of the Hellentistic economy specifically, the differences between them are noteworthy. Cf. Davies (2001).

[19] I agree fully here with Descat's conclusions (2003:168).

[20] On this parade, see Thompson (2000b).

[21] On the military, cf. Baker (2003). For festivals, see Perpillou-Thomas (1993).

The sources of Ptolemaic revenue compare, broadly, with the second book of the well-known *Oikonomika*, attributed to one or more students of Aristotle.[22] This treatise, composed probably at the end of the fourth century BC, reveals much about the mentality and the taxation policy of Hellenistic states, whether the Seleukid kingdom is the specific subject of the treatise or not (Descat 2003:154–56). In the most recent discussion of the text,[23] it has been argued that this treatise on revenue comes not from observation of the Persian Empire but from the early Seleukid economic system. Revenue streams in order of importance were:

(1) revenue from land
(2) revenue from natural resources
(3) revenue from markets
(4) sale taxes from the movement of commodities and property
(5) revenue from animals
(6) revenue from capitation taxes
(7) "extraordinary" revenue, war booty and the like

Officials were also responsible for creating new revenue streams, and even for decreasing spending in some areas where possible. An equilibrium between the king and constituent groups was recognized as crucial with respect to revenue.[24]

Whatever the source of the text, and for whatever purpose it was written, Book II of the *Oikonomika* outlines the same categorical pattern as was followed by Ptolemaic state revenue. In most respects the nature of the state's income did not differ from royal income in the New Kingdom or in the Late Period. There was one important exception: the income in cash generated by the Ptolemaic system. It came in various forms, initially as war booty; of which third-century external warfare must have supplied an important component.[25] With the gradual loss of empire over the course of the third century, internal revenue, and revenue collection mechanisms probably played an increasingly important role in Ptolemaic finance.

---

[22] See Descat (2003) on possible authorship of some of the work. Note that the role of satrap in the text does not compare well with late fourth-century Egypt: Rostovtzeff (1941:444).

[23] Aperghis (2004:117–35).

[24] Cf. the remarks of Descat (2003:165) concerning a third-century inscription from Aiolis in Asia Minor, and Ma (2003:186), who also effectively utilizies the concept of equilibrium in discussing the relationship between kings and local communities.

[25] See Austin (1986); Chaniotis (2005:129–27). In one famous case, war booty has been estimated to amount to 10 percent of total income under Ptolemy III (Préaux 1978/1:367). For booty from the Third Syrian War: *FGrH* 160.ii. Cf. Austin (1986:465).

In Rostovtzeff's view, the Ptolemies continued the tradition of ownership of the land by the king and the compulsory labor system, the "twin
pillars" of an Oriental state."[26] All land was either "royal land," directly
managed by the king, or it was "conceded" to others to work, and could
be confiscated by the king as he desired. Many scholars have assumed an
erosion of state power over land from the third to the second and first
centuries BC.[27] But this theory rests on two false assumptions. The first is
that the king claimed all of the land in Egypt by royal right. This idea is
supported by the terminology used in official documents, which divides
the land into two large classes: royal land directly controlled by the crown
and conceded land. This fiscal terminology, however, reflects neither the
maintenance of traditional landholding patterns in the Thebaid nor the
limited state intervention there. A recently published text confirms widespread private holding of land in the south, albeit at best though the taxation of that land compares to the taxation of royal land in the Fayyum.[28]
State, or "public" revenue was distinguished from the personal revenue
of the king and from the private income of others. I would not, however
insist on an absolute distinction between public and private in all spheres
(cf. Briant 2006).

We have also seen that the kings were involved in establishing new
settlement patterns and in founding cities. There the Ptolemies honored
Greek traditions of democracy and autonomy and showed concern for
the prosperity of the citizens and for public harmony, although that was
not always achieved.[29] But in both of these cases, there were other players
involved. Political relationships between the king and ruling coalitions
evolved and changed, and the actions of individuals closer to the scene
were often more important than royal activity.

As in other area's of social life, the evolution of economic institutions
in Egypt was driven by the intentions of the kings and their policies operating in a broader context of the society and its larger forces: demographic change, war, geography and climate, the interests of social groups,
to name a few. The new economic regime established by Ptolemy I and II
would affect Egypt for many centuries to come. The initial expansion of
the state was impressive. Had some of the buildings of Ptolemaic Alexandria or Ptolemaïs survived, as did some of the Ptolemaic-period temples
along the southern Egyptian Nile, it might appear that there was an early
"Ptolemaic economic miracle" that presaged by some thirteen centuries,
though on a smaller scale certainly, the Fatimid "miracle."[30]

---

[26] Rostovtzeff (1941:271).

[27] Lewis (1986:33); Taubenschlag (1955:235). Cf. Husson and Valbelle (1992:260–61).

[28] Christensen (2003).

[29] Austin (2003).

[30] The phrase "the Fatimid miracle" is Goitein's (1967:33).

In terms of policy and its effects, as Runciman points out (1989:286), it is more often than not the unintended consequences that prove most decisive in the evolution of institutions. Ptolemaic rule in Egypt created a new system, with new territorial boundaries and new economic institutions. If the state was, like other premodern states, weak in intensive power (its capacity to organize internally to solve particular problems) as I suggested in the last chapter, what then explains the evolution of Egyptian society in this period? The answer to that question is complex, and it will require an analysis not only of the actions of the king, but also of the intricate temporal and spatial interactions of a variety of social groups and indeed individual actors with respect to loyalty and the state's enforcement costs.[31]

Eisenstadt (1993:121) identified three main goals of rulers: (1) to monopolize or at least to guarantee the mobilization of resources for the purpose of achieving the goals of the regime and to maintain services; (2) to continuously control and regulate economic resources; and (3) to maintain political control. The key to success was the ability of the state to obtain "free-floating" resources that provided both for royal power and for constituent groups in the society.

In the middle of the third century, Ptolemy II Philadelphos, as the embodiment of the Ptolemaic state, was probably the wealthiest man in the world. "So great are the revenues that come every day and from every direction to his rich store," the poet Theocritus gushed in his famous encomium to the king (Hunter 2003:87). Of course, as in earlier Egyptian history, the taxation system was a motor that created demand in the economy. But unlike previous regimes, that revenue consisted of two principal components, revenue in grain and revenue in cash, generated by a "new kind of economic machine" (Davies 2006:82) that was primed largely by cash. Coinage was the product of policies of the early kings, particularly of Ptolemy II and his major fiscal reforms (von Reden 2007), and it enabled the Ptolemies to assert sovereignty over the whole of the country in an easier, more efficient manner.

State revenue, the subject of nearly the whole of Préaux's (1939) classic treatise on the Ptolemaic economy, was large, although, as with expenditures, we can only make an approximate quantitative guess given the state

---

[31] Bingen has stressed individual actors. This follows the Weberian tradition of course, and serves as a counterweight to the "top down" approach in the analysis of social systems. That point with respect to ancient Egyptian society has been well made by Lehner (2000:339), and Eyre (forthcoming). The opportunity to observe individual actors in society is one of the great appeals of the papyrological sources. For a good illustration, see *SB* XX 14708 (Theadelphia, 151 BC), documenting the private extortion racket of a local official in the guise of tax collection. For an English translation of the text, see Bagnall and Derow (2004, text 98).

of our knowledge of the population and the amount of land under cultivation at any one time.[32] The need to create "free-floating resources," driven
by the military concerns of the king, was one among several variables.
Only literary texts furnish us with numbers, and they are, of course, sus-
pect. Moreover it is not always easy to know if the figures recorded are
total production, state revenues, personal revenues of the king, or something else. Jerome's oft-quoted figures for Ptolemy II's annual revenue of
14, 800 talents and 1.5 million artabas (assuming 1 *artaba* at ca. 40 liters,
or 32 kg.) of wheat are difficult to judge; the figure for wheat is considered
too low by some scholars.[33] It is, therefore, difficult to guess at the streams
of early Ptolemaic revenue, to know how closely this tracked the *Oikonomika,* and in particular to estimate how much revenue came from war
booty during the third century.[34]

If modern minimum consumption estimates are anywhere near accurate for Ptolemaic Egypt, 1.5 million *artabas* of Jerome's figure would feed
192,000 persons.[35] If Préaux's estimate that 8 million *artabas* of wheat per
year is a better estimate of Ptolemaic state revenues, that would mean that
state income in wheat could sustain over one million persons per year. The
cash revenue, based on an average third-century wage, would purchase
roughly 500,000 to 750,000 man-years of labor.[36] The annual revenue in
money of Ptolemy II would then be roughly equivalent to the total public
wealth of the Athenian economy at its height ca. 430 BC.[37] The population
of Egypt was considerably larger than that of Atens, of course, but at least
we get some idea of how potentially wealthy the Ptolemaic state was. As
Préaux (1978/1:365) rightly stressed, that revenue does not represent an

[32] For the accumulated wealth of private individuals and kings in the Hellenistic world:
Rostovtzeff (1941:1143–59).

[33] Préaux (1978/1:364–65); Bowman (1986:27). Cf. the comments by Rostovtzeff
(1941:1150–53). Muhs (2005a:10–11) considers the figures too high, because he argues
that grain and capitation taxes were the main sources of revenue in the early Ptolemaic
period. We have of course no way of knowing either actual income or expenditures for such
projects as the building of Alexandria, which would have been considerable. On the problem of ancient grain measures, see Stroud (1998:54–55).

[34] An important text known as the "Bulletin" (= *FGrH* 160; Wilcken, *Chrest.*, text 1;
trans. Burstein [1985, text 98]), referring to an event during Third Syrian War of Ptolemy
III, suggests that at Seleukeia 1,500 silver talents were seized, 10 percent of the annual state
revenue as reported by Jerome. Préaux (1978/1:366–67). Cf. Austin (1986). On the Third
Syrian War, see Huß (2001:338–52), with extensive bibliography.

[35] For the modern subsistence estimates, based on developing world studies, I rely on
Hopkins (1995/96:197, n. 11).

[36] For a rough calculation of the order of magnitude, see Préaux (1978:364–66). Cf. New
Kingdom temple offerings of Ramses II and III amounting to one million liters annually, or
1/60th of Jerome's figure for the grain income of Ptolemy II. Haring (1997:389); Warburton
(2000).

[37] Goldsmith (1987:23). On Athenian revenues, see further Möller (2007:375–80.

exorbitant percentage of the total wealth of the country. Préaux reckoned a taxation rate of 16 percent, roughly the figure I reached of state revenue amounting to between 14 and 21 percent of overall minimum GDP (Manning 2003a:135, n. 21). That is an impressive number if one compares it to the Roman taxation level estimates of Hopkins (1995, 1996) of about half that level. If these estimates are anywhere near the truth, the Ptolemies must count as among the most impressive taxing powers and mobilizers of resources in antiquity.

INSTITUTIONAL STRUCTURE OF THE PTOLEMAIC STATE

Most analyses of the Ptolemaic state begin with a description of the basic structure of the state as essentially a pharaonic structure of governance through what were called in Greek "nomes," or administrative districts, with an overlay of Greek officials who sat atop this time-honored structure connecting villages to nomes to the capital.[38] The ancient administrative division of the country is thought to have become, in this period, an ideal state order, a fixed "sacred" geography. Pseudo-Aristotle's *Oikonomika* (II.2.33) does mention nome governors in charge of taxation in their districts at the end of the fourth century BC, but these officials became increasingly unimportant in the Ptolemaic system as new tax districts were created.[39] "Tax divisions," or toparchies, were created to facilitate the collection of taxes at scale.[40] It is easier to understand the Ptolemaic administrative system in the Fayyum since it was imposed *de novo* on a newly developed area. Upper Egypt, a more complex region, seems to have been at first administered as a region and later to have been divided into toparchies (Clarysse and Thompson 2006/2:118). Demotic documents from the Third Intermediate and Saïte periods suggest that the temple of Amun operated with its own administrative staff, renting out its vast lands and collecting rents and taxes on them.[41] As far as these documents permit us to see, the temple seems to wholly administer its own holdings.

[38] On the activities of Saïte nomarchs, see *Nitocris Adoption Stela*, line 10. There each "nomarch" (Eg. *h3ty-c*) was responsible for providing sustenance for the traveling princess as she made her way up-river to Thebes. See Caminos (1964:84). For the text, see chapter 1. On Saite administration in general, see Lloyd (1983:332–37).

[39] On the Greek administrative terminology, see the discussion by Falivene (1991:208–15).

[40] See Clarysse and Thompson (2006/2:101–22) on administrative geography.

[41] See *pReinhardt* (tenth century BC) published by Gasse (1988); Vleeming (1993); the Louvre papyri dated to 568–533 BC, reign of Amasis, published by Donker van Heel (1995). See also Hughes (1952) on temple leases of land.

Overall administrative patterns appear to have continued along traditional lines under the early Ptolemies, but gradually new institutions appeared that show a shift in the flow of taxes in Thebes, and in Edfu where we have documentation. Large temple estates were historically part of the state, the interconnections between crown and temple being intricate, linked by ritual and theology as well as by the cycle of wage payments to temple servants, soldiers, and officials from the agricultural production of the temple lands.[42] Those connections continued and indeed were encouraged by the Ptolemies with one major distinction. Temples gradually became subordinated to the royal bureaucracy. By the end of the third century, "royal" scribes replaced temple scribes at Thebes, and temple granaries used for storage of the harvest were replaced (presumably in name only) by royal granaries, with Ptolemaic officials in charge of issuing tax receipts. Temple taxes appear to have been subordinated to the state by syntaxis payment.[43] The traditional "first fruits" tax on orchards and vineyards given to temples was replaced by a system that inserted tax farmers as intermediaries in the system, the temples being then in theory paid by these state officials.[44]

When it comes to the economy, the old view of a highly directed, centralized state economy has given way to a subtler view of the relationship of the state to the economy. Increasingly, the state's role is seen as more reactive to conditions and particular needs than planned out and directed from the center. The single most important shift in economic policy of the Ptolemies as compared to earlier regimes was the shift from the control of labor and the taxation of labor service to a taxation system dedicated to raising revenue in cash.[45] This shift brought with it several important new institutions: banking, coinage, tax farming, and the census.

The most plentiful documents left us by these new institutions are taxation receipts. They were normally recorded on ostraca, small shards of pottery or stone chips, and were a regular feature of taxation, at least in the Thebaid, where they are mainly attested.[46] A small number of receipts written on papyrus are known from the Fayyum.[47] The local nature of tax receipts is suggestive of the targeting of local economies.[48] It was the

[42] On temple economies, see Haring (1997).

[43] See the analysis by Vandorpe (2000a). On the funding of temples, known as the syntaxis, see Vandorpe (2005).

[44] On this apomoira tax, see Clarysse and Vandorpe (1998); Vandorpe (1995).

[45] The point is well made by Clarysse and Thompson (2006/2:34).

[46] Muhs (2005a).

[47] Vandorpe (1996:237). There are cases in which bank receipts from Upper Egypt were written on papyrus, e.g. pHaun I 11 (158 BC).

[48] Cf. Ma (2000).

Figure 8. A demotic tax receipt from Thebes, dated to the late Ptolemaic period. The text was published in Wångstedt (1954:80-8; oWångstedt 1 = Museum Gustavianum Victoriamuseet Uppsala, inv. 87).

number and the variety of the taxes collected, and the complexity of the system, that was so impressive to Préaux, as a testament that the state asserted sovereignty across the entire range of the productive economy (1939:427).

Writing and contract ensure trust and stability, and predictability, and thus, in theory, more revenue. Here we can observe a likely improvement on, or at least an extension of, the ancient Egyptian system that, like the Ptolemaic system, relied on village hierarchies and social obligations. The alleged abuse of farmers by officials is reported in literary texts and in official decrees in ancient Egypt. The state attempted to counter the problem through force of morality, and increasingly, by the routinization of the administrative process via written records, already a standard practice in the early New Kingdom.[49] The introduction of tax receipts into the Ptolemaic system, attested very early at Thebes, may have been intended to protect taxpayers from overzealous collectors.[50] The practice of issuing

---

[49] See e.g., *The Duties of the vizier*, van den Boorn (1988). Eyre (forthcoming).
[50] For the early Theban receipts, see Depauw (2000:168–93). The earliest are *pTeos* 4 and 5 (311 BC). They are house sale tax receipts.

receipts was not entirely new; for example, harvest tax receipts issued by the temple of Amun at Thebes are known from the Saïte period,[51] by the Ptolemaic use of them as a state institution was new.

Vandorpe documents clearly another significant aspect of Ptolemaic taxation history, namely, the link between politics, language, and tax collection. Northern disturbances such as the invasion of Antiochus IV had consequences in the upper reaches of the Egyptian Nile as well as in the Fayyum where some of his soldiers damaged temples (*pTebt*. III 781) The switch from the use of demotic to Greek in the tax receipts may perhaps be linked to the imposition of stronger state control of the south in the wake of a series of rebellions. Vandorpe derives the following historical scheme: After the revolt of the Thebaid (208–186 BC), taxes were again collected, by Egyptian officials. After another brief period of unrest in the 160s BC, Greek officials were in charge of tax collection while Egyptian scribes were reduced to countersigning the tax receipts. By around 160, the collection of taxes was split between several different collection points. But the collection appears never to have been stable over the long run, with problems emerging again in the early first century. The extensive use of tax receipts linked to royal banks was one of the fiscal innovations of the Ptolemies, and while a study of them shows a strong correlation between state control and tax collection, the absence of receipts in periods of unrest may not mean that taxes were not collected, but merely that they were not recorded, or that the tax revenue went somewhere other than into state banks.

COINAGE

It has generally been assumed that the use of coinage had profound effects on social relations While any assessment of the impact of Ptolemaic coinage must take into account the fact that Egypt had been partially monetized long before the Ptolemies, Ptolemaic documentation supports the this view.[52] Bingen (1978b) gives a famous example of Egyptian beekeepers and stresses the dependence that the monetary system created. The profit motive of Greeks clashed with the "traditional networks of the old Egyptian economy." Bingen also suggested that the use of surety documents, a kind of performance bond in which a thirty party guaranteed that work would be performed in certain industries, such as beer making,

---

[51] Receipts are not strictly new with Ptolemaic rule. For Saïte period harvest tax receipts written on papyrus, see Donker Van Heel (1995:88–91; 169–75; 183–91). Other pre-Ptolemaic demotic receipts are listed by Thissen (1980).

[52] On the difference between coinage and money, see van Reden 2007:4–5.

reflects state pressure to generate cash and a social response that reinforced "group solidarity." But such texts, for the moment, are limited in
time (mainly to the reign of Ptolemy III) and in space (to the Themistos
district of the Arsinoite nome, i.e. the Fayyum).[53] Nevertheless, the Ptolemaic monetary system and the demand for cash in the taxation system
probably did have profound social effects.

Metals were used as a medium of exchange, a store of value, and a
means of payment for more than a millennium before coins. Gold rings
and copper blades, as well as grain, were well known in New Kingdom
transactions, and a nominal exchange rate between copper and silver was
(usually) fixed at 1:60.[54] An important Ramesside period letter shows, for
example, that the harvest tax collected on private land was paid in "gold
into the treasury of Pharaoh."[55] The term "gold" in this text is susceptible
to several interpretations, and it is at least plausible that it refers in a
general sense to "money" (cash), and that taxes in grain were conceived
of in monetary terms. A silver standard was in place by the end of the
New Kingdom. Under the Persians, the treasury of Ptah in Memphis was
the guarantor of a silver bullion standard, and this standard may have
been more widely accepted than in earlier times.[56] In the so-called Third
Intermediate period (1069–664 BC), taxes were beginning to be monetized. A 10 percent sales tax, for example, is known from a few documents.[57] Greek and Persian silver coinage was certainly around, although
it was used as bullion; i.e., its value reckoned by weight.[58]

Increased monetization seems to be associated with the higher volume
of trade with Greece that began in the seventh century BC, at the same
time as the Greek trading colony was established at Naukratis in the
western Delta.[59] The bulk of the coin hoards found in Egypt to date come
from either the Delta or the Memphis region, reflecting northern Egypt's
stronger connections to the Mediterranean. It is therefore not surprising
to see an increase in coin hoards beginning in the sixth century BC. If

[53] For these documents, see de Cenival (1973).

[54] Summaries describing the pharaonic Egyptian economy (i.e., primarily the New Kingdom economy, when the documentary evidence is at its densest) may be found in Warburton
(1997); Menu (1998); and in Kemp (2006). Barter exchange measured against fixed value
of a commodity (silver, copper/bronze, grain) is well known in ancient Egypt and well described by Janssen (1975b) and by Kemp (2006:319–26).

[55] pValençay 1; discussed by Gardiner (1951); Katary (1989:207–16); Warburton
(1997:136–37).

[56] See e.g., the demotic marriage contract dated to the reign of Darius I from Saqqara,
published by Martin (1999); Vleeming (1991:89).

[57] On the history of the transfer tax, see Depauw (2000:58–63); and briefly Muhs
(2005a:3–4).

[58] E.g., pRyl.dem.9.15.15–19.

[59] Muhs (2005:4).

Kim's suggestion (2002) is correct, the pattern of small change use in the Greek world speaks to a deeply embedded institution across the range of the social hierarchy and, as a Greek institution, one that would have been familiar to Greek immigrants in Egypt by the late fourth century. As Muhs rightly (2005:4) argues though, monetized transactions were still limited to a small elite circle. Money as coinage was first introduced in the sixth century BC—the Greek loan word *stater* appears in demotic by the end of the that century—and by end of the fourth century, the evidence for the use of bronze coins in small transactions increases, at least in Lower Egypt.[60]

The use of coined money in the taxation system, as payment of wage labor, and in small transactions was a new feature of the Egyptian economy under the Ptolemies. The establishment of a mint at Alexandria by 315 BC at the latest shows that coinage was a feature of the Ptolemaic system from the very beginning. Taxes were divided into two types: those collected (or at least calculated) in terms of grain, and those for which payment in coin was demanded. Certain taxes on agricultural production were required in cash. The most important of these were the *apomoira*, a tax on vineyards, a tax on fruit trees, and a tax on fodder crops.

Certainly by the second century BC, and probably before, Egyptian temples were fully involved in the cash game. Recently published texts from Edfu, for example, suggest that temples were involved in the marketing of wine.[61] Other forms of business, beekeeping among them, were cash businesses in which the state normally received cash rents.[62] But as both von Reden and Rowlandson have recently pointed out, the persistence, for pragmatic reasons, of the Roman policy of collecting the tax on grain-bearing land in kind shows that there were in practice limits to monetizing the economy in coin.

The fixing of the value of each coin and the determination of how many of each denomination should circulate was an additional, and important, source of the sovereign power of kings (Pseudo-Aristotle, *Oikonomika* II.1.3). Accordingly, policies concerning the use of coins and their circulation are strongly linked to the early Ptolemaic project to integrate the royal economy with the ancient institutional structure of Egypt. A taxation system that demanded payment in coin was an imposition of state authority on villages just as, in earlier times, the king established order in rural areas by setting nome (i.e., district) boundaries. The act of de-

---

[60] On *stater* in demotic, see Chauveau (2000). See further Duyrat's (2005) analysis of Egyptian coin hoards, with his maps, pp. 47–50. Between 333 and 300 BC, only the Coptos hoard comes from Upper Egypt.

[61] *pCarlsb.* 409 and 410, for which see Schentuleit (2006).

[62] See the comments by Bingen (1978b).

manding coin was an act of sovereignty, a constraint on the hinterland, and a means by which state authority was imposed, at least in theory, in a uniform or standardized way. Thus the requirement that coinage be used in the payment of taxes and in small transactions was part of the imposition of a larger political order, analogous, for example, to the Ptolemaic legal system, which blended both Greek and Egyptian legal traditions into one state system. The process in Ptolemaic Egypt is rather different from that described by Seaford (2004) for the Greek *polis*, as it did not involve so great a threat against the local elite as to undermine traditional society.[63]

Ptolemaic fiscal control of Egypt differed from the fiscal policy of earlier states in its demand for cash, but it took some time, presumably, for coins to become available and for the idea of coinage to take hold in the countryside. Nevertheless, Egyptians switched to the new system (Rowlandson 2001:154) even if the amount of coinage in circulation fell short of the nominal amount of taxes in money demanded by the Ptolemaic fiscal system.[64] The state's demand for tax payments in coin was, in fact, the principal engine of Ptolemaic monetization.

The single most important tax, known in early Ptolemaic demotic sources as the "yoke tax" and subsequently as the "salt tax," was assessed per capita, and it applied to animals as well. The *apomoira* tax on vineyards was instituted to raise money for temples as well as for the cult of Arsinoë II (Clarysse and Vandorpe 1998). The state continued to collect the tax, however, thus keeping the collection of this revenue in state hands as a kind of "insurance" against shortfalls of other revenues.[65] A whole host of small taxes on professions and transactions were also collected in coin, either silver or bronze.[66]

Coinage may not have transformed the Egyptian countryside but, as Bingen has shown, the Ptolemaic taxation system with its new fiscal institutions, must have affected social relationships to some degree as the rural population came to terms with the new ways. The establishment of state banks was surely one of the key "political strategies" of the early Ptolemaic state.[67] Banks replaced the traditional economic function of temples as payment centers in areas such as the Thebaid, where tax receipts are documented by the end of the reign of Ptolemy I.

Lending at interest appears to have been an institution late in coming to Egypt. It is not documented until around 900 BC, much later than in

---

[63] Cf. the remarks of von Reden (2002:165–66).
[64] von Reden (2002).
[65] Walbank (1993).
[66] See von Reden (2007) for the details.
[67] von Reden (2001:66, n. 10).

the Near East.[68] Strictly speaking this applies only to written loan contracts, as loans with interest are well known before this date from the
New Kingdom village of Deir el-Medina.[69] There are only a handful of
pre-Ptolemaic money loan contracts, however, and thus it is not possible
to establish the extent of private lending of money, or to determine the
standard rate of interest.[70]

Loans in kind, despite the introduction of coinage, are still the majority
of recorded, preserved loan contracts of the Ptolemaic period. Most of
these are from the Thebaid and are dated to the second century BC, but
the distribution can in no way demonstrate secular trends in private lending; i.e., we cannot use the increased number of documented loans of the
second century to suggest that private loans became more common in the
later Ptolemaic period.

Coinage certainly represented the authority of the king, and it is significant that coins bore images that were invariably dynastic and never
Egyptian, unlike some recently discovered bronze tokens that have both
Egyptian and Greek motifs.[71] The king's authority was couched not only
in the demand for taxes but in his power to assign tenure to land, to
survey fields, to establish nome boundaries, to conduct censuses of men
and animals, to guarantee justice, to establish weights and standards, and
so on.[72] Coinage, then, was a new institution brought to bear in the ancient power struggle between central and local authority in Egypt, and
the establishment of the Ptolemaic mint in Alexandria was an important
signal by a new sovereign state. Demotic legal texts show us the history
of the relationship between money and the state in the first millennium
BC rather clearly. In Saïte demotic documents, as well as Aramaic ones,
sums of money are calculated in terms of pieces of silver weighed against
a certain weight standard established by temple authority: "silver, x *deben*
of the Treasury of Ptah, refined". The Egyptian standard weight was
known as the *deben*, and it was at the treasury of the most important
temple of the Saïte-Persian period, that of the god Ptah at Memphis, that
its weight was fixed. This important role of the temple was replaced in
the Ptolemaic period when the phrase "silver, x *deben* of the Treasury of
Ptah, refined" had become an archaism with the new meaning not of a
standardized weight but of a specific amount of silver in Ptolemaic coins.[73]

[68] Van de Mieroop (2005).

[69] E.g., *P. Turin PR 9* mentioning a loan of grain with 50 percent interest. On the history
of lending in Egypt, see Menu (1994, 1998).

[70] See briefly Depauw (1997:146–47).

[71] On the tokens, see Picard (1999).

[72] Hicks (1969:63–80). The public auction was a new mechanism introduced by the Ptolemies to assign tenure to land and to assign rights to tax farming contracts.

[73] See Vleeming (1991:88–89), with literature.

This marks a subtle yet important shift of political and economic power away from Egyptian temples and into the hands of the Ptolemaic kings.

A group of demotic Egyptian papyri from Asyut, now in the British Museum, provides valuable insights into financial dealings in an Egyptian village in Upper Egypt. They preserve the transcript and supporting documentary evidence of a legal dispute between two half-brothers over the inheritance of two small plots of land. The dispute took place in the early second century BC and was brought before judges in the temple of the local god.[74] During the course of the oral proceedings, a complete list of the property of the priestly family is listed. All of it, as it turns out, is either real property or shares of offices (priesthoods or scribes). There is no trace of the new Ptolemaic economy in coin, and we can only guess if any revenue from local storehouses was generated in coin or in kind.

Important evidence on lending practices in the Egyptian countryside comes from the late second-century archive of Dionysios son of Kephalas.[75] Napthali Lewis has made a good case that this Dionysios, scion of a Greco-Egyptian military family, used his social connections within the military to lend money and grain. Far from being in a debt trap, as has been supposed, Dionysios was rather a "master of sharp practice."[76] He owned and rented land in the area around the garrison town at Akoris, but it is his role as lender that is the dominant subject of the papers that have come down to us. Two-thirds of the archive is devoted to his lending activities, and most of the loans were grain loans. In three cases, money loans were designated as repayable in kind. Since the interest rate on loans in kind was traditionally set at 50 percent, it would seem there was incentive, intentional or not, to lend in kind rather than in cash, and to convert the grain to cash only when and if necessary.[77]

In both the case of the Asyut priests and Dionysios, access to real assets either through the temple or the new royal economy that privileged soldiers and state officials would allow persons to convert hard assets to liquid ones.[78] It is hardly surprising, that elites took advantage of eco-

[74] Manning (2003a:201–205); and see chapter 6 and Appendix.

[75] Boswinkel and Pestman (1982); Lewis (1986:124–39).

[76] Lewis (1986:131). There are a number of grain loans, repayable in kind preserved in Dionysios' archive. Upon first glance, it appears that he was borrowing money to pay off a previous loan. But a new study of the archive reveals a subtler picture of his business affairs. Dionysios, it seems, was borrowing large amounts of grain to be paid off with next year's harvest. Meanwhile from the borrowed grain, he made out loans of grain to others at advantageous prices, and sold grain as well. In other words, Dionysios was something of a commodities broker.

[77] For some cases of variable interest rates in loans in kind, see Vandorpe (1998).

[78] For loans in kind and in money for the military community at Pathyris in Upper Egypt, see the important discussion by Vandorpe (2002:105–217).

nomic opportunities as they presented themselves. Soldiers receiving salaries could be instruments of monetization, but as Bingen (1984) has shown, for other Greeks, access to land, and in particular to the all-important wheat crop, was only an ad hoc and irregular feature of the royal economy. In Bingen's view, the Greek *mentalité* of a monetary economy came straight up against an ancient agricultural regime that was only partly altered by the new institutions within the royal economy. As the Dionysios archive shows, the credit market still relied on personal contacts and trust between individuals within a family, or within a status group.

Much attention has been paid to the effect of the monetary economy on the lower strata of society. Such is the case with the surety documents from the Fayyum in which small amounts of cash were paid to guarantee that work would be performed in certain industries such as beer-making.[79] Mummification was another cash business, and Egyptian temples also raised cash in other ways which was accounted for by the Ptolemaic officials known as the *praktor*, and the *lesonis*, a temple priest charged with oversight of the temple's fiduciary responsibility to the state. If the third-century archive of Milon from Edfu with which I began this chapter is any guide, the industrial activities of Egyptian temples (*inter alia* beer-making and the manufacturing of linen and papyrus) were in general such vital generators of cash (and hence of taxes for the state) that officials, such as the *lesonis*, were personally liable for shortfalls in expected income.

Gauging the extent to which coinage was used, not only in taxation but also in small private transactions, is really a matter of assessing the degree to which the royal economy had penetrated into village and household economies. Alan Samuel (1984) has stressed that traditional peasant mentality clung to barter transactions, with little resort to market or "public" transactions, and thus with little use for coinage. Two levels were in place, even during the second century when bronze coins were available for small transactions. On the one hand the Ptolemaic coinage system was fully embedded in practice as a unit of account. On the other hand, Egyptian peasants were more engaged with social relationships in their village that used barter to establish the relative value of goods to be exchanged. As Samuel puts it:

> While the introduction of silver currency in Egypt by the Ptolemies was a century old by the time our second-century texts were written, the practice of using silver as the standard of exchange had by no means overwhelmed the long-established practice of reckoning in

[79] Bingen (1978b).

kind, and indeed, may even have receded to some extent after the first influx of Greeks into the countryside.[80]

Thus we may say that by the second century, coinage had penetrated into most Egyptian households, but coins never became all-purpose money. They remained, rather, one means of payment, and never fully replaced reckoning in kind.[81] Furthermore, many (perhaps even most) of Egyptian sales dating to the Ptolemaic period were probably not cash sales at all, but transfers of rights within families.[82] In other words, even though the language of these contracts expresses the fact that a satisfactory "price" has been paid by the "purchaser," this language could be applied to a wide variety of transfers of property rights, from sales that involved a transfer of cash to intra-family transfers that conveyed rights without payment. On the other side of the coin, as it were, are undocumented cash sales. These would include, for example, the sale of animals of which there is extremely little trace in the surviving Ptolemaic record, for reasons I have laid out elsewhere.[83] Egyptian marriage "contracts" were also monetized, but they had been since the sixth century BC.[84] They specified a cash sum that would be payable to the woman upon divorce, and also the value of her dowry in terms of silver, and later under the Ptolemies, in terms of Ptolemaic coinage. Demotic documents, therefore and perhaps surprisingly, are probably not good gauges of cash transactions in Egyptian villages and towns.

There may well have been, in the third century BC especially, a regional difference between the newly exploited area of the Fayyum and the Thebaid, which was still dominated by ancient temple estates and was perhaps slower to accept the new monetary system.[85] The types of taxes also varied regionally.[86] While we cannot be sure, the extensive documentary evidence for wine (not only in the Fayyum) and fruit tree production is, perhaps, a good proxy measure of the reach of the Ptolemaic money economy into the countryside. Those were cash businesses and would have generated taxes in coin as well.

The documented history of coinage under the Ptolemies seems to track rather closely the history of other Ptolemaic state institutions.[87] Given the

[80] Samuel (1984:202).

[81] Cf. Bingen (1978b:212).

[82] For one cash sale of land purchased at a public auction, see *pHausw. 16* (Edfu, 221–220 BC) discussed by Manning (1999).

[83] Manning (2002–2003).

[84] See Lüddeckens (1960:289–321) on monetary values expressed in demotic marriage contracts.

[85] Reekmans (1948:22–23.)

[86] On the impressive range of taxes, see Préaux (1939:591–95); Muhs (2005a) for the Thebaid.

[87] See von Reden (2007) for the details of monetary integration and disintegration.

elite and state bias of the documents, this is perhaps no surprise. But the extent of the use of coinage can stand for both the success of Ptolemaic state formation, with its quest for standardization and predictability, and the flip side of this, the variable rate at which the population adopted the new rules. It does appear to be the case, as Samuel has argued, that the elites (Greeks, Greek-speaking members of the bureaucracy, soldiers, and Egyptian priests) were more likely to buy into the Ptolemaic system and its institutions than peasant farmers. But we must remember that this dichotomy was not entirely synonymous with that of Greek versus non-Greek. As we saw in the third-century Milon archive from Edfu, Egyptian priests in the south were fully involved in the cash economy. Temple building projects there, beginning with the great Horus temple constructed at Edfu in 237, may have stimulated, in conjunction with the new tax system, increased circulation of coin through the cycle of wage payments. Whatever the extent of private cash transactions, however, the Ptolemaization of Egypt, including the acceptance of coins as a medium of exchange and their use in the general accounting of state revenue and payments, was both successful and thorough by the end of the third century, despite the fact that the supply of coins no doubt lagged behind their use as a unit of account and as a symbol of royal sovereignty. The persistence of the natural economy may also have allowed people to disguise private economic activity, but we will never know the full extent of this practice.

CITIES

The growth of Alexandria by immigration, and of other places as well, must have effected the organization of food Egypt's supply. No figures survive on the pre-Ptolemaic population of Egypt, but most scholars assume growth under the Ptolemies due largely to immigration into the newly founded urban centers.[88] The usually accepted estimate for the first century BC, including the city of Alexandria, lies between 3.5 and 4.5 million, on a theoretical maximum agricultural base of nine million *arouras* (1 aroura = ca. two-thirds of an American acre, or 2756 m²; the total land under cultivation would be then around six million acres, 24,793 KM²), roughly comparable to Egypt's agricultural land at the beginning of the nineteenth century AD.[89] Greeks amounted to about 10 percent of the population.

[88] For a recent treatment of the ancient Egyptian population, see Kraus (2004).

[89] Population estimates differ significantly. On various methods of estimation, see Rathbone (1990:109–15); Scheidel (2001). Estimates based on the papyri are usually lower. For example, Clarysse (2003:21) estimates a total population of 2.8 million, extrapolating on

The growth of Alexandria and the reclamation of the Fayyum were without question the two most impressive developments of the period. The city of Alexandria, occupied by 311 BC, was the first "urban giant" in the Mediterranean.[90] The centralization of political power in the city, the rent-seeking behavior of its Greek elites, and its role as a trading center all played their part in concentrating a population of around 200,000 by the middle of the third century BC (and by the early Roman period that figure would more than double to perhaps 500,000[91]). We know very little about the grain supply to the city. It seems likely that market exchange, as in Memphis, played an important role. The ancient capital city of Memphis, an important political center since the unification of the Egyptian state ca. 3000 BC, remained a vital economic center of manufacture, distribution and shipping under the Ptolemies.[92] The population of the city was something on the order of 50,000–60,000.[93]

In addition to these achievements in the urban sphere, the Ptolemies could boast the reclamation of land and the settlement of new populations in the Fayyum and in the Herakleopolite and Oxyrhynchite nomes as great accomplishments of the early Ptolemaic period. New land in the Fayyum was perhaps trebled (the exact figure is debated). Ptolemaic expansion was centered in the Fayyum for two main reasons: (1) it was possible to reclaim land there; and (2) the Ptolemies could directly project state power on the new land and new settlements, important both for revenues and for building loyalty among key groups.[94] Expansion in this area allowed the Ptolemies to establish, as it were, new rules, and direct management of the land, although the process itself was a combination of the state and private initiative. The amount of royal land in the area was probably higher than elsewhere, and it became a kind of "showcase" of state power (the density of banks and of the military population were notable).[95] Fayyum villages are believed, on average, to have been larger than those in the Nile valley, and the census registers suggest a total popu-

the basis of burial records from Edfu. The estimate of seven million by Turner (1984:167) taken Diodorus Siculus is too high. Clarysse and Thompson (2006/2:100–102) on the basis of the census returns suggest a total population in the mid-third century of about 1.5 million. The total arable and total cropped area would have fluctuated, and it was no doubt considerably less than this maximum. The figure comes from a temple (Edfu) text, but it should not be dismissed outright. The lower estimates do accord well with the fact that throughout the period there was a labor shortage on the land.

[90] Ades and Glaeser (1995). Scheidel (2004) offers a model of urban growth in Alexandria.

[91] Delia (1988), Rathbone (1990: 120), Scheidel (2001).

[92] Thompson (1988).

[93] The lower estimate of Thompson (1988:32–5); cf. Rathbone (1990:141, n. 41).

[94] Rathbone (1996, 1997).

[95] Rathbone (1990).

lation in the Fayyum of between 85,000 and 100,000 in the mid-third century BC.[96]

The most important center in the Thebaid was Ptolemaïs Hermeiou, which we discussed in the last chapter. Strabo (17.1.42) states that it was not smaller in size than Memphis, and Akhmim (Panopolis), in the same area, may also have been a town of considerable size. In both cases, lack of real information limits our ability to quantify. Greeks from throughout the Greek world, and other members of other groups, continued to be settled there for some time after its foundation.[97] Greeks came in smaller numbers to Thebes, a city of very roughly 50,000.[98]

The Ptolemies inherited a sophisticated economic structure that connected state finance to a regionally and hydraulically diverse agrarian environment based on flood recession agricultural production.[99] This was a localized system centered on "small independent basins" (Eyre 2004:161) controlled and managed with almost no state interference except in the collection of tax. Access to land, its registration and survey, and the control of labor, were the key drivers in ancient Egypt's economic history, were all determined by variable local conditions. All of this was dependent on adjustments to changing conditions of water and soil. The potentially very rich agricultural region of Middle Egypt, for example, was subject to cyclical Nile flood patterns and was therefore more prone to instability. Historically this was the region that was subject to continuous "colonization" of the soil, often by soldiers (Eyre 2004:161–62). The relationship between the central state and ever-present local power bases could be tipped by fluctuations in the average annual Nile discharge (Butzer 1984).

In the last chapter, I asserted that the Ptolemaic state was "built to control" rather than "built to last," a fact that stemmed from the state being a "capstone" established on top of populations, able to *prevent*, but unable to *organize* well. The documentation of the Ptolemaic economy also fits this premodern pattern very well. Much of the economic organization was local. The central institutional concern of the early Ptolemies was to regulate, or "gate," revenue flows. We have already observed the interest in "gating" trade flows (with the foundation of the city of Ptolemaïs and the attention paid to Edfu), and the new fiscal institutions introduced by the first two kings also served to gate revenue. This was

---

[96] Clarysse and Thompson (2006).

[97] Plaumann (1910:3), *SEG* XX 665 discussed in Fraser (1960), a Roman copy dated to the second century AD.

[98] Clarysse (1995).

[99] Models of the ancient Egyptian economy have been much discussed in recent years. For one such model, see Warburton (2000).

literally true, for example, in the case of taxes imposed on the trade that flowed in and out of the Fayyum via the desert roads. One had to go through gates (Gr. *pylai*) and pay a transit tax.[100] Much the same thing happened at the port of Memphis, which controlled traffic between Upper and Lower Egypt. Here we can observe the Ptolemaic state reaching down into rural structures.

THE STATE'S ENCOUNTER WITH THE INDIVIDUAL

Egypt, with its very well defined boundaries, and its sharp contrast between cultivation and harsh desert was, perhaps, the easiest place on earth to tax. The primary point of contact between the state and the individual was, in fact, in the collection of taxes and in the related institution of the census, which in turn formed the basis of Ptolemaic wealth.[101] The Ptolemies, just as the earlier pharaohs, "were obsessed with order."[102] Indeed the entire society was based upon the concept of order. That order, of course, which could be seen in the form of "rational" accounting of persons and of crops, in the bureaucratic hierarchy, in the social order, and in the reckoning of time, was in essence an idealistic (and very ancient) expression of the state's ideology. Put another way, it was an extension of the theological system. The divine order of the cosmos became a part of royal ideology. The king, as guarantor of order on earth was considered omniscient. Social harmony was order, and order was knowledge. The state wanted to count and control the movement of humans, animals and transactions. The individual, by contrast, wanted nothing more than to remain invisible—or at the very least to be counted as one of a privileged group that was treated, and taxed, preferentially.

The tension between the terror that the state projected and the desire for avoidance by the individual is certainly observable in earlier Egypt. Weber described it in melodramatic terms:

We know how an Egyptian tax levy was made: the officials arrived unexpectedly, the women began to cry; and soon a general flight and hunt began; those liable for taxes were hunted down, beaten, and tortured into paying what was demanded by the officials, who were themselves held responsible for quotas based on the official cadaster. This was the guise in which the state appeared to the peasants in the Near East, and as it appeared in modern times to Russian peasants.[103]

[100] Sijpesteijn (1987).
[101] I rely here on the magisterial study of Clarysse and Thompson (2006).
[102] Eyre (2004:159).
[103] Weber (1909 [1998]:131).

Many details of the intricate Ptolemaic taxation system are still not perfectly understood.[104] Its complexity, and the competitiveness of tax farming arrangements may have aided in the collection of greater revenue for the state, but they also served the interest of the king by creating new organizations within the state that prevented collective action against him.[105] Clarysse and Thompson (2006/2:348), in summarizing the new tax collection system, conclude:

> The degree to which such forms of adaptation are to be seen in the Hellenistic world more generally is hard to evaluate but complexity appears a characteristic feature of how things were done in Ptolemaic Egypt.

Cross-listing of registration of persons by both household and by occupation might have served to reinforce solidarity along household and ethnic lines, and the increasing exemptions from the salt tax in the reign of Ptolemy III might suggest some success at small-scale collective action. A system of tax collection that was both local and competitive may have worked to focus attention on local figures and away from the central authority, thus minimizing the impetus for large-scale resistance to the king. The documentation shows that the economic relationship between temples and the Ptolemies was also less direct in the third century, and the increase in the number of tax receipts in the period after the Theban revolt suggests stronger administrative control or, perhaps, a change in practice.[106] The land measurement receipts, again for the moment confined to the Thebaid, might suggest that the tax receipts by analogy also served to protect individual taxpayers by clearly establishing, in writing, that their obligations were fulfilled. While many of these ostraca come from a restricted group of people, they include receipts for the payment of a wide array of different taxes, including the salt tax, which suggests that the issuance of tax receipts was a standard procedure.[107]

The tax on persons that was for unknown reasons called the "salt tax" and taxes on professions, were the main sources of tax revenue in money.[108] The salt tax, introduced by Ptolemy II can be documented from 263 through 217 BC but was probably collected through the middle of the second century. Salt tax rates decreased over time as more and more exemptions were granted (Clarysse and Thompson 2006 2:88–89). In addition to being a source of revenue (smaller than the Roman poll tax), it

---

[104] Préaux (1939) provides an index listing the wide array of taxes.
[105] See chapter 4.
[106] For the demotic receipts, Kaplony-Heckel (2000), Muhs (2005a).
[107] Muhs (2005a).
[108] For the salt tax, see Clarysse and Thompson (2006/1:36–89).

was thus also a means to enhance loyalty between the ruler and the new elite. "Hellenes" were exempt from another largely symbolic tax, the obol tax, which was associated with the salt tax; and after 256, those with special status in the Greek cultural sphere (teachers, coaches, actors, victors in the Alexandrian athletic games) were entirely exempt from the salt tax, while others were taxed at a lower rate. Exemption became a marker of Greek cultural status. In the reign of Ptolemy III, priests, and even animals belonging to temples, as well as others associated with temples, were exempt from the salt tax.

The way in which taxes were collected can be documented through the granary tax receipts from the Thebaid, and it is only in this region that we can be certain of the process.[109] There may well have been regional differences in collection methods, and much primary work remains to be done before an overall assessment is possible. The evidence from the Thebaid shows that grain taxes were usually paid at state granaries in installments throughout the year after the grain harvest, and a receipt was issued and countersigned by state officials for the taxpayer.[110] This method of payment applied to Upper Egypt as well as the Fayyum.[111] On the basis of the dates of the grain tax receipts, the taxes were paid after the harvest, were due in full by the end of the regnal year, and were transported to the royal granary by the taxpayer. This issuance of receipts, as far as we know, is a new aspect of the traditional grain tax process, and may have been designed to protect taxpayers from overzealous tax collectors. Because of the scattered survival of the receipts, it is very difficult to assess the overall revenue in any one area. Clearly though, there was a shift from the use of demotic to Greek for the receipts that was concomitant with the installation of Greek officials in the Thebaid after Antiochus IV's invasion in 168 BC.[112] But this shift in language was not permanent, and it is interesting to note that demotic as a "fiscal" language used in receipts emerges again in the early Roman period.[113] On the basis of the published tax receipts from Pathyris, it seems clear that there is a correlation between tax collection and the installation of loyal state officials working in the granaries. It is abundantly clear that the collection of taxes was a major problem for the Ptolemaic state over the long term.[114]

[109] Packman (1968), Vandorpe (2000a,2000b).

[110] Packman (1968:62–63); Keenan and Shelton (1976:9). On installments for the grain tax, cf. *pSiut* 10597 (Asyut, 171BC).

[111] Cf. Keenan and Shelton (1976:9).

[112] Vandorpe (2000b).

[113] Demotic was common in early Roman Theban banking receipts, but in AD 33 "Greek became the normal language of the Theban banks." Vandorpe and Clarysse (2008:166).

[114] Clarysse and Thompson (2006/2:36–89).

The Ptolemies exacted a tax on property transfers. Known as the *en-kuklion* in Greek documents, it was in fact a continuation of an Egyptian tax on transfers that was in the control of local temples. This tax has been studied recently by Depauw in his publication of an early Ptolemaic demotic family archive from Thebes.[115] A complex document (much in it remains obscure) from Thebes, dated 291 BC, hints that taxes, in this case funerary taxes, were already being farmed in Thebes in the very early Ptolemaic period.[116] If the current understanding of the text is correct, it provides important documentary evidence that either the Ptolemaic tax system was established quite early in the south, or, in my view more likely, that the Ptolemaic system retained earlier economic institutions. The history of the transfer tax and related structures (banks, tax farmers, receipts) shows the nature of the fiscal reforms begun by Ptolemy II.

Census taking, of people and animals, was not new with the Ptolemies. A preoccupation with counting people and things, and with the accuracy of that count, was characteristic of the ancient Egyptian state. The biennial cattle census, for example, goes back at least as far as the Old Kingdom. As is so often the case, Persian and Athenian antecedents may also have reinforced the Ptolemaic institution. But the main interest of the Ptolemies was in the new money-raising capacity of the census.

We do not know the details of how the census was conducted, nor do we know its frequency. It is also uncertain whether the system was dependent on persons showing up at a records office to make a declaration, or whether an inspection by scribes took place, or perhaps both. There may well have been urban/ rural and ethnic distinctions on how the operation was actually conducted (Clarysse and Thompson 2006/2:27). Profession also mattered, the military, for example, seems to have been in charge of the survey of soldiers' households and property.

It was likely the case that census lists were updated at some regular interval (Clarysse and Thompson 2006/2:19). An irregular census would have enormously complicated the collection process and the determination of payments. Already a notable feature of the documentation for the census is its lack of uniformity and standardization (Clarysse and Thompson 2006/2:66). The carrying over of old information, the lack of an audit, and the bilingual nature of the system, reinforce the view that the bulk of the material that survives reflects tax liability rather than actual amounts collected (Clarysse and Thompson 2006/2:74). What is true of the census is also true of the bureaucratic system as a whole, and it should be remembered that both were established in response to the state's desire

---

[115] Depauw (2000).

[116] The text is *pBMGlanville* 10528, originally published in Glanville (1939). It was republished and discussed by Depauw (2000:70–74).

Royal court in Alexandria (inter alia the *dioiketes*)

Regional officials

Nome officials (*strategos*, *oikonomos*, royal scribe)

District officials (*toparchs*)

Village officials (village scribe, police)

Figure 9. The basic structure of the Ptolemaic bureaucracy.

for information, and both met with a variable response at local levels. There may have been some training of responsible personnel, but we know very little about this. One might speculate that circular letters were sent from the central authorities (or the king?), such as those used to inform officials of state expectations and their particular duties, another ancient feature taken over from the Egyptian bureaucracy.

The Individual's Encounter with the State

Voluntary encounters between individuals and the state usually took place at the level of the local bureaucracy or, in the case of petitions to the king, were presented to royal officials to initiate legal proceedings.[117] Egypt and China, the two historical examples of what Hicks (1969:20) called "classical bureaucracies," show similar patterns in the maintenance of a general state framework throughout their dynastic histories, even when taken over by outside groups.[118] The framework of the Egyptian bureaucracy is known to us from literary and funerary texts that emphasize expected behavior and the maintenance of the hierarchy. The Nile river communications corridor provided good conditions for bureaucratic administration, and the Ptolemies were able to retain the basic structure of the ancient bureaucracy along with its parallels to the classical Chinese system (Deng 1999).

A principle point in which the Ptolemaic bureaucracy did differ from earlier systems is of course in its bilingual Greco-Egyptian nature.[119] The survival of documentary papyri from Egypt tend to give the impression

---

[117] See chapter 6.

[118] For a classic account of the later Chinese bureaucracy, see Huang (1981).

[119] On earlier bureaucracy in Egypt, see Kemp (2006:163–92).

that the bureaucracy was massive, and unique to Egypt, but this impression is probably due in large part to the fact that so very few documents survive from elsewhere in the Hellenistic world. It is an artifact of the luck of survival. Thompson (1994) has argued that the increase in the number of documents that survive is probably a proxy measure of an increase in the size of the bureaucracy as well as an increase in literacy rates, which together produced an "intensified bureaucratic form of government" (1994:83). Such an "overproliferation of central bureaucracy" (Baines and Yoffee 1998:223) had a parallel in the expanding Middle and New Kingdoms in ancient times. Be that as it may, fourth-century literacy rates in demotic, based on an assumption of the number of Egyptians having some ability to read and write, have been estimated at approximately 7% (Ray 1994), and assuming an increase, mainly of literate Greeks, the numbers in the Ptolemaic period may have been something on the order of 7 to 10% of the population (approximately 245,000–350,000 persons), though only a tiny fraction of this number would have been fully literate in demotic. This is comparable in scale to literacy rates in early China, and provides an upper boundary for the bureaucracy's size.[120] We must, however, remain cautious in assessing a growth in the writing habit, not least because so little has come down to us from earlier periods. Consider for example, the strong emphasis on both the recording and publishing of a wide variety of official acts that was already evident in the Old Kingdom.[121]

All the same, a wider range of contract forms, an increase in the use of written correspondence (Depauw 2006), evidence that more scribes were employed in accounting and checking and counterchecking, the issuance of bank receipts, the apparent emphasis on written rules governing conduct and personal relationships within hierarchies of power—all of these factors give the impression of an increase in the use of writing and in the size of the bureaucratic system. That there was a contemporary sense of an over-inflated bureaucracy we know from the way in which it was parodied in the famous Letter of Aristeas that recounts the historical background to the creation of the Septuagint.[122] Yet very little of this structure

---

[120] For China: Deng (1999).

[121] The variety of texts and officials involved are discussed by Redford (2001:146–50). The New Kingdom text known as the *Duties of the Vizier* also emphasizes the use of written documents.

[122] On the letter, which has generated a mountain of scholarship, see Gruen (1998: chapter 6). For written rules, see e.g., *pRev.*, *pEleph*.Gr.14 on the rules of an auction. For a good example of the acceptance by an official of the obligation to undertake certain functions in writing, and the personal relationships involved, see Geens (2008:139), discussing *pFouad Crawford 3* (= *SB* I 5680, = Bagnall and Derow [2004, text 84]).

appears to be new. The demotic *Petition of Petiese*, dating to the reign of Darius I, highlights the complex relationships between state and temple officials, the scale of adminsistrative capacity, and the writing habit in the context of property and legal disputes in the Saïte and early Persian periods.[123]

The Ptolemaic bureaucracy was, then, broadly speaking a continuation of earlier practice as derived from the Egyptian historical experience. Its growth, beyond what was proportional to demographic expansion, would have been in the banking and military sectors. It must have taken time to establish loyal Greek-speaking officials throughout the state, but we know little about this issue in the reign of Ptolemy I, whether because the king was primarily occupied with overseas events (Hölbl 2001:28), or through the accidents of preservation. We begin to hear about efforts to develop a bureaucracy in the reign of Ptolemy II because of the significant amount of papyri preserved from his reign through the re-use of papyri as mummy cartonnage. It was built on an ancient structure and was over-whelmingly concerned with revenue, but the resolution of legal disputes was also a key function, as we will see when we discuss Horemheb's de-cree in the next chapter.[124] The bureaucracy was, as we have noted, bilin-gual, with a basic division between Greek and Egyptian "functions" de-pending on the level in the administrative hierarchy. Egyptian-named persons function at the lowest levels of administration, while officials with Greek names are found at the nome level and higher, and in the context of tax collection.[125] We should not forget that the bureaucracy, along with the army, represents the employment function of the state. Overall the system was "hellenized" to the extent that the important functions of state service were occupied by persons having Greek names and probably sufficient knowledge of Greek to function within the system. In many cases scribes and other officials were Egyptians who adapted to the new system. Tensions existed between the traditional practice of inherited of-fice and the state's desire to control loyalty. The chief of state finances, the *dioikêtês*, was certainly an office that existed before the Ptolemies, as were officials known as nomarchs in the Greek texts, albeit they served a different function under the Ptolemies. The size and the operation of the Ptolemaic bureaucracy come into sharp focus in a famous mid-second century text from Saqqara.

---

[123] On this petition, see the literature cited above, chapter 1 (Persian Period).

[124] For an overview, see Bagnall and Derow (2004:285–88); Falivene (1991). For legal disputes, see chapter 6.

[125] Falivene (1991:217).

In 158 BC, writing from his retreat inside the ancient necropolis at Saqqara, a certain Ptolemy, the son of a soldier, who is for some reason living "in seclusion" inside the temple walls, addressed a petition to the Ptolemaic monarchs who were visiting the area.[126] The petition was an attempt to get his younger brother enrolled in the army. It generated at least thirty-two more documents, and took five months to crawl its way through two parallel bureaucracies, one civil, and the other military.[127] We can follow the machinations of the fully developed bureaucracy here, observing its complexity, its specialized scribes, and its specialized documents. In the end the petition was, it seems, quickly approved with a rather terse "Do it, but report how much [it will cost]" scribbled in, perhaps in the king's own hand. There follows, though, an account of a personal adventure that took the petitioner and a messenger on several trips to various scribes, to get the order approved.[128]

We tend to imagine the bureaucracy as being rationally conceived and structurally consistent, from the top down. Bureaucracy, and the bureaucratic "attitude of mind," (Kemp 2006:182), arrived early in Egypt, and it is of course the surviving products of the bureaucracy, its administrative documents, that scholars have relied on to build their pictures of the pharaonic and Ptolemaic states. The bureaucracy was surely never anything like "perfected" (Hölbl 2001:25). Indeed it was probably quite variable and fluid, and therefore there was no doubt considerable competition over turf. Clarysse and Thompson's detailed study of the census records is important for many reasons, but perhaps of utmost importance is the evidence these texts provide for the evolution of the bureaucratic system. We see that, for example that the new system still relied on demotic scribes to some extent; use of demotic was slowly replaced by Greek at local levels, but not uniformly so. In fact in some areas, like the Lykopolite nome in the south, demotic continued to be quite important in the local administrative machinery (Clarysse and Thompson 2006, 2:6–7).

Alan Samuel, in a series of influential articles, has argued that scholars should be wary of using the administrative papyri to draw too many conclusions, because realities were probably quite different from the intentions expressed by the officials. This idea continued a line of thought developed by Crawford (1978), who believed that there was no effective

---

[126] For the background and on the petitioner's status, see the masterful study by Thompson (1988:212–65); Ray (2002:130–52). Cf. Bevan (1968:137–39) stressing the "immense complexity" of the bureaucratic system.

[127] *UPZ* I, 14.

[128] Lewis (1986:78); Shipley (2000:227). The Chinese story "The Wan Family's Lawsuit," by Chen Yuanbin provides the flavor of an individual's encounter with the many layers of a bureaucratic state. The story subsequently became a movie, "The Story of Qiu Ju," directed by Zhang Yimou.

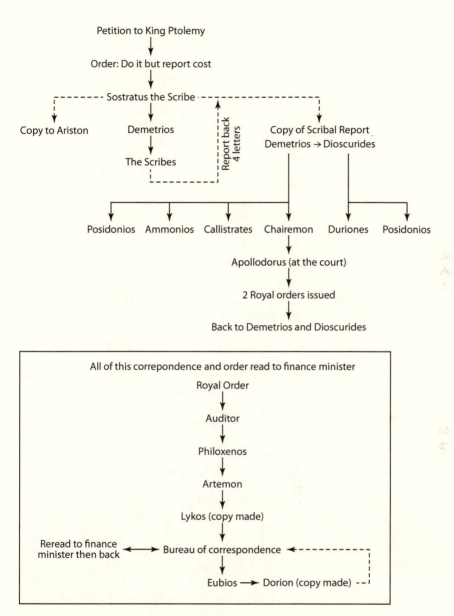

Figure 10. The flow of Ptolemy's petition through two bureaucracies.
From *UPZ* I 14.

means of distinguishing public from private sectors, because the same official might operate in both, sometimes in a private and sometimes in a public capacity.[129] In many ways Samuel's views were a radical departure from established views of Ptolemaic institutions. He held, for example, that the kleruchic system was not a means primarily to "compensate" soldiers (in fact it avoided that directly) but rather a way to establish loyal, Greek taxpayers throughout Egypt. The two, of course, are not mutually exclusive. The granting of land to soldiers was an ancient practice in Egypt, but the terminology used in Ptolemaic times was entirely Greek, and this is important. The need to have a ready fighting force inside Egypt was a perceived advantage, as was having loyal Greek-speaking tax payers established throughout Egypt. Here Samuel's emphasis is correct, and the contrast between the structure of the Seleukid and Ptolemaic kingdoms is clear. The Ptolemaic aim of establishing "royal areas" was successful.

By contrast, the Ptolemaic bureaucracy as a whole appears to Samuel to have been irrational and incoherent, modified when "circumstances required" (1993:175), and suffering from a perennial "shortage of personnel" (1966:229). As the Ptolemies' political problems began to accumulate, their ad hoc, irrational, and dysfunctional bureaucratic system made a bad situation worse by adding economic difficulties to the mix of troubles. The Ptolemaic system evolved haphazardly in response to local officials' pragmatic needs and to the needs of local populations. There was none, or little guidance from the capital, and no distinctions were drawn between official and private functions (1993:178). Ptolemaic officials, in Samuel's view, were making it up as they went along.[130] There was an effort to put in place a hierarchy of officials, but there were many problems in establishing it, not the least of which was the shortage of manpower.[131] There is indeed no reason to assume that the Ptolemaic system devolved from a well-organized, centralized bureaucracy at the beginning to one in which local officials slowly gained power for themselves.

Alan Samuel stressed the ad hoc nature of the Ptolemaic system, and hence what he called its "irrationality." This "irrationality," though, and what has been seen as bureaucratic dysfunction, arise from a distinctively modern, and orientalist, view of the ancient Egyptian bureaucracy. The system was neither "irrational" nor "dysfunctional." It was merely more limited in its reach and effect than the modern mind might conceive.[132] It

---

[129] Samuel (1966b, 1983, 1989, 1993).

[130] The view finds support in some of the records of Menches, village scribe at Kerkeosiris toward the end of the second century.

[131] On this last point, see especially Samuel's critique in Samuel (1966).

[132] I am very much informed here by Kemp's treatment of the pharaonic bureaucracy (2006:163–92).

is true that the Ptolemies had ambitions of creating a systemized bureau-cracy with clear lines of authority. There were however some things that they could not alter: the local character of the bureaucracy, the inherent overlap between religious, fiscal and administrative responsibilities, and the tensions between royal authority and hereditary claims to offices (cf. Lloyd 1983:332). There is in fact little in the structure of the bureaucracy itself that differs from the Persian period. But whether or not the Ptole-maic bureaucracy enjoyed greater autonomy from central management than in ancient times (Eisenstadt 1993:389), the administrative system did continue to evolve throughout the period.

The difficulty of enforcing rules and the problem of officials abusing their positions were outlined already by Préaux (1939) and stressed more recently by Samuel (1993:179). The nature of bureaucratic changes was in part determined by the behavior of local officials; the king was only a part of the overall system, coexisting not only with the bureaucratic hier-archy but also with the military and indeed with the Egyptian priests (Samuel 1993:180). All of these problems and limitations on Ptolemaic political power led Samuel to downplay the role of Ptolemy II. "We can no longer understand Philadelphus' kingship," Samuel concluded, "as worked out in terms of his establishment of administrative control over the land" (1993:180).

It was the shift in administrative language, from what would have tech-nically been Aramaic under Persian rule to Greek that marks the most important and substantive change. Aramaic certainly had some impact on Egypt's language, its literature, and its institutions (Ray 1994; Clarysse 1987), but that impact was probably not great (Ritner 2002; Depauw 2006:292). The shift to Greek under the Ptolemies, however, had pro-found and long-lasting affects, and John Ray's observation (1994:62) that Ptolemaic demotic consistently filtered out Greek loan words that must have been common in the spoken language tells us much about cultural politics under the Ptolemies. Greek was certainly in everyday use, increas-ingly, in the administrative centers, and an examination of the technical vocabulary developed by administrative scribes shows the extent of the imposition of a new economic system, at least in the Fayyum (Thompson 1994:77). Over the course of Ptolemaic history, however, the deliberate selection of Greek or Egyptian in tax receipts in the south shows that language was very much a part of political control or the lack thereof.[133] In this sense the settlement of Greeks, and the establishment of the admin-istrative center at Ptolemaïs served to "hellenize" Egypt, in terms of the

---

[133] On the language of tax receipts in the south, see Vandorpe (2000b) and Clarysse and Vandorpe (2008).

language of administration and also of scribal practice.[134] But kings had their place in setting reforms in motion, and it is one king above all who was instrumental in the shaping of the state.

PTOLEMY II AND THE REFORMS

In Turner's treatment (1984) of the Ptolemaic economy, Ptolemy II is assigned a dual role as both the builder of the new economic system and the cause of its ruin. A clear shift in tax collection practices, for example, can be observed in the documents from his reign, with Greek *stratêgoi* being placed in charge of taxes in the nomes (Falivene 1991). At some point between 265 and 261, the bronze coinage was also reformed. A wider variety of denominations was introduced, and an increase in their circulation is documented.[135] These fiscal reforms have usually been understood as a move to finance the Second Syrian War (Turner 1984). But they were probably part of larger state reforms begun indeed by Ptolemy I to gain control over Egyptian society, and many of the institutions involved in the process were familiar to key Greek constituencies. It was also at this time that the Egyptian priest Manetho's history of Egypt was written, an important text that ended with the new Egyptian dynasty of the Ptolemies and thus established the legitimacy of the Ptolemies.[136] Although military finance certainly occupied the lion's share of the state budget, we need not understand all of this activity as an effort to pay for one particular war. The Ptolemaic fiscal system, based on the Greek institution of tax farming, had broader designs and longer-lasting effects.

TAX FARMING

The farming of certain taxes, and the related institutions of money, banking, and public auction, all derived from fourth century BC Greek, especially Athenian, experience.[137] The terminology of Ptolemaic tax farming documents is fourth-century Athenian, and the early Ptolemaic adaptation shows that the kings relied on all of the Greek precedents that had

---

[134] Greek writing instruments were in place by 230 BC, after which the Egyptian reed brush became quite rare. See Clarysse (1993); Depauw (2006: 297).

[135] See Lorber (2005).

[136] For a good overview of Ptolemy II's reign, see Thompson (forthcoming). On the salt tax, a commonly taxed item in antiquity, but associated with the capitation tax only in Egypt, see Clarysse and Thompson (2006 1:36–89).

[137] Xen., *Ways* 4.19–20.

been established during the fourth century, and attempted to apply them to the new setting of Egypt. We do not know how early tax farming was first introduced, but it is full operation by the middle of the third century.[138] The scale of the Egyptian countryside naturally altered the Athenian system substantially. The desire of the ruler was of course to create stable revenue streams, i.e., to smooth income, in an environment of information asymmetry. The way in which the mechanisms of tax farming were applied reveals much about the nature of the Ptolemaic reforms of the economic system. Although the system had its advantages, all of the theoretical predictions about the perils of tax farming—that it would give rise to bribery, collusion, evasion, and information problems—are borne out by the Ptolemaic documentation.

The key text is the well-known Revenue Laws Papyrus (*pRev.*). The preserved sections of this very large text, dated to 259 BC, are concerned with the farming of money taxes; that is, the taxes on orchards and vineyards, two oil crops (sesame and castor oil), and banks.[139] The text does not cover all types of revenue that were collected by tax farming, however.[140] Thus the Ptolemaic system, as in Republican Rome, would seem to combine both direct (i.e., taxes on production) and indirect taxation. The taxation of the land itself, being the most valuable asset in the state, was left to the ancient system of state agent collection (cf. Kiser 1994:293). Bingen's (1978a) perceptive analysis has demonstrated that the text is not a codified treatment of the new economy, as Rostovtzeff (1922) once suggested but, rather, a whole series of texts collected together that imply that tax farming was a recursive or "experimental" process, with problems being solved as they arose in real time.[141]

Unlike in fourth century Athens, where tax farmers were responsible for the entire system, the functions of tax farming and tax collection were

---

[138] An early Ptolemaic demotic text (*pBM* Glanville 10528, Thebes, 291 BC), published by Glanville (1939); Depauw (2000:70–74) has often been suggested to be a tax farming agreement. Its early date would be important evidence for Ptolemaic penetration of the southern Egyptian economy. However, as far as I can determine, nothing in the text suggests a tax farming agreement. Rather, it mentions local agents collecting a certain type of tax on behalf of the state.

[139] For *pRev.*, see Grenfell and Mahaffy (1896), Préaux (1939:65–93), Bingen (1952, 1978). On Ptolemaic intentions, see Samuel (1983).

[140] Other areas subject to the farming of taxes include beer and natron production, and the tax on sales transactions (*enkuklion*).

[141] Parts of *pRev.*, written in several different hands, show corrections and changes. The experimental nature of some aspects of Ptolemaic tax farming that is suggested by *pRev.* is predicted by agency theory, and derives from the need of the ruler to optimize (or stabilize?) revenue in an environment of assymetric information. Cf. Kiser (1994:293).

Figure 11. *pRev.*, 24, 4–25, 2. This is one of the most important Ptolemaic economic documents. It dates to 259 BC, and has been understood by some previous scholars as a systematic treatise on revenue collection and central state planning. Bingen's (1978a) work has shown that it is in fact a compilation of seven separate texts, and should be regarded as an ad hoc practical solution for economic administration that established the rules for a Greek fiscal institution, tax farming, and the contractual obligations and expectations of both tax farmers and tax payers.

very often decoupled in the Ptolemaic system.[142] As Préaux (1939:450) has observed, the tax farming system would at first seem to be superfluous given the bureaucracy in charge of collecting the various taxes. In most tax farming systems, tax collection devolved either to state agents or to the tax farmers themselves.

The Ptolemaic system was, however, a hybrid, like so much else in the Ptolemaic world. Certain taxes were farmed but then collected by state agents (*logeutai*), a traditional position within the tax collection bureaucracy in Egypt and widespread in the Hellenistic world.[143] So why the decoupling? The standard answer has been that the Ptolemies were solving one of the state's basic problems with tax farming—distrust of tax collectors' loyalty. That may be part of the answer. But the political economy of the state, the variety of taxes collected, and the state's need for cash may also be factors. The early kings needed to attract Greeks familiar with a monetary economy in order for them to extract the revenue that the kings needed to maintain their power base. Tax farming created an incentive structure that aligned the interest of individuals with the ruler's and, at the same time, aided the ruler in maintaining a monopoly on political power in the capital. A large state and the presence of Greek agents of the king spread throughout the countryside and ready to be mobilized "wherever they were and for whatever need presented itself" (Bingen 1978a:168) shaped the system.

Tax farming was often used where monitoring and transaction costs are high, poor communication conditions exist, and reliable record keeping is not available (Kiser and Kane 2007). Kiser's (1994) study of early tax farming systems suggests that several factors typically weighed in favor of introducing the system; among which were the size of the state and the fact that the taxed asset possessed high variability and mobility and it was easily measured.

In Kiser's model, the ruler has the aim of maximizing revenue and will choose the taxation system that produces the most efficient solution to the agency problem. The Ptolemaic solution fits this model, but it was the creation of stable and predictable, rather than maximal, revenues that the Ptolemies were after. The need for efficiency in raising the cash required to finance military operations, may be an explanation here. Tax farmers were expected to make their payments to the crown in money, and being

---

[142] For the Athenian tax farming system, see Stroud (1998); and Rhodes and Osborne (2003) discussing a very interesting Athenian inscription (*SEG* xlvii 96, 374/3 BC) that records a law concerned with the grain supply to Athens utilizing tax farming. On the decoupling, see the remarks by Bingen (1978a:166).

[143] On the role of state agents in collecting revenue, see Polyb. 22.13.2 on the viceroy of Cyprus.

in most cases Greeks, they had knowledge and access to capital that would enable them to make loans of a sort to the ruler (in advance of actually collecting the revenues due) (Kiser 1994:289).

The introduction of banks played an important role in the collection and payments of farmed taxes.[144] There were three types: state or royal banks, "concessionary" banks licensed by the state, and private banks that emerged in the second century and appear to have replaced "concessionary" banks.[145] It is the royal banks that concern us here. They formed, along with the tax farmers and the state granaries that collected taxes in kind, the intermediary between production and state revenues. The granaries received payments in grain and held deposits of individual taxpayers. The state granaries were also an important means by which of the local state bureaucracy was paid.

Public bids for the right to collect a certain tax for the short term (one year, or in some cases for longer periods) in a specific territory were posted by the tax farmers at royal banks. The auction process served not only to guarantee revenues but also may have functioned as a recruiting device to bring persons into the bureaucratic structure (Eisenstadt 1993:129). The competitive nature of the system provided an incentive to collect the tax.[146] We might expect, in such a short-term system, that there would have been an incentive to overcollect. But *pRev.* 1–22, fragmented as it is, suggests that the use of written contracts carefully specified the rights and duties of the tax farmers. Despite the administrative theory expressed in the papyrus, however, abuses by tax farmers are reported. "Now many people are coming down river to the city (Alexandria)," one complaint goes, "and are lodging complaints against you [a financial official in the Memphite nome], your subordinates, and especially the tax farmers, for abuses of power and fraudulent exactions, and some even allege blackmail."[147]

The sale of a tax farm occurred in the name of king at a public auction, conducted in both Greek and Egyptian.[148] Such sales were organized at the nome and toparchic level; the name and nationality of the successful

---

[144] Now summarized in Bogaert (1994, 2001). See also Geens (2008); Vandorpe and Clarysse (2008).

[145] Bogaert (1998–99); Geens (2008).

[146] A sense of the atmosphere of an auction is conveyed by *PLBat*, vol. 20, 30.10–15 (142/141 BC); *pKöln* VI 260 (213 BC). On tax farming, see Harper (1934); Préaux (1939:450–59), Rostovtzeff (1941:328–30); Bingen (1978a); Turner (1984). The rules of tax farming are laid out in *pRev.*, 1–22. For an English translation, see Bagnall and Derow (2004:181–95). Cf. *UPZ* 112 (Oxyrhynchite nome, 204/03 BC), an announcement of the auction for the annual tax farming contract in a nome.

[147] *UPZ* 113 (156 BC). Trans. Austin (2006:text 321).

[148] Préaux (1939:451), with bibliography.

bidder was declared in front of the *oikonomos*. Written tenders preceded the bidding, and the successful bid was often secured by personal guarantors and by the taking of a royal oath.[149]

Tax farmers were required to pay into royal banks monthly, through the tax collectors. The royal banks were the instruments of state control, and the tax farming system, by incentivizing collection, insured the smooth inflow of funds to the royal coffers throughout the year and over the longer term. We would expect to find the farmers of the tax and the collectors working together, and indeed there is good evidence to suggest that this is what happened (Clarysse and Thompson 2006 1:77). Information was important to the success of the system (cf. Rostovtzeff 1941:329); and just as in ethnic group social organization, tax collection organization may have reinforced group identity. Tax farmers, it must be remembered, could be jailed in the case of failure of collection.[150] The system had built into it very powerful incentives to performance and these were no doubt reinforced by personal relationships.[151] About the overall performance of the system we are almost wholly ignorant.

TECHNOLOGY

Despite Hellenistic advances and the impressive scientific output of Alexandria, productivity was probably only marginally improved by technological innovations.[152] Much has been made of the new technologies of the period, but as far as evidence permits us to see, new machines were little used in the Egyptian countryside.[153] The waterwheel and the Archimedean screw, certainly attested for the first time in the Ptolemaic period, would have intensified local irrigation possibilities, mainly in orchards and vineyards, but, like double cropping, they were not widely disseminated before the Roman period.[154]

Innovation it seems, whether in the form of machines or the alphabetization of census registers, was slow to reach the countryside.[155] Some advancement in irrigation equipment, and perhaps an increase in the use

---

[149] Cf. the elaborate process of a land auction detailed in *pEleph* 14 (ca. 223 BC, Edfu; = *Select papyri* 2, text 233).

[150] *pTebt*. III 772 (236 BC = Bagnall and Derow [2004], text 101).

[151] *pTebt*. I 40 (117 BC = Bagnall and Derow [2004], text 97) showing a patron-client relationship.

[152] On Alexandrian science, see Fraser (1972). Cf. Préaux (1966).

[153] Wilson (2002), Lewis (1997). On the relationship of technology to economic development in the ancient world, see Schneider (2007).

[154] Samuel (1983:58); Rowlandson (1996:20). See Rathbone (2007:701, n. 13).

[155] Alphabet: Clarysse and Thompson (2006/2:69).

of draft animals, may have had some impact on agricultural productivity on marginal land and in gardens.[156] The introduction of iron into Egypt for agricultural implements and other tools is documented in the mid-third-century Zenon and Kleon archives, but its use was likewise limited, probably restricted to state-directed construction projects.[157] Irrigation in the Fayyum did not depend on water-lifting machines alone; the ancient basin irrigation system (relying on the annual flood of the river) was also used there. Taxation of the land was, therefore, more important for the economy than technological improvements in Ptolemaic productivity. Hellenistic building technology was, however important in the construction of new villages in the Fayyum.

The paucity of price data preserved in the papyri is a serious barrier to understanding the long-term performance of the Ptolemaic economy. There are significant gaps in our information about basic commodities (e.g., for the price of wheat from the mid-third century to 209 BC).[158] And what references there are can be confusing. Small items such as hoes are rarely given values, for example, and even when they are, we are cannot always be sure whether a price is reckoned in silver or bronze. The data derived from penalty clauses in contracts can also mislead, since they may not reflect anything meaningful in terms of commodity price; they may simply be arbitrary figures.

Difficulties in tracing the long-term history of commodity prices are exacerbated by our lack of knowledge about the amount of money in circulation and the velocity of its circulation.[159] The supposed price inflation that occurred in the reign of Ptolemy IV Philopator has received extensive comment and various explanations.[160] Earlier analyses pinned blame on either the reduction of precious metal in the silver coins, on a new bookkeeping system, or on a reduction of the weight of the bronze drachma and a consequent increase in the value of coin in circulation.[161] Much of the so-called price inflation, however, is derived not from a single new bronze accounting standard but from multiple re-tariffings of the bronze coins against silver and gold.[162] An independent bronze standard was introduced at the end of the third century.

---

[156] Bonneau (1993:106).

[157] Rostovtzeff (1941:362–63, 1197); *pPetr.* III 42 C 2–3 (= *SB* XVIII 13881; Mertens [1985]), a text from the Kleon archive containing a complaint by workers that their iron tools are being worn out by hard rock. On this archive, see the overview by Lewis (1986). The entire archive, including several previously unpublished texts, is to be republished by Bart van Beek.

[158] Samuel (1984). For the gap in wheat prices, see Cadell & Le Rider (1997).

[159] Bagnall (1999).

[160] Reekmans (1951); Maresch (1996); Cadell & Le Rider (1997); Bagnall (1999).

[161] Reekmans (1951).

[162] Bagnall (1999) 198; von Reden (2007).

Egypt's Fayyum depression was an area that underwent land reclamation and the intensification of agriculture on a significant scale during the Ptolemaic period, a state of affairs coinciding very likely with the fact that prior claims to land in the valley made taking over such land politically difficult. Other areas (the eastern Delta and the region around Alexandria) were also developed or received renewed attention, and there were new settlements in the Herakleopolite and Oxyrhynchite nomes as well.[163] This process was probably already underway in the reign of Ptolemy I Soter, although once again the lack of documentary evidence for his reign limits certitude.[164] Documentation of reclamation and settlement is extensive for the reign of Ptolemy II, who visited the area on at least two occasions.[165]

We are hampered by both the qualitative and quantitative differences between third-century BC data from the Fayyum and from Upper Egypt, and this dampens our hopes of presenting a testable hypothesis. Nevertheless some broad facts can be stated. In the early Ptolemaic period, land in the Fayyum was reclaimed under state direction, and new settlements of soldiers and Egyptians were established. No similar "investment" is known in the Nile valley. The Ptolemaic maintenance of an old land tenure regime in the Thebaid, where the right to convey land already existed, the granting of land to important new constituents, and the use of agents to collect taxes all combined to reduce state revenues, but this was unavoidable; it followed from the political necessity of seeking legitimacy from old institutions, and loyalty from the bureaucracy and the army.[166] The traditional temple-administered estates appear to have continued, held privately by soldiers and temple dependents and leased out to others on short-term leases.[167] The picture of regional differences in the early Ptolemaic regime is the result of historic patterns of land exploitation. The private archives from Upper Egypt suggest, however, that soldiers became well established in the south during the second century.

The transmission of property, both real property and rights to income from offices, by written legal instruments had a long history before the Ptolemies. Even so, most transactions probably occurred within family and social groups without written legal instrument. Such "paperless"

---

[163] On the Delta, see Davoli (2001). For new Upper Egyptian foundations in the second century, see Vandorpe (1995:233); Kramer (1997).

[164] See Thompson (1999b: 125). Cf. Diod. Sic. 18.33.

[165] *PSI* 4 354 (253 BC); *pPetr.* II 13, 18a (253 BC, on the date see Clarysse (1980) 85; *pPetr.* II 39 e 3 (247–245 BC?). The first visit may be tied to kleruchic settlement in the area; see Clarysse (1980, 2000a).

[166] For the problem of limited Greek access to land, and the consequent problems affecting royal revenues, Bingen (1984).

[167] Manning (2003a).

transactions would have reduced clerical costs, but they also reflect limited market mechanisms, and they must have created considerable uncertainty. The advantage to the state was that the holding of land by families and other groups saved the state the cost of defining and enforcing individual property rights, something that we know from recorded disputes was difficult.

Access to land and to the market in land was limited, but this does not mean that land was not potentially available. The shortage of labor that could be applied to the land was a serious long-term problem that no doubt reduced the amount of productive land.[168] The price of land was in fact historically low, a low multiple of the value of a year's harvest, which is another indication of the limited "market alienability" of land—it was the rights to the income from land ("economic rights") rather than individualized "legal rights" to the land itself that were "owned."[169]

The land survey established the state's authority as well as private interest in the land. But this authority, and therefore the economic power of the state, rested on the knowledge of local officials who performed and recorded the survey. Land surveying was one the oldest state institutions in Egypt, and centralized knowledge of the exact extent of each nome, measured by its length along the Nile—in essence a theological statement asserting political control over Egypt—can be traced back to the Middle Kingdom (Dynasty 12, ca. 1991–1783 BC).[170] The difficulty for the Ptolemaic state, as for other states, was in obtaining accurate information each year on local agricultural production. This once again required both the loyalty and the accuracy of the village scribe and his assistants in charge of land survey and registration, and that loyalty and accuracy was not always forthcoming.[171] The survey of standing crops and the fixing of rents, of course, give the impression of accurate measurement and recording, but there are examples of figures being carried over from old records, and of land being misclassified.[172]

A key to royal revenues was the tenancy on royal land of so-called "royal farmers."[173] Royal farmers were direct tenants of the king, leasing the land they worked from year to year under terms adjusted to take account of fluctuating conditions. What were technically short-term grants of land later became stable, and tenure could be passed to heirs.

---

[168] Samuel (1989).

[169] On the distinction between economic and legal rights, see Barzel (1997). On prices of land in the Greek papyri, Cadell (1994).

[170] Manning (2003a:146–48).

[171] Verhoogt (1998).

[172] Crawford (1971) 20–23; Verhoogt (1998:132, n. 121).

[173] Rowlandson (1985).

The term "royal farmer" was used in official contexts not as an indicator of class but as a status designator,[174] and it was a status that was sought after, not forced upon the farmer.[175] It was later applied to a wide range of men from peasants to priests, the status providing them access to land and capital and to an array of other benefits, including protection from military billets, a guarantee that they could only be brought before Greek courts, and the right to be left undisturbed during sowing and harvest time.[176] So desirable was this status in fact that groups of men were known to take on leases of small plots of royal land simply to obtain it. (The size of plots of royal land was generally small, but there are documented royal leases of up to 160 *arouras*.[177]) Clearly individuals with this status exploited it.[178] Recently published documents from the Fayyum, however, show that the terms of the leases of royal land could be changed frequently, that rent fluctuated with annual production, and that transfers between farmers were frequent. This suggests that the Ptolemaic system was probably much more flexible and more adaptive to the realities of rural Egypt than Rostovtzeff's view admits.[179]

The early Ptolemaic kings decided to settle Greek soldiers on land in Egypt in order to retain a loyal fighting force available for call up when needed. At the same time, the placing of military men in the countryside served to pacify, in theory, troublesome areas and to get marginal land under cultivation. Soldiers were given plots of land (*kleroi*) according to their rank. The 100-aroura cavalrymen were the largest group of third-century kleruchs.[180] Other kleruchs had smaller plots of land; thirty *arouras* for infantry soldiers for example. This class of landholding evolved into hereditary tenure, leaving Greeks, in the main, in a better position on the land than their Egyptian counterparts. The kleruchic system had a long-term impact on the land in those parts of Egypt that had a large contingent of military settlers, forming a major part of what was classed as private land in the Roman period.[181]

---

[174] Rowlandson (1985:331).

[175] *Pace* de Ste. Croix (1983:153). See Lá' da and Papathomas (2003) and their treatment of *pVindob* G 60499 (mid-second century BC) for a recently published example illustrating the privileges of a royal farmer.

[176] Shelton (1976:118). *pTebt*. I5 (= *Select Papyri*, vol. 2, text 210; *C. Ord. Ptol.* 53; [118 BC], 221–26), Rowlandson (1985: 331).

[177] *pLille* 8, 4 (third century BC). On the range, see Shelton (1976:152).

[178] On the extent and variety of the business activity of one royal farmer, see Boswinkel and Pestman (1982), Lewis (1986:124–39).

[179] The papyri discussed by Shelton 1976 (esp. *pTebt*.IV 1103, 1105, 1107) are crucial in demonstrating, for example, that the rate of cessions of royal land was as high as one-third from year to year. This contrasts sharply with Rostovtzeff (1941:284–87). See the remarks of Rowlandson (1985:337), Shelton (1976:120–21), and Verhoogt (1998:27).

[180] Uebel (1968), Clarysse and Thompson (2006).

[181] Rowlandson (1996:45–46).

The gift of large estates to high officials, not new with the Ptolemies, enabled sizeable tracts of land to be developed quickly. The land was a temporary grant by the king, called a "gift estate" (*dorea*) in the papyri, and could not be transferred privately. The ephemeral nature of tenure on this class of land shows that such estates were essentially royal land, created as a means of providing revenue for the king and his circle. The land was then "ceded" by the king to others for their use, and they were of course obliged to pay taxes to the crown on their production. The estate of the *dioikêtês* (the chief financial officer of the state) Apollonios, near Philadelphia, is the most famous example. This was a kind of "model estate," or "experimental farm."[182] Like other large estates, it took advantage of economies of scale in developing these estates, as well as the private initiative and capital of ambitious officials and immigrants.[183] The "gift" of land in fact created a potential revenue stream for Apollonius; it was up to him to take advantage of this potential. By all accounts, he seems to have done so, at least for the ten or so years that that surviving estate records document. His involvement in the management of the estate appears to have waned after only a couple of years, however, if we may judge by his correspondence preserved in the archive.

We can also see that the size of the operation took advantage of the centralization of information. Unlike Apollonius' estate in the Memphite nome, which was composed of discrete plots of land scattered around several villages, his estate at Philadelphia was one large parcel. Apollonius at first kept a close watch on operations, even though the land was leased out and even turned over to others to manage.[184] Each year, for example, he sent out memos to his manager telling him what seed and what amounts were available.[185] Some at least of the account records suggest that these instructions were not followed particularly closely.[186] The estate seems also to have been a place where experiments could be tried, although many appear to have failed.[187] Economic activity was particularly dedicated to commercial operations in viticulture and later in oil crops.[188]

[182] Edgar (1931:12).

[183] Cf. Rostovtzeff (1922:145).

[184] In the latter case, it seems that kleruchs were given land from the estate itself. See further Crawford (1973:240–41). A group of Egyptian farmers who had come to Philadelphia from the ancient center at Heliopolis took a lease of 1,000 *arouras* within the estate. See *pLond.* VII 1954 (Philadelphia, 257 BC), Rostovtzeff (1922:73–75); Thompson (1999b:136).

[185] *pCair. Zen.* 59292, 420–430, cited by Crawford (1973:236).

[186] This is especially true in the case of over-producing what was specified and with important crops like poppy. So Crawford (1973:245).

[187] On the experimental nature of the estate, see Orrieux (1983:77–97).

[188] On viticulture, Clarysse and Vandorpe (1997), Préaux (1947) 22–26; and for oil crops, Sandy (1989).

Poppy cultivation was also attempted on the Philadelphia estate, largely on marginal land, but its success appears to have been short-lived.[189]

Estates of this kind were in decline by the end of the third century. Their purpose was certainly to establish the state's direct control over new land, to settle new populations, to establish revenue streams for state officials, and to exact as much new revenue as possible.

CONCLUSION

The Ptolemaic state has often been regarded as highly centralized, with descriptions conjuring up the image of a despotic ruler who commanded the economy and all those within the state, from the top down. But a distinction should be drawn here between "centralized" and "bureau-cratic," and between the direct revenue of the king and the revenue of the state. State revenues were no doubt impressive by ancient standards, but there were limits on the degree to which economic production could ever be centralized (i.e., planned, or commanded from the center), given the nature of the Nile valley, the distances between center and periphery, and the nature of irrigation, which dictated local control and placed a high value on local knowledge of agricultural conditions. There were certainly interventions by the state in an effort to improve the irrigation system and increase the amount of arable land, but links between central state planning and irrigation practice were always indirect.

The bureaucracy was a double-edged sword. On the one hand, it kept the rulers in power, but on the other it probably had a dragging effect, stifling development and growth, similar to what happened in China (Deng 1999). The bureaucracy was organized and coercive; it controlled the "merchant class" and siphoned off resources. This is a slightly differ-ent picture than Rostovtzeff gave for the evolution of power in the later Ptolemaic period. Using documents like the first-century asylum decrees (Bingen 1989), he saw real power shift from the king and his ministers to a small "clique of selfish, greedy, and lawless officials who formed a new, wealthy, and influential aristocracy of the kingdom" (Rostovtzeff 1941:896). This social trend was actually broader than Rostovtzeff's lan-guage admits (cf. Bingen 1989).

The ability of the Ptolemaic state to direct new irrigation work that trebled the land base in the Fayyum is a classic example of state interven-tion in the economy. The impetus for a project of this magnitude came from the pressures of population growth and from the need to settle a loyal fighting force within the country. The Ptolemaic bureaucracy was

---

[189] On cultivation of the poppy: Crawford (1973:248).

large, and it is not surprising therefore that the taxation regime was far more extensive and successful than in earlier Egyptian history. Yet the management of the irrigation regime remained diffused and in charge of local officials. Earlier historians of the Ptolemaic state have posited a central-planning or estatist model for the Ptolemaic agrarian economy, but the evidence we have gathered suggests that it was rather more reactive, or ad hoc, than centrally planned.

The path of economic change in the Ptolemaic period can be traced back to Saïte (650–525 BC) social and political reforms, and to Persian imperial rule. Ptolemaic taxation policy, which demanded that some taxes be paid in coin, certainly increased the amount of revenue captured by the state. There were, however, strong structural constraints on the development of the economy. The framework of the ancient property regime remained intact, initially at least, in areas such as the Thebaid, although over the long term it was altered by land grants to soldiers, and, to a certain extent, through the use of public auction. Taxation in kind of agricultural production on grain-bearing land limited the ability to monetize the economy.[190] There were new fiscal institutions that allowed greater capture of revenue, at least over the short term, but the continuation of ancient structures, the structure of the bureaucratic system that was developed over the course of the third century, and concessions to local elites, severely limited potential for sustained per capita economic growth. But sustained per capita growth was not, after all, the aim of the regime.[191] The Ptolemies sought instead an equilibrium that was anchored in an ancient system in which the pharaoh guaranteed justice in exchange for revenue.

The legal system under the Ptolemies has usually been studied as a separate institution, but law was intimately linked to the political economy of the state, and to its economic structure. I turn now, therefore, to an examination of the Ptolemaic legal system.

[190] Rowlandson (2001).
[191] Samuel (1983:41).

Chapter 6

ORDER AND LAW

SHAPING THE LAW IN A NEW STATE

In despotic states, where there are no fundamental
laws, neither is there a depository of laws.
—*Montesquieu*, Spirit of the laws, *Part I, Book 2.4*

The state pretends to regulate everything and
in fact regulates nothing.
—*Hopkins (1987:98)*

THIS CHAPTER is concerned with the connections between the king, Egyptian society, the law, and the economy.[1] Earlier approaches to the Ptolemaic legal system and Ptolemaic legal reforms have, in the main, been focused, on royal activity and, thus on formal aspects of the law.[2] This "legal centralist tradition," an heir to Hobbes' *Leviathan*, and enshrined in Weber's notion of the state as the monopolizer of legitimate violence, considers states as "the chief sources of rules and enforcement efforts."[3] But the Ptolemaic kings did not impose a Greek legal order on Egypt. Rather, while asserting their sovereignty over Egyptian institutions, and building a new administrative framework, they continued, at the same time, the traditions of private law that new populations like the Greeks

[1] For an excellent orientation to some of the issues addressed here, see Swedberg (2003:189–217).

[2] Previous studies of Ptolemaic law: Taubenschlag (1955); Seidl (1962); Préaux (1978/1:271–80, 1978/2:587–601); Rupprecht (1994: Chapter 3, especially for document typology). Wolff (1966, 1978, and 2002) remain the standard surveys, mainly from an administrative point of view. For demotic Egyptian law, see Manning (2003b). Pierce (1972) remains an important study of demotic contracts and their relationships to Greek contract forms. See also Mélèze-Modrzejewski (1995) on the judiciary. Ptolemaic law, by his own admission, was not discussed by Turner (1984:155) in his historical summary of the period. Cf. Frier and Kehoe (2007); Kehoe (2007). Cf. the general treatment of the sociology of law and the economy in Edelman and Stryker (2005).

[3] Ellickson (1991:138). The term "legal centralism" comes from the economist Oliver Williamson (1983). Ellickson (1991:138–55) provides an excellent summary of legal centralist notions, and the orientations of the "Law and Economics" and the "Law and Society" schools of thought with respect to the debate over the role of social norms vs. state-centered positive law in creating order.

brought with them, and that the Egyptians had developed for centuries. "Ptolemaic law," by which I mean the variety of legal traditions current in the Ptolemaic period, was shaped by three main forces: royal legislation that attempted to establish a legal order based on the new social conditions, the underlying legal traditions of the population and, finally, by the bureaucracy that adjudicated the law.

My orientation is informed by two considerations. The first is taken from Ellickson's work on informal social norms, which argues against the idea that the state was the "dominant" or even the "exclusive controller" of the social order.[4] And the second consideration is suggested by Friedman's thesis that "major legal change follows and depends on social change" (Friedman 1975:269). More specifically, I would only add that legal change in the Ptolemaic period followed social *and* economic change.[5]

Having stated my orientation to Ptolemaic law, I do not wish to diminish the role of the king to zero. The king, after all, was historically the embodiment of social norms and the font of law as the guarantor of *Ma'at* (justice, order). The king could make law known though decrees and administrative decisions. But such royal decrees or decisions were not comprehensive statements of law, but rather, ad hoc pronouncements and responses, and they were not promulgated without reference to social norms, social relationships, or to the interests of particular groups. The role of the king (or the state if you will) was as creator of a "cognitive framework," a drawer of boundaries. Neither ruler (nor "state") can be analyzed apart from the wider society. The heterogeneous population of Ptolemaic Egypt made the assertion of sovereignty over local legal traditions an important aspect of state reforms. Of course, even in a relatively well-documented ancient society like Ptolemaic Egypt, we cannot measure the extent to which individuals bargained and resolved disputes outside of the formal framework of the legal entitlements of either royal law or local norms. We might guess that such "informal" or "self help" solutions were extensive. If "large segments of social life are located and shaped beyond the reach of law" (Ellickson 1991:4) in a modern American context, how much more is this likely to have been true in an ancient one? This is one area where brilliant fieldwork in a modern society simply yields richer and subtler results than a study of the papyri, which cannot capture the whole of legal activity, can ever hope to produce.

As in other premodern states, the provision of law and the guarantee of justice, were critical to the creation of a political equilibrium and to

[4] Ellickson (1991), a brilliant analysis of dispute resolution using informal rules in a contemporary American setting.
[5] Cf. Huang's (1996) very lucid account of Qing dynasty China.

the extraction of resources, law being an important component of both state power and legitimacy, as well as, certainly, a key to political longevity, and, like religion, a means by which the state penetrated local society. Major changes occurred in the area of public law that concerned state revenues. In the area of private law, as we will see, the Ptolemaic state provided a framework for the continuity of local norms, but such norms and the scribal traditions reflected in the written legal documents evolved considerably under Ptolemaic rule.

The most important feature of the age was the multiethnic character of Ptolemaic law in toto, the legal traditions of many ethnic groups being recognized by the kings. This incorporation of local traditions into the state system is important in understanding the Ptolemaic state's role in the adjudication of local disputes.

Law in ancient Egypt did not exist, despite the search for it by some scholars, as a formal, public, *written* codified system of law. It was rather a complex system that joined royal decree, i.e., royal *authority*, with norms and practices that developed at the local level. The Ptolemies, as the new pharaohs, became the embodiment of law writ large, but disputes were adjudicated by local elites (village elders, priests), and enforcement was the job of the local police force.[6]

There were major attempts at establishing a hierarchy of law and defining the jurisdictions of courts in the early Ptolemaic period, and these efforts must be associated with the fiscal changes that I surveyed in the last chapter. Indeed these legal reforms were a sine qua non for the extraction of "free floating" resources. Over the course of Ptolemaic rule, it appears that the bureaucracy, under the umbrella of the sovereignty of the state, began to supersede traditional authority. The clearest example of such state penetration of local society is found in purely Egyptian disputes where Ptolemaic officials appeared as mediators. Consider the following example.

In Psinteo, a small village in the southern Fayyum, on the 12th of May 171, Herieus, a "royal farmer," i.e., a cultivator of royal land, and thus of some importance to the revenues of the king, petitioned the *stratêgos*, a local government official.[7] In the petition he described, laconically, being violently treated (whether in a physical or strictly in a legal sense is unclear) by a woman and two men, one of whom seems to have been something of a local heavy. A plot of undeveloped land, which he had inherited from his father while still young (the petition tells us), had been illegally seized, and a tower (a dovecote?) built on it. Herieus, the plaintiff, and

---

[6] On the Ptolemaic police, see the overview in Thompson (1997b); Clarysse and Thompson (2006/2:165–77).

[7] *pTebt.* III/1 780. For the status of royal farmer, see chapter 5.

Thareus, the woman who had committed the wrong, were both Egyptians. After the illegal seizure of land, Thareus died, and her heirs, a man and his sister, probably children of Thareus, now laid claim to the property. A petition was made to the *stratêgos* by Herieus to resolve the dispute. But in this petition there is a somewhat unexpected twist. Instead of appealing directly to Egyptian law or to a local tribunal, which we would expect to adjudicate a case of this nature, the plaintiff petitions the state through a local official. Herieus makes reference to a decree of the king, a *diagramma*: "But the legislation (*diagramma*) declares, 'If any person build upon the land of another, let him be deprived of the building'." Herieus requests that the offending parties be summoned before the *stratêgos* and an investigation made, and if the accused are found guilty that they be forced to abandon the property. The end of the document has a note, presumably by the *stratêgos*, to another official requesting that he summon the two parties involved. We do not, as so often, know the outcome of the dispute.

This minor property dispute in a small village raises two important points for understanding Ptolemaic law. First, appeal is made to a Ptolemaic regional official, not to a village head or to a local court, even though the dispute is a local matter and involves an issue in Egyptian property law. Nonetheless, appeal is made to the king's justice, through a local official, the *stratêgos*. The dispute, probably a typical one in the villages, shows us that at this period, the state was expected to play a role in adjudicating private disputes. (Clearly this case was a matter of "adjudication" rather than "arbitration," although arbitration certainly existed, especially in the days before the Ptolemaic court system had been established.[8]) The second important point that the trial highlights is the fact that the plaintiff makes an appeal to a generalized Ptolemaic law called the *diagramma*. This "legislation" is referred to many times in the Greek papyri in the context of private legal disputes.[9]

The many references to different sections of this "legislation" in Ptolemaic documents led Wolff to suggest that the effort was a comprehensive, even "planned," attempt to promulgate a state legal framework that incorporated both Egyptian law and new state rules. According to Wolff (1960:210) this framework established an "integrated legal system, depending on and sanctioned by royal will, and was one of the conditions prerequisite to the attainment of the political goal," namely sovereignty over Egypt. Importantly though, the system was "integrated" only in the sense that the two different sources of law, the Greek and the Egyptian,

---

[8] The two types of dispute resolution. See Gulliver (1979); discussed by Harries (1999). On Ptolemaic arbitration, see the observations of Wolff (1962).

[9] On this "legislation," see Wolff (1960); Mélèze-Modrzejewski (1995,2001:190–93).

established as *lex fori*, were subsumed under royal sovereignty.[10] That fact is well illustrated in the Asyut family dispute discussed below. There the king directly influenced what would be the law for those members of the population who were classed as "Hellene" through a new court (*dikastê-rion*). With respect to Egyptian law, Ptolemaic sovereignty was certainly asserted by the presence of a royal representative (*eisagogeus*) at trials.[11]

The Ptolemies, then, were active in shaping a new legal framework to accommodate the new social realities of their multiethnic state, and, like the Persians before them, in "reauthorizing" or "restating" local law within a new state framework.[12] That framework, in turn, implies that the law was not unilaterally imposed from above in the manner usually supposed in Wittfogel's (and classical Marxist) despotic theory, but was established also per community and through the state's reaction to "law on the ground." The intent was, by asserting sovereignty over local norms, to create a more orderly and predictable system of state-sanctioned dispute resolution, and perhaps also a better means of insuring the protection of private rights.[13] Before examining the Ptolemaic impact on local law, I turn to a brief overview of Egyptian law.

LEGAL TRADITIONS IN EGYPT

In the legal system of ancient Egypt, the concept of justice is closely associated with the concept of *Ma'at*, usually translated as "order," or "justice."[14] Its core meaning is closer to "harmony," or indeed "social equilibrium," the consensus that bound the lowest member of the community to the king himself. In that social sense, Egypt did indeed come close to being a nation, an "imagined community, to borrow Benedict Anderson's phrase, in which all members viewed themselves as joined together by language, custom, and *Ma'at*.[15] While written legal texts, especially those concerned with property, are well attested from the Old Kingdom period

[10] Wolff (1960:212). See further below on Egyptian codes.

[11] Whether we agree with Allam's (2008) argument that the office of *eisagogeus* was merely a continuation of ancient practice or not, this official's actions during and after the Asyut trial treated further below and translated in the Appendix show quite clearly that we are dealing here with official state presence at the resolution of an Egyptian dispute. Wolff (1960:205) suggests that the official in both Greek and Egyptian courts was responsible for the "composition of the court."

[12] The literature on "Persian imperial authorization" of the *Torah* is enormous. See Schmid (2007) with previous literature cited.

[13] For Ptolemaic Egypt, e.g., Green (1990:188): Ptolemaic rule "did not in any sense depend on a willing consent, much less active choice, by the governed."

[14] Assmann's conception of "connective justice."

[15] Cf. the remarks by Kemp (2006:19–25).

onward, emphasis was also placed on the oral argument, and on maintaining a sense of equity between two disputants. Written collections of "laws" (Egyptian *hpw*) are also known from early times, but the decree of each king was paramount. Several kings in the New Kingdom are referred to as "establishers of laws" (*smn hpw*), and even earlier, regional officials (nomarchs) were also known as "makers of laws" in their districts.[16] A papyrus from the late Middle Kingdom cites several "laws": "the law pertaining to those who desert," "the law pertaining to one who flees the prison," etc., suggesting that these citations may go back to a larger criminal code (Hayes 1955:51–52), or perhaps simply to a body of royal decrees. The term *hp* in the papyrus need not refer to codified law at all. It may simply refer to a procedural rule, or even to a royal decree, an ambiguity that illustrates the extent to which the Egyptian language lacked a technical legal vocabulary. Kruchten (2001:278) concludes that the word *hp* connotes:

> every kind of rule, either natural or juridical, general or specific, public or private, written or unwritten. That is, in an administrative or legal context, every source of rights, such as "law," "decree," "custom," and even "contract."

There was no independent judiciary in pre-Ptolemaic Egypt, and no distinction was made between the administrative and legal functions of state officials. This overlapping of official functions continued under the Ptolemies. Ideals of justice were well established in literary texts, in the tomb biographies of officials, and in the expressed ideology of kingship as protector as "justice." Obtaining justice for private wrongs, however, was contingent, depending on the patronage of an official and often on a large dose of patience. Private disputes were often settled informally in the village by elders, or between representatives of the families involved. Throughout Egyptian history, enforcement remained a serious problem, and confessions to were an essential element of guilt finding. The ideal in Egyptian law, Eyre concludes, was social order not statute, and the Egyptian state was not strong enough to impose royal law and judgment throughout the state. Priests and temples had come to play a critical role in resolving legal disputes by New Kingdom times.

Far from being static, Egyptian law underwent major changes during the first millennium BC, as did other aspects of society, and it continued to evolve under the Ptolemies. Like the cuneiform documents from Hellenistic Babylonia, the changes were stimulated not by royal fiat but by the specific needs of notary scribes.[17] The tradition of private order con-

---

[16] Eyre (2004).
[17] On the cuneiform documents, see Van der Spek (1995).

tracting formalized in writing goes far back into Egyptian history. Beginning in Dynasty 18, agreements were formalized in writing. Major reforms occurred at the end of Dynasty 25 and during Dynasty 26, the Saïte period, in a process that Menu (1994:224) has called the "juridicisation of relationships of exchange." Two elements of a written sales contract come together in the seventh century BC: the acknowledgement of receipt of a sale price and the cession of the item of sale and the rights pertaining thereto. The obligation of the seller in sales is stressed: the seller must protect the rights of the buyer against all others, and the sales document will serve as title to the object conveyed.[18] Formal, written agreements are well documented from the Saïte period onward. Such agreements, which usually concern private property in houses, land, or priestly income, were crucial in establishing legal title to property, and it is for this reason that they are preserved in family "archives."[19]

Another key reform that we can certainly attach to the reign of Amasis is related to the spread of demotic Egyptian. An examination of the demotic texts from Thebes during Amasis' reign shows that all of the new features of demotic legal documents were established in the south during his reign (Martin 2007).[20] Two things are clear in this reform. (1) The vector of influence was from the north, which had a "more developed legal tradition" (Martin 2007:28) than the south; and (2), the process of establishing the demotic script and its legal forms was gradual. The adoption of the new administrative language, no doubt a key part of political consolidation, was not imposed directly but was probably accepted by different scribal families at different times.[21] By the middle of the fourth century BC at the latest, corresponding to the Nectanebid flourishing, the fully developed demotic sale document well known from the third century BC, is documented as far south as the Elephantine island.[22]

CODIFICATION

Eisenstadt (1993:137–40) laid out three basic aspects of the codification of the law in bureaucratic states. The act of codifying the law advanced

---

[18] The private demotic archive of Tsenhor, ranging from 556–487 BC, provides excellent testimony for an already "mature" demotic legal tradition. See Pestman (1994).

[19] On such documents as title deeds, see Pestman (1983b).

[20] See also Malinine (1953); Allam (1991).

[21] For a discussion of the texts and one particular scribal family that document the process, see Donker van Heel (1994); Martin (2007).

[22] The text is *pMoscow* 135 (Elephantine, 349 BC). It is a sales document with four witness copy texts used to transfer priestly income. For the text, see Martin (1996:356–59). On the demotic witness copy form of contract, see Depauw (1999).

the state's goal of gaining control of "traditional groups and strata," it promoted "differentiated legal institutions" and, at the same time, it attempted to gain control over the "autonomous growth" of these institutions. The act of codification was a means by which the state defined a cognitive framework and gained control of society. By its nature then, the codification of law took account of the constituent groups in a society.

It has often been remarked that ancient Egypt has not produced a law code to rival the other Near Eastern collections of laws. Egypt would in fact appear to be unique among the major civilizations of the ancient Near East in not producing any formal *public* written code of laws, of which the *Codex Hammurabi* is the most famous example.[23] We possess publicly published local laws from other Mediterranean civilizations dating to the sixth and fifth centuries BC, but none from Egypt. Amasis' reforms and the tradition of Darius' codification of Egyptian law discussed below suggest, however, that Egypt was also part of this larger trend.[24] Indeed there is good evidence that both state reforms by kings and collections of legal rules and procedures were part of Egyptian tradition.

TRADITIONS OF CODIFICATION

That the codification of laws, seen as a means of creating political consensus, did take place in Egypt, is suggested by the first-century BC historian Diodorus Siculus (I. 94–95), who preserves a tradition of great Egyptian "lawgivers" (Greek *nomothêtai*)[25] that extends all the way back to the beginning of Egyptian history.[26] He mentions six rulers of Egypt specifically. The list begins with Mnevis (i.e., Menes, the founder of a united Egypt, ca. 3050 BC) at the very beginning of Egyptian history, and continues with kings of the Old and Middle Kingdoms, down to the obscure Bocchoris (Bakenrenef) of Dynasty 24, who ruled over the Delta from ca. 720 to715 BC, Amasis of the Saïte period, and finally the Persian king Darius. Identifying a tradition of specific "lawgivers" in Egypt was probably Diodorus' "attempt to 'hellenize' an Egyptian institution for foreign consumption" (Redford 2001:136).[27] Redford argues that the concept of

[23] On Near Eastern codified law, Roth (1997); Bottero (1992); and the debate between Westbrook (1994) and Otto (1994).

[24] On the increased evidence for law codes in the first millennium BC, see Knoppers and Harvey (2007).

[25] This is a different use of the Greek word *nomothetai* than the standard definition in the context of Athenian law, where it refers to the legislators who reviewed and proposed changes to the laws.

[26] Redford (2001, 2004:81) rejects the tradition recorded by Diodorus out of hand.

[27] Cf. the remarks of Rütersworden (1995), who understands the tradition of Darius' codification of Egyptian law as an historical projection back from the Hellenistic period.

a "lawgiver" is not a legitimate aspect of Egyptian kingship. But as we have seen above, there is a strong tradition of kings, and officials, promulgating the law by decree or by other means. What is perhaps most striking in Diodorus' treatment of "lawgivers" is the complete absence of any Ptolemaic king from the list.

Much of what Diodorus tells us about the early lawgivers is rather innocuous. For him, just as for Herodotus, what was remarkable about Egyptian lawgivers was their "unusual and strange" customs. There is nothing in the Egyptian sources that directly attests to something resembling legislation, a systematic body of law, in the manner in which Diodorus conceives it, until the New Kingdom text known as the *Decree* or *Edict of Horemheb*, a royal decree erected prominently in the Karnak temple in Thebes, that reorganized state institutions, including the judiciary, and focused especially on abuse by state officials in the wake of the Amarna episode.[28]

> Now, as for any official or any priest (concerning whom) it shall be heard, saying: "He sits, to execute judgment among the official staff appointed for judgment, and he commits a crime against justice therein;" it shall be against him a capital crime. Behold, my majesty has done this, to improve the laws of Egypt, in order to cause that another should not be [. . . .]

> [Behold, my majesty appointed] the official staff of the divine fathers, the prophets of the temples, the officials of the court of this land and the priests of the gods who comprise the official staff out of desire that they shall judge the citizens of every city. My majesty is legislating for Egypt, to prosper the life of its inhabitants; when he appeared upon the throne of Re. Behold, the official staffs have been appointed in the whole land [. . .] all [. . .] to comprise the official staffs in the cities according to their rank. [29]

Throughout the decree, emphasis was placed on royal revenue and justice. This is of course not to say that no private law existed in Egypt. Quite the contrary. The use of written legal instruments to record all private legal agreements is well documented from the Old Kingdom period onward, although even in much later times when our documentation for legal practice is quite good, we cannot say conclusively that the use of written legal instruments was the norm.[30]

The organization of the Egyptian bureaucracy, which we can see was already elaborate by the end of the Old Kingdom, must have relied on

---

[28] On this decree, see Breasted (1906–1907/3:22–33).

[29] Translation of Breasted (1906–1907/32).

[30] A survey of later Egyptian written legal instruments may be found in Manning (2003b).

formal rules of procedure, whether written down and in that sense "codified" or not. Egyptian tradition is often passed on by what is called "instruction literature," typically couched as a father speaking to his son on
proper behavior in a variety of social and professional settings. The same
literary form existed within the Ptolemaic bureaucracy. To be sure, written documents conveying a set of rules of procedure are preserved in two
tombs of high officials of the New Kingdom who were responsible for the
administration of justice in Egypt. The text, known as the "Duties of the
Vizier," lays out in some detail expectations as to the performance of such
officials. It is indeed nothing less than a "code" of conduct for such high
officials (van den Boorn 1988). The traditions of codification per se in
Egypt, then, were extensive. The king could legislate, and the bureaucracy
could collect rules and norms of behavior. The traditional view of historians, however, is that such collections do not constitute law codes.

The question of what constitutes an ancient code has been among the
most intensely debated subjects in ancient law. The debate has revolved
around two main issues: the comprehensiveness of the code (for some, a
"true code" must be comprehensive), and whether the rules it contains
are prescriptive (Lindgren 1995:150, n. 3). In fact this understanding of
a legal "code" as a comprehensive or exhaustive treatment of the law,
often with the most extreme examples, the Code of Justinian or the *Code
civil* of Napoleon in mind, is too narrow.[31] There were many types of
codification in antiquity, and indeed even the briefest of examinations of
the well-known Near Eastern law "collections" shows that they are quite
heterogeneous.[32] For my purposes here, a written collection of rules or
norms fulfills the definition of a code, whatever the purposes for which it
was published. By this standard it is beyond doubt that the tradition of
collections of law extended far back into Egyptian history.[33] Egyptian examples need not have looked like Hammurabi's code. It is important to
keep in mind, however, that Hammurabi's code and the demotic Egyptian
texts discussed below have in common that they are, in their essence,
school texts.[34] In the former, the king's relationship to "law" is stressed,
whereas in the demotic collections, there is no royal presence.

What does the term *nomothêtai* used by Diodorus mean? The term
occurs in the context of Athenian law where it refers to a body of judges
whose job it was to accept or reject proposed changes or amendments to
existing law (MacDowell 1978:48–49). Diodorus clearly does not have
this technical usage in mind in his treatment of Egyptian law. His meaning

---

[31] Cf. Mélèze-Modrzejewski (1995:5).
[32] On the ancient Near Eastern tradition, see Roth (1997).
[33] Cf. Pestman (1983a); Mélèze-Modrzejewski (1995).
[34] On the Near Eastern codes, see Otto (1994); Roth (1997).

is rather a broad one, covering a range of royal activities, from abolishing existing laws to amending them to issuing very wise judgments.

As we have noted, the important reforms or compilations of the Egyptian legal system dating to the first millennium BC were, according to Diodorus, those of Bocchoris (Bakenrenef), Amasis, and Darius. Bocchoris, the founder and sole member of Dynasty 24, reigned for six years (720–715 BC) and controlled important cities in the Delta and the strategic town of Herakleopolis in Middle Egypt. He is credited by Diodorus not only with "craftiness" but also with specific changes to the law of written contracts. We cannot verify Diodorus' account here, and it is likely that the entire tradition is a fabrication for some specific purpose. Shifts in the language of contracts are certainly documented, however, particularly with the rise and spread of the Egyptian script known as demotic ca. 650 BC.[35] And during the Third Intermediate Period (1069–664) we can notice "practical developments towards a notary system and the professionalisation of legal procedures"(Eyre 2004:93).

The next king mentioned by Diodorus is the much more important historical figure Amasis (570–526 BC), the greatest king of the Saïte period during which time major political recentralization and major cultural changes took place in Egypt. Diodorus reports that Amasis' legal reforms consisted of rules governing the officials responsible for the administration of Egypt as a whole and those in charge of districts (nomes). The consolidation of the use of the demotic script throughout Egypt and the institution of a census were also of major achievements of Amasis' rule, though neither is mentioned by Diodorus.[36] In the broad sense, it seems beyond doubt that Amasis was a "lawgiver."

While Diodorus names Darius as a lawgiver, he does not attribute to him any specific reforms. Rather, the Persian king is contrasted with the "lawlessness" of his predecessor Cambyses, and is said to have studied theology with Egyptian priests, no doubt a nod for the careful treatment of Egyptian temples. More specific information about Darius' impact on local legal tradition in Egypt comes from an Egyptian source of the Ptolemaic period. The text is known as the *Demotic Chronicle* and its main subject is a series of proverbs that associate particular events with "good" and "bad" kings of Egypt. It has justifiably been compared to the *Book of Deuteronomy* (Assmann 2002:378–88, with literature).

On the verso of this text, mention is made of a letter that was sent by Darius to the Persian governor of Egypt requesting that there be assembled Egyptian priests, soldiers, and scribes to "write down the law of Egypt which had formerly been valid until the forty-fourth (i.e., the last)

---

[35] On Bocchoris as lawgiver, see Markiewicz (2008).
[36] See chapter 1, "Saïtes."

year of Amasis." It is telling that a commission of soldiers, scribes, and priests were assembled to inform the Persian king of existing law, a clear sign that the law was a consensus of the customs and norms of a variety of communities, and not established by the king. In other words, what Darius wanted was to record the customs and legal norms that existed just before the Persian conquest. He was not producing a unified, written code, nor new legislation, but rather a collection of prevailing customs and scribal usages derived from a variety of key groups, namely "priests, soldiers, and scribes."[37] The Persian king required this information (in writing) as an aid to the work of political consolidation.[38] This Persian practice of recording is also attested in the Old Testament *Book of Daniel* (6:8):

> O King, issue the ordinance and have it put in writing, so that it may be unalterable, for the law of the Medes and Persians stands forever.[39]

The process of collecting the legal traditions ordered by Darius, we are told, took sixteen years and resulted in a code of Egyptian law, divided into "public," "temple," and "private" law that was written down in demotic Egyptian and in Aramaic, the lingua franca of Persian administration.[40] It is this Persian act of "codification" that some scholars have seen as the model for the later Ptolemaic codification of law.[41] The image of the legal and political order that Darius' codification of Egyptian law presents, however, contrasts with the actual functioning of the legal system during his reign as we see it revealed in a well-known text, *The Petition of Petiese*, a rambling, remarkably detailed account by an elderly priest of his struggles to assert rights to a priestly office in the Amun temple at Teudjoi in Middle Egypt.[42]

Darius would seem to be the very model for the early Ptolemaic kings who wanted to root themselves firmly within the Egyptian traditions of

[37] Cf. Seidl (1968).

[38] The so-called "Frei thesis" of Persian "imperial authorization" of the Pentateuch is explored in Watts (2001); and for the codification of Egyptian law specifically, see therein the articles by Frei and Redford. For more recent treatments of this lengthy controversy, essentially a debate about the connection between royal power and local scribal traditions in the law, see *Zeitschrift für Altorientalische und biblische Rechtsgeschichte* 1 (1995); Schmid (2007) with an excellent summary of the literature. See also Knoppers and Harvey (2007).

[39] See further Bedford (2001).

[40] On Darius' "codification," see inter alia Reich (1933); Bresciani (1985); Mélèze-Modrzejewski (1995); Redford (2001).

[41] On Ptolemaic demotic "codes," and for strong arguments in favor of them being the result of Saite and Persian period codifications of law, see Lippert (2004a), and further below.

[42] For this text, see Griffith (1909); and the superb new edition of the text by Vittmann (1998). A good overview is provided by Ray (2002:97–112)

kingship, and to insert their dynasty into the *longue durée* of Egyptian history. What is fascinating, and perhaps telling, about Diodorus' account is that the Ptolemies are not mentioned at all. Indeed for Diodorus they are destroyers of the ancient social fabric (Diod. Sic. I 95.6). Diodorus' attitude can no doubt be attributed to his idealization of Egypt, Macedonian defeats at the hands of Rome, and the overall problems of first-century Egypt. The papyri, however, afford us a very different view of Ptolemaic legal evolution.

THE PTOLEMIES AS SHAPERS OF THE LAW

In the last chapter, we saw that the Ptolemies introduced new fiscal institutions that had profound and long-lasting effects on Egypt. The new economic system was codified in the specific sense that the kings, or their agents, issued written instructions of various kinds defining and clarifying expectations for those who had official functions in the economic sphere.[43] Ptolemaic governance also attempted to shape the law by decrees, administrative rulings (*prostagmata*), and in many other ways.[44] As I will outline below, however, in every area of legal activity, the Ptolemies acted well within the Egyptian tradition of royal sovereignty.

Local norms and scribal practice, deeply embedded in Egyptian society, as well as newer Greek traditions, were included in the new order.[45] There was very real need for the Ptolemies to reshape the law within their new sovereign state given the demographic diversity of its population, which while in large measure already in place before the Ptolemies, had now to compete for resources in the new world of the Ptolemaic economy.

New immigrant communities—Greeks, Jews, and others—brought their legal traditions with them to Egypt.[46] The two major systems of law that we know best, the Egyptian and Greek (a hybrid in this period), and the court systems that adjudicated the law of these traditions, were not

---

[43] The classic texts are *pRev.* and *pTebt.* 703. See above, Introduction, "Ptolemaic Egypt: Beyond Préaux and Rostovtzeff?" Rostovtzeff (1922:165–66) went too far, however, in suggesting that *pRev.* was a single "Codex . . . published by order of the king." See the comments by Bingen (1978a).

[44] They have been assembled and studied by Lenger (1964). On the weakness of the enforcement of Ptolemaic decrees, see Préaux (1936).

[45] On local law in pharaonic Egypt, Redford (2001:144); and Macdowell (1990) for the well documented New Kingdom village at Deir el-Medina, western Thebes.

[46] *pEleph.* 1, for example, is a Greek marriage contract, dated 310 BC (and therefore the earliest dated Greek document from Egypt) that preserves old Greek legal forms (e.g., "upon all property . . . both land and sea") and might well also preserve a Dorian Greek legal tradition. See further Porten and Farber (1996:408–10).

fused into one system but remained formally separate traditions.[47] That formal separation of legal traditions, which has tempted some scholars to view Ptolemaic society in toto as a kind of apartheid system, was breached every day by people living their lives in a multiethnic state.[48] The bilingual (Greek and demotic Egyptian) family archives from the period, provide ample testimony of persons choosing and utilizing two distinct legal traditions in contract forms and notarization. The reason for the selection of language, and presumably in some cases at least the selection of the applicable law, is not always clear to us. But that this had become common by the second century BC is shown by the royal decree (how effective it was is another question) mentioned above that attempted to redraw the jurisdictional lines between Greek and Egyptian law by deciding that the language of the contract should determine the court.[49] The flexibility in choice of contract was such that there was no concept of "legal personality" by which one's ethnicity determined the controlling law of contract.

The Ptolemaic state was particularly active in setting up legal regulations governing the economy, but there could be no formal separation between law and economics.[50] Indeed it is in the economic sphere, particularly with respect to revenue, that the Ptolemaic state most actively shaped the law. This is a tradition that, as we have seen, goes back at least to Horemheb. The organization of the court system and the adjudication of disputes were also major foci of Ptolemaic legal reform. The stratêgos, as the title suggests, was originally a military officer, but the responsibility of this official quickly gravitated to the resolution of disputes in the nomes.[51]

Other cases show that royal officials could also issue administrative decisions with the force of law and could sit jointly in judicial proceedings.[52] Clearly there existed a difference between the civic laws of the

[47] For the status of Greek law in the period, see Wolff (2002). On the concept of legal pluralism: Wolff (1960, 1998:38–41). Préaux (1978/2:587) rightly against Taubenschlag's (1955:27) thesis of a fusion into "Greco-Oriental" law. A basic summary of the differences between Greek and Egyptian law in the period may be found in Préaux (1978/2:590–94). On legal pluralism elsewhere in the Hellenistic world, see Van der Spek (1995) treating cuneiform law under the Seleukids. On the supposed "personality" doctrine, see Wolff (1966); Préaux (1978/2:595–98).

[48] Cf. the remarks of Wolff (1966:71).

[49] pTebt. I 5, 207–20.

[50] Paralleled by Seleukid policy. See the remarks of Van der Spek (1995:175)

[51] On the office and its evolution, see pHib. II 198 (ca. 240 BC) and the comments by Bagnall (1969).

[52] Fraser (1972:11), discussing pHal. 1 and the dioikêtês' letter concerning the remission of the salt tax for certain groups. Cf. Wolff (1962:178). On joint judicial proceedings with officials, see Samuel (1966b).

Greek cities in Egypt, which the king controlled directly, and Egyptian villages in which traditional norms and customs prevailed. Hence there was a difference in clarity between the law that governed citizens of the Greek cities in Egypt and those "Hellenes" living in other locations. In the area of civil, or private, agreements and transactions, the law was not imposed from above, but determined by the community. The king intervened in certain matters, above all those concerned with revenue. At other times, local law prevailed undisturbed.

PTOLEMAIC LEGISLATION

The Ptolemaic kings were heirs to several traditions: Egyptian law, of course; the assembly of legal traditions that played a fundamental part in Persian imperial governance; and, finally, the theoretical study of legal systems of the fourth century BC as described in the writings of Aristotle and his pupils, particularly Theophrastus—and indeed made reality by Demetrius of Phaleron.[53] The Greek cities were subject to both a separate body of civic law and to the royal edicts regulating behavior.[54] Selected passages of such a "civil code" for Alexandria are preserved in a document that probably furnished "justifications" (*dikaiomata*) for legal arguments in several legal disputes.[55] In other cases royal law pertaining to specific matters was promulgated via decrees and orders—*diagrammata* and *prostagmata*.[56] Ptolemaic law, however, was not instrumental. It did not seek to "release economic energy" as was, for example, the deliberate goal of nineteenth-century American law making (Hurst 1956).[57] Rather, Ptolemaic activity in the sphere of the law was intended to preserve the status quo and to assert sovereignty throughout Egypt.

The great historian of ancient law Hans Julius Wolff argued (1960: 209–10) that Ptolemy II Philadelphus was the principal reformer of the legal system. Like Turner (1984) who saw Philadelphus as the creator (and bankrupter) of the economic system, Wolff argued that Ptolemaic law was formed by a legislative act of this same king, ca. 275 BC. It was in his view, like the royal economy, the work of a single king. Ptolemy II's "legislation" (*diagramma*) organized the jurisdictions of the court sys-

---

[53] See Fraser (1972:108–15) on the background of Ptolemaic lawmaking.

[54] *pGurob* 2 (ca. 275 BC; = *CPJud*. I 19) is the main text.

[55] *pHal*. (= *Bagnall and Derow* text 124), a mid-third-century papyrus deriving from the opposite end of the country, Elephantine. The papyrus also contains other forms of law, such as a letter from Ptolemy to an official clarifying the procedure for the billeting of soldiers. The text requires a new study. It has been summarized by Fraser (1972:109–10).

[56] Fraser (1972:107); Lenger (1964); Müller (1968).

[57] On Willard Hurst as a legal historian, see Flaherty (1970).

tem around "Greek" and Egyptian law under the sovereignty of the king.
"The king's objective," Wolff concluded,

> in launching his project of judicial reform was not simply the organi-
> zation of a regular judiciary and the promulgation of a set of rules
> which would guide the courts and other authorities in their endeavor
> to secure the use of fair and orderly means by persons seeking ful-
> fillment of their private interests. He was striving to solidify into per-
> manent and normal government under the supreme authority of the
> king what up to then had hardly been more than a machinery de-
> signed for mere economic exploitation and backed by nothing but
> the power of the armed forces, as far as the native population was
> concerned, and purely personal bonds of military command and alle-
> giance, as regarded the alien element.

While the third century as a whole was probably characterized by a series
of gradual changes as the state responded to a dynamic social environment, the documentary and literary evidence for the reign of Ptolemy II
does tend to the conclusion that major attempts at judicial reforms were
made, and that these were, almost certainly, related to structural reforms
of the economy, including the introduction of the salt tax, the use of status
designations in contracts, and the land reclamation project in the Fayyum,
among others. War, both direct and by proxy, was endemic in these years
and may well have been a major driver in reshaping the state.[58]

Whether the attempt at systemization recorded in the *diagramma* occurred on one occasion or over the course of many years is unclear. As in
certain areas of economic reform, however, there is little doubt that the
reign of Ptolemy II saw the beginnings of serious attempts at organizing
law. Two caveats are in order. First, we must remain cautious, for reasons
I have laid out, about assigning the reforms exclusively to one king, let
alone to this one king specifically. Second, we must also guard against
understanding the process of creating state economic and legal institutions as happening over a short span of time. It seems more likely that
state reforms were gradual.[59] When it comes to Ptolemy II, we may be
easily misled by the abundance of material dating to his reign.[60] Like all

[58] Cf. Thompson (forthcoming); Fischer (2008). For the First and Second Syrian Wars
(274–271 BC and 260–253? BC) against the Seleukids in particular, see Heinen (1984). On
the "ubiquity" of war in the Hellenistic period generally, see Chaniotis (2005:5–12).

[59] *pHibeh* II 198 (242 BC, reign of Ptolemy III) preserves a decree that organizes judicial
competence. Cf. *pMich Zenon* 70 (237 BC).

[60] Earlier treatments of Ptolemy II's activity are Lenger (1964) and Müller (1968). Specific
actions associated with the reign of Ptolemy II abound, e.g., legislation on slavery, on which
see Müller (1968:70–86). It is perhaps also connected to the *diagramma*.

kings, he would of course have wanted to project an image of order in whatever documents he did issue, regardless of the true situation. [61]

Ptolemy II's legislation, as reconstructed by Wolff from citations in various secondary texts, treated legal procedure as well as substantive law. Some of the citations refer to quite detailed points of law. The aim of this legislation seems have been primarily to furnish "a code of instructions concerning the activities of the courts" (Wolff 1960:220), and the dual nature of the Greco-Egyptian judiciary was a "conscious" effort (Wolff 1966:75). Of course, it must be added that from the point of view of society, the king had little choice but to observe what was already in existence.

Ptolemy II's main activity was to organize the judiciary along the following lines. He created three separate courts and a hierarchy of laws that subordinated Greek and Egyptian law to royal law. *Dikastêria* courts heard cases of Greek-speaking parties. The *chrêmatistai*, a court that represented royal authority and grew to be the main state court by the second century, heard cases on an ad hoc basis. The *laokritai*, composed of Egyptian priests, heard cases involving Egyptians. And a fourth court, the *koinodikion*, only attested during the third century (and then not very well), adjudicated cases involving Greeks and Egyptians through equity.[62] For the Jewish population, Mélèze-Modrzejewski argues (1995:8–10), probably correctly, the *Septuagint* translation of the *Torah* became the body of law in Egypt.[63] By the end of the second century, however, the language of legal documents was beginning to replace the ethnicity of the parties involved as the determinant of the court of jurisdiction.[64]

Ptolemy's "legislation" also deferred to "equity" in cases where the *diagramma* did not specify substantive law, a practice that came directly out of the Athenian system.[65] On the whole the function of royal involvement was to establish the legal traditions that would be enforced, to establish courts and their jurisdictions, and to publicize the legal procedures of the state, the roles of officials, and so on. What happened in the legal sphere is, therefore, analogous to the economic instructions issued in the mid-third century, which put particular rules in place all the while adapt-

---

[61] In some cases, the concern with order may stem from the state's reaction to very poor Nile flooding and the subsequent chaos that this invariably caused. So Turner (1984:158) in discussing *pHib*. II 198. This would have been a very ancient concern of kingship.

[62] On the development of the Ptolemaic courts, see above all Wolff (1962, 2002:84–85); Mélèze-Modrzejewski (1995, forthcoming).

[63] The tradition, largely formed on the basis of the *Letter of Aristeas*, is that the *Septuagint* was written in the third century BC, and specifically at the request of Ptolemy II. This is a much-debated point. On the state of the debate, see Mélèze-Modrzejewski (1995); Pearce (2007); van der Kooij (2007).

[64] *pTebt*. I 5, 207–220; Pestman (1985b); Wolff (2002:85–86).

[65] Aristot., *Pol*. III.1282b. See the discussion by LeFebvre (2006:156, n. 37).

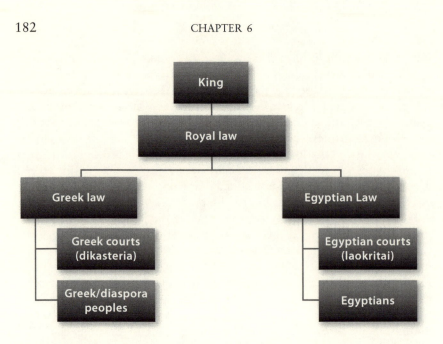

Figure 12. A hierarchical model of the sources of law in the Ptolemaic system. Adapted from LeFebvre (2006:159).

ing to preexisting traditions.[66] In Egyptian law, for example, informal dispute outside of the *laokritai* courts continued to take place, seemingly without state interference. A common type of demotic text known as a "temple oath" shows that local disputes could also be adjudicated in the context of a local temple.[67] The king, then, as in the economy, played a central, coordinating role in creating a "cognitive framework," while leaving much in place.

Ptolemaic "legislation" raises important issues about the origin of law. It has, as I have already indicated, often been viewed through the lens of legal centralism, with an emphasis on codes and rules arising from the command, or "legislation," of the sovereign (Figure 12). In fact, however, the king's "legislation" aligned with the interests of the ruling coalitions. The *diagramma*, with respect to private Egyptian law, was probably no more than a confirmation of preexisting law, comparable to the Persian "codification" of Egypt's legal structures.

Unlike the Persian "codification," however, the Ptolemaic *diagramma* with respect to Egyptian law, appears to have been far more wide-

---

[66] See above, Introduction, "Ptolemaic Egypt: Beyond Préaux and Rostovtzeff?"

[67] On temple oath texts, see Kaplony-Heckel (1963). Many such texts have been published since Kaplony-Heckel's fundamental study. Temples as locations of trials: Quaege-

ranging, although as Wolff (1960:20) correctly stressed, Ptolemaic activity was not an attempt at a comprehensive overhaul. It did not, for instance, tamper with existing private law or procedure. The presentation of legal custom in the guise of royal legislation was in keeping with pharaonic tradition. As we have seen, a major part of this new legislation was concerned with the rules of procedure and of enforcement, and therefore focused on the court systems. Wolff noted, however, that there are references in the literature to some aspects of substantive law, and this suggested to him that the Ptolemies were aiming to create an *integrated system* of law.[68] This stretches the evidence too far. We do not in fact know if the Ptolemies had any long-term interest in placing Egyptian courts under Ptolemaic sovereignty, outside of monitoring them. We do know that Egyptian and Greek law never merged. There was no Ptolemaic law.[69] What the Ptolemaic kings aimed at here, just as in the translation into Greek of the *Torah*, was clarity and predictability.[70] Whether this legislation was the work of Ptolemy II alone or, more likely in my view, part of a longer iterative process between the king acting within Greco-Egyptian society (Figure 13) over the course of the third century, it is clear that early Ptolemaic reforms reflected important changes in society.[71]

Those social changes were driven by fiscal changes and by the new bureaucratic structure that, over time, took over the judicial functions originally defined by early Ptolemaic kings, and by the evolution of society itself. We see the transition completed in the second-century case discussed above in which the plaintiff Herieus, or the scribe who wrote his petition, citing a specific section of the *diagramma*, not Egyptian law directly; it would moreover be a government official and not a tribunal of priests who would decide Herieus' case. An appeal to Ptolemaic officials to settle a local dispute may also have been prompted by the desire for a quicker path to "adjudication" by the application of the administrative rules laid out in the *diagramma*. But there is a stronger reason. Just as in the second-century Asyut inheritance dispute, the initial instinct of the complainant was to petition the *stratêgos* although it was quite a local

---

beur (1993). Priests as judges: el-Aguizy (1988); Manning (2003a:204). On pharaonic law courts, see Allam (1991).

[68] Wolff (1960:216) already qualified his remarks by stating: "It was not of course a 'system' in the sense of a unified body of coordinated institutions equal in rank. . . . The private law system of Ptolemaic Egypt was rather a combination of several complexes of legal norms, with each complex belonging to a definite sphere where under certain conditions the precepts comprised in it had the force of binding rules."

[69] That point is forcefully made by Wolff himself (1966).

[70] For the various theories behind the Greek translation of the Pentateuch, see van der Kooij (2007).

[71] Cf. Wolff (1960:206).

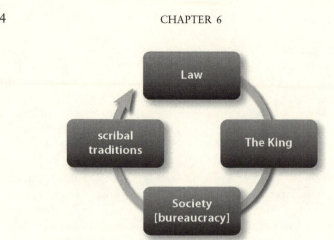

Figure 13. A "law and society" model of the evolution of Ptolemaic law. Cf. Swedberg (2003:191) discussing Friedman (1975).

matter. An initial appeal to the Ptolemaic bureaucracy (before being sent back to the local Egyptian court), may have been an attempt at obtaining a fair hearing by a neutral party, or it may have been done in hopes that the enforcement of an eventual ruling might be swifter under state than local authority.[72] The presence in the Egyptian court of a state official, the *eisagogeus*, also indicates state bureaucratic supervision; but we need not, with Wolff (1960:211), assume that this was the original intention of the early Ptolemaic legislation. By the second century, Egyptian society had evolved, and there was no longer a clear-cut distinction between Greek and Egyptian law based on court jurisdiction.

CODIFICATION OF EGYPTIAN LAW UNDER THE PTOLEMIES?

The published evidence for collections of legal rules and the proper forms for documents written in demotic is confined to the Ptolemaic period, most of these dated to the third century BC. These texts raise many questions, some of which we cannot answer. Were they, for example, the result of Saïte reforms and Persian "imperial authorization," or part of an older independent legal tradition, or were they perhaps generated more directly by Ptolemaic efforts at systemization? Are these texts, fragmentary though they may be, evidence of fuller codification of law?

The most important of these texts is the so-called *Hermopolis Legal Code* (= *pMattha*). Since its discovery in 1938–39 "in a partially broken

[72] On the Asyut case, see Appendix.

Text	Origin	Date
pBerl. 23757 recto[a]	Akhmim	late 3rd century BC(?)
Codex "S"[b]	Hermopolis Magna(?)	late 3rd/early 2nd century BC[c]
pCarlsb. 236[d]	?	3rd century BC
pCarlsb. 301 + pFlorence[e]	Tebtunis	Late Ptolemaic/Early Roman
pBerl. 23890a-b, d-g recto[f]	Fayyum (Soknopaiou Nesos?)	1st century BC
pCarlsb. 628[g]	Tebtunis?	Mid-Ptolemaic

Figure 14. Published demotic legal collections from the Ptolemaic and Roman periods.

Sources: [a]Lippert (2004a). See also Stadler (2004); [b]= pBerl. 13621a-d + pCairo 50108a + b recto+ pGießen UB 101.3 II–IV, VIb, VII recto. For this text, now split between three collections, see Mrsich (1984); Lippert (2003); [c]For the date, based on paleography, see Lippert (2003:94); [d]Tait (1991); [e]Bresciani (1981); Chauveau (1991); [f]Lippert (2004b:389–403); [g]Lippert (2004b:403–04).

jar in the debris of a ruined building opposite the room of mummification" (Mattha 1975:xi) at Hermopolis and its subsequent publication in 1975, the Hermopolis code has received much attention among scholars of demotic Egyptian.[73] In its surviving fragmentary state, the text is written in ten columns. It is dated by paleography to the early Ptolemaic period, usually to the reign of Ptolemy II. A mathematical treatise is written on the verso. The milieu for the creation of such a text has been supposed to have been a "house of life"—a temple scriptorium where important books on religion and traditional learning were copied. (Quaegebeur 1982).

A Greek papyrus (pOxy. 3285) from the second century AD shows marked similarities to the Hermopolis text, and it is clearly a translation of it. The original of the Greek version is certainly to be sought in the Ptolemaic period, and perhaps, like pMattha, in the reign of Ptolemy II. Its survival into the Roman period shows that Egyptian law, in its translated Greek form, continued to survive.[74] The Greek translation of an

[73] The *editio princeps* of the text is Mattha and Hughes (1975). It has been updated with some corrections by Donker van Heel (1990), who also provides a bibliography. Grunert's (1982) study provides a translation of the Hermopolis text and translations of other Ptolemaic legal documents as illustrations of Egyptian law in the Ptolemaic period.

[74] pCarlsb. 236 is the 44th column of a second century AD demotic text from Tebtunis, suggesting a massive compilation of Egyptian law.

Egyptian body of law, whether "authorized" by a Ptolemaic king or not, was the result of the adjudication of Egyptian law within a Greek bureaucratic context. The use of Greek versions of local law is well documented in the famous Hermias dispute discussed below.

The surviving text of *pMattha*, 80 percent of which is concerned with rights in real property and 20 percent with inheritance law (Johnson 1994:157, n. 33), covers the following specific areas of law:

Lease of arable land and lessor/lessee disputes
Return of a mortgaged house
Lease of houses/other property
Collection of the remainder of the purchase price of a house
The law of annuities
The method of asserting rightful title
The use of force against another's property
Hindering others from building on private property
Litigation between neighbors
Inheritance/rights of an oldest son[75]

There are clearly some organizational legal principles suggested here: leases, sales, legal title, inheritance rules. There can be little doubt that the rules collected in the text had real force in Ptolemaic times, although some of the passages preserve unusual or at least difficult cases rather than normative ones.[76] The emphasis on property rights in the text preserves the Egyptian tradition, but it contrasts to some degree with the Ptolemaic realities of access to land (Bingen 1984).

There has been vigorous debate about the nature of this text, whether it is in fact a code similar to the Near Eastern codes, a legal commentary, a "manual" (Mélèze-Modrzejewski 1995:5) used by judges to decide cases, or a collection "written as a guide to good practice" (Eyre 2004:94).[77] The original editors of the text understood it as merely one part of a "great code" yet to be discovered.

The text as we have it outlines various procedures and presents boilerplate legal forms, contracts, oaths, and so on. The grammar style of the text suggests general rules or legal customs that should be followed. I give here a representative sample:

---

[75] Caution is required in making overall conclusions about what the text covered in toto since it is only partially preserved.

[76] Ritner (2004:498–501); Mélèze-Modrzejewski (1995:6).

[77] See the summary of the debate and the literature on the Hermopolis text by Mélèze-Modrzejewski (1995:5). A new demotic compilation and discussion of the issue may be found in Lippert (2004a).

DOCUMENT FORM

If a man acquires land and if a lease is made for him to ensure its being clear for him, <this is> a form for the lease which shall be made:"A has said to B, ' You have leased to me such-and such land. . . .'[78]

RULES OF PROCEDURE

If a man makes a lease concerning the fields, and if the owner of the fields gives him seed-corn, and if the man who made the lease does not till the fields, and if he takes (or 'gets') the seed-corn after the fields have been inundated and are enriched, he is required to give the harvest from the seed-corn according to the lease he made.[79]

This genre of text, in some respects, resembles what is called a *Restatement of Law* in the modern American legal system. The collection of rules and acceptable forms of contract, although lacking the legal analysis of modern *Restatements*, clarified the law, and could be used by scribes and judges as an aid in deciding cases, and by students as well. In some cases these collections may have served as school texts of a kind to educate judges and the scribes who drew up legal documents.[80] They are, thus, authoritative without necessarily being authorized by the king himself, and they bear strong similarities to Near Eastern legal collections.[81] What we cannot know, given the fragmentary nature of the text, is how much of Egyptian law the text originally covered.

Such "restatements" might explain the context in which these Ptolemaic period demotic legal collections were used. It has been argued, however, that they derive from an older tradition. Pestman, for example, believes (1983a) that the Hermopolis text is merely a Ptolemaic copy of a text that originated in the eighth century BC during the reign of king Bocchoris, one of Diodorus' supposed "lawgivers." Others have wanted to connect the text to the tradition of Darius' "codification" of Egyptian law. But the text as we have it certainly dates to the third century BC, as do at least three other similar demotic collections of legal statements. The case for an earlier date of composition is based on three incomplete dates in the papyrus that may refer back to a date between 645 and 582 BC, a reference to a pre-Persian form of marriage contract (Johnson 1994:157) and, in a few places in the text, archaic orthography. Others have argued

---

[78] *pMatha* II 27–28. Trans. a composite from Donker van Heel (1990:21).

[79] *pMattha* II 9–10. Trans. a composite from Donker van Heel (1990:13).

[80] *pBerl.* 23757 and *pCarlsb.* 301, Lippert (2004a:173–74). It is perhaps, then, no coincidence that the verso of *pMattha* contains a mathematical treatise, as Lippert points out.

[81] Roth (1997:4).

forcefully that texts such as *pMattha* were written in the Ptolemaic period and reflect current law.[82] These are not mutually exclusive ideas.

We cannot, at the moment, connect any of the Ptolemaic demotic "restatements" to the early Ptolemaic legal reforms, and none of the demotic collections mention the Ptolemies by name. If we are correct in believing that the early Ptolemaic kings, or even Ptolemy II specifically, "reauthorized," that is formally accepted local Egyptian legal norms as positive law, it seems logical that such a process would have put pressure on the scribes who drew up legal documents and adjudicated disputes to set down in writing their customary forms and procedures.

In his treatment of legal reforms, it is interesting to note that Diodorus does not mention the Ptolemies as lawgivers other than to disparage changes wrought after the Macedonian conquest:

> The system, then, of law used throughout the land was the work, they say, of the men just named, and gained a renown that spread among other peoples everywhere; but in later times, they say, many institutions which were regarded as good were changed, after the Macedonians had conquered and destroyed once and for all the kingship of the native line. (Diod. Sic. I 95.6, Trans. Oldfather).

This is a rather harsh critique of Ptolemaic rule, and was no doubt colored by the author's own feelings and by the actualities of late Ptolemaic times, which, by all accounts, were difficult both politically and economically.[83] Diodorus' years in Egypt, between 60 and 56 BC, were not happy ones. Documents both before and after this time make clear that there were serious agricultural problems: communication lapses in the administration, flight from the land, and crop failure, culminating apparently in 48 BC, when the historian Pliny the Elder (*HN* V.58) noted the lowest flood level known to him (7.5 feet), no doubt part of a longer and unpleasant trend. But as I have just outlined, the Ptolemies not only maintained many of the ancient legal institutions, they were also quite involved in the law at both the state and the local level.

The evolution of interaction between the state and local levels of society can be traced in the social relationships documented in "private order contracts." Persian period animal sales (Cruz-Uribe 1985), and "abnormal hieratic" contracts (Donker van Heel 1995) from Thebes show that Ptolemaic private legal instruments evolved directly out of two earlier Egyptian scribal traditions. A late fourth-century contract for the sale of a house in Thebes, for example, already shows a fully developed Ptolemaic

---

[82] Mrsich (1984:256–57).

[83] He may have harbored a more general dislike of the Ptolemies. On Diodorus' attitude, see Murray (1970).

demotic instrument of sale, of a somewhat archaic type (in its use of so-called "witness copy."[84] The centralizing tendencies of the Saïte and Ptolemaic periods did not displace local traditions. The language of contracts was not uniform in time or place, and there are ancient contractual clauses in the boilerplate of Ptolemaic legal texts.[85]

Ptolemaic demotic documents do show some differences in form from earlier contracts. Private law, and the law of private contracts, however, "remained mostly outside of the orbit of statute law to the end of the Ptolemaic period and beyond" (Wolff 1966:69). What changes there were in contract forms were in large measure due to the state's interest in the registration and the taxation of transactions. The dating formula at the beginning of Ptolemaic demotic private contracts, for example, utilizes an elaborate version of the standard dating protocol (Year X, month Y, day Z of King A) based on the reigning monarch, but with the important addition of the names of Ptolemaic dynastic priests. The first important change in the form of the contracts involves the specification of the day on which the contract was made.[86] Before 186 BC the day of the month was not specified in demotic contracts; after 186 the day's date was required. This additional detail in contracts is symptomatic of an increased specificity in documentation that can be seen elsewhere in the Ptolemaic system and probably goes back to fiscal reforms of Ptolemy II associated with registration and the use of tax receipts (Clarysse and Thompson 2006/1:18).[87] Some demotic contracts, for example, have full physical descriptions of the parties involved, a more regular feature of Greek contracts.[88]

Another distinctive feature of Ptolemaic demotic sales instruments is that they typically consisted of two separate documents, a document of "sale" acknowledging the receipt of a satisfactory price, and a quitclaim stating that all rights to the property have been conveyed to the new owner. These agreements were often written side by side on the same piece of papyrus, but nonetheless were quite distinct in legal conception. This "split" sale and quitclaim evolved out of an earlier form of single document. As with mortgages, which used the form of a sales contract to pledge property, the Ptolemaic split sale may have developed to provide

---

[84] *pTeos* 1 (326 BC), published by Depauw (2000:77–109).

[85] Cf. the remarks comparing early demotic legal contracts with Ptolemaic examples in Vleeming (1991:147).

[86] This is perhaps not a change at all. Earlier cursive hieratic, as opposed to early demotic texts, did write out the day of the month.

[87] On the introduction of day dates in Egyptian contracts, see Manning (2003a:211).

[88] Clarysse (1991:49–55). For the demotic texts, all from the second-century Theban area, see Mairs and Martin (forthcoming).

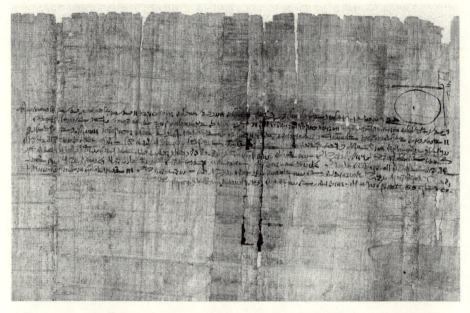

Figure 15. A Ptolemaic demotic marriage contract (*pHearst* 6, formerly pBMFA 38–2063a, published by Parker [1963]). The text comes from Dendera and is dated 2 February 186 BC. It is significant that the dating protocol is expressed in terms of Ptolemy V Epiphanes, as the text marks the restoration of Ptolemaic control over Upper Egypt after the Theban revolt (206–187 BC) was put down. During the revolt the drawing up of legal instruments in the name of the king was temporarily halted in the south.

Note: E.g., *pCarnavon* 2 (203 BC, Theban region) is dated year 4 of Haronnophris, one of the rebel kings who controlled the Theban region from 206 to 187 BC.

more flexibility in the use of property, the definition of which became more secure during the Saïte period.

There are other notable features of Ptolemaic contracts. The standard demotic sale contained a list of sixteen witnesses written on the verso of the document, testifying to the agreement. Earlier Egyptian contracts had eight or even four witnesses. By around 200 BC, the use of what is called a "witness copy contract," a verbatim copy of the contract written out by some of the witnesses as an act of attesting to the accuracy of the agreement, became obsolete.[89] The abandonment of this ancient instrument may be related to the state's requirement that private agreements be registered through state notaries. The state was becoming

[89] Depauw (1999).

a third party to the transaction, as we shall see below. It would be difficult to understand how otherwise to account for such a change in scribal practice. But once again, the change results from adjustments in economic realities and the need for predictability. The proper witnessing of private agreements was critical when it came time to enforce those agreements, as both the Asyut probate dispute and the trial of Hermias (below) show, where improper witnessing of contracts played a role in the disputes and their resolution.

We note also a rapid and systematic decline in the use of certain types of contract forms such as the "double document," in which the contents of the contract are written twice, once at the top of the instrument, impressed with a seal to protect the integrity of the text; and then a second time beneath the first. Around 120 BC, the upper, or "inner" text began to have only an abstract of the contents, another modification likely explained by the new state policy on notarizing private agreements.[90] In both cases, the change in contract forms came from the state's interest in regulating and enforcing private agreements, and, we presume, in the interest of creating revenue, in this case for the local state records offices.

RECEIPTS AND REGISTRATION

The issuance of receipts and the registration of private agreements was an important aspect of Ptolemaic legal procedure. We have already discussed tax receipts and their probable function within the economy. There the Ptolemies appear to have continued and extended an ancient tradition. Another example of such an extension is the use of receipts of payment to workers. In the case of Egyptian workers and Greek supervisors, the receipts were written in both Greek and Egyptian so that the text could be understood by both parties, and then sealed with an impression by the workmen and kept by the payer.[91]

The existence of official registers to record documents such as land records goes far back into Egyptian history. In pharaonic times it was the vizier who supervised the deposit of important documents in official archives. We know that private agreements were registered by the Third Intermediate period, a practice perhaps tied to the collection of the sale tax (Muhs 2005a:19). Our knowledge of early Ptolemaic state practices is scanty due to the paucity of records, but it seems likely that by the end of the third century state records offices were receiving and recording private agreements. By the reign of Ptolemy II, Greek subscripts added to

---

[90] On the double document: Pestman (1968); Yiftach-Firanko (2008).
[91] On such texts, see the discussion by Vandorpe (1996).

demotic sale contracts from Upper Egypt (Thebes[92] and Edfu[93]), Memphis,[94] and in the Fayyum (Hawara[95]) note that text has been "deposited in the box," perhaps a reference to the official registration of the contract. Here again the function of registration appears to have been tied to the collection of the sale tax.[96] In addition to being notarized, private demotic contracts were also recorded in registers. A third century demotic register illustrates an advanced recording system:

> Day 21: a document of division of a third share of an empty plot . . . made by. . . . Day 22: a lease of one aroura of land . . . made by so-and-so, whose mother is. . . .[97]

Even private receipts are noted in this fascinating if fragmentary text, which shows us also that such records of private agreements, better known from the early Roman period, were already kept in the third century BC. Notary offices also seem to have been involved in the enforcement of loan agreements, as in some cases loans are not only registered as made, but also as repaid. As far as the evidence permits us to say, there does not appear to have been bureaucratic uniformity in how private agreements were registered.[98] Occasionally, for example, red stamps were used as a means of authentication on some Greek contracts, bank receipts, and petitions.[99] While contracts written in Greek were drawn up and recorded according to a different tradition, there were some Ptolemaic innovations. Notary scribes, called *agoranomoi*, are attested by the third century, though they are best known from mid-second century documents from the Pathyrite nome (from 141 BC at Krokodilopolis, and by 136 at a branch of the Krokodilopolis office in Pathyris).[100] Contracts notarized by these scribes replace older forms of contracts that required witnesses and,[101] as noted above, these public scribes may have played a role in the development of Egyptian contracts, obviating the need for the ancient Egyptian system of recording private agreements with sixteen wit-

---

[92] *pPhila.* 14 (264 BC).

[93] *pHausw.* 2 (240 BC).

[94] *PLeiden* I 379.

[95] e.g., *pChicHawara* 9 (239 BC; Hughes and Jasnow 1997: 52–58)

[96] Muhs (2005a:20).

[97] *pSorb* inv. 264 + 265 (Ghoran, Fayyum), de Cenival (1987),

[98] It is clear that there is some amount of regional variation in scribal traditions. At Pathyris and Krokodilopolis, the notary office is called the *archeion*; on which see Vandorpe (2004).

[99] Vandorpe (1996:254–55).

[100] E.g., *pHib.* I 29. On these scribes, see Seidl (1962:62–63); Pestman (1985c); Vandorpe (2000c), with previous literature, and (2004).

[101] The Greek "six-witness agreements." See Wolff (1978:571).

nesses (this though private demotic agreements continued to be written throughout the third and second centuries). An important observation about these scribes is that despite the fact that such contracts are written in Greek, on high quality papyrus, and the scribes have Greek names, the scribes that Pestman (1985c) has studied were Egyptians. A *public* state system, with Egyptian scribes involved, was encroaching on earlier *private* scribal traditions.

In 145 BC, an administrative order was published that required demotic instruments to be registered in order to be valid, that summaries in Greek of the contents of such agreements to be made alongside the demotic text, and that another summary in Greek and Egyptian be deposited in the records office.[102] A recently published register of contracts from the agoranomic office in Pathyris dated to 110 BC, however, contains complete copies of agreements, minus the dating protocol, not just abstracts.[103] We cannot be certain, given the current state of the evidence, whether such public notary documents were designed to replace an earlier system of registering demotic Egyptian contracts, or were merely an attempt to make the system more uniform.[104]

It is the case that demotic begins to decline as a language of contract in the second half of the second century BC.[105] At some point in the second century (it would be nice to be able to fix an exact date but we cannot), a notice went out to recruit scribes who could write demotic contracts and to fix the fees for drawing up such contracts.[106]

The Adjudication of "Ptolemaic" Law

The workings of the parallel court system that determined jurisdiction of adjudication by the language of case documents can be clearly seen in a later Ptolemaic decree sorting out jurisdictional boundaries of contractual agreements written in Greek and Egyptian.[107] The ancient system of property rights, inheritance, and contracting was left largely intact but, like the Egyptian temples, these institutions were gradually incorporated into the state system through the medium of the Greek language.

The record of a mid-second-century trial held before priest-judges of the local temple (the *laokritai* court) in the Upper Egyptian town of Asyut

---

[102] *pPar.* 65; analyzed by Pestman (1985c). Note that the agoranomic register from Pathyris dated to 110 BC records copies of contracts, not just abstracts of them.

[103] Vandorpe (2004).

[104] Cf. the comments of Muhs (2005:21).

[105] Manning (2003a:173–77).

[106] *pRyl.* IV 572, 30–64.

[107] *pTebt.* I 5 (118 BC).

Figure 16. A Greek translation of a demotic contract, *pTebt*. I 164 (Kerkeosiris, Fayyum, 112 BC). On the basis of the handwriting, Verhoogt (1998:51) has suggested that the text is a scribal exercise.

(Appendix), is an important record of an Egyptian trial proceeding. It demonstrates very well that the Ptolemies maintained the Egyptian legal institutions of marriage and property rights through the local, traditional institutional structures. At the same time, the dispute and its resolution also demonstrate that Egyptian legal trials were regulated and monitored by the Ptolemaic state.[108] In fact the most important aspects of the Asyut case are that it began with a petition to the Ptolemaic *stratêgos*, and that the entire process was monitored by state agents. There is also ample evidence of state involvement in Upper Egyptian legal proceedings. The Ptolemaic state monitored both the Greek and the Egyptian judiciary. Ptolemaïs, the administrative center of the district and the seat of the *chrêmatistai*, ultimately played a dominant role as a clearing-house for legal petitions that came from throughout Upper Egypt, especially from soldiers residing in the south.[109] Even a dispute involving two sides of an Upper Egyptian family that began with a petition to state officials residing in Ptolemaïs, was, after its resolution by a local tribunal, heard again on appeal by priest-judges at Ptolemaïs.[110]

On two occasions during the dispute proceedings, sections of presumably codified law are cited. The plaintiff refers to a general law pertaining to Egyptian marriage practice:

> Now it is written in the law of year 21 that if a man marries a woman and he has a son with her, and he divorces her, and he marries another woman, and he writes for her an endowment deed, and he has a son with her, and the said man dies, (as for) his property—it is to the children of the first wife for whom he wrote the first endowment deed that it is given.

The term used for "law" in the citation of the law was the Egyptian word *ḥp*, which as we have seen has a wide array of meanings. Wolff (1960:212–13) argued that the law cited here was not part of Ptolemaic *diagramma* but part of an earlier Egyptian codification.[111] The *diagramma*, Wolff argued, was set out to govern the non-Egyptian population. In the case of the Tebtunis property dispute with which I began this

---

[108] Cf. Wolff (1962:48–53).

[109] Abd el-Ghani (2001:23).

[110] One might compare *pVindob* G 60499 (mid-second century BC), a request to the local *stratêgos* from an Egyptian "royal farmer," asking the official to intervene in a private lawsuit with another Egyptian by postponing a trial before the local Egyptian tribunal, the *laokritai*. See further La'da and Papathomas (2003). This was clearly a case, though, of administrative procedure rather than adjudicating law. Cf. Samuel (1966b).

[111] So also Seidl (1962:7), who suggests an underlying pharaonic law, perhaps reformulated into demotic here: "*Die Sprache deutet wohl auf einen Ptolemäerkönig, doch kann es sein, daß dieser Recht, das schon in der Perserzeit in Geltung war, in eine neue Form ge-*

chapter, an Egyptian cited not Egyptian law in its Egyptian form, but the *diagramma* (Wolff 1960:221). The reason was that it was standard procedure for private parties seeking the resolution of a dispute to petition state officials, at least initially, and it would have been easier to cite the law in its Ptolemaic, Greek form. In the Asyut trial, the law cited was stated in demotic, perfectly reasonable given the Egyptian context of the court.

It is clear that the reference to a "law of year 21" refers to the reign of a king. There is no reason to exclude the possibility that it refers specifically to a regnal year of a Ptolemy, although most have assumed that we are dealing with the citation of an ancient Egyptian legal source. Nor can we altogether exclude the possibility that the "law" referred to is a demotic Egyptian law created under the Ptolemies. There is a second citation of Egyptian law in the trial, the "sixth paragraph law" (at the very end of Tefhape's response, which some have interpreted as a reference to codified law, a "pharaonic code of old" (Wolff 1960:213), although as we have seen there is no evidence for any such a document (unless we accept Darius' "codification").[112]

Whether we take the citation in the Asyut case as a referring to the *diagramma* or to earlier Egyptian law, there are other examples to demonstrate the wide-ranging and long lasting effects of the Ptolemaic organization of Egypt's legal system. Consider the case of two Jewish litigants, a man and a woman, from the Fayyum (dated 226 BC).[113] The man sues the woman before the local Greek court at Krokodilopolis for insulting him in public, for tearing his cloak and causing monetary damages. The man did not appear in court in the end, but the woman filed among her documents in response to the suit a section of the *diagramma* stipulating that the failure of a plaintiff to appear would result in the automatic dismissal of the case.

The most important Ptolemaic text illustrating an attempt by the state to reestablish legal rules on a systematic scale is a royal decree promulgated at the end of the most serious civil war of the period.[114] The document is in fact a series of decrees that attempt to reaffirm preexisting law and social order. The decrees are termed in the text "benefactions," when

---

bracht hat. Ja, wir können nicht einmal ausschließen, daß der Grundgedanke dieses Zitats nicht schon aus dem NR kommt. Der echt ägyptische Charakter dieses Gesetzes ist nicht zu bezweifeln." Cf. Lippert (2004:170), viewing the citation as part of a larger work: " . . . *nicht ein einzelnes Gesetz, sondern ein ganzes Faszikel einer Gesetzsammlung mit den in diesem Jahr erlassenen Gesetzen."*

[112] Perhaps Diodorus Siculus' I.75 reference to "eight volumes of law refers to the same code.

[113] *pPetr.* II 219 + *pGurob* 2 (=*CPJud* I 19).

[114] *pTebt.* I 5 (= *C.Ord.Ptol* 53). Translation and literature in Austin (2006, text 290).

in fact what is being decreed are concessions to various social groups: the remission of taxes, privileges granted to royal workers, and the recognition of the Egyptian clergy as a key component of the state. Many of the ordinances in fact simply repeat earlier rules.[115] The "amnesty decree," as it is called, shows massive confusion in the taxation system and in the functioning of official state office holders. "Networks competing with the king for the revenues of the arable land and for its resources of manpower and goods" were, according to Bingen (1984:199) the by-product of the Ptolemaic policy of promoting organizations that competed with each other. As Bingen goes on to point out, it was not strictly speaking a matter of Greek against Egyptian, although Ptolemaic royal policy and its bureaucracy was oriented in those terms because its goal was the collection of revenue. Greeks competed with other Greeks, just as Egyptians competed against other Egyptians for scarce resources.

Perhaps no other example better illustrates the contours of Ptolemaic law— judicial competence, the interaction of different ethnic groups with different legal traditions, the state's efforts in coping with a complex legal landscape and its support of Egyptian law—than the well-known case brought by Hermias, a high-ranking military officer from Kom Ombo, against an Egyptian family of low level mortuary priests (*choachytes*). The trial, which took place in Thebes in 117 BC, stands in sharp contrast in its orderliness to the "amnesty decree" issued a year earlier. The dispute was a rather complex affair, the details of which were recorded in full in one of the most illuminating and important papyri of the Ptolemaic period.[116]

Hermias' case first came before royal officials and a Greek tribunal, the *chrêmatistai*, originally an itinerant royal court created to hear disputes, which became a regular feature of nome governance in the second century (Préaux 1978/1:279). The trial was held before an administrative tribunal headed by the *epistatês of the nome*, and was Hermias' seventh (!) and final (as far as we know) attempt in ten years to gain control over part of a house compound that he claimed to own as a legacy from his father who had fled Thebes at the outbreak of the great Theban revolt of 205 BC. The trial is noteworthy for many reasons. Among the most important are the complexity of the proceedings, which required the use of "lawyers," certainly a new feature of the Ptolemaic legal system, and the variety of bilingual legal sources cited, which included royal ordinances, de-

---

[115] Bingen (1984).

[116] *pTor.Choach*. 12 (=*pSurvey* 48; *UPZ* II 162, 117 BC), truly one of the most outstanding documents from the ancient world. English translation in Bagnall and Derow (2004, text 132). The entire archive of which this text forms a part was assembled by Wilcken (1935) and is treated by Pestman (1993). The dispute itself is discussed in full by Pestman (1992), with excellent photographs of the papyrus.

motic Egyptian contracts, and law derived from "common Greek law" (*politikoi nomoi*). Egyptian legal documents were translated into Greek for use as evidence, a necessity as the Greek-speaking officials would otherwise have been unable to understand the Egyptian documentation of property ownership.[117]

Despite the status of the complainant, the Ptolemaic officials decided the case in favor of the Egyptian priests and against their fellow Greek. The Egyptian's "lawyer," one Deinon, claimed that the priests had (1) held the property unchallenged and in common for thirty-seven years; and (2) had tax receipts for the property. Possession was enough, according to a royal decree he then cited, to prove ownership. More decisive still was the fact that (3) the Egyptian defendants produced written contracts of sale showing that a clear title of ownership had passed to them from the seller. Egyptian law was overwhelmingly in favor of the Egyptians. For his part, Hermias could produce neither evidence of possession nor written evidence of title.[118] Neither ethnicity nor personal status mattered in the adjudication of the property rights at stake in the case. Proof of the priestly family's ownership was properly established through valid Egyptian contracts. The dispute, and the mixture of law cited in its resolution, represents the culmination of the evolution of Ptolemaic law. In the third century, courts were divided into two branches, one adjudicating "Greek" law, the other Egyptian. By the middle of the second century, this system had evolved into a larger, "bureaucratized" legal apparatus that incorporated both legal traditions, as well as royal decrees and edicts.[119]

Conclusions

In his recent essay on the Greek legacy in Egypt, Alan Bowman (2006:210) concluded:

> But early in the Ptolemaic period an internal Egyptian chronological 'narrative' was constructed, was used by classical historians such as Diodorus, and is still used, as is too rarely explicitly stated, as the basis of the modern chronology of dynastic Egypt. This was created in the third century BC in the ambience of the Ptolemaic court by an Egyptian priest of Isis, Manetho of Sebennytos (in the Delta), writing

---

[117] On the translation of demotic documents in the context of dispute resolution before Greek judges, see also *UPZ* II 185 (= *pSurvey* 19), and *pLeiden* 413 with the comments by Mairs and Martin (forthcoming). I thank the authors for providing their article in advance of publication.

[118] *UPZ* II 162 9.5–7. Pestman (1983b:294).

[119] See Mélèze-Modrzejewski (1975).

in Greek, who alone 'represents a complete and systematic version of the Egyptian tradition.' Egyptian history was thus captured or re-invented within a classicizing historiographical framework possibly with the encouragement, if not instruction, of Ptolemy II Philadelphus, the monarch who founded that factory of classical scholarship, the Alexandrian Museum.

The early Ptolemaic kings were concerned with, and indeed spent much energy on, their political position, conforming their image insofar as possible to that of earlier legitimate regimes while distancing themselves from Persian rule. Of course it was typical in Egyptian history for new dynasties to stress their connections to previous ones. Even the Persians had wanted to be seen as legitimate successors of the Saïtes, though the later period of their rule certainly erased any good will that the early Persian administration might have fostered. Indeed an actively anti-Persian policy was followed by the Ptolemies (Gozzoli 2006). They wanted to build on the Saïte consolidation and to stress their pharaonic pedigree. And they very much wanted to know about proper Egyptian practice. Ptolemaic attempts at writing their new dynasty into Egyptian history, above all reflected in the work of Hecataeus and Manetho, were motivated by the need to legitimize their control of society.[120] The effects of this historicizing, and of this Ptolemaic search for order had, however, much larger consequences for Egypt.

The "codification" of the legal system, essentially an incomplete process of bureaucratization of both positive laws and royal decisions, was one of the main channels through which the Ptolemies exerted control. In this regard they no doubt found useful the traditions of justice and the guaranteed access to the of law that formed an integral part of pharaonic kingship. By upholding these ancient traditions the Ptolemies were able to build a crucial bridge between their economic aims and Egyptian society. Above all, though, it is the growth and the promiscuousness of the Ptolemaic bureaucracy that must be held responsible for much of the change wrought by the Ptolemaic legal system. The Ptolemaic project clearly had

[120] Murray (1970); Burstein (1992); Verbrugghe and Wickersham (1996:120); more recently Dillery (1999:93–116); Lloyd (1999); Gozzoli (2006). I am simplifying a complex issue here: as Verbrugghe and Wickerham note (p. 119), there is no evidence for the view that this was history written to order for Ptolemy Philadelphus. Dillery (112–13) characterizes it as "a narrative history of Egypt constructed out of a traditional method of preserving the past that had existed for millennia" (citing the king lists) and one that "also contained narratives that offered another way to present the history of Egypt, one that concerned both the past and the future and which privileged the role of the native priest." He concludes that "the incentive to write the work, indeed perhaps the model itself of the combined king list and narrative, evidently came from the Greek world."

roots in the Saïte recentralization that, importantly, utilized the new script known as demotic to establish administrative control throughout Egypt. In short, as Redford summarized (2001:153), under the Saïtes, "property law, contract law and tax law were brought to a peak of refinement and based on ancient precedent and modern adaptation." Darius, and the Ptolemies after him, probably sought no more than consensus on what was already in existence.

The existence of multiple sources of law—Greek law for citizens in the Greek cities, Egyptian law, royal decrees, and administrative decisions—and parallel court systems, tell us much about the shape of the early Ptolemaic state. As in other areas (Turner 1984:146–47), there were limits to state centralization, and very likely limits to the ability of the state to integrate the diverse elements of Ptolemaic Egyptian society. These limits would in turn have been major factors working against economic performance, especially when it came to the enforcement and adjudication of property rights. There was no single legislative act by which Ptolemy established the legal system of the new state. Rather, Ptolemaic legal policy was to legislate in areas that concerned revenue, but to accept the various legal traditions that were represented by the diverse population. The Hermias trial demonstrates two important points: the hybridity (and complexity) of Ptolemaic law in the second century BC, and, following from this, that the law was more comprehensive than earlier, attempting to protect not only royal revenues but also certain traditions of private property rights.

The Hermias trial, and the petition of Horos that I mentioned in the last chapter, also show us that bureaucratic routine determined, if it did not in fact supercede, both proper procedure and the applicable law.[121] This shifting of judicial powers to the discretion of local functionaries coincides with developments in the economy and in society at large. Royal law, that is the law adjudicated by royal courts and tribunals, increasingly took precedence over the law as administered by local Egyptian courts (the *laokritai*).[122] This supercession of independent local law corresponds with the apparent decline in the use of demotic as a language of contract. The state's desire for greater uniformity and predictability in contracting played a (small) part in this development, but I follow Kehoe in believing that, as in the Roman period, the "state's power to regulate the rural economy [was] limited" (Kehoe 2007:132), as was the state's ability to limit the "autonomous growth" (Eisenstadt 1993:138) of bureaucratic legal institutions. Bureaucratic officials may indeed have been "freer" to decide cases than the judges in the court system, whose powers were more

---

[121] Wolff (1960); Préaux (1978/1:280).
[122] Mélèze-Modrzejewski (1975).

narrowly defined, and the Egyptian courts may have had less power to enforce their decisions than state institutions. Ptolemaic Egyptian society evolved, and the law and with it the court system, evolved as well.[123]

In creating a state built to control, the Ptolemies established a system in which people competed for legal rights and for rents. They put in play all three strategies for forming a ruling coalition that I mentioned in chapter 4—terror, cooptation, and raising the cost of collective action. The early rulers co-opted elites and created institutions that competed against each other, thus making coordination at the local level difficult. Whether intentional or not, this competitive structure was far from "irrational" as it allowed the Ptolemies to sustain their rule for three centuries. If we take a simultaneous view of Ptolemaic legislation and the underlying social realities of Egypt with which the legislation had to reckon, we see how similar the Ptolemies were to the pharaohs. The "structural tensions" that Bingen (1984) has observed in Ptolemaic society with respect to revenue collection are also a feature of Ptolemaic law. As Bingen noted, however, this "incoherence," or to repeat Samuel's term, the "irrationality" of the Ptolemaic system created "positive outcomes" not only for "the big contractors" but also for the Ptolemaic kings themselves.[124]

Finally, the study of the law under the Ptolemies shows that it was not just the aims of the king that we must consider, but also how Egyptian society responded to these aims. Much like the spread and adoption of demotic by scribes in Saïte times, the creation and consolidation of religious texts, and the recording of temple ritual and theology (best observed at the Edfu temple), implementing the Ptolemaic "codification" of the law involved a more complex process than a mere command from above.[125] Indeed one can trace the "codification" of Egypt back to Saïte reforms, and to Herodotus. The Ptolemaic kings, then, stand at the end of a long evolution and, as the last pharaohs, binding themselves to ancient traditions and engaging with local society, they helped to shape Egypt's complex legacy.

---

[123] Cf. The remarks of Wolff (1966:77). See also Samuel (1966b) on "administrative decisions."

[124] Bingen's (2007:190, n. 2) remark in his lightly revised version of his 1984 article.

[125] On the adapation of the demotic writing system, see chapter 1, "Saïte Period."

Chapter 7

CONCLUSIONS

To some extent it [the system of government] linked
onto the old system of the pharaohs, though when
Ptolemy I took over the country, only ruins of that
system were left, after generations of Persian rule and
chaotic periods of struggle and rebellion.
—*Bevan (1968)*

Ptolemaic rule never really caught on in Egypt.
—*Green (1990:192)*

THIS BOOK has been concerned with Ptolemaic state making. I have argued that we should eschew modern state analogies and treat the Ptolemies as a premodern state. The Ptolemies took a path to state centralization that bargained with and incorporated key constituent groups. This
state-making model explains much about how Ptolemaic society evolved.
I have also stressed the strong institutional continuities, both those found
already operating in Egypt when Alexander arrived, and those Greek fiscal institutions derived from fourth-century Athenian experience. The re-
sulting Ptolemaic dynasty was a hybrid state that attempted to combine
ancient social structures with new fiscal institutions.

Recent scholarship has substantially altered our understanding of the
Ptolemies' relationship to Egypt's past in several areas. This paradigm
shift, can be generally characterized as placing greater stress on institutional continuity, and it has been based in the main on a significantly
larger corpus of available evidence. Whereas Bevan, Préaux, and Rostovtzeff relied heavily on Greek documentary papyri, we now have at our
disposal a greater number of demotic Egyptian and hieroglyphic texts and
more archaeological material as well. Today our attempts to understand
local society better balance the concerns emphasized, and in my view overemphasized, by the scholars of the past, namely an analysis of state aims
that takes no account of the political relationships between the king and
Egyptian society.

The new material, combined with the Greek papyri, provides a fuller
and richer picture of the interaction of the kings with Egyptian society.
Our picture of Hellenistic debt to fourth-century Greek experience is

clearer as well. The Aristotelian *Oikonomika*, whatever its specific context, was as much a part of Ptolemaic as of Seleukid economic mentality.
We have the state's need for finance, which comes immediately out of
fourth-century BC Greek thinking and the exigencies of the post-Alexander
world, dictated by military competition between states. Going deeper into
the past, we have set the Ptolemaic state within the context of Egyptian
history. The Ptolemaic political economy, as I have stressed, must be understood in the light of Saïte reforms and reactions to the imperial rule of the
Persians and then the Ptolemies.

Ptolemaic rule brought many changes, not the least of which was the
use of Greek language in the administration of Egypt. The changes were
not, however, transformative. Fifth- and fourth-century Greek, that is
Athenian, financial theory, some of it no doubt taken from Persia, was
superimposed on an ancient agricultural society. There seems to have been
little technical or social innovation. This Ptolemaic project produced a
wide range of responses, from collaborative acceptance by some, to outright resistance by others. But the reaction of the bulk of the population
(though of course not well documented) was probably more muted, verg-
ing on indifference. At the beginning of this book I raised the "geographic/
institutions" debate of Acemoglu et al. (2002). Although we are not able
to measure incomes in the Ptolemaic period, it would seem probable that
Ptolemaic governance continued and indeed extended an ancient pattern
of expansion that resulted only in static growth. Egypt under Roman rule,
at least initially, may well have experienced a "reversal of fortune."[1]

The overall style of governance was pharaonic, conservative, and reac-
tionary. By adopting pharaonic patterns of rule and propping up an elite
of soldiers, priests and bureaucrats, the Ptolemies reinforced, indeed rein-
vigorated an ancient system. The Ptolemaic period in Egypt represented
an "efflorescence," to borrow from Jack Goldstone, that broadly bears
similarities to the Middle and New Kingdoms of ancient Egypt. The state
was in an expansive mode, with (probably) a rising population, new
building programs, new cities, and new settlements on newly reclaimed
land, as well as increased warfare and a burgeoning bureaucracy. There
was what Eric Jones (1988) has famously termed "extensive growth."
There was probably no "intensive" or real economic growth, no increase
in the standard of living (though of course new archaeological evidence
may alter this picture). The state's new taxation institutions, and its bureaucrats, very likely absorbed any increases in production. There was
also a notable expansion of "high culture" (Baines and Yoffee 1998:257)
as evidenced by the building of temples for example, but Egyptian civiliza-

---

[1] On the Roman takeover, see Capponi (2005); Monson (2008).

tion became "provincialized." Sacred texts, written with a vast and arcane inventory of hieroglyphic signs, could still be seen on the walls of the Ptolemaic temples of course, but they were understood by fewer and fewer. The Roman administration would take even greater advantage of the Greek/non-Greek dichotomy and it would continue to be a foil for early Christian religious leaders in Egypt as well.

We have seen in previous chapters that kingship was revitalized, and to some extent redefined, by Ptolemaic rule. The attempt to impose a sovereign order over Egypt produced a cultural response, including the written recording of Egypt's traditions in law, in theology, in literature, and in other fields as well. Darius' consolidation of Persian rule in Egypt after the death of Cambyses built on Saïte reforms to some extent. The codification of Egyptian temple tradition, including the recording of cult practice on the walls of temples themselves, is seen in its fullest expression at Edfu, but for the first time in Darius I's temple at Kharga (cf. Assmann 2002:419). This consolidation of tradition continued under the Ptolemies.[2]

The Ptolemaic centralization of the state differed in some respects from the Saïte reforms. The Saïte kings wanted to establish a more uniform administrative system by replacing the scribal and legal traditions in the south of the country with the demotic script and its legal formulas. These reforms were begun by Psammetichus and in place under Amasis, whose long reign allowed for the political consolidation of the country. That took something on the order of eighty years. We do not know enough about differences in economic organization, but it is certain that in Upper Egypt the temples were the economic engines in their territory.

The Ptolemies, by contrast, consolidated and extended Greek fiscal and ancient Egyptian traditions. There were other traditions as well, not the least of which were those of the Jewish populations in Alexandria and elsewhere. The new urban structures stimulated by Ptolemaic governance added to an already complicated social system. Greek was of course the language of the Ptolemaic administration. And like early demotic under the Saïtes, it took time to establish the new language in the local offices of the new administrative apparatus. Given the nature of the evidence, we have to make guesses, but the time frame was probably roughly the same as for the "demoticisation" (Martin 2007) of Egypt under the Saïtes. Importantly though, demotic was never completely replaced by Greek under the Ptolemies in the same way as the hieratic tradition was.

---

[2] See, for example, the Ptolemaic period text *pJumilhac*, Vandier (1961), which records priestly ritual in a consolidated form.

The Ptolemies are directly responsible for some of the greatest achievements of the ancient world, not the least of which is the building of Alexandria—the first "urban giant" (Ades and Glaeser 1995) of the ancient world, home to the greatest center of learning in Mediterranean antiquity and to the famed lighthouse, among many other significant monuments. This book offers a new perspective on the connections between Greek and Egyptian civilization, by trying to understand Egyptian civilization in its own terms, examining the manner in which the Ptolemies established themselves within Egyptian traditions, and the dynamic interactions between the two cultures during Ptolemaic rule. Ptolemaic governance incorporated (and overwrote the history of) Egypt into larger political frameworks beginning with Persian and ending with Roman rule. One of the most important trends in recent years has been the weight given to Egyptian culture, which has been seen as vital, indeed even revivified, in the period. That trend has been driven primarily by the publication of things Egyptian: private sculpture, architecture, demotic papyri, and inscriptions. And as a result we can now see clearer than before that Egypt in the first millennium BC was far from leading what Breasted (1905:595) called an "artificial existence."

The response to Ptolemaic rule has been an underestimated force in Ptolemaic history. I have argued in this book that while the king played an important role as an agent of change, he was not the only actor on the stage. Much of the process of change is not well documented. Take for example the Egyptian temples built in the period, or the hieroglyphic writing that covers the walls of these magnificent structures. No one would deny their fundamental Egyptianness, yet these temples, and the Ptolemaic-period hieroglyphics carved into them, are different from those of the pre-Ptolemaic traditions. Egyptian society had adapted and evolved here. We do not know enough to decide whether this was internal change alone, or whether it took place in combination with reactive forces putting pressure on Egyptian society, but whatever drove the change, change there was.

In the shaping of law, the Ptolemies played an important role. Over the course of the three centuries of their rule, the state, from the point of view of local society, appears to have been reasonably effective at enforcing its aims while maintaining local traditions and adjudicating local disputes. Over time the royal courts seem to have crowded out the local courts and state bureaucracy replaced more traditional methods of dispute resolution in the countryside. If we can rely on the documentary evidence, the demotic tradition declined. Older forms of contract disappeared, and new Greek-influenced forms came into use, with adjustments sometimes driven by Ptolemaic registration practices and by their fiscal interest in taxing transactions. In the main, however the Ptolemies did not tamper with the essence of local legal traditions. There was some movement to organize these traditions into written texts, whether we call them "codes" or not. Importantly, however, there appears to have been very little in the way of new legislation or innovation. Ptolemaic law, and Ptolemaic legal culture, is a counterexample to the Weberian principle that law can enable or direct new modes of behavior.[3] The Ptolemies appear merely to have fixed legal custom in place.

If the introduction of coinage by the Ptolemies helped to impose a uniform political and economic system on Egypt, it was only part of a larger project to merge the new political order with the ancient institutional structure of Egypt. The early kings often issued rules of expected behavior for officials; rules were also written down for the performance of specific functions and in particular for regulating the new fiscal institutions.

Finally, but not least in historical importance, Ptolemaic rule captured Egyptian civilization in a form that would become its canonical image until just a little less than two centuries ago. Then, with the help of one of the trilingual Ptolemaic synodal decrees, the Memphis decree of 196 BC that we now know as the Rosetta Stone, a brilliant French scholar began to decipher the Egyptian language, both the hieroglyphic and the demotic writing systems. It took another couple of generations before a German scholar working on another Ptolemaic priestly document, the Kanopos decree, confirmed Champollion's basic system. From that point on we could begin to understand Egyptian civilization on its own terms. Nevertheless the systemization of Egyptian society that was a response to Ptolemaic rule in Egypt remains at the foundation of our understanding of Egyptian history, its basic chronology, its temple rituals, even its geography and the name of most of its towns. Ptolemaic Egyptology is very much with us today, as we witness ancient Alexandria come to light before our eyes.

---

[3] Swedberg (2003).

Appendix

THE TRIAL RECORD OF THE PROPERTY
DISPUTE HELD AT THE TEMPLE OF
WEPWAWET IN ASYUT, UPPER EGYPT, 170 BC
BEFORE THE LOCAL *LAOKRITAI*-JUDGES

pSiut 1 (=pBM inv. 10591, recto)

BIBLIOGRAPHY

The *editio princeps* of this text, along with the other documents that comprise a small archive, was published by Thompson (1934). Two documents that were originally part of the archive were published later by Shore and Smith (1959). A modified translation of the text was published by Seidl (1967). For an analysis of the text, see also Seidl and Stricker (1937). Some corrections to the readings are now collected in den Brinker et al. (2005:87–95). Additional comments may be found in Seidl (1962); Johnson (1987); Vleeming (1989); Allam (1990).

Author's Note: The following is my own rough-and-ready and slightly abridged translation of the text. It can in no way stand for a serious edition of this complex text. I hope by this merely to give the reader a sense of what is an extremely important legal document. There are many obscure or diffcult passages, and the whole text requires more scholarly attention.

A copy, after the protocol {and the words that were written afterward}. Year 11, day 21 of the month of *Pachons* of pharaoh Ptolemy, son of Ptolemy, as the judges—the priests of *Wepwawet*, (and the priests of) the gods Adelphoi, Euergetes, Philopatores, Epiphanes, and the gods Philometores, their name(s) *rmn-hry-hbs-khepr.w*, the gods Euergetai, Philopatores, the gods Epiphanes:

> *Djed-Djehuty-efankh* son of *Neshor*
> *Patiamunipy* son of *Djed-Djehuty-efankh*
> *Patiamunipy* son of *Tut*

three persons, were seated in the court in Siut, (and) *Andromachos*, the *eisagogeus*, was seated with them.

[FIRST PLEA]—

The endowed woman *Chratianch*, daughter of *Petiwepwawet*, is the one who speaks before her lords the judges, the priests of *Wepwawet*, and the gods who dwell with him. "Greetings! May they live! I am bringing a complaint against *Tefhape*, the lector-priest, son of *Petetum*. There is a deed of endowment in the treasury of Ptah of full value which the eldest son of an endowed woman, *Tut*, son of *Petetum*, my husband, made in year 21 of pharaoh, father of the ever-living pharaoh, while *Petetum*, son of *Tuot*, his father, confirmed the said deed, saying: 'Accept the said deed from the eldest son of an endowed woman, *Tuot*, son of *Petetum*, my eldest son. Let him act according to everything in it. My heart is satisfied with them.' The above-mentioned document is in my possession. If it is needed, I will bring it. It happened in year 25, second month of *Phaopi* of pharaoh, father of the ever-living pharaoh. Now *Petetum* was about to die. He made a division to *Tefhape*, son of *Petetum*, whom I am suing, the younger son of *Tut*, son of *Petetum*, my husband—he is a child of the father, but not of the mother—concerning the one-third share of his property. Now there does not belong to him legal control over the property, neither he nor any son, on account of the endowment deed that he made to *Tsheretenash*, the mother of *Tut*, son of *Petetum*, my husband. Now it is written in the law of year 21 that if a man marries a woman and he has a son with her, and he divorces her, and he marries another woman, and he writes for her an endowment deed, and he has a son with her, and the said man dies, his property—it is to the children of the first wife for whom he wrote an endowment deed first that it is given. Furthermore, the said man died before I (*l*. he) completed the said division with witnesses. I made three public protests at the request of *Patiwepwawet*, son of *Tut*, against the (said) document. It happened that in year 8 of the ever-living pharaoh, *Tefhape*, son of *Petetum*, mentioned above, complained (against) my husband to *Theomnestos*, who was *stratêgos* of the district of Thebes. It happened that *Dionysius* was his herdsman and *Hor* his camel keeper—the brother of the mother of *Tefhape*, son of *Petetum*, the above-mentioned man whom I am suing. They threw *Tut*, son of *Petetum*, my husband, in jail. They caused that he made an apportionment amounting to a one-third share of the property of *Petetum*, his father, under duress. They caused that I endorsed it as a result of the force that they were using against me. Afterwards, it happened that *Theomnestos* went North. [I] related to *Timarchos*, the *stratêgos* of the district of Siut, the above-mentioned matter. I made a report to *Numenios*, the *stratêgos* of the nome, to stop the illegal acts that they did against me. I asked that he write to you to hear my plea against him. There are ten (arouras) of land that belong to *Tut*, son of *Petetum*, my husband, he being in possession of them since his father died, and he was leasing it out, and annual rent was given to him, they (the land) being security for (my) endowment document. *Tefhape*, against whom I am complaining, had already leased the said land to *Heraclides*, who is in the cavalry, while I did not know that he received protection against me, and did not allow me to have the ability of approaching them (*scil.* the land). I am asking: 'May you cause that the above-mentioned man be sent (for) and that you hear my plea against him, and that you place a restraining order concerning any property belonging to *Petetum*, the father of *Tut*. (It) happens that it belongs to *Patiwepwawet*, son of *Tut*, my eldest son, along with his brothers, because of the endowment deed which was made to me by the eldest son of an endowed woman, *Tut*, son of *Petetum*, my husband, it being confirmed through his father according to that which is written in the law about which I have already cited above. The above-mentioned man—I have another complaint that I will present against him. This is my first plea, written year 11, month of Pharmouthi, day 22."

[RESPONSE]

His response. Its copy.

It is the son of an endowed woman, *Tefhape* son of *Petetum*, who speaks before his superiors, the judges—the priest of *Wepwawet*, and (and the priests of) the gods Adelphoi, Euergetes, Philopatroes, Epiphanes. "Hail! May they live! The words which *Chratianch*, daughter of *Patiwepwawet*, sent before the judges, making a claim against me, there is falsehood in them. The rest is my justification. The testimony that she made:

'It happened in year 21, month of Phaopi, day 25 of pharaoh, the father of the ever-living pharaoh, that *Petetum* was about to die. He assigned a share to *Tefhape*, son of *Petetum*, whom I am suing, who is the younger brother of *Tut*, son of *Petetum*, my husband as child of the father, but not of the mother, concerning the one-third share of his property, while he does not have legal control over the property, neither he nor any son regarding the deed of endowment which he made to *Tshenese*, mother of *Tut*, son of *Petetum*, my husband. It is written in the law of year 21 that if a man marries a woman, and he writes for her an endowment, and he has a son by her, and he divorces her and marries another woman, and he writes for her an endowment and he has a son by her, and the said man dies—his property, it is to the children of the first woman for whom he writes the deed that his property goes as a prior document. Moreover, the said man died while he did not complete the division with witnesses. I made three public protests at the request of *Petewepwawet*, son of *Tut*,

my eldest son after the said deed.' These things—there is falsehood in
them. It happens that there is a (deed) of endowment consisting of 50
pieces (of silver) of the treasury of Ptah, of full value, along with its food
and clothing (allowance) which *Petetum*, son of *Tut*, my father, gave to
Ewe, daughter of *Wepwawet*, my mother, in year 25 of pharaoh, the father of the ever-living pharaoh, which was confirmed by *Tut*, son of *Petetum*, her husband, in whose name she is coming (to court). It is subscribed
at the bottom (of the document) in his own hand. It is in my possession
today. If it is needed, I will bring it before the judges as well as the deed
of division which my father *Petetum* gave to me for my share of everything
belonging to him, they being listed in year 25, second month of Phaopi
of pharaoh, the father of the ever-living pharaoh, which was confirmed
by *Tut*, son of *Petetum*, and subscribed at its foot in his own hand, completed with sixteen witnesses. If it is needed, I will bring it before the
judges. The testimony which she made: 'It happened in year 8 of the ever-
living pharaoh that the aforementioned *Tefhape*, son of *Petetum*, brought
suit against *Tut*, son of *Petetum*, my husband; *Theomnestos* was *stratêgos*
of the Theban nome. It happened that *Dionysius* was his herdsman and
Hor his camal keeper—the brothers of the mother of *Tefhape*, son of
Petetum, whom I am suing. They caused that *Tut*, son of *Petetum*, my
husband, be put in jail. He caused that he made an apportionment of one-
third of the property of *Petetum*, his father, under duress. They caused
that I confirmed it because of the force on me that they were using.' What
she said is false. They did not throw *Tut*, son of *Petetum*, in jail. Also, he
has not made for me a deed of apportionment while *Themnestos*, the
stratêgos of Thebes, was here in the district of Siut. I actually made a
petition (to) *Themnestos*, the *stratêgos* in year 8, month of Pharmouthi,
day 15. He wrote on my behalf to *Timarchos*, the *stratêgos* of the district
of Siut, to hear my complaint against him (*scil. Tut*). The communication
that he made to me is in my possession, and a copy of the petition that I
made to him. The aforesaid man found that it was he who is defrauding
me. He was not able to come to the registration office with me. He made
a deed of apportionment in year 8, month of Pachons, day 2, for the one-
third share of everything and all property belonging to *Petetum*, my father, which was confirmed by his wife. The said deed is in my possession
today. If it is needed, I will bring it, showing the deed of apportionment
that my father made for me in year 25 [which is proof against the] ruse
that she is using, while they completed the said deed with witnesses in the
dromos of *Wepwawet*. This testimony which she made: 'It happened that
Theomnestos went North; *Timarchos*, the *stratêgos* of the district of
Thebes, made a report concerning the matter; likewise I gave (a report)
to *Numenios*, the *stratêgos* of Thebes, regarding the illegal acts which
were done against me. I caused that he be sent before you to hear my

complaint against him.' Concerning this, there is no truth in it. When anyone reports to the *stratêgos*, he will write on their behalf to hear pleas according to the law. This statement that she made: 'There are ten arouras of land belonging to *Tut*, son of *Petetum*, my husband. He has been in possession of them since his father died, while they made for him a lease concerning them, while they got rent annually, they being security for my endowment deed. *Tefhape*, whom I am suing, already leased the said land to *Heraclides*, who is in the cavalry. He (*l.* I) did not know that he received protection against me, not allowing me to be able to approach them.' This is not true. The said land, it belongs to me. (I) worked it with *Tut* in year 9. In year 10, I leased them to *Agylos*, son of *Lysimachos*, the cavalryman. It happens that they farm most of the plot with clover. He made a lease in the names of two men, such that one-third was for me, two-thirds for *Tut*. We made their rent as shares for us. In year 11, I leased my own one-third to *Heraclides*, the cavalryman. *Aguilas* and *Apylus*, who are in the infantry, are the ones who farm the other two-thirds at the behest of *Tut*, son of *Petetum*, my brother. This testimony that she made: 'There is a deed of endowment of 50 pieces of silver of the treasury of Ptah of full value together with its food and clothing which *Tut*, son of *Petetum*, my husband, made for me in year 21, month of Paopi, and *Petetum*, his father, confirmed the said deed.' This is a lie. *Petetum*, my father, did not confirm the said deed at all. I am requesting that you dismiss the aforementioned *Chratianch*, daughter of *Petewepawet*, from me in this false claim against me, and in which she has no (legal) justification.

Written in year 11, month of Pharmouthi, day 22."

[Chratianch's response]

The endowed woman *Chratianch*, daughter of *Petwepwawet*, is she who says: "I repeat my words. The response that *Tefhape*, son of *Petetum*, wrote to the judges being the reply to the first plea that they allowed him, it is untrue. The rest—he has no (legal) justification in them. The testimony that he made: 'There is a deed of endowment of 50 pieces of silver of the treasury of Ptah of full value with its food and clothing which *Petetum*, son of *Tut*, my father, already made to *Ewe*, daughter of *Wepwawetewe*, my mother, in year 25, month of Phaopi of the pharaoh, father of the ever-living pharaoh, which is confirmed by *Tut*, son of *Petetum*, through whom she has come, signed at the bottom in his own hand. I have it in my possession today. If it is needed I will bring it before the judges (as well as) the deed of division which *Petetum*, my father, made for me concerning the one-third share of everything and all property belonging to him, listed in year 25, month of Phaopi of pharaoh, father of the ever-living pharaoh, confirmed by *Tut* son of *Petetum*, inscribed at the bottom in his own hand, complete with sixteen witnesses. It is in my possession today. If it is needed, I will bring it.' These things—there is no (legal) justification in them. There is no matter concerning me about what is written in the law. It happens that the deed of endowment of 50 pieces of silver of the treasury of Ptah of full value, with its food and clothing which, *Tut*, son of *Petetum*, the eldest son of an endowed woman, my husband, made for me in year 21, month of Phaopi of the father of the ever-living pharaoh, while *Petetum*, his father, confirmed the said deed saying: 'Accept the said deed from the eldest son son of an endowed woman *Tut*, son of *Petetum*, my eldest son. Let him do in accordance with everything above. My heart is satisfied with it.' The said deed is in my possession today. If it is wanted I will bring it before the judges concerning what I wrote in it in the first plea. The said deed is prior (in time) by five years to a deed that he says was made for *Ewe*, my mother. *Petetum*, his father, does not have legal control over the property belonging to him or any man, while I have not confirmed it according to what is written in the law. Likewise, *Tut* son of *Petetum*, my husband does not have legal control over the confirmation of the deed to give property to any one. The property of *Petetum*, his father, they are security for the deed of endowment according to what I wrote in my first plea, and also the deed of apportionment. There are three public protests which *Petewepwawet*, my eldest son, made in pursuance of it. If they want them, I will bring them according to what I wrote in my first plea. This statement which he made: 'They did not throw *Tut*, son of *Petetum*, in jail, he did not make for me a deed of apportionment when *Dionysius* the *stratêgos* of the Theban nome was here in the district of Siut. I petitioned *Themnestos*, the proper (*stratêgos*), in year 28, month of Pharmouthi, day 15. He wrote on my behalf to *Timarchos*, the *stratêgos* of the district of Siut, to hear my plea with him. The letter that he wrote on my behalf is in my possession, along with the copy of the petition that I gave to him. The aforesaid man found that it was he who defrauded me. He was not able to come to the registration office with me. He made for me a deed of apportionment of the one-third share of everything and all property belonging to *Petetum*, his father, confirmed by *Chratianch*, his aforementioned wife.' These things are untrue. Dionysius who was the herdsman of *Theomnestos* and *Hor* his camel keeper—the brothers of the mother of the aforementioned *Tefhape* are the ones who placed *Tut*, son of *Petetum*, my husband in jail, compelling him to make an apportionment under duress, causing me to confirm it out of fear for my life, as I wrote in my first plea. If it happens that there is a letter in his hand which was made (to) *Timarchos*, it was they who caused that it be made for him also—I have nothing to do with it, The statement that he made: 'The said land is mine, I ploughed it with *Tut* in year 9. In year 10 we leased them to *Agylos*, son of *Lysimachos*, the cavalryman. It happens that they farm most of it with clover. He made a lease for us in both our names according to one-third for me, two-thirds for *Tut*. We made their rent as a share for ourselves. In year 11, I made a lease of my own one-third share to *Heraklides*, the cavalryman, while *Agylos* and *Apylos*, who are in the infantry, are the ones who ploughed the other two-thirds share of *Tut*, my brother.' This is not true. *Heraklides*, the cavalryman, farmed it, he did not make a lease for us concerning it. *Tefhape* had already given a petition to *Shepmin*, the *oikonomos*, and likewise to *Timarchos*, the *stratêgos*. The testimony that he made: '*Petetum*, my father did not confirm the said deed ever.' This is an outright lie. The deed of endowment of 50 pieces of the treasury of Ptah of full value, and its food and clothing, which the eldest son of an endowed woman made for me, confirmed by *Petetum*, his father, signed at the bottom on his own hand. It is in my possession. If it is needed, I will bring it. I request that you not allow *Tefhape*, son of *Petetum*, whom I am suing, control over the property belonging to *Petetum*, father of *Tut*, my husband. It so happens that it is mine, belonging to *Petewepwawet*, my eldest son, and his brothers. The land is security for my deed of endowment. Concerning the said man, I have another matter that I shall speak against him. This is my second plea. Written year 11, month of Pharmouthi, day 29."

[His reponse. Its copy.]

The son of an endowed woman, *Tefhape*, son of *Petetum*, is he who says: "My words are still my words. The words which *Chratianch*, daughter of *Petewepawet*, wrote before the judges, complaining against me today in her second plea, they are not true. The rest is my justification. The testimony that she made: 'I have nothing to do with them. He has no justification in them either concerning that which is written in the law.' She writes lies in them. It happens that she wrote in her first plea: '*Petetum* was about to die. He made an apportionment to *Tefhape*, son of *Petetum*, the younger brother of *Tut*, son of *Petetum*, my husband—that is, a son of the father but not of the mother— whom I am suing above, concerning the one-third share of his property, he not having dominion over his property, neither he nor anyone else.' The testimony which she further made: 'The said man died while he (*l.* I) had not completed the apportionment with witnesses. I made a protest at the behest of *Petewepwawet*, son of *Tut*, my son.' Concerning this matter—it is not true. It happens that there is a deed of endowment of 50 pieces of the treasury of Ptah of full value, with its food and clothing, which *Petetum*, son of *Tut*, my father, made for *Ewe*, daughter of *Wepwawetew*, my mother, in year 25, month of Phaopi of pharaoh, father of the ever-living pharaoh, he writing upon the said document: 'It is to you and the children which you have born to me and those who you will bear to me (that goes the) one-third share of everything and all property which is mine, and those things I will acquire.' It was confirmed by *Tut*, son of *Petetum*, and signed at the bottom in his own hand, in whose name she has come. The said document is in my hand today. If it is wanted I will bring it before the judges, and likewise the deed of apportionment which *Petetum*, my father, made for me of the one third share of everything and all property which is his, listed on the verso, in year 25, month of Paophi of pharaoh, father of the ever-living pharaoh, confirmed by *Tut*, son of *Petetum*, signed at the bottom in his own hand, and completed with 16 witnesses. I have it in my hand today. If it is wanted, I will bring it before the judges in accordance with that which is written in the law. The testimony which she made: 'It happened that the deed of endowment of 50 pieces of the treasury of Ptah, of full value, with its food and clothing, which the eldest son of an endowed woman *Tut*, son of *Petetum*, made for me, confirmed by Petetum his father.' What she said is untrue. *Petetum*, my father, did not confirm to her a deed at all. Besides these things, *Tut*, in whose name she is coming, does not have legal control (over any of) the shares except his share. The testimony that she made: "*Dionysius* who was a herdsman of *Themnestos* and *Hor* his camel keeper—the brothers of the mother of *Tefhape*, were those who caused to throw *Tut*, son of *Petetum*, my husband, in jail, forcing him to make a deed of apportionment under duress, and making me confirm it.' As for these things, I have already said that they are all false. They did not throw *Tut*, son of *Petetum*, in jail. He did not make for me a deed of apportionment until year 8, month of Pachons, day 2 of the ever-living pharaoh, while it was *Themnestos* to whom she is speaking here in the district of Siut, while they completed the said deed with witnesses in the dromos of *Wepwawet*, showing me the deed of apportionment which my father made for me previously on it, and the deed of endowment which he made to *Ewe*, my mother. Now you (*scil.* the judges) know that they will expel anyone who would make a document with another party saying that they were made to make it under duress. Besides these things, of the said document which he made when we approached the law of the elders of the association (?) of the temple of *Wepewawet*. The testimony that she made: 'The said lands—*Heraclides*, the cavalryman, ploughed them at his (*scil. Tefhape's*) behest, without causing a lease to be made for us concerning them.' What she said is untrue, as I wrote in my first plea. The one-third share of the said lands is what I made a lease to *Heraclides*, the cavalryman. The two-thirds share of *Tut*—*Agylos* and *Apylos* are those who are working it. I request that the aforementioned *Chratianch* be dismissed in her unjustified claim against me, and that it happen according to the 6th? law for me. I have another matter (which I will speak) against her. This is my second plea. Written year 11, month of Pachons, day 1."

Their complaints were completed. The scribe of the judges read them out before them (scil. the judges) while they were standing between (them, *scil.* the parties).

[Examination by the judges]

They said to them: "These things—are these your words which you spoke?" They spoke: "Our (lit. your) words are what we said." They questioned *Chratianch, daughter* of *Petewepwawet*: "Is there a man who makes your plea?" She said: "*Ouertes* is the one who makes my plea. My plea is his plea. If he is right, I am right. If he is wrong, I am wrong." They questioned *Ouertes* who is pleading for *Chratianch*. He said: "There is a *diagraphe* which was made for *Tut*, son of *Petetum* , the husband of *Chratianch* (by the) chief (of police) of pharaoh in year 11, month of Mesore, for 1 1/2 arouras of land as an excess of land which they found in relation to them besides these which are written for the tax. He handed over the deliveries to the royal bank. We sued him concerning them. Let them judge concerning our plea. Our justification (relies) on them." He finished speaking. They questioned *Tefhape*, son of *Petetum*, concerning that which is written above. He said: "The testimony which she made: 'There is a *diagraphe* which was made to *Tut* by the chief of police of pharaoh in year 6, month of Mesore concerning 1 1/2 arouras of land which was found being in excess of measurement about it [. . . .] while the deed of year 8, month of Pachons, day 2 was made for us for the 1/3 of ten arouras of land which is 3 1/41/8, writing their boundaries. If my 3 1/41/8 completes the remainder before them according to what is written on my documents, let them judge according to my documents—upon them is my justification. There is nothing more which I will say.'"

They closed his mouth. They said to *Tefhape*, son of *Petetum*: "Bring the deed that *Petetum*, your father, made for *Ewe*, your mother, and the deed of apportionment which was made for you." He brought a deed of endowment before us.
[A verbatim copy is placed in the record]
They questioned *Chratianch* concerning the said document. She did not deny it. He brought a deed of apportionment.
[A verbatim copy is placed in the record]
[Legal review of the evidence by the judges]

[JUDGEMENT]

We have decided that the above-mentioned *Tefhape*, son of *Petetum*, should be placed in possession of all of the property that is described in the deed of division that is appended and that proves his (rightful) 1/3 share of his father's property. We have ordered *Horimhotep*, the bailiff of *Andromachos*, the *eisagogeus*, to put *Tefhape*, son of *Petetum*, in possession of the property so described, which *Tut*, son of *Petetum*, signed over to him in the aforementioned year 8 with respect to the 1/3 share of his father's property. This was confimed by the aforementioned *Chratianch*, daughter of *Patewepwawet*. (We further order that) he give the aforementioned quitclaim deed as proof of title because of the claim made by her. Written by *Tut*, son of *Harsiese*, one of the scribes who writes on behalf of the priests of *Wepwawet* and the gods who dwell with him.

[**Signatures of the three judges**]

BIBLIOGRAPHY

Abd el-Ghani, Mohammed. 2001. The role of Ptolemais in Upper Egypt outside its frontiers. In *Atti del XXII Congresso internazionale di Papirologia, Firenze, 23–29 agosto 1998*, vol. 1, ed. Isabella Andorlini et al., 17–33. Florence: Instituto papirologico G. Vitelli.

Acemoglu, Daron and James A. Robinson. 2006. *Economic origins of dictatorship and democracy.* Cambridge: Cambridge University Press.

Acemoglu, Daron, Simon Johnson, and James A. Robinson. 2002. Reversal of fortune: Geography and institutions in the making of the modern world income distribution. *The Quarterly Journal of Economics* 117/4:1231–94.

Ades, Alberto F. and Edward L. Glaeser. 1995. Trade and circuses: Explaining urban giants. *The Quarterly Journal of Economics* 110/1:195–227.

El-Aguizy, Ola. 1988. A Ptolemaic judicial document from *Hwt-Nsw. BIFAO* 88:51–62.

———. 1992. About the origins of early demotic in Lower Egypt. In *Life in a multi-cultural society: Egypt from Cambyses to Constantine and beyond*, ed. Janet H. Johnson (Studies in Ancient Oriental Civilization 51), 91–102. Chicago: Oriental Institute.

Alcock, Susan E. 1994. Breaking up the Hellenistic world: Survey and society. In *Classical Greece: Ancient histories and modern archaeologies*, ed. Ian Morris, 171–90. Cambridge: Cambridge University Press.

Alcock, Susan E., Jennifer E. Gates, and Jane E. Rempel. 2005. Reading the landscape: Survey archaeology and the Hellenistic *oikoumene*. In *A companion to the Hellenistic world*, ed. Andrew Erskine, 354–72. Malden, MA: Blackwell.

Allam, Schafik. 1990. Women as holders of rights in ancient Egypt (during the Late Period). *JESHO* 32:1–34.

———. 1991. Egyptian law courts in pharaonic and Hellenistic times. *JEA* 77:109–27.

———. 2002. Elders (*presbyteroi*)-notables-great men rmt.w c3yw=hl-c3.yw. In *Acts of the seventh international conference of demotic studies, Copenhagen, 23–27 August 1999*, ed. Kim Ryholt, 1–26. Copenhagen: Museum Tusculanum Press.

———. 2008. Regarding the *eisagogeus* at Ptolemaic law courts. *JEH* 1:1–19.

Alleaume, Ghislaine. 1992. Les système hydrauliques de l'Égypte pré-moderne. Essai d'histoire du paysage. In *Itinéraires d'Égypte. Mélanges offerts au père Maurice Martin, s.j.*, ed. Christian Décobert, 301–22. Cairo :Institut français d'Archéologie orientale.

Allen, James P. 2002. *The Heqanakht Papyri.* Publications of the Metropolitan Museum of Art Egyptian Expedition 27. New York: Metropolitan Museum of Art.

Anagnostou-Canas, Barbara. 1994. La colonization du sol dans l'Égypte ptolémaïque. In *Grund und Boden in Altägypten. (Rechtliche und sozio-ökonom-*

ische Verhältnisse), ed. Schafik Allam, 355–74. *Akten des internationalen Symposions Tübingen 18/–20. Juni 1990.*

Anquetil-du Perron, Abraham-Hyacinthe. 1778. *Législation orientale.* Amsterdam.

Aoki, Masahiko. 2001. *Toward a comparative institutional analysis.* Cambridge: MIT Press.

Aperghis, G. G. 2004. *The Seleukid royal economy: The finances and financial administration of the Seleukid empire.* Cambridge: Cambridge University Press.

———. 2005. City building and the Seleukid royal economy. In *Making, moving and managing: The new world of ancient economies, 323–31 BC*, ed. Zofia H. Archibald, John K. Davies, and Vincent Gabrielsen, 27–43. Oxford: Oxbow Books.

Archibald, Zofia. 2001. Away from Rostovtzeff: A new SEHHW. In *Hellenistic Economies*, ed. Zofia H. Archibald, John Davies, Vincent Gabrielsen, and G. J. Oliver, 379–88. London: Routledge.

Arnold, Dieter. 1999. *Temples of the last pharaohs.* New York: Oxford University Press.

Ashton, Sally-Ann. 2001. *Ptolemaic royal sculpture from Egypt: The interaction between Greek and Egyptian traditions.* Oxford: Archaeopress.

———. 2003. The Ptolemaic royal image and the Egyptian tradition. In *Never had the like occurred: Egypt's view of its past*, ed. John Tait, 213–23. London: UCL Press.

Assmann, Jan. 2002. *The mind of Egypt: History and meaning in the time of the pharaohs.* New York: Henry Holt and Company.

———. 2000. *Herrschaft und Heil. Politische Theologie in Altägypten, Israel und Europa.* Munich: Hanser.

Aufrère, Sydney H. 2000. *Le propylône d'Amon Rê Montou à Karnak-Nord.* Cairo: Institut français d'Archéologie orientale.

Austin, M. M. 1986. Hellenistic kings, war, and the economy. *CQ* 80 n.s. 36: 450–66.

———. 2003. The Seleukids and Asia. In *A companion to the Hellenistic world*, ed. Andrew Erskine, 121–33. Malden, MA: Blackwell.

———. 2006. *The Hellenistic world from Alexander to the Roman conquest: A selection of ancient sources in translation.* Second augmented edition. Cambridge: Cambridge University Press.

Azzoni, Annalisa and Sandra Luisa Lippert. 2000. An Achaemenid loanword in the Legal Code of Hermopolis: *3bykrm. Enchoria* 26:20–30.

Baer, Klaus. 1962. The low price of land in ancient Egypt. *JARCE* 1:25–45.

———. 1963. An eleventh dynasty farmer's letters to his family. *Journal of the American Oriental Society* 83:1–19.

———. 1971. Land and water in ancient Egypt. Paper presented at the Twenty-eighth International Congress of Orientalists, Canberra. Unpublished manuscript in the archives of the Oriental Institute, Chicago.

Bagnall, Roger S. 1969. Some notes on P. Hib. 198. *BASP* 6:73-118.

———. 1976. *The administration of the Ptolemaic possessions outside Egypt.* Leiden: E. J. Brill.

———. 1992. Landholding in late Roman Egypt: The distribution of wealth. *JRS* 82:128–49.

———. 1993. *Egypt in late antiquity.* Princeton: Princeton University Press.

———. 1995. *Reading papyri, writing ancient history.* London: Routledge.

———. 1997. Decolonizing Ptolemaic Egypt. In *Hellenistic constructs: Essays in culture, history and historiography,* ed. Paul Cartledge, Peter Garnsey, and Erich Gruen, 225–41. Berkeley: University of California Press.

———. 1999. Review of Hélène Cadell and Georges Le Rider, *Prix du blé et numéraire dans l'Égypte Lagide de 305 à 173.* (Papyrologica Bruxellensia 30. Brussels, 1997). *Swiss Numismatic Revue* 78:197–203.

———. 2001. Archaeological work on Hellenistic and Roman Egypt, 1995–2001. *AJA* 105:227–43.

———. 2005. Egypt and the concept of the Mediterranean. In *Rethinking the Mediterranean,* ed. William V. Harris, 339–47. Oxford: Oxford University Press.

———. 2007. Introduction: Jean Bingen and the currents of Ptolemaic history. In Jean Bingen, *Hellenistic Egypt. Monarchy, society, economy, culture,* 1–12. Berkeley: University of California Press.

Bagnall, Roger and Peter Derow, eds. 2004. *The Hellenistic period: Historical sources in translation.* 2nd ed. Oxford: Blackwell.

Bagnall, Roger S., J. G. Manning, S. E. Sidebotham, and R. E. Zitterkopf. 1996. A Ptolemaic inscription from Bir 'Iayyan. *CdE* 71:317–30.

Baines, John. 1996. On the composition and inscriptions of the Vatican statue of Udjahorresne. In *Studies in Honor of William Kelly Simpson,* ed. P. D. Manuelian, 83–92. Boston: Museum of Fine Arts.

———. 2004. Egyptian elite self-presentation in the context of Ptolemaic rule. In *Ancient Alexandria between Egypt and Greece,* ed. W. V. Harris and Giovanni Ruffini, 33–61. Leiden: E. J. Brill.

Baines, John and Norman Yoffee. 1998. Order, legitimacy, and wealth in ancient Egypt and Mesopotamia. In *Archaic states,* ed. Gary M. Feinman and Joyce Marcus, 199–260. Santa Fe: School of American Research Press.

Baker, Patrick. 2003. Warfare. In *A companion to the hellenistic world,* ed. Andrew Erskine, 373–88. Oxford: Blackwell.

Bang, Peter Fibiger. 2007. Trade and empire: In search of organizing concepts for the Roman economy. *Past and Present* 195:3–54.

Barkey, Karen. 1994. *Bandits and bureaucrats: The Ottoman route to state centralization.* Ithaca: Cornell University Press.

Bar-Kochva, Bezalel. 1976. *The Seleucid army: Organization and tactics in the great campaigns.* Cambridge: Cambridge University Press.

Barry, William D. 1993. The crowd of Ptolemaic Alexandria and the riot of 203 B.C. *Echos du Monde classique* 37 n.s. 12:415–31.

Barzel, Yoram. 1997. *Economic analysis of property rights,* 2nd ed. Cambridge: Cambridge University Press.

Bathish, Nisreen and Anthony Löwstedt. 1999. Apartheid: Ancient, past and present. Paper presented at the conference: The TRC: Commissioning the past. Jointly organized by the History Workshop at the University of Witwatersand and the Centre for the Study of Violence and Reconciliation, Johannesburg.

Bedford, Peter R. 2001. *Temple restoration in early Achaemenid Judah*. Leiden: E. J. Brill.

Bell, Barbara. 1971. The dark ages in ancient history: I. The first dark age in Egypt. *AJA* 75:1–26.

———. 1975. Climate and the history of Egypt: the Middle Kingdom. *AJA* 223–69.

Bell, Lanny. 1985. The Luxor temple and the cult of the royal Ka. *JNES* 44/4: 251–94.

Bendix, Reinhard. 1978. *Kings or people: Power and the mandate to rule*. Berkeley: University of California Press.

Bernard, A. and O. Masson. 1957. Les inscriptions grecques d'Abou Simbel. *Revue des Études grecques* 70:1–20.

Bevan, Edwyn R. [1927] 1968. *The house of Ptolemy: A history of Hellenistic Egypt under the Ptolemaic dynasty*. Chicago: Ares.

Bianchi, Robert S. 1983. Satrapenstele. In *LÄ* 5, 492–93. Wiesbaden: Otto Harrassowitz.

Bierbrier, M. L. 1975. *The late New Kingdom in Egypt (c. 1300–664 BC): A genealogical and chronological investigation*. Warminster:Aris and Philips.

Bingen, Jean. 1952. *Papyrus Revenue Laws*, nouv. éd. du texte. Sammelbuch griechischer Urkunden aus Ägypten, Beiheft 1. Göttingen: Hubert.

———. 1978a. *Le papyrus Revenue-Laws: Tradition grecque et adaptation hellénistique*. Opladen. Republished as The revenue laws papyrus: Greek tradition and hellenistic adaptation, in Jean Bingen 2007, 157–88.

———. 1978b. Économie grecque et société égyptienne au IIIe siècle. In *Das ptolemäischen Ägypten*, ed. H. Maehler and V. M. Strocka, 211–19. Mainz: Philipp von Zabern. Reprinted in Jean Bingen 2007, 215–28.

———. 1984. Les tensions structurelles de la société ptolémaïque. In *Atti del XVII Congresso internazionale di papirologia* (Napoli, 19–26 maggio, 1983), 3/921–37. Naples: Centro internazionale per lo Studio dei papyri Ercolanesi. Reprinted in Jean Bingen 2007, 189–205.

———. 1989. Normalité et spécificité de l'épigraphie grecque et romaine de l'Égypte. In *Egito e storia antica dall'ellenismo all'età araba*, ed. L. Criscuolo and G. Geraci,15–35. Bologna: CLUEB. Reprinted in Jean Bingen 2007, 256–78.

———. 2007. Ptolemy I and the quest for legitimacy. In *Hellenistic Egypt: Monarchy, society, economy, culture*, ed. with an introduction by Roger S. Bagnall, 15–30. Berkeley: University of California Press. Originally published: 1988. Ptolémée I Sôter ou la quête de la légitimité. *Academie royale de Belgique de la Classe des Lettres et des Sciences morales et politiques*, 5 ser. 74:34–51.

Bin Wong, R. 1997. *China transformed: Historical change and the limits of European experience*. Ithaca: Cornell University Press.

Blanton, Richard E. 1998. Beyond centralization: Steps toward a theory of egalitarian behavior in archaic states. In *Archaic states*, ed. Gary M. Feinman and Joyce Marcus, 135–72. Santa Fe: School of American Research Press.

Blaut, J. M. 2000. *Eight eurocentric historians*. New York: The Guilford Press.

Bleeker, Claas Jouco. 1967. *Egyptian festivals: Enactments of religious renewal*. Leiden: E. J. Brill.

Block, Fred and Peter Evans. 2005. The state and the economy. In *The Handbook of Economic Sociology*, 2nd ed., ed. Neil J. Smelser and Richard Swedberg, 505–26. Princeton: Princeton University Press.

Boardman, John. 2006. Greeks in the east Mediterranean (South Anatolia, Syria, Egypt). In *Greek colonisation: An account of Greek colonies and other settlements overseas* 1, ed. Gocha R. Tsetskhladze, 507–34. Leiden: E. J. Brill.

Bogaert, Raymond. 1994. *Trapezitica Aegyptiaca: Recueil de Recherches sur la Banque en Égypte Gréco-romaine*. Papyrologica Florentina 25. Florence: Edizione Gonnelli.

———. 1998–1999. Les operations des banques de l'Égypte ptolémaïque. *Ancient Society* 29:49–145.

———. 2001. Les Documents bancaires de l'Égypte Gréco-romaine et Byzantine. *Ancient Society* 31:173–288.

Bokovenko, N. A. 2004. Migrations of early nomads of the Eurasian steppe in a context of climatic changes. In *Impact of the environment on human migration in Eurasia*, NATO Science Series 4, Earth and environmental sciences, ed. E. M. Scott et al., 21–33. Kluwer Academic Publishers. (Electronic Resource.)

Bonneau, Danielle. 1993. *Le Régime administratif de l'eau du Nil dans l'Égypte grecque, romaine et byzantine*. Leiden: E. J. Brill.

Boswinkel, E. and P. W. Pestman. 1982. *Les archives privées de Dionysios, fils de Kephalas: Textes grecs et démotiques*. PLBat 22. Leiden: E. J. Brill.

Bottéro, Jean. 1992. The code of Hammurabi: Writing, reasoning and the gods. Trans. Zainab Bahrani and Marc van de Mieroop, 156–84. Chicago: The University of Chicago Press.

Bowersock, Glenn W. 1986. Rostovtzeff in Madison. *The American Scholar* 55 (Summer, 1986):391–400.

———. 1990. *Hellenism in late antiquity*. Ann Arbor: University of Michigan Press.

Bowman, Alan B. 1986. *Egypt after the pharaohs*. Berkeley: University of California Press.

———. 2001. Documentary papyri and ancient history. In *Atti del XXII congresso internazionali Papirologia, Firezne, 23–29 agosto, 1998*, vol. 1, ed. Isabella Andorlini et al., 137–45. Florence: Istituto papirologico G. Vitelli.

———. 2006. Recolonising Egypt. In *Classics in Progress: Essays on ancient Greece and Rome*, ed. T. P. Wiseman, 193–224. British Academy Centenary Monographs. Oxford: Oxford University Press.

———. 2007. Egypt in the Graeco-Roman world: From Ptolemaic kingdom to Roman province. In *Regime change in the ancient near east and Egypt: From Sargon of Agade to Saddam Hussein*. Proceedings of the British Academy 136:165–81.

Braudel, Fernand. 1981. *Civilization and capitalism, 15th–18th centuries* 2: The wheels of commerce. Translation from the French revised by Siân Reynolds. New York: Harper and Row.

Braun, T.F.R.G. 1982. The Greeks in Egypt. In *CAH* 3, pt. 3, 32–56. Cambridge: Cambridge University Press.

Breasted, James Henry. 1905. *A history of Egypt: From the earliest times to the Persian conquest*. New York: Charles Scribner's Sons.

———. 1906–1907). *Ancient records of Egypt. Historical documents from the earliest times to the Persian conquest, collected, edited and translated with commentary.* 5 vols. Chicago:University of Chicago Press.

Breger, Claudia. 2005. Imperialist fantasy and displaced memory: Twentieth-century German Egyptologies. *New German Critique* 96:135–69.

Bresciani, Edda. 1981. Frammenti da un 'prontuario legale' demotico da Tebtuni nell' istituto papirologico G. Vitelli di Firenze. *EVO* 4:201–15.

———. 1985. The Persian occupation of Egypt. In *The Cambridge History of Iran* 2, ed. Ilya Gershevitch, 502–28. Cambridge: Cambridge University Press.

———. 1995. L'égypte des satrapes d'après la documentation araméenne et égyptienne. In *Académie des Inscriptions et Belles-Lettres*, Comptes rendus des séances de l'Année 1995, 97–108.

———. 1998. L'Egitto achemenide: Dario I e il canale del mar Rosso. *Transeuphratène* 14:103–11.

Brett, Michael. 2001. *The rise of the Fatimids: The world of the Mediterranean and the Middle East in the fourth century of the Hijra, tenth century* CE. Leiden: E.J. Brill.

Briant, Pierre. 1982. *Rois, tribus et paysans.* Paris: Les Belles Lettres.

———. 2002. *From Cyrus to Alexander: A History of the Persian Empire*, trans. Peter T. Daniels. Winona Lake, IN: Eisenbrauns. Originally published as *Histoire de l'Empire perse de Cyrus à Alexandre*, 2 vols, vol. 10: Achaemenid History. Leiden: Nederlands Instituut voor het Nabije Oosten, 1996.

———. 2003. Quand les rois écrivent l'histoire: la domination achéménide à travers les inscriptions officielles lagides. In *Événement, récit, histoire officielle: L'écriture de l'histoire dans les monarchies antiques*, ed. N. Grimal and M. Baud, 173–86. Paris: Cybele.

———. 2006. L'Économie royale entre privé et public. In *Approches de L'Économie hellénistique*, 343–51. Saint-Bertrand-de-Comminges: Musée archéologique de Saint-Bertrand-de-Comminges.

Briant, Pierre and Raymond Descat. 1998. Un registre douanier de la satrapie d'Égypte à l'époque achéménide. In *Le commerce en Égypte ancienne*, ed. B. Menu, 59–104. Cairo: IFAO.

den Brinker, A. A., B. P. Muhs, and S. P. Vleeming, eds. 2005. *A Berichtigungsliste of demotic documents. Papyrus editions.* Louvain: Peeters.

Buck, Carl D. 1946. The dialect of Cyrene. *CP* 41/3:129–34.

Burstein, Stanley. 1985. *The Hellenistic age from the battle of Ipsos to the death of Kleopatra VII*, Translated documents from Greece and Rome, vol. 3. Cambridge: Cambridge University Press.

———. 1992. Hecataeus of Abdera's History of Egypt. In *Life in a Multi-cultural society: Egypt from Cambyses to Constantine and beyond*, ed. Janet H. Johnson, 45–49. Chicago: Oriental Institute.

———. 1996a. Ivory and Ptolemaic exploration of the Red Sea: The missing factor. *Topoi* 6:799–807.

———. 1996b. Images of Egypt in Greek historiography. In *Ancient Egyptian literature: History and forms*, ed. Antonio Loprieno, 591–604. Leiden: E. J. Brill.

————. 2000. Prelude to Alexander: The reign of Khababash. *Ancient History Bulletin* 14.4:149–54.

Buruma, Ian (2007). "Tyranny in the twenty-first century," *Financial Times* 8 January 2007:13.

Butzer, Karl. 1976. *Early hydraulic civilization in Egypt: A study in cultural ecology*. Chicago: University of Chicago Press.

————. 1980. Long-term Nile flood variation and political discontinuities in pharaonic Egypt. In *The causes and consequences of food production in Africa*, ed. J. Desmond Clark and Steven A. Brandt, 1–36. Berkeley: University of California Press.

————. 1996. Irrigation, raised fields, and state management: Wittfogel redux? *Antiquity* 70:200–204.

Cadell, Hélène. 1994. Le Prix de Vente des Terres dans l'Égypte ptolémaïque d'après les Papyrus grecs. In *Grund und Boden in altägypten. (Rechtliche und Sozio-Ökonomische Verhältnisse). Akten des internationalen Symposions Tübingen 18.–20 Juni 1990*, ed. Schafik Allam, 289–305.

Cadell, Hélène and Georges Le Rider. 1997. *Prix du blé et numéraire dans l'Égypte de 305 à 173*. Papyrologica Bruxellensia 30. Brussels.

Caminos, Ricardo. 1964. The Nitocris Adoption Stela. *JEA* 50:71–101.

Carrié, Jean-Michel. 2003. Jean de Nikiou et sa Chronique: une écriture 'égyptienne' de l'histoire? In *Événement, récit, histoire officielle: L'écriture de l'histoire dans les monarchies antiques*, ed. N. Grimal and M. Baud, 155–72. Paris: Cybele.

Cartledge, Paul. 1997. Introduction to *Hellenistic constructs: Essays in culture, history and historiography*, ed. Paul Cartledge, Peter Garnsey, and Erich Gruen, 1–19. Berkeley: University of California Press.

Chaffee, John W. 1995. *The Thorny Gates of Learning in Sung China: A Social History of Examinations*, 2nd ed. Albany: State University of New York Press.

Chamoux, François. 2001. *Hellenistic Civilization*. Oxford: Blackwell.

Chaniotis, Angelos. 2005. *War in the Hellenistic world: A social and cultural history*. Oxford: Blackwell.

Charles, R. H. [1916] 2007. *The chronicle of John, Bishop of Nikiu. Translated from Zotenberg's Ethiopic text*, new ed. Merchantville, N.J.: Evolution Publishing.

Chaudhuri, K. N. 1990. *Asia before Europe: Economy and civilisation of the Indian Ocean from the rise of Islam to 1750*. Cambridge: Cambridge University Press.

Chauveau, Michel. 1991. P. Carlsberg 301: Le manuel juridique de Tebtynis. In *The Carlsberg Papyri*, vol. 1, Demotic texts from the collection, 93–101. Copenhagen: CNI Publications.

————. 2000. La première mention du statere d'argent en Égypte. *Transeuphratène* 20:137–43.

Christensen, Thorolf. 2003. P. Haun. inv. 407 and cleruchs in the Edfu nome. In *Edfu, an Egyptian provincial capital in the Ptolemaic period*, ed. Katelijn Vandorpe and Willy Clarysse, 11–16. Brussels: Koninklijke Vlaamse Academie von Belgie voor Wetenschappen en Kunsten.

Clarysse, Willy. 1980. A royal visit to Memphis and the end of the Second Syrian War. In *Studies on Ptolemaic Memphis, Studia Hellenistica* 24:85–89.

———. 1987. Greek loan-words in demotic. In *Aspects of demotic lexicography*, ed. S. P. Vleeming, 9–33. Louvain: Peeters.

———. 1988. A new fragment for a Zenon papyrus from Athens. In *Proceedings of the XVIII International Congress of Papyrology, Athens, 25–31 May 1986*, vol. 2, 77–81. Athens: Greek Papyrological Society.

———. 1991. *The Petrie Papyri*, vol. 1: *The Wills*, 2nd ed. Collectanea Hellenistica, vol. 2. Brussels: Koninklijke Academie voor Wetenschappen, Letteren en Schone Kunsten van België.

———. 1993. Egyptian scribes writing Greek. *CdE* 68:186–201.

———. 1994. Nephorites, founder of the 29th Dynasty and his name. *CdE* 69: 215–17.

———. 1995. Greeks in Ptolemaic Thebes. In *Hundred-Gated Thebes. Acts of a colloquium on Thebes and the Theban area in the Graeco-Roman period*, ed. S. P. Vleeming, *PLBat* 27:1–19. Leiden: E. J. Brill.

———. 1997. Nomarchs and toparchs in the third century Fayyum. In *Archeologia e papiri nel Fayyum. Storia della ricerca, problemi e prospettive*. Atti del convegno internazionale, Siracusa, 24–25 Maggio 1996, 69–76. Siracusa: Istituto internazionale del Papiro.

———. 1998. Ethnic diversity and dialect among the Greeks of Hellenistic Egypt. In *The two faces of Graeco-Roman Egypt*, ed. A.M.F.W. Verhoogt and S. P. Vleeming, 1–13. Leiden: E. J. Brill.

———. 2000a. The Ptolemies visiting the Egyptian chora. In *Politics, administration and society in the Hellenistic and Roman worlds*, ed. Leon Mooren, Proceedings of the International Colloquium, Bertinoro 19–24 July 1997, *Studia Hellenistica* 36:29–53.

———. 2000b. Ptolémées et temples. In *Le décret de Memphis, Colloque de la Fondation Singer-Polignac à l'occasion de la célébration du bicentenaire de la découverte de la Pierre de Rosette*, Paris 1 Juin 1999, ed. Dominique Valbelle and Jean Leclant, 41–65. Paris: De Boccard.

———. 2001. Het Griekse millennium: 500 C.C. tot 500 N.C., *Academiae Analecta*, Nieuwe reeks, nr. 7. Koninklijke Vlaamse Academie van België voor Wetenschappen en Kunsten.

———. 2003. The archive of the praktor Milon. In *Edfu, an Egyptian provincial capital in the Ptolemaic period*, ed. Katelijn Vandorpe and Willy Clarysse, 17–27. Brussels: Koninklijke Vlaamse Academie von Belgie voor Wetenschappen en Kunsten.

Clarysse, Willy and Eddy Lanciers. 1989. Currency and the dating of demotic and Greek papyri from the Ptolemaic period. *Ancient Society* 20:117–32.

Clarysse, Willy and Dorothy J. Thompson. 2006. *Counting the people in Hellenistic Egypt*, 2 vols., Cambridge Classical Studies. Cambridge: Cambridge University Press.

Clarysse, Willy and Katelijn Vandorpe. 1995. *Zenon, Un Homme d'Affairs grec a l'Ombre des Pyramides*. Louvain: Louvain University Press.

———. 1997. Viticulture and wine consumption in the Arsinoite nome (P. Köln V 221). *Ancient Society* 28:67–73.

———. 1998. The Ptolemaic Apomoira. In *Le Culte du Souverain dans l'Égypte ptolémaïque au IIIe Siècle avant notre Ére*, Actes du colloque international, Bruxelles 10 mai 1995, ed. Henri Melaerts, *Studia Hellenistica* 34:5–42.

———. 2008. Egyptian bankers and bank receipts in Hellenistic and early Roman Egypt. In *Pistoi dia tèn technèn: Bankers, loans and archives in the ancient world. Studies in honour of Raymond Bogaert*, ed. Koenraad Verboven, Katelijn Vandorpe, and Véronique Chankowski, *Studia Hellenistica* 44:153–68.

Clarysse, Willy, G. Van der Veken, and S. Vleeming. 1983. *The eponymous priests of Ptolemaic Egypt*, PLBat 24. Leiden: E. J. Brill.

Cohen, Getzel M. 2006. *The Hellenistic settlements in Syria, the Red Sea basin and North Africa*. Berkeley: University of California Press.

Crawford, Dorothy J. 1971. *Kerkeosiris: An Egyptian village in the Ptolemaic period*. Cambridge: Cambridge University Press.

———. 1973. The Opium Poppy: A Study in Ptolemaic Agriculture. In *Problèmes de la terre en Grèce ancienne*, ed. Moses I. Finley, 223–51. Paris: Mouton.

———. 1978. The Good Official of Ptolemaic Egypt. In *Das ptolemäische Ägypten, Akten des Internationalen Symposions 27.–29. September 1976 in Berlin*, ed. Herwig Maehler and Volker Michael Strocka, 195–202. Mainz: Philipp von Zabern.

———. 1980. Ptolemy, Ptah and Apis in Hellenistic Memphis. In *Studies in Ptolemaic Memphis*, ed. W. Peremans, *Studia Hellenistica* 24:1–42.

Crone, Patricia. 2003. *Pre-Industrial societies: Anatomy of the premodern world*. Oxford: Oneworld Publications.

Cruz-Uribe, Eugene. 1985. *Saïte and Persian demotic cattle documents: A study in legal forms and principles in ancient Egypt*, American Society of Papyrologists 26. Chico, CA: Scholar's Press.

Cuvigny, Hélène. 1985. *L'arpentage par espèces dans l'Égypte ptolémaïque d'après les papyrus grecs*. Papyrologica Bruxellensia 20. Brussels: Fondation égyptologique Reine Élisabeth.

El-Daly, Okasha. 2005. *Egyptology: The missing millennium—Ancient Egypt in medieval Arabic writings*. London: UCL Press.

Darnell, John C. 2007. The antiquity of Ghueita temple. *GM* 212:29–32.

Davidson, James. 1998. Review of Cartledge et al. 1997. *Classical Review* 48/2:380–83.

Davies, John K. 1984. Cultural, social and economic features of the Hellenistic world. In *CAH* 7/1, 2nd ed., 257–320. Cambridge: Cambridge University Press.

———. 2001. Hellenistic economies in the post-Finley era. In *Hellenistic Economies*, ed. Zofia H. Archibald, John Davies, Vincent Gabrielsen, and G.J. Oliver, 11–62. London: Routledge.

———. 2002. The interpenetration of Hellenistic sovereignties. In *The Hellenistic world: New perspectives*, ed. Daniel Ogden, 1–21. London: Classical Press of Wales.

———. 2006. Hellenistic economies. In *The Cambridge companion to the Hellenistic world*, ed. Glenn R. Bugh, 73–92. Cambridge: Cambridge University Press.

Davoli, Paola. 1998. *L'archeologia urbana nel Fayyum di èta ellenistica e romana*, Missione Congiunta delle Università di Bologna e di Lecce in Egitto. Naples: G. Procaccini.

———. 2001. *Saft el-Henna: Archeologia e storia di una città del Deltaorientale*. Imola: Editrice La Mandragora.

Dawdy, Shannon Lee. 2005. Review of Gosden 2004. *AJA* 109/3:569–70.

de Cenival, Françoise. 1972a. *Les associations religieuses en Égypte d'après les documents démotiques*. Bibliothèque d'étude 46. Cairo: Institut français d'archéologie orientale.

———. 1972b. Un acte de renonciation consecutive à un partage de revenus liturgiques memphites (P. Louvre E 3266). *BIFAO* 71:11–65.

———. 1973. *Cautionnements démotiques du début de l'époque ptolémaïque*, Société d'histoire du Droit: Collection d'histoire institutionnelle et sociale, vol. 5. Paris: Éditions Klincksieck.

———. 1987. Répertoire journalier d'un bureau de notaire de l'époque ptolémaïque en démotique (P. dem. Lille 120). *Enchoria* 15:1–9.

de Morgan, U. Bouriant, and G. Legrain. 1894. *Les carrières de Ptolemais*. Paris: Ernest Leroux.

de Spens, R. 1998. Droit international et commerce au début de la XXIe dynastie: Analyse juridique du rapport d'Ounamon. In *Le commerce en Égypte ancienne*, ed. N. Grimal and B. Menu, 105–26. Cairo: Institut français d'Archéologie orientale.

Delia, D. 1988. The population of Roman Alexandria. *TAPA* 118:275–92.

———. 1993. Response to Alan Samuel 1993:192–204 (q.v.).

Deng, Gang. 1999. *Premodern Chinese economy: Structural equilibrium and capitalist sterility*. London: Routledge.

Depauw, Mark. 1997. *A companion to demotic studies*. Brussels: Fondation égyptologique Reine Élisabeth.

———. 1999. Demotic witness-copy-contracts. *RdE* 50:67–105.

———. 2000. *The archive of Teos and Thabis from early Ptolemaic Thebes*. Turnhout: Brepols.

———. 2006. *The demotic letter: A study of epistolographic scribal traditions against their intra- and intercultural background*, Demotische Studien 14. Sommerhausen: Gisela Zauzich.

Depuydt, Leo. 1995. Murder in Memphis: The story of Cambyses's mortal wounding of the Apis bull (ca. 523 B.C.E.). *JNES* 54/2:119–26.

Derchain, Philippe. 1987. *Le dernier obélisque*. Brussels: Fondation égyptologique Reine Élisabeth.

———. 2000. *Les impondérables de hellenisation: Littérature d'hierogrammates*. Turnhout: Brepols.

Derda, Tomasz. 2006. *Arsinoites Nomos: Administration of the Fayum under Roman rule*. Journal of Juristic Papyrology, Supplement 7. Warsaw.

Descat, Raymond. 2003. Qu'est-ce que l'économie royale? In *L'Orient méditerranéen de la mort d'Alexandre aux campagnes de Pompée: Cités et royaumes à l'époque hellénistique*, ed. Francis Prost, 149–68. Rennes: Presses universitaires de Rennes.

Descat, Raymond and Pierre Briant. 1998. Un registre douanier de la satrapie d'Egypte à l'époque achéménide (TADC3.7). In *Le commerce en Égypte ancienne*, ed. N. Grimal and B. Menu, 59–104. Cairo: Institut français d'Archéologie orientale.

Devauchelle, Didier. 1995. Les sentiments anti-perse chez les anciens égyptiens. *Transeuphratène* 9:67–80.

Diamond, Larry. 2002. Elections without democracy: Thinking about hybrid regimes. *Journal of Democracy* 13/2:21–35.

Dietze, Gertrud. 2000. Temples and soldiers in southern Ptolemaic Egypt: Some epigraphic evidence. In *Politics, administration and society in the Hellenistic and Roman worlds*, ed. Leon Mooren. Proceedings of the International Colloquium, Bertinoro 19–24 July 1997, *Studia Hellenistica* 36:77–89.

Dillery, John. 1999. The first Egyptian narrative history: Manetho and Greek historiography. *ZPE* 127:93–116.

———. 2005. Cambyses and the Egyptian *Chaosbeschreibung* tradition. *Classical Quarterly* 55/2:387–406.

Dobias-Lalou, Catherine. 2000. *Le dialecte des inscriptions grecques de Cyrène*, Karthago 25.

Donker van Heel, Koenraad. 1990. *The legal manual of Hermopolis [P. Mattha]: Text and translation.* Leiden: Papyrologisch Instituut.

———. 1994. The lost battle of Peteamonip son of Petehôrresne. In *Acta Demotica, Acts of the Fifth International Conference for Demotists, Pisa, 4th–8th September 1993*, ed. E. Bresciani, 115–24. Egitto e Vicino Oriente 17.

———. 1995. *Abnormal hieratic and early demotic texts collected by the Theban choachytes in the reign of Amasis: Papyri from the Louvre Eisenlohr Lot.* Leiden.

Dothan, Trude and Moshe. 1992. *People of the sea: The search for the Philistines.* New York: Macmillan.

Duyrat, Frédérique. 2005. Le Trésor de Damanhour (*IGCH* 1664) et l'évolution de la circulation monétaire en Égypte hellénistique. In *L'exception égyptienne? Production et échanges monétaires en Égypte hellénistique et romaine*, ed. Frédérique Duyrat and Olivier Picard, *Études alexandrines* 10:17–51. Cairo: Institut français d'Archéologie orientale.

Eckstein, Arthur M. 2008. *Rome enters the Greek East: From anarchy to hierarchy in the Hellenistic Mediterranean, 230–170 BC.* Oxford: Blackwell.

Edelman, Lauren B. and Robin Stryker. 2005. A sociological approach to law and economy. In *The Handbook of Economic Sociology*, 2nd ed., ed. Neil J. Smelser and Richard Swedberg, 527–51. Princeton: Princeton University Press.

Edgar, Campbell Cowan. 1931. *Zenon Papyri in the University of Michigan Collection*, University of Michigan Studies, Humanistic Series 24. Ann Arbor: University of Michigan Press.

Egberts, A.B.P. Muhs and J. van der Vliet, eds. 2002. *Perspectives on Panopolis.* Leiden: E. J. Brill.

Eide, Tormod, T. Hägg, R. Holton Pierce, and L. Török, eds. 1994. *Textual sources for the history of the Middle Nile Region between the eighth century BC and the sixth century AD.* Fontes Historiae Nubiorum, vol. 1: *From the eighth to the mid-fifth century BC.* Bergen: University of Bergen Department of Classics.

Eisenstadt, S. N. [1963] 1993. *The political systems of empires*, with a new foreword by the author. New Brunswick: Transaction Publishers.

El-Daly, Okasha. 2005. *Egyptology, the missing millennium: Ancient Egypt in Medieval Arabic writings*. London: UCL Press.

Ellickson, Robert C. 1991. *Order without law: How neighbors settle disputes*. Cambridge: Harvard University Press.

Ellis, Frank. 1993. *Peasant economics: Farm households and agrarian development*, 2nd ed. Cambridge: Cambridge University Press.

Elvin, Mark 1973. *The pattern of the Chinese past*. Stanford: Stanford University Press.

Empereur, Jean-Yves, ed. 1998. Commerce et artisanat dans l'Alexandrie hellénistique et romanine. Actes du colloque d'Athènes 11–12 décembre 1988. Bulletin de Correspondance hellénique Supplément 33. Athens.

Erskine, Andrew. W. 1995. Culture and power in Ptolemaic Egypt: The Museum and the Library of Alexandria. *Greece and Rome* 42:38–48.

Erskine, Andrew W., ed. 2003. *A companion to the Hellenistic world*. Oxford: Blackwell.

Eyre, Christopher. 1994. The water regime for orchards and plantations in pharaonic Egypt. *JEA* 80:57–80.

———. 2004. How relevant was personal status to the functioning of the rural economy in pharaonic Egypt? In *Le dépendance rurale dans l'Antiquité égyptienne et proche-orientale*, ed. Bernadette Menu, 157–186. Cairo: Institut français d'Archéologie orientale.

———. Forthcoming. Provincial government. In *Oxford Handbook of Egyptology*, ed. James Allen and Ian Shaw. Oxford: Oxford University Press.

Fahmy, Khaled. 1998. The era of Muhammed 'Ali Pasha, 1805–1848. In *The Cambridge history of Egypt*, vol. 2: Modern Egypt from 1517 to the end of the twentieth century, ed. M. W. Daly, 139–79. Cambridge: Cambridge University Press.

Falivene, Maria Rosaria. 1991. Government, management, literacy: Aspects of Ptolemaic administration in the early Hellenistic period. *Ancient Society* 22:203–27.

Farid, Adel. 1993. *Die demotischen Inschriften der Strategen*. San Antonio: Van Siclen.

Feinman, Gary M. and Joyce Marcus, eds. 1998. *Archaic states*. Santa Fe: School of American Research Press.

Felber, Heinz. 1997. *Demotische Ackerpachtverträge der Ptolemäerzeit*. Wiesbaden: Otto Harrassowitz.

———. 2002. Die demotische Chronik. In *Apokalyptik und Ägypten: Eine kritische Analyse der relevanten Texte aus dem griechisch-römischen Ägypten*, ed. A. Blasius and B. U. Schipper, Orientalia Lovaniensia Analecta 107:65–111. Louvain: Peeters.

Ferguson, Niall. 2001. *The cash nexus: Money and power in the modern world, 1700–2000*. New York: Basic Books.

Finley, M. I. 1965. Technological innovation and economic progress in the ancient world. *Economic History Review* 18:29–45.

————. 1976. Colonies—an attempt at typology. *Transactions of the Royal Historical Society* 5th ser. 26:167–88.

————. 1978. Empire in the Greco-Roman world. *Greece and Rome* 25/1:1–15.

————. 1985. *Ancient History. Evidence and models*. New York: Penguin.

————. 1999. *The Ancient Economy*, 2nd ed., updated with a new foreword by Ian Morris. Berkeley: University of California Press.

Fischer, Christelle. 2008. *Army and society in Ptolemaic Egypt*. Ph.D. dissertation, Stanford University.

Fischer, H.G. 1977. "Gaufürst," s.v. in *Lexikon der Ägyptologie*, vol. 4, ed. W. Helck and W. Westendorf, 408–17. Wiesbaden: Otto Harrassowitz.

Flaherty, David H. 1970. An approach to American History: Willard Hurst as legal historian. *The American Journal of Legal History* 14/3:222–34.

Fowler, Richard. 2007. Kingship and banditry: The Parthian empire and its western subjects. In Rajak et al. 2007, 147–62.

Fox, Robin Lane. 2007. Alexander the Great "Last of the Achaemenids"? In *Persian responses: Political and cultural interaction with(in) the Achaemenid empire*, ed. Christopher Tuplin, 267–311. Swansea: Classical Press of Wales.

Frandsen, Paul John. 1979. Egyptian imperialism. In *Power and Propaganda: A symposium on ancient empires*, vol. 7: Mesopotamia, ed. Mogens Trolle Larsen, 167–90. Copenhagen: Akademisk Forlag.

Franke, D. 1991. The career of Khnumhotep III of Beni Hasan and the so-called "decline of the nomarchs." In *Middle Kingdom Studies*, ed. S. Quike, 51–67. New Malden: Sia Publications.

Franko, George Fredric. 1988. Sitometria in the Zenon archive: Identifying Zenon's personal documents. *BASP* 25:13–98.

Fraser, P.M. 1958. *Berytus* 12:120–27.

————. 1960. Inscriptions from Ptolemaic Egypt. *Berytus* 13:123–61, pl. 29.

————. 1972. *Ptolemaic Alexandria*, 3 vols. Oxford: Clarendon Press.

Friedman, Lawrence. 1975. *The legal system: A social science perspective*. New York: Russell Sage Foundation.

Frier, Bruce W. 1989. A new papyrology? *BASP* 26:217–26.

xFrier, Bruce W. and Dennis Kehoe. 2007. Law and economic institutions. In *The Cambridge economic history of the Greco-Roman world*, ed. Walter Scheidel, Ian Morris, and Richard Saller, 113–43. Cambridge: Cambridge University Press.

Froidfond, Christian. 1971. *Le Mirage égyptien dans la literature grecque d'Homère à Aristote*. Aix-en-Provence: Ophrys.

Furubotn, Eirik G. and Rudolf Richter. 2000. *Institutions and economic theory: The contribution of the new institutional economics*. Ann Arbor: University of Michigan Press.

Furuoya, Tomohiro. 2005. Excavated documents and their genetic context in ancient Japan. In *Genesis of historical text: Text/context*, ed. Shoichi Sato, Proceedings of the fourth international conference, 21st Century COE Program, 23–30. Nagoya: Nagoya University Graduate School of Letters.

Gabrielsen, Vincent. 2003. Piracy and the slave-trade. In *A companion to the Hellenistic world*, ed. Andrew Erskine, 389–404. Oxford: Blackwell.

Gardiner, Alan H. 1937. *Late Egyptian Miscellanies*, Bibliotheca aegyptiaca, vol. 7. Brussels: Fondation égyptologique Reine Élisabeth.

——. 1951. A protest against unjust tax demands. *RdE* 6:115–33.

——. 1953. The coronation of Haremhab. *JEA* 39:13–31.

——. 1961. *Egypt of the pharaohs: An Introduction*. Oxford: Clarendon Press.

Gasse, Annie. 1988. *Données nouvelles administratives et sacerdotales sur l'Organisation du Domaine d'Amon xxᵉ–xxiᵉ dynasties, à la lumière des papyrus Prachov, Reinhardt et Grundbuch (avec édition princeps des Papyrus Louvre AF 6345 et 6346–7)*, 2 vols. Cairo: Institut français d'Archéologie orientale du Caire.

Gates-Foster, Jennifer. 2006. Hidden passage: Graeco-Roman roads in Egypt's eastern desert. In *Space and spatial analysis in archaeology*, ed. E. Robertson et al., 315–22. Calgary: University of Calgary Press.

Geens, Karolien. 2008. Financial archives of Graeco-Roman Egypt. In *Pistoi dia tèn technèn: Bankers, loans and archives in the ancient world, Studies in honour of Raymond Bogaert*, ed. Koenraad Verboven, Katelijn Vandoorpe, and Véronique Chankowski, 133–51. Louvain: Peeters.

Geertz, Clifford. 1980. *Negara: The theatre state in nineteenth-century Bali*. Princeton: Princeton University Press.

Gellner, Ernest. 1983. *Nations and nationalism*. Ithaca: Cornell University Press.

Glanville, S.R.K. 1939. *A Theban archive of the reign of Ptolemy I Soter*, Catalogue of Demotic papyri in the British Museum, vol. 1. London: British Museum.

Goddio, Franck. 1995. Cartographie des vestiges archéologiques submerges dans le Port East d'Alexandrie et dans la Rade d'Aboukir. In *Alessandria e il mondo ellenistico-romano, I centenario del Museo greco-romano: Alessandria, 23–27 novembre 1992, atti del II Congresso internazionale italo-egiziano*, ed. Amedeo Tullio, Cristina Naro, and Elisa Chiara Portale, 172–75. Rome: L'Erma di Bretschneider.

——. 1998. *Alexandria: The submerged royal quarters*. London: Periplus Publishing.

——. 2006. *Egypt's sunken treasures*. Munich: Prestel.

Goelet, Jr., Ogden. 2002. Fiscal renewal in ancient Egypt: Its language, symbols, and metaphors. In *Debt and economic renewal in the ancient Near East*, ed. Michael Hudson and Marc Van de Mieroop, 277–326. Bethesda: CDL Press.

——. 2004. Accounting practices and economic planning in Egypt before the hellenistic era. In *Creating economic order: Record-keeping, standardization, and the development of accounting in the ancient Near East*, ed. Michael Hudson and Cornelia Wunsch, 215–68. Bethesda, MD: CDL Publishing

Goitein, S. D. 1967. *A Mediterranean society: The Jewish communities of the Arab world as portrayed in the documents of the Cairo Geniza*, vol. 1: Economic foundations. Berkeley: University of California Press.

Goldsmith, Raymond W. 1987. *Premodern financial systems. A historical comparative study*. Cambridge: Cambridge University Press.

Goldstone, Jack A. 2006. A historical, not comparative, method: Breakthroughs and limitations in the theory and methodology of Michael Mann's analysis of power. In *An anatomy of power: The social theory of Michael Mann*, eds. John A. Hall and Ralph Schroeder, 263–82. Cambridge: Cambridge University Press.

Golvin, J.-C. 1995. Enceintes et portes monumentales des temples de Thèbes à l'époque ptolémaïque et romaine. In *Hundred-gated Thebes. Acts of a colloquium on Thebes and the Theban area in the Graeco-Roman period*, ed. S. P. Vleeming, *PLBat* 27:31–41. Leiden: E. J. Brill.

Gosden, Chris. 2004. *Archaeology and colonialism: Cultural contact from 5000 BC to the present*. Cambridge: Cambridge University Press.

Gozzoli, Roberto B. 2006. *The writing of history in ancient Egypt during the first millennium BC (ca. 1070–180 BC): Trends and perspectives*. London: Golden House Publications.

Green, Peter. 1990. *Alexander to Actium: The historical evolution of the Hellenistic age*. Berkeley: University of California Press.

———. 1993. Response to Samuel 1993:209–10 (q.v.)

Greene, Molly. 2000. *A shared world: Christians and Muslims in the early modern Mediterranean*. Princeton: Princeton University Press.

Greenfield, Jonas C. and B. Porten. 1982. *The Bisitun Inscription of Darius the Great: Aramaic Version*, Corpus Inscriptionum Iranicarum 1: Inscriptions of Ancient Iran. London: Lord Humphries.

Greif, Avner. 2006. *Institutions and the path to the modern economy: Lessons from medieval trade*. Cambridge: Cambridge University Press.

Grenfell, B. P. and J. P. Mahaffy. 1896. *The Revenue laws of Ptolemy Philadelphus*. Oxford: Clarendon Press.

Griffith, Francis Llewellyn. 1909. *Catalogue of the demotic papyri in the John Rylands Library Manchester*, 3 vols. Manchester: University Press.

Grimal, Nicholas. 1981. *La stèle triomphale de Pi('ankh)y au Musée du Caire, JE 48862 et 47086–47089*. Cairo: Institut français d'archéologie orientale.

Grimm, Günter. 1998. *Alexandria: Die erste Königsstadt der hellenistischen Welt*. Mainz: Philipp von Zabern.

Gruen, Erich. 1984. *The Hellenistic world and the coming of Rome*. Berkeley: University of California Press.

———. 1996. Hellenistic kingship: Puzzles, problems, and possibilities. In *Aspects of Hellenistic Kingship*, ed. P. Bilde, et al., 116–25. Aarhus: Aarhus University Press.

———. 1998. *Heritage and Hellenism: The reinvention of Jewish tradition*. Berkeley: University of California Press.

Grunert, Stefan. 1982. *Der Kodex Hermopolis und ausgewählte private Rechtsurkunden aus dem ptolemäischen Ägypten*. Leipzig: Verlag Phillip Reclam.

Gulliver, P. H. 1979. *Disputes and negotiations: A cross-cultural perspective*. New York: Academic Press.

Gygax, Marc Domingo. 2005. Change and continuity in the administration of Ptolemaic Lycia: A note on *pTebt*. I 8. *BASP* 42:45–50.

Gyles, Mary Francis. 1959. *Pharaonic policies and administration, 663 to 323 BC*. Chapel Hill, NC: University of North Carolina Press.

Haber, Stephen. 2006. Authoritarian Government. In *The Oxford Handbook of Political Economy*, ed. Barry Weingast and Donald Wittman, 693–707. Oxford: Oxford University Press.

Habermann, Wolfgang and Bernhard Tenger. 2004. Der Wirtschaftsstil der Ptole-
    mäer. In *Wirtschaftssyteme im historischen Vergleich*, ed. B. Schefold, 271–333.
    Stuttgart: Franz Steiner Verlag.
Habicht, Christian. 1958. Die herrschende Gesellschaft in den hellenistischen
    Monarchien. *Vierteljahrschrift für Sozial- und Wirtschaftsgeschichte* 45:1–16.
Haldon, John F. 1993. *The state and the tributary mode of production*. London:
    Verso.
Hannity, Sean. 2005. *Deliver us from evil: Defeating terrorism, despotism and
    liberalism*. New York: Harper Collins.
Haring, B.J.J. 1997. *Divine households: Administrative and economic aspects of
    the New Kingdom royal memorial temples in western Thebes*. Leiden: Neder-
    lands Instituut voor het Nabije Oosten.
Harper, G. M. 1934. Tax contractors and their relation to tax collection in Ptole-
    maic Egypt. *Aegyptus* 14:49–64.
Harries, Jill. 1999. *Law and empire in late antiquity*. Cambridge: Cambridge Uni-
    versity Press.
Harris, William V. 2005. The Mediterranean and ancient history. In *Rethinking
    the Mediterranean*, ed. W. V. Harris, 1–42. New York: Oxford University Press.
Hauben, Hans. 1987. Cyprus and the Ptolemaic Navy. *Report of the Department
    of Antiquities, Nicosia, Cyprus* 65, 213–26.
Hawass, Zahi. 2000. *Valley of the golden mummies*. New York: Abrams.
Hayes, William C. 1955. *A papyrus of the Late Middle Kingdom in the Brooklyn
    Museum*. Brooklyn: Brooklyn Museum.
Hazzard, R.A. 1995. *Ptolemaic coins: An introduction for collectors*. Toronto:
    Kirk and Bentley.
Heinen, Heinz. 1984. The Syrian-Egyptian wars and the new kingdoms of Asia
    Minor. Chapter 11 in *CAH* 7/1, 2nd ed., 412–45. Cambridge: Cambridge Uni-
    versity Press.
———. 1987. L'Égypte dans l'historiographie moderne du monde héllenistique.
    In *Egitto e storia antica dall'ellenismo all'Età Araba: Bilanco di un confronto*,
    ed. L. Criscuolo and G. Geraci, 105–35. Bologna: CLUEB.
———. 2003. *Geschichte des Hellenismus. Von Alexander bis Kleopatra*. Mu-
    nich: C. H. Beck.
Helmis, Andréas. 1990. Despotisme et repression: Les limites du pouvoir ptolé-
    maïque. In *Symposion 1988: Vorträge zur griechischen und hellenistischen
    Rechtsgeschichte*, eds. Giuseppe Nenci and Gerhard Thür, 311–17. Cologne:
    Böhlau Verlag.
Hennig, D. 2003. Sicherheitskräfte zur Überwachung der Wüstengrenzen und
    Karawanenwege im ptolemäischen Ägypten. *Chiron* 33:145–74.
Hens, H. 1979. *De Kyreners in Ptolemaeisch Egypte*. MA thesis, Katholieke Uni-
    versiteit Louvain.
Herman, Gabriel. 1980–81. The 'friends' of early Hellenistic rulers: Servants or
    officials? *Talanta* 12–13:103–49.
Hicks, John. 1969. *A theory of economic history*. Oxford: Oxford University
    Press.
Hobsbawm, Eric. 1969. *Bandits*. London: Liedenfeld and Nicholson.

Hobson, Deborah. 1985. House and household in Roman Egypt. *YCS* 28: 211–29.

Hodges, Donald and Ross Gandy. 2002. *Mexico under siege: popular resistance to presidential despotism*. London: Zed Books.

Hoffmann, Friedhelm. 2000. *Ägypten Kultur und Lebenswelt in griechisch-römischer Zeit: Eine Darstellung nach den demotischen Quellen*. Berlin: Akademie Verlag.

Hölbl, Günther. 2001. *A History of the Ptolemaic empire*, trans. Tina Saavedra. London: Routledge. Originally published as *Geschichte des Ptolemäerreiches* (Darmstadt: Wissenschaftliche Buchgesellschaft, 1994).

Hopkins, Keith. 1995/96. Rome, taxes, rents and trade. *Kodai* 6–7:41–75. Reprinted in Walter Scheidel and Sitta von Reden, eds. *The Ancient Economy*, 190–230. London: Routledge.

Horden, Peregrine and Nicholas Purcell. 2000. *The corrupting sea: A study of Mediterranean history*. Oxford: Blackwell.

Hornblower, Simon. 1994. Persia. in *CAH* 6, 2nd. ed., 45–96. Cambridge: Cambridge University Press.

———. 1996. "Hellenism, Hellenization," in the *Oxford Classical Dictionary*, *3rd* ed., ed. Simon Hornblower and Antony Spawforth, 677–79. Oxford: Oxford University Press.

Houston, Stephen, John Baines and Jerrold Cooper. 2003. Last writing: Script obsolescence in Egypt, Mesopotamia and Mesoamerica. *Comparative Studies in Society and History* 45/3:430–79.

Huang, Philip C.C. 1996. *Civil justice in China: Representation and practice in the Qing*. Stanford: Stanford University Press.

Huang, Ray. 1981. *1587, a year of no significance: The Ming Dynasty in decline*. New Haven: Yale University Press.

Hübsch, Gerbert. 1968. Die Personalangaben als Identifizierungsvermerke im Recht der gräko-ägyptischen Papyri. *Berliner juristische Abhandlungen* 20. Berlin: Duncker und Humblot.

Hughes, George R. 1952. *Saïte demotic land leases*. SAOC 28. Chicago: Oriental Institute.

———. 1984. The So-Called Pherendates Correspondance. In *Grammata demotika: Festschrift für Erich Lüddeckens*, ed. H.-J. Thissen and K.-Th. Zauzich, 75–88. Würzburg: Gisela Zauzich Verlag.

Hughes, George R. and Richard Jasnow. 1997. *Oriental Institute Hawara papyri: Demotic and Greek texts from an Egyptian family archive in the Fayyum (fourth to third century BC)*. Oriental Institute Publications 113. Chicago: Oriental Institute.

Hunter, Richard. 2003. *Theocritus: Encomium of Ptolemy Philadelphus*. Berkeley: University of California Press.

Hurst, Willard. 1956. *Law and the conditions of freedom in the nineteenth-century United States*. Madison: University of Wisconsin Press.

Huß, Werner. 1990. Die Herkunft der Kleopatra Philopator. *Aegyptus* 70: 191–203.

———. 1991. Die in ptolemaïscher Zeit verfaßten Synodal-Dekrete der ägyptischen Priester. *ZPE* 88:189–208.

Huß, Werner. 2001. *Ägypten in hellenistischer Zeit, 332–30 v. Chr.* Munich: C. H. Beck.

Husson, Genevieve and Dominque Valbelle. 1992. *L'État et les Institutions en Égypte des premiers pharaons aux empereurs romains.* Paris: A. Colin.

Irwin, Robert. 2006. *Dangerous knowledge: Orientalism and its discontents.* Woodstock: Overlook Press.

Issar, Arie S. 2003. *Climate changes during the Holocene and their impact on hydrological systems.* Cambridge: Cambridge University Press.

Jansen, H. Ludin. 1950. *The Coptic story of Cambyses' invasion of Egypt.* Avhandlinger utgitt av Det Norske Videnskaps-Akademie i Oslo. II Hist.-Filos. Klasse 1950, no. 2.

Janssen, Jac. J. 1975a. Prolegomena to the study of Egypt's economic history during the New Kingdom. *SAK* 3:127–85.

———. 1975b. *Commodity prices from the Ramessid period.* Leiden: E. J. Brill.

———. 1979. The role of the temple in the Egyptian economy during the New Kingdom. In ed. E. Lipinski, *State and temple economy in the ancient Near East*, vol. 2, 505–15. Louvain: Peeters.

Jasnow, Richard. 1999. Remarks on continuity in Egyptian literary tradition. In *Gold of praise: Studies on ancient Egypt in honor of Edward F. Wente*, ed. Emily Teeter and John A. Larson, 193–210. Chicago: Oriental Institute.

Johnson, Carl. 2000. Ptolemy I's *epiklesis* SWTHR: origin and definition. *Ancient History Bulletin* 14:102–06.

Johnson, Janet H. 1974. The Demotic Chronicle as an historical source. *Enchoria* 4:1–17.

———. 1987. Ptolemaic bureaucracy from an Egyptian point of view. In *The Organization of Power: Aspects of Bureaucracy in the Ancient Near East*, ed. McGuire Gibson and Robert C. Biggs, Studies in Ancient Oriental Civilization 46: 141–49. Chicago: Oriental Institute.

———. 1994. The Persians and the continuity of Egyptian culture. In *Achaemenid History* 8: *Continuity and change*, ed. Heleen Sancisi-Weerdenburg, Amélie Kuhrt, and Margaret Cool Root, 149–59. Leiden: Nederlands Intituut voor het Nabije Oosten.

Jones, Eric. 1988. *Growth recurring: Economic change in world history.* Ann Arbor: University of Michigan Press.

Kaiser, Brooks A. 2007. The Athenian trierarchy: Mechanism design for the private provision of public goods. *Journal of Economic History* 67/2:445–80.

Kamal, Ahmed. 1905. *Stèles ptolémaïques et romaines.* Catalogue général des antiquités égyptiennes du Musée du Caire 12. Cairo: Imprimerie de l'Institut français.

Kanawati, Naguib. 1990. *Sohag in Upper Egypt: A glorious history.* Giza: Prism Publications.

———. 1999. "Akhmim," in *The encyclopedia of the archaeology of ancient Egypt*, ed. Kathryn A. Bard, 124–28. New York: Routledge.

Kaplony-Heckel, Ursula. 1963. *Die demotischen Tempeleide*, Ägyptologische Abhandlungen 6. Wiesbaden: Otto Harrassowitz.

———. 2000. Demotic ostraca from Thebes: Percentages and relations between pharaoh and the temple. *JARCE* 37:75–80.

Katary, Sally L. D. 1989. *Land tenure in the Ramesside period*. London: Kegan Paul International.

Keenan, James G. and John C. Shelton. 1976. *The Tebtunis papyri*, vol. 4, Graeco-Roman Memoirs 64. London: Egypt Exploration Society.

Kehoe, Dennis P. 1988. *The economics of agriculture on Roman imperial estates in North Africa*. Hypomnemata 89. Göttingen: Vandenhoeck.

———. 2007. *Law and the rural economy in the Roman Empire*. Ann Arbor: University of Michigan Press.

Kemp, Barry J. 1978. Imperialism and empire in New Kingdom Egypt. In *Imperialism in the ancient world: The Cambridge University research seminar in ancient history*, ed. P.D.A. Garnsey and C. Whitaker, 284–97. Cambridge: Cambridge University Press.

———. 1989. *Ancient Egypt: Anatomy of a civilization*. London: Routledge.

———. 1995. How religious were the ancient Egyptians? *Cambridge Archaeological Journal* 5:1:25–54.

———. 2006. *Ancient Egypt: Anatomy of a civilization*, 2nd rev. ed. London: Routledge.

Kienitz, F. 1953. *Die politische Geschichte Ägyptens vom 7. bis zum 4. Jahrhundert vor der Zeitwende*. Berlin: Akademie-Verlag.

Kim, H. S. 2002. Small change and the moneyed economy. In *Money, labour and law: Approaches to the economies of ancient Greece*, ed. Paul Cartledge, Edward C. Cohen, and Lin Foxhall, 44–51. London: Routldge.

Kiser, Edgar. 1994. Markets and hierarchies in early modern tax systems: A principal-agent analysis. *Politics and Society* 22/3:284–315.

Kiser, Edgar and Danielle Kane. 2007. The perils of privatization: How the characteristics of principals affected tax farming in the Roman Republic and empire.*Social Science History* 31/2:191–212.

Kitchen, Kenneth A. 1986. *The Third Intermediate Period in Egypt (1100–650 B.C.)*, 2nd ed. with Supplement. Warminster: Aris and Phillips.

Klotz, David. 2006. *Adoration of the ram: Five hymns to Amun-Re from Hibis temple*. Yale Egyptological Studies 6. New Haven: Yale Egyptological Seminar.

Knoppers, Gary N. and Paul B. Harvey, Jr. 2007. The Pentateuch in ancient Mediterranean context: The publication of local lawcodes. In *The Pentateuch as Torah: New models for understanding its promulgation and acceptance*, ed. Gary N. Knoppers and Bernard M. Levinson, 105–41. Winona Lake: Eisenbrauns.

Koenen, Ludwig. 1968. Die prophezeiungen des "Topfers." ZPE 2:178–209.

———. 1977. *Eine agonistische Inschrift aus Ägypten und frühptolemäische Königsfeste*, Beiträge zur klassischen Philologie 56. Meisenheim am Glan: Hain.

———. 1985. Die Adaptation ägyptischer Königsideologie am Ptolemäerhof. In *Egypt and the Hellenistic world, Proceedings of the international colloquium, Louvain, 24–26 May 1982*, ed. E. Van 't-Dack, P. van Dessel, and W. van Gucht. *Studia Hellenistica* 27:143–90.

———. 1993. The Ptolemaic king as a religious figure. In *Images and ideologies: Self-definition in the Hellenistic world*, ed. A. Bulloch et al., 25–115. Berkeley: University of California Press.

Koenen, Ludwig. (2007). Papyrology, Ptolemaic Egypt and Byzantine Palestine. In *Akten des 23. Internationalen Papyrologenkongresses, Wien, 22.–28. Juli 2001*, ed. Bernhard Palme, Papyrologica Vindobonensia 1:5–13. Vienna: Verlag der Österreichischen Akademie der Wissenschaften.

Kornemann, Ernst. 1925. Die Satrapenpolitik des ersten Lagiden. In *Raccolta di scritti in onore di Giacomo Lumbroso (1844–1925)*, 235–45. Milan: Aegyptus.

Kraeling, Carl. 1962. *Ptolemais, city of the Libyan Pentapolis*. Oriental Institute Publications 90. Chicago: Oriental Institute.

Kramer, Bärbel. 1997. Der *ktistes* und der Einrichtung einer neuen Stadt. *Archiv für Papyrusforschung* 43/2:315–39.

Kraus, Jürgen. 2004. *Die Demographie des Alten Ägypten: Eine Phänomenologie anhand altägyptischer Quellen*. PhD. dissertation, Georg-August-Universität Göttingen.

Kruchten, Jean-Marie. 2001. Law. In *The Oxford encyclopedia of ancient Egypt*, ed. Donald B. Redford, 277–82. Oxford: Oxford University Press.

Kuhlmann, Klaus P. 1983. *Materialien zur Archäologie und Geschichte des Raumes von Achmim*. Mainz: Philipp von Zabern.

Lá' da, Csaba. 2002. *Foreign ethnics in Hellenistic Egypt. Studia Hellenistica* 38.

Lá' da, Csaba and Amphilochus Papathomas. 2003. A Ptolemaic petition by a royal farmer concerning the postponement of legal proceedings before the *laokritai*. *AfP* 49/2:183–92.

Lajtar, Adam. 2006. *Deir el-Bahari in the Hellenistic and Roman periods: A study of an Egyptian temple based on Greek sources*. Journal of Juristic Papyrology, Supplement 4. Warsaw.

Lansing, J. Stephen. 1991. *Priests and programmers: Technologies of power in the engineered landscape of Bali*. Princeton: Princeton University Press.

Laronde, André. 1987. *Cyrène et la Libye hellénistique*. Paris: Éditions du Centre de la Recherche Scientifique.

Launey, M. 1949–1950. *Recherches sur les armées hellénistique*, 2 vols. Paris: E. de Boccard.

Laurens, Henry. 1987. *Les Origines intellectuelles de l'Expédition d'Égypte: L'orientalisme islamisant en France (1698–1798)*. Istanbul: Editions Isis.

Leahy, Anthony. (1985). The Libyan period in Egypt: An essay in interpretation. *Libyan Studies* 16:51–65.

LeFebvre, Michael. 2006. *Collections, codes, and Torah: The re-characterization of Israel's written law*. New York: T & T International.

Lehner, Mark. 2000. Fractal house of pharaoh: Ancient Egypt as a complex adaptive system, a trial formulation. In *Dynamics in human and primate societies. Agent-based modeling of social and spatial processes*, ed. T. Kohler and G. Gumerman, 275–353. Oxford: Oxford University Press.

Lenger, Marie-Thérèse, ed. 1964. *Corpus des Ordonnances des Ptolémées (C. Ord. Ptol.)*. Mémoires, 2nd series, vol. 57/5. Reissued with corrections in 1980. Brussels: Académie royale de Belgique.

Lev, Yaacov. 1991. *State and society in Fatimid Egypt*. Leiden: E. J. Brill.

Levi, Margaret. 1988. *Of rule and revenue*. Berkeley: University of California Press.

Lewis, M.J.T. 1997. *Millstone and hammer: The origins of water power.* Hull: University of Hull Press.

Lewis, Napthali. 1986. *Greeks in Ptolemaic Egypt: Case studies in the social history of the Hellenistic world.* Oxford: Clarendon Press.

Lichtheim, Miriam. 1976. *Ancient Egyptian literature*, vol. 1: The Old and Middle Kingdoms. Berkeley: University of California Press. Reissued in 2006.

———. 1980. *Ancient Egyptian literature*, vol. 3: The Late Period. Berkeley: University of California Press. Reissued in 2006.

Lindgren, James. 1995. Measuring the value of slaves and free persons in ancient law. *Chicago-Kent Law Review* 71/1:149–215.

Lippert, Sandra Luisa. 2003. Die sogenannte Zivilprozessordung: Weitere Fragmente der ägyptischen Gesetzessammlung. *Journal of Juristic Papyrology* 33:91–135.

———. 2004a. *Ein demotisches juristisches Lehrbuch: Untersuchungen zu Papyrus Berlin P 23757 rto*, Ägyptologische Abhandlungen. Wiesbaden: Otto Harrassowitz.

———. 2004b. Fragmente demotischer juristischer Bücher (pBerlin 23890 a-b, d-g rto und pCarlsberg 628). In *Res severa verum gaudium: Festschrift für Karl-Theodor Zauzich zum 65. Geburtstag am 8. Juni 2004*, ed. F. Hoffmann and H. J. Thissen, 389–405. Louvain: Peeters.

Lippert, Sandra L. and Maren Schentuleit. 2006. *Demotische Dokumente aus Dime*, 2 vols. Wiesbaden: Otto Harrassowitz.

Lloyd, Alan B. 1969. Perseus and Chemmis (Herodotus II 91). *JHS* 89:79–86.

———. 1977. Necho and the Red Sea: Some considerations. *JEA* 63:142–55.

———. 1982. The inscription of Udjahorresnet: A collaborator's testament. *JEA* 68:166–80.

———. 1983. The Late Period, 664–323 BC. In *Ancient Egypt: A social history*, ed. B. G. Trigger, B. J. Kemp, D. O'Connor, and A. B. Lloyd, 279–348. Cambridge: Cambridge University Press.

———. 1988a. Herodotus on Cambyses: Some thoughts on recent work. *AchHist* 3:55–66.

———. 1994. Egypt, 404–332 B.C.. In *CAH* 6, 2nd ed., 337–60. Cambridge: Cambridge University Press.

———. 1999. Manetho. In *Encyclopedia of the archaeology of ancient Egypt*, ed. Kathryn Bard, 464–65. London: Routledge.

———. 2000. Saite navy. In *The sea in antiquity*, ed. G. J. Oliver, R. Brock, T. J. Cornell, and S. Hodkinson. *British Archaeological Reports*, international series 899, chapter 8. Oxford: Hadrian Books.

———. 2002. The Egyptian elite in the early Ptolemaic period: Some hieroglyphic evidence. In *The Hellenistic world: New perspectives*, ed. Daniel Ogden, 117–36. London: Classical Press of Wales.

———. 2003. The Late Period (664–332 BC). In *The Oxford history of ancient Egypt*, ed. Ian Shaw, new paperback edition, 364–87. New York: Oxford University Press.

———. 2007. Darius I and Egypt: Suez and Hibis. In *Persian responses: Political and cultural interaction with(in) the Achaemenid empire*, ed. Christopher Tuplin, 99–115. Swansea: Classical Press of Wales.

Lloyd, Alan, B., trans. 1975. *Herodotus Book 2*, vol. 1. Leiden: E.J. Brill.

———. 1988b. *Herodotus Book 2*, vol. 3. Leiden: E. J. Brill.

Lorber, Catherine C. 2005. Development of Ptolemaic bronze coinage in Egypt. In *L'exception égyptienne? Production et échanges monétaires en Égypte hellénistique et romaine*, ed. Frédérique Duyrat and Olivier Picard, *Études alexandrines* 10, 135–57. Cairo: Institut français d'Archéologie orientale.

Lüddeckens, Erich. 1960. *Ägyptische Eheverträge*, Ägyptologische Abhandlungen, vol. 1. Wiesbaden: Otto Harrassowitz.

Lyons, H. G. and L. Borchardt. 1896. Eine trilingue Inschrift von Philae. *Sitzungberichte Berlin. Akad.* 462:82.

Ma, John. 2000. *Antiochos III and the cities of western Asia Minor*. Oxford: Oxford University Press.

———. 2003. Kings. In *A companion to the Hellenistic world*, ed. Andrew Erskine, 177–95. Oxford: Blackwell.

Macdowell, Andrea G. 1990. *Jurisdiction in the workman's community of Deir el-Medina*. Leiden: Nederlands Instituut voor het Nabije Oosten.

MacDowell, Douglas M. 1978. *The law of classical Athens*. Ithaca: Cornell University Press.

Mairs, Rachel and Cary J. Martin. Forthcoming. A bilingual 'sale' of liturgies from the archive of the Theban choachytes: P. Berlin 5507, P. Berlin 3098 and P. Leiden 413. *Enchoria*.

Malinine, Michel. 1953. *Choix de Textes juridiques en hiératique anormal et en démotique (xxv–xxvii dynasties)*. Paris: Librairie ancienne honoré Champion.

Malkin, Irad. 2004. Postcolonial concepts and ancient Greek colonization. *Modern Language Quarterly* 65.3:341–64.

Mann, Michael. 1986. *The sources of social power*. Cambridge: Cambridge University Press.

Manning, J. G. 1999. The Auction of Pharaoh. In *Gold of praise: Studies in Honor of Edward F. Wente*, ed. John Larsen and Emily Teeter, 277–84. Chicago: Oriental Institute.

———. 2002–2003. A Ptolemaic agreement concerning a donkey with an unusual warranty clause: The strange case of P. dem. Princ. 1 (inv. 7524). *Enchoria* 28:46–61.

———. 2003a. *Land and power in Ptolemaic Egypt: The structure of land tenure*. Cambridge: Cambridge University Press.

———. 2003b. Demotic law. In *A history of near eastern law*, vol. 2, ed. Raymond Westbrook, 819–62. Leiden: E. J. Brill.

———. 2003c. Edfu as a central place in Ptolemaic history. In *Edfu: An Egyptian provincial capital in the Ptolemaic period*, ed. Katelijn Vandorpe and Willy Clarysse, 61–73. Brussels: Koninklijke Vlaamse Academie van België voor Wetenschappen en Kunsten.

———. 2007. Hellenistic Egypt. In *The Cambridge economic history of the Greco-Roman world*, ed. Walter Scheidel, Ian Morris, and Richard Saller, 434–59. Cambridge: Cambridge University Press.

Manning, J. G. and Ian Morris, eds. 2005. *The ancient economy. Evidence and models*. Stanford: Stanford University Press.

Manuelian, Peter Der. 1994. *Living in the past: Studies in archaism of the Egyptian twenty-sixth dynasty*. London: Kegan Paul International.

Maresch, Klaus. 1996. *Bronze und Silber. Papyrologische Beiträge zur Geschichte der Währung im ptolemäischen und römischen Ägypten bis zum 2. Jahrhundert n. chr*. Papyrologica Coloniensia:25. Abhandlungen der Nordrhein-Westfälischen Akademie der Wissenschaften, Cologne.

Markiewicz, Tomasz. (2008). Bocchoris the lawgiver. Or was he really? 12:309–30. *JEH*.

Marquaille, C. 2001. *The external image of Ptolemaic Egypt*. Unpublished PhD thesis, King's College London.

Marsot, Afaf Lutfi al-Sayyid. 1984. *Egypt in the reign of Muhammed Ali*. Cambridge: Cambridge University Press.

Martin, Cary J. 1996. The demotic texts. In *The Elephantine papyri in English: Three millennia of cross-cultural continuity and change*, ed. Bezalel Porten. Leiden: E. J. Brill. Pp. 277–385.

———. 1999). A twenty-seventh dynasty "marriage contract" from Saqqara. In *Studieson ancient Egypt in honour of H. S. Smith*, 193–99. London: Egypt Exploration Society.

———. 2007. The Saïte "demoticisation" of southern Egypt. In *Literacy and the state in the ancient Mediterranean*, ed. Kathryn Lomas, Ruth D. Whitehouse, and John B. Wilkins, 25–38. London: Accordia Research Institute.

Mattha, Girgis. 1945. *Demotic ostraka from the collections at Oxford, Paris, Berlin, Vienna and Cairo*. Textes et Documents 6. Cairo: Publications de la société Fouad I de Papyrologie.

Mattha, Girgis and George R. Hughes. 1975. *The demotic legal code of Hermopolis West*. Bibliothèque d'Études 45. Cairo: Institut français d'archéologie orientale.

McClellan, Murray C. 1997. The economy of Hellenistic Egypt and Syria: An archaeological perspective. In *Ancient economic thought*, ed. B. B. Price, 172–87. London: Routledge.

McGing, B. C. 1997. Revolt Egyptian Style: Internal Opposition to Ptolemaic Rule. *AfP* 43:273–314

McKechnie, Paul. 1989. *Outsiders in the Greek cities in the fourth century BC*. London: Routledge.

McKenzie, J. S. 2003. Glimpsing Alexandria from archaeological evidence. *JRA* 6:35–61.

Meeks, Dimitri. 1972. *Le grand texte des donations au temple d'edfou*. Cairo: Institut français d'archéologie orientale.

Mélèze-Modrzejewski, Joseph. 1975. Chrématistes et laocrites. In *Le monde grec: pensée, littérature, histoire, documents. Hommages à Claire Préaux*, ed. J. Bingen, G. Cambier, and G. Nachtergael, ULB Fac. Philos. Let. 52, Brussels, 699–708.

———. 1995. Law and justice in Ptolemaic Egypt. In *Legal documents of the Hellenistic world: Papers from a seminar*, ed. Markham J. Geller and Herwig Maehler, 1–19. London: Warburg Institute.

———. 2001. The Septuagint as Nomos: How the Torah Became a "Civic Law" for the Jews of Egypt. In *Critical Studies in Ancient Law, Comparative Law, and Legal History*. Essays in honour of Alan Watson, eds. J. W. Cairns and O. F. Robinson, 183–99. Oxford: Oxford University Press.

———. Forthcoming. Ptolemaic justice. In *Law and society in Egypt from Alexander to the Arab Conquest, 332 BC–640 AD*, ed. J. G. Keenan, J. G. Manning, and Uri Yiftach-Firanko. Cambridge: Cambridge University Press.

Menu, Bernadette. 1988. Les Actes de Vente en Égypte ancienne, particulièrement sous les rois Kouchites et Saïtes. *JEA* 74:165–81.

———. 1994. Modalités et réglementation du prêt en Égypte à l'époque de la première domination perse. In *Colloque international de l'ASPEP*, Paris. Reprinted in *Recherches sur l'histoire juridique, économique et sociale de l'ancienne Égypte*, vol. 2, *Bibliothèque d'étude* 122 (1998), 385–99. Cairo: Institut français d'archéologie orientale.

———. 1998. Le système économique de l'Égypte ancienne. *Méditerranées. Revue de l'association Méditerranées, publiée avec le concours de l'Université de Paris X-Nanterre* 17:71–97.

Merkelbach, Reinhold. 1977. *Die Quellen des griechischen Alexanderromans*. Munich: C. H. Beck.

Mileta, Christian. 2002. The king and his land: Some remarks on the royal area (*basilike chora*) of Hellenistic Asia Minor. In *The hellenistic world: New perspectives*, ed. Daniel Ogden, 157–75. London: Classical Press of Wales.Millar, Fergus. 1998. Looking east from the classical world: Colonialism,culture, and trade from Alexander the Great to Shapur I. *International History Review* 20/3:507–31.

Miller, Margaret C. 1997. *Athens and Persians in the fifth century BC: A study in cultural receptivity*. Cambridge: Cambridge University Press.

Minas, Martina. 1998. Die *kanephoros*: Aspekte des ptolemäischen Dynastiekults. In *Le culte de souverain dans l'Égypte ptolémaïque au IIIe siècle avant notre ère*. Actes du colloque international, Bruxelles 10 mai 1995. *Studia Hellenistica* 34, ed. Henri Melaerts, 42–60.

———. 2005. Macht und Ohnemacht. Die Representation ptolemäischer königinnen in ägyptischen Tempeln. *AfP* 51:127–54.

Möller, Astrid. 2000. *Naukratis: Trade in archaic Greece*. New York: Oxford University Press.

———. 2007. Classical Greece: Distribution. In *The Cambridge economic history of the Greco-Roman world*. ed. Walter Scheidel, Ian Morris, and Richard Saller, 362–84. Cambridge: Cambridge University Press.

Momigliano, Arnaldo. 1966. *Studies in historiography*. London: Weidenfeld and Nicolson.

———. 1976. *Alien wisdom: The limits of hellenization*. Cambridge: Cambridge University Press.

Monson, Andrew. 2008. *Agrarian institutions in transition: Privatization from Ptolemaic to Roman Egypt*. PhD thesis, Stanford University.

Montesquieu. [1748] 1989. *The spirit of the laws*, ed. Anne M. Cohler, Basia C. Miller, and Harold S. Stone, Cambridge texts in the history of political thought. Cambridge: Cambridge University Press.

Mooren, Leon. 1975. *The aulic titulature in Ptolemaic Egypt: Introduction and prosopography*. Brussels: Paleis des Academiën.

────. 1983. The nature of Hellenistic monarchy. In *Egypt and the Hellenistic world: Proceedings of the international colloquium, Leuven, 24–26 May 1982*, ed. E. Van 't-Dack, P. van Dessel, and W. van Gucht, *Studia Hellenistica* 27: 205–40.

Mooren, Leon, ed. 2000. *Politics, administration and society in the Hellenistic and Roman world: Proceedings of the international colloquium, Bertinoro 19–24 July 1997. Studia Hellenistica* 36.

Morony, Michael G. 1984. *Iraq after the Muslim conquest*. Princeton: Princeton University Press.

Morris, Ian. 1994. Archaeologies of Greece. In *Classical Greece. Ancient histories and modern ideologies*, ed. Ian Morris, 8–47. Cambridge: Cambridge University Press.

────. 2005. Archaeology, standards of living, and Greek economic history. In *The Ancient economy: Evidence and models*, eds. J. G. Manning and Ian Morris, 91–126. Stanford: Stanford University Press.

Mørkholm, Otto. 1980. Cyrene and Ptolemy I. *Chiron* 10:154–59.

Moyer, Ian S. 2002. Herodotus and an Egyptian mirage: The genealogies of the Theban priests. *JHS* 122:7–90.

Mrsich, Tycho. 1984. Eine Zwischenbilanz zum "zivilprozessualen" Abschnitt des demotischen Rechtsbuches 'S' (P. Berl. 13621 Rc Col. II). In *Gedächtnisschrift für Wolfgang Kunkel*, ed. D. Nörr and D. Simon, 205–82. Frankfurt: V. Klostermann.

Mueller, Katja. 2006. *Settlements of the Ptolemies: City foundations and new settlement in the Hellenistic world. Studia Hellenistica* 43.

Muhs, Brian P. 2001. Membership in private associations in Ptolemaic Tebtunis. *Journal of the Economic and Social History of the Orient* 44/1:1–21.

──── (2005a). *Tax receipts, taxpayers, and taxes in early Ptolemaic Thebes.* Oriental Institute Publications 126. Chicago: Oriental Institute.

────. (2005b). The grapheion and the disappearance of demotic contracts in early Roman Tebtynis and Soknopaiou Nesos. In *Tebtynis und Soknopaiou Nesos: Leben im römerzeitlichen Fajum*, ed. Sandra Lippert and Maren Schentuleit, 93–104.. Wiesbaden: Otto Harrassowitz.

Müller, Bernd Jürgen. 1968. *Ptolemaeus II: Philadelphus als Gesetzgeber*. PhD dissertation, Köln.

Murray, G. W. 1967. Trogodytica: The Red Sea littoral in Ptolemaic times. *Geographical Journal* 133/1:24–33.

Murray, Oswyn. 1970. Hecataeus of Abdera and pharaonic kingship. *JEA*56:141–71.

Muszynsky, M. 1977. Les Associations religieuses en Égypte d'après les sources hiéroglyphiques, démotiques et grecques. *Orientalia Louvanensia Periodica* 8:145–74.

Nesbitt, M. and D. Samuel. 1995. From staple crop to extinction? The archaeology and history of the hulled wheats. In *Hulled wheats; Proceedings of the first internationl workshop on hulled wheats 21–22 July 1995*. Castelvecchio Pascoli, Tuscany, Italy, eds. S. Padulosi, K. Hammer and J. Heller, 41–100. Rome: International Plant Genetic Resources Institute.

Nicolet, Claude. 2003. *La fabrique d'une nation: La France entre Rome et les Germains*. Paris: Perrin.

North, Douglass C. 1990. *Institutions, institutional change and economic performance*. Cambridge: Cambridge University Press.

———. 1981. *Structure and change in economic history*. New York: Norton.

O'Brian, Martin. 1998. The Sociology of Anthony Giddens: An introduction. In Anthony Giddens and Christopher Pierson, *Conversations with Anthony Giddens*, 1–27. Stanford: Stanford University Press.

O'Connor, David and David P. Silverman, eds. 1995. *Ancient Egyptian Kingship*. Probleme der Ägyptologie, vol. 9. Leiden: E. J. Brill.

O'Leary, Brendan. 1989. *The Asiatic mode of production: Oriental despotism, historical materialism and Indian history*. Oxford: Blackwell.

Ogden, Daniel. 2002. From chaos to Cleopatra. In *The hellenistic world: New perspectives*, ed. Daniel Ogden, ix–xxv. London: Classical Press of Wales.

Ogilvie, Sheilagh. 2007. "Whatever is, is right?" Economic institutions in preindustrial Europe. *Economic History Review* 60/4:649–84.

Olson, Mancur. 1982. *The rise and decline of nations*. New Haven: Yale University Press.

———. 2000. *Power and prosperity: Outgrowing communist and capitalist dictatorships*. New York: Basic Books.

Onasch, Hans-Ulrich. 1994. *Die Assyrischen Eroberungen Ägyptens*, 2 vols. *Ägypten und Altes Testament* vol. 27. Wiesbaden: Otto Harrassowitz.

Orrieux, Claude. 1983. *Les Papyrus de Zenon: L'horizon d'un grec en Égypte au IIIe siècle avant J.C.* Paris: Macula.

———. 1985. *Zéno de Caunos, parépidémos, et le destin grec*. Paris: Belles Lettres.

Otto, Eckart. 1994. Aspects of legal reforms and reformulations in ancient cuneiform and Israelite law. In *Theory and method in Biblical and cuneiform law: Revision, interpolation, and development. Journal for the Study of the Old Testament*, Supplement Series 181, ed. Bernard Levinson, 160–96. Sheffield: Sheffield Academic Press.

Owen, Roger. 1972. Egypt and Europe: From French Expedition to British Occupation. Reprinted in *The modern Middle East: A reader*, ed. Albert Hourani, Philip S. Khoury, and Mary Christina Wilson, 111–24. London: I. B. Tauris.

Packman, Zola M. 1968. *The taxes in grain in Ptolemaic Egypt: Granary receipts from Diospolis Magna 164–88 B.C.* American Studies in Papyrology 4. New Haven: American Society of Papyrologists.

Park, Thomas K. 1992. Early trends toward class stratification: Chaos, common property, and flood recession agriculture. *American Anthropologist* 94:90–117.

Parker, Richard A. 1963. A demotic marriage document from Deir el-Ballas, *JARCE* 2:113–16.

Parkinson, R.B. 1991. *The tale of the eloquent peasant*. Oxford: Griffith Institute.

Pearce, Sarah. 2007. Translating for Ptolemy: Patriotism and politcics in the Greek Pentateuch? In *Jewish perspectives on hellenistic rulers*, ed, Tessa Rajak, Sarah Pearce, James Aitken, and Jennifer Dines, 165–89. Berkeley: University of California Press.

Peden, Alexander J. 2001. *The graffiti of pharaonic Egypt: scope and roles of informal writings (c.3100–332 BC)*. Leiden: E. J. Brill.

Peremans, W. 1977. Un groupe d'officiers dans l'armée des Lagides. *Ancient Society* 8:175–85.

Perpillou-Thomas, Françoise. 1993. *Fêtes d'Égypte ptolémaïque et romaine d'après la documentation papyrologique grecque*. Studia Hellenistica 31.

Pestman, P.W. 1968. Eine demotische Doppelurkunde. In *Antidoron Martino David oblatum: Miscellanea Papyrologica*, ed. E. Boswinkel, B. van Groningen, and P. Pestman, 100–111. *PLBat* 17. Leiden: E. J. Brill.

———. (1978). L'agoranomie: Un avant-poste de l'administration grecque enlevé par les Égyptiens. In *Das ptolemäische Ägypten*, ed. Herwig Maehler and Volker Michael Strocka, 203–10. Mainz: Philipp von Zabern.

———. 1981. *A guide to the Zenon archive*. PLBat 21. Leiden: E. J. Brill.

———. 1983a. L'Origine et l'extension d'un manuel du Droit égyptien: Quelques réflexions à propos du soi-disant Code d'Hermopolis. *JESHO* 26:14–21.

———. 1983b. Some aspects of Egyptian Law in Graeco-Roman Egypt: Title-deeds and 'upallagma. In *Egypt and the Hellenistic world*, ed. E. Van 't Dack, P. van Dessel, and W. Van Gucht, *Studia Hellenistica* 27:281–302.

———. 1985a. Le démotique comme langue juridique. In *Textes et études de papyrologie grecque, démotique et copte*, ed. P.W. Pestman, *PLBat* 23, 198–203. Leiden: E. J. Brill.

———. 1985b. The competence of Greek and Egyptian tribunals according to the decree of 118 BC. *BASP* 22:265–69.

———. 1985c. Registration of demotic contracts in Egypt: P. Par. 65, 2nd cent. B.C. In *Satura Roberto Feenstra sexagesimum quintum annum aetatis complenti ab alumnis collegis amicis oblata*, ed. J. Ankum, J. E. Spruit, and F.B.J. Wubbe, 17–25. Fribourg: Éditions universitaires.

———. 1992. *Il Processo di Hermias e altri documenti dell'archivio dei Choachiti (P. Tor. Choachiti)*, Catalogo del Museo Egizio di Torino, Serie Prima-Monumenti e Testi 6. Turin: Ministerio per I Beni Culturali e Ambientali.

———. 1993. *The archive of the Theban choachytes (Second century B.C.): A survey of the demotic and Greek papyri contained in the archive*. Leiden: E. J. Brill.

———. 1994. *Les papyrus démotiques de Tsenhor (P. Tsenhor): Les archives privées d'une femme égyptienne du temps de Darius Ier*. Louvain: Peeters.

Peters, F. E. 1970. *The harvest of Hellenism: A history of the Near East from Alexander the Great to the triumph of Christianity*. New York: Simon and Schuster.

Pfeiffer, Stefan. 2004. *Das Dekret von Kanopos (238 v.Chr.): Kommentar und historische Auswertung eines dreisprachigen Synodaldekretes der ägyptischen Priester zu Ehren Ptolemaios' III. und seiner Familie, Archiv für Papyrusforschung und verwandte Gebiete*, Beiheft 18. Munich: K. G. Saur.

———. 2008. *Herrscher- und Dynastiekulte im Ptolemäerreich: Systematik und Einordnung der Kultformen*. Münchener Beiträge zur Papyrusforschung und antiken Rechtsgeschichte 98. Munich: Beck.

Picard, Olivier. 1999. Un monnayage Alexandrin énigmatique: Le trésor d'Alexandrie 1996. In *Travaux de numismatique grècque offerts à George Le Rider*, ed. M. Amandry and S. Hurter, 313–21. Paris: Spink and Son.

———. 2004. L'apport des monnaies des fouilles d'Alexandrie. In *L'exception égyptienne? Production et échanges monétaires en Égypte hellénistique et romaine*, ed. Frédérique Duyrat and Olivier Picard, *Études alexandrines* 10, 81–90. Cairo: Institut français d'Archéologie orientale.

Pierce, Richard Holton. 1972. *Three demotic papyri in the Brooklyn Museum: A Contribution to the study of contracts and their instruments in Ptolemaic Egypt, Symbolae Osloensis* 24. Oslo: Universitetsforlaget.

Plaumann, Gerhard. 1910. *Ptolemais in Oberägypten: Ein Beitrag zur Geschichte des Hellenismus in Ägypten*. Leipzig: Quelle and Meyer.

Pomeroy, Sarah B. 1994. *Xenophon, Oeconomicus: A social and historical commentary*. Oxford: Clarendon Press.

Porten, Bezalel and J. J. Farber. 1996. The Greek texts. In *The Elephantine papyri in English: Three millennia of cross-cultural continuity and change*, ed. Bezalel Porten, 386–568. Leiden: E. J. Brill.

Posener, Georges. 1936. *La première domination perse en Égypte*. Bibliothèque d'Études 11. Cairo: Institut français d'archéologie orientale.

———. 1953. On the Tale of the Doomed Prince. *JEA* 39:107.

———. 1960. De la divinité du Pharaon. *Cahiers de la Société asiatique* 15. Paris.

Préaux, Claire. 1936. Un problem de la politique des Lagides: la faiblesse des edits. In *Atti del IV Congresso internazionale di Papirologia, Firenze, 28 aprile–2 maggio 1935*. 185–93. Milan: Aegyptus.

———. 1939. *L'Économie royale des Lagides*. Brussels: Edition de la Fondation égyptologique Reine Élisabeth.

———. 1947. *Les Grecs en Égypte d'après les archives de Zénon*. Brussels: Office de Publicité.

———. 1966. Sur la Stagnation de la Pensée scientifique à l'époque héllènistique. In *Essays in honor of C. Bradford Welles*, *American Studies in Papyrology* 1, 235–50. New Haven: American Society of Papyrologists.

———. 1971. Greco-Roman Egypt. In *The legacy of Egypt*, 2nd ed., ed. J. R. Harris, 323–54. Oxford: Clarendon Press.

———. 1978. *Le Monde hellénistique: La Grèce et l'Orient de la mort d'Alexandre à la conquête romaine de la Grèce (323–146 av. J.-C.)*, 2 vols. Paris: Presses Universitaires de France.

———. 1983. L'attache à la Terre: Continuities de l'Égypte ptolémaïque à l'Égypte romaine. In *Das römisch-byzantinische Ägypten: Akten des internationalen Symposions 26.–30. September 1978 in Trier*, ed. G. Grimm et al., 1–5. Mainz: Philipp von Zabern.

Pringsheim, Fritz. 1949. The Greek sale by auction. In *Scritti in onore di Contardo Ferrini pubblicati in occasione della sua beatificazione* 4, ed. Gian Gualberto Archi, *Publicazioni dell'universita' cattolica del sacro cuore*, new series 28, 284–343. Milan.

Quack, Joachim. 2004. Review of Vittman (2003). *JAOS* 124.2:360–61.

Quaegebeur, Jan (1979). Documents égyptiens et rôle économique du clergé en Égypte hellénistique. In *State and temple economy in the ancient Near East*,

Proceedings of the International Conference organized by the Katholieke Universiteit Leuven from the 10th to the 14th of April 1978, vol. 2, ed. Edward Lipinski, 707–29. Louvain: Departement Oriëntalistiek.

———. 1982. Sur la 'loi sacrée' dans l'Égypte gréco-romaine. *Ancient Society* 11–12:227–40.

———. 1993. La Justice à la Porte des Temples et le Toponyme Premit. In *Individu, société et spiritualité dans l'Égypte pharaonique et Copte: Mélanges offerts au Professeur Aristide Théodoridès*, ed. C. Cannuyer and J.-M. Kruchten, 201–20. Ath: Illustra.

Rajak, Tessa, Sarah Pearce, James Aitken, and Jennifer Dines, eds. 2007. *Jewish perspectives on Hellenistic rulers*. Berkeley: University of California Press.

Rathbone, Dominic. 1989. The ancient economy and Graeco-Roman Egypt. In *Egitto e storia antica dall'ellenismo all'età araba: Bilancio di un confronto*, ed. Lucia Criscuolo and Giovanni Geraci, 159–76. Bologna: Editrice CLUEB. Reprinted in *The ancient economy*, ed. Walter Scheidel and Sitta von Reden, 155–69.

———. 1990. Villages, land and population in Graeco-Roman Egypt. In *Proceedings of the Cambridge Philological Society* 216, n.s. 36:103–42.

———. 1996. Toward a historical topography of the Fayum. In *Archaeological research in Roman Egypt*, The Proceedings of the Seventeenth Classical Colloquium of the Department of Greek and Roman Antiquities, British Museum, ed. Donald M. Bailey, *Journal of Roman Archaeology*, Supplementary Series 19:50–56.

———. 1997. Surface survey and the settlement history of the ancient Fayum. In *Archeologia e Papiri nel Fayyum: Storia della Ricerca, Problemi e Prosettive. Atti del Convegno internazionale*, 7–20. Siracusa: Istituto internazionale del Papiro.

———. 2000. Ptolemaic to Roman Egypt: The death of the *dirigiste* state? In *Production and public powers in classical antiquity*, ed. E. Lo Cascio and D. W. Rathbone, Cambridge Philological Society, Supplementary vol. 26:44–54. Cambridge: Cambridge University Press.

———. 2007. Roman Egypt. In *The Cambridge economic history of the Greco-Roman world*, ed. Walter Scheidel, Ian Morris, and Richard Saller, 698–719. Cambridge: Cambridge University Press.

Ray, John. 1976. *The archive of Hor*: Texts from Excavations, Second Memoir. London: Egypt Exploration Society.

———. 1987. Egypt: Dependence and independence (425–343 BC). In *Achaemenid History*, vol. 1: *Sources, structures and syntheses, Proceedings of the Groningen 1983 Achaemenid history workshop*, ed. Heleen Sancisi-Weerdenburg, 79–95. Leiden: Nederlands Instituut voor het Nabije Oosten.

———. 1988. "Egypt 525–404 B.C.," in *CAH*, vol. 4, 2nd ed. Cambridge: Cambridge University Press. Pp. 254–86.

———. 1994. Literacy and language in Egypt in the Late and Persian periods. In *Literacy and power in the ancient world*, 51–66. Cambridge: Cambridge University Press.

———. 2002. *Reflections of Osiris: Lives from ancient Egypt*. Oxford: Oxford University Press.

Ray, John. 2005. *Demotic papyri and ostraca from Qasr Ibrim*. London: Egypt Exploration Society.

Redford, Donald B. 1970. *A study of the biblical story of Joseph (Genesis 37–50)*. Leiden: E. J. Brill.

———. 1986. *Pharaonic king-lists, annals and day-books*. Mississauga: Benben Publications.

———. 2001. The so-called "codification" of Egyptian law under Darius I. In *Persia and Torah: The theory of imperial authorization of the Pentateuch*, ed. James W. Watts, 135–59. Atlanta: Society of Biblical Literature.

———. 2004. *From slave to pharaoh: The black experience of ancient Egypt*. Baltimore: Johns Hopkins University Press.

Reed, Joseph D. 2000. Arsinoe's Adonis and the poetics of Ptolemaic imperialism. *TAPA* 130:319–51.

Reekmans, Tony. 1948. Monetary history and the dating of Ptolemaic papyri. *Studia Hellenistica 5*.

———. 1949. Economic and social repercussions of the Ptolemaic copper inflation. *CdE* 48:324–42.

———. (1951). The Ptolemaic copper inflation. *Studia Hellenistica 7*: 61–119.

Reger, Gary. 1994. *Regionalism and change in the economy of independent Delos, 314–167 B.C.* Berkeley: University of California Press.

Reich, Hermann. 2004. Die 'Orientalische Despotie'. In *Wirtschaftssysteme im historischen Vergleich*, ed. Bertram Schefold, 493–542. Stuttgart: Franz Steiner.

Reich, Nathaniel J. 1933. The codification of the Egyptian laws by Darius and the origin of the "Demotic Chronicle." *Mizraim* 1:178–85.

Rhodes, P. J. and Robin Osborne. 2003. *Greek historical inscriptions: 404–323 BC*. Oxford: Oxford University Press.

Ricketts, Linda M. 1982–83. The *epistrategos* Kallimachos and a Koptite inscription: SB V 8036 reconsidered. *Ancient Society* 13/14:161–65.

Ritner, Robert K. 1999. Implicit models of cross-cultural interaction. A question of noses, soap and prejudice. In *Life in a multi-cultural society: Egypt from Cambyses to Constantine and beyond*, ed. Janet H. Johnson, 283–90. Chicago: Oriental Institute.

———. 2002. Third Intermediate Period antecedents of demotic legal terminology. In *Acts of the seventh international conference of demotic studies, Copenhagen, 23–27 August 1999*, ed. Kim Ryholt, 343–59. Copenhagen: Cartsen Niebuhr Institute of Near Eastern Studies.

———. 2003. The Satrap Stela. In *The literature of ancient Egypt: An anthology of stories, instructions, stelae, autobiographies, and poetry*, 3rd ed., ed. William Kelly Simpson, 392–97. New Haven: Yale University Press.

———. 2004. A selection of demotic ostraca in the Detroit Institute of Arts. In *Res severa verum gaudium: Festschrift für Karl-Theodor Zauzich zum 65. Geburtstag am 8.Juni 2004*, ed. F. Hoffmann and H. J. Thissen, 497–508. Louvain: Peeters.

Roeder, Günther. 1959. *Die ägyptische Götterwelt*. Zürich: Artemis.

Rostovtzeff, Michael. 1920. The foundations of social and economic life in Egypt in Hellenistic times. *JEA* 6:161–78.

———. 1922. *A large estate in Egypt in the third century* B.C.*: A study in economic history.* Madison, WI: University of Wisconsin Press.

———. 1941. *The social and economic history of the Hellenistic world*, 3 vols. Oxford: Clarendon Press.

Roth, Martha T. 1997. *Law collections from Mesopotamia and Asia Minor*, 2nd ed. Atlanta: Scholar's Press.

Rowlandson, Jane. 1985. Freedom and subordination in ancient agriculture: The case of the *Basilikoi Georgoi* of Ptolemaic Egypt. *History of Political Thought* 6:327–47.

———. 1996. *Landowners and tenants in Roman Egypt: The social relations of agriculture in the Oxyrhynchite nome.* Oxford: Oxford University Press.

———. 2001. Money use among the peasantry of Ptolemaic and Roman Egypt. In *Money and its uses in the ancient Greek world*, ed. Andrew Meadows and Kirsty Shipton, 145–55.. New York: Oxford University Press.

———. 2003. Approaching the peasantry of Greco-Roman Egypt: From Rostovtzeff to rhetoric. In *Views of ancient Egypt since Napoleon Bonaparte: Imperialism, colonialism and modern appropriations*, ed. David Jeffreys, 147–52. London: UCL Press.

———. 2005. Town and country in Ptolemaic Egypt. In *A companion to the Hellenistic world*, ed. Andrew Erskine, paperback version of 2003 edition, 249–63. Oxford: Blackwell.

———. 2007. The character of Ptolemaic aristocracy: Problems of definition and evidence. In *Jewish perspectives on hellenistic rulers*, ed. Tessa Rajak, Sarah Pearce, James Aitken, and Jennifer Dines, 29–49. Berkeley: University of California Press.

Rubensohn, O. 1907. *Elephantine-papyri*. Berlin: Weidmann.

Runciman, W. G. 1989. *A treatise on social theory*, vol. 2: *Substantive social theory.* Cambridge: Cambridge University Press.

Rupprecht, Hans-Albert. 1994. *Kleine Einführung in die Papyruskunde*. Darmstadt: Wissenschaftlichen Buchgesellschaft.

Rüterswörden, Udo. 1995. Die persische Reichsautorisation der Thora: Fact of fiction?" *Zeitschrift für Altorientalische und biblische Rechtsgeschichte* 1: 47–61.

Rutherford, Ian. 2005. Downstream to the cat-goddess: Herodotus on Egyptian pilgrimage. In *Pilgrimage in Graeco-Roman and Early Christian antiquity: Seeing the Gods*, ed. Jas Elsner and Ian Rutherford, 131–50. Oxford: Oxford University Press.

Said, Edward. 1978. *Orientalism*. New York: Random House.

Sallares, Robert. 1991. *The Ecology of the ancient Greek world*. Ithaca: Cornell University Press.

Saller, Richard. 2002. Framing the debate over growth in the ancient economy. In *The ancient economy*, ed. Walter Scheidel and Sitta von Reden, 250–69. London: Routledge. Reprinted in *The ancient economy: Evidence and models*, ed. J. G. Manning and Ian Morris, 223–42. Stanford: Stanford University Press.

Salmenkivi, Erja. 2002. *Cartonnage papyri in context: New Ptolemaic documents from Abu Sir al-Malaq. Commentationes Humanarum Litterarum* 119. Helsinki: Societas Scientarum Fennica.

Samuel, Alan E. 1966a. The internal organization of the nomarch's bureau in the third century BC. In *Essays in honor of C. Bradford Welles, American Studies in Papyrology* 1, 213–29. New Haven: American Society of Papyrologists.

———. 1966b. The judicial competence of the *oikonomos* in the third century BC. *Atti dell' XI Congresso internazionale di Papirologia* Milan: Istituto Lombardo di Scienze e Lettere.

———. 1971. P. Tebt. 703 and the *oikonomos*. In *Studi in onore di Edoardo Volterra*, Pubblicazioni della Facoltà di giurisprudenza dell'Università di Roma, vol. 2, 451–60. Milan: Giuffrè.

———. 1983. *From Athens to Alexandria: Hellenism and social goals in Ptolemaic Egypt. Studia Hellenistica* 26.

———. 1984. The money economy and the Ptolemaic peasantry. *BASP* 21: 187–206.

———. 1989. *The shifting sands of history: Interpretations of Ptolemaic Egypt.* Publications of the Association of Ancient Historians. Lanham: University Press of America.

———. 1993. The Ptolemies and the ideology of kingship. In *Hellenistic history and culture*, ed. Peter Green, 168–210. Berkeley: University of California Press.

Sanders, Paula A. 1994. *Ritual, politics, and the city in Fatimid Cairo*. Albany: State University of New York Press.

———. 1998. The Fatimid state, 969–1171. In *The Cambridge history of Egypt*, vol. 1: Islamic Egypt, 640–1517, ed. Carl F. Petry, 151–74. Cambridge: Cambridge University Press.

Sandy, D. Brent. 1989. *The production and use of vegetable oils in Ptolemaic Egypt. BASP*, Supplement vol. 6.

Sargent, Thomas J. and François R. Velde. 2002. *The big problem of small change.* Princeton: Princeton University Press.

Scheidel, Walter. 2001. *Death on the Nile: Disease and the demography of Roman Egypt.* Leiden: E. J. Brill.

———. 2004. Creating a metropolis: A comparative demographic perspective. In *Ancient Alexandria between Egypt and Greece*, ed. W. V. Harris and Giovanni Ruffini, 1–31. Leiden: E. J. Brill.

Schentuleit, Maren. 2006. *Aus der Buchhaltung des Weinmagazins im Edfu-Tempel: Der demotische P. Carlsberg 409.* Copenhagen: Museum Tusculanum Press.

Schipper, Bernd Ulrich. 2005. *Die Erzählung des Wenamun. Ein Literaturwerk im Spannungsfeld von Politik, Geschichte und Religion. Orbis Biblicus et Orientalis* 209. Fribourg : Academic Press.

Schmid, Konrad. 2007. The Persian imperial authorization as an historical problem and as a biblical construct: a plea for distinctions in the current debate. In *The Pentateuch as Torah: New models for understanding its promulgation and acceptance*, ed. Gary N. Knoppers and Bernard M. Levinson, 22–38. Winona Lake, IN: Eisenbrauns.

Schnebel, M. 1925. *Die Landwirtschaft im hellenistischen Ägypten, Münchener Beiträge zur Papyrusforschung und antiken Rechtsgeschichte*, vol. 7. Munich.

Schneider, Helmuth. 2007. Technology. In *The Cambridge economic history of the Greco-Roman world*, ed. Walter Scheidel, Ian Morris, and Richard Saller, 144–71. Cambridge: Cambridge University Press.

Schroeder, Ralph. 2006. Introduction: the IEMP model and its critics. In *An anatomy of power: The social theory of Michael Mann*, 1–16. Cambridge: Cambridge University Press.

Schulman, Alan Richard. 1988. *Ceremonial execution and public rewards: some historical scenes on New Kingdom private stelae. Orbis Biblicus et Orientalis* 75. Freiburg: Universitätsverlag.

Scott, W. Richard. 2001. *Institutions and organizations*, 2nd ed. Thousand Oaks, CA: Sage Publications.

Scullard, H.H. 1974. *The elephant in the Greek and Roman world*. Ithaca: Cornell University Press.

Seibert, J. 1972. Nochmals zu Kleomenes von Naukratis. *Chiron* 2:99–102.

Seidl, Erwin. 1932. Die demotischen Zivilprozessordnung u. die griechischen Rechtsurkunden. *CdE* 7:210–26.

———. 1962. *Ptolemäische Rechtsgeschichte, Ägyptologische Forschungen* 22. Glückstadt: J. J. Augustin.

———. 1967. Der Prozeß Chrateanch gegen Tefhape im Jahre 170 v. Chr. *Zeitschrift für vergleichende Rechtswissenschaft* 69:96–117.

———. 1968. *Ägyptische Rechtsgeschichte der Saiten- und Perserzeit*. Glücksadt: J. J. Augustin.

Seidl, Erwin and B.H. Stricker. 1937. Studien zu Papyrus BM eg. 10591. *ZSS-RA* 57:272–308.

Seidlmayer, S.J. 2001. *Historische und moderne Nilstände: Untersuchungen zu den Pegelablesungen des Nils von der Frühzeit bis in die Gegenwart*. Berlin: Achet.

Sethe, Kurt and Joseph Partsch. 1920. *Demotische Urkunden zum ägyptischen Bürgschaftsrechte vorzüglich der Ptolemäerzeit*. Leipzig: B. G. Teubner.

Sewell, Jr., William H. 2005. *Logics of history: Social theory and social transformation*. Chicago: University of Chicago Press.

Shaw, Brent D. 1984. Bandits in the Roman Empire. *Past and Present* 105:3–52.

———. 1992. Under Russian eyes. *JRS* 82:216–28.

Shaw, Ian, ed. 2000. *The Oxford history of ancient Egypt*. Oxford: Oxford University Press.

Shelton, John. 1976. Land Register: Crown tenants at Kerkeosiris. In *Collectanea Papyrologica: Texts published in honor of H. C. Youtie*, ed. Ann Ellis Hanson, 111–52. Bonn: R. Habelt.

Sherwin-White, Susan. 1987. Seleucid Babylonia: A case study for the installation and development of Greek rule. In *Hellenism in the East: The interaction of Greek and non-Greek civilizations from Syria to Central Asia after Alexander*, ed. Amélie Kuhrt and Susan Sherwin-White, 1–31. Berkeley: University of California Press.

Sherwin-White, Susan and Amélie Kuhrt (1993). *From Samarkhand to Sardis: A new approach to the Seleucid Empire*. Berkeley: University of California Press.

Shipley, Graham. 2000. *The Greek world after Alexander, 323–30 BC*. London: Routledge.

Shipton, Kirsty. 2000. *Leasing and lending: The cash economy in fourth-century BC Athens*. London: Institute of Classical Studies.

Shore, A. F. and H. S. Smith. 1959. Two unpublished demotic documents from the Asyut archive. *JEA* 45:52–60.

Sidebotham, S. E. 2000. From Berenike to Koptos: Recent results of the desert route survey. *Topoi*, Supplement 3:415–38.

Sidebotham, S. E. and W. Z. Wendrich. 1996. *Berenike 1995: Preliminary report of the excavations at Berenike (Egyptian Red Sea coast) and the survey of the eastern desert*. Leiden: Research School, CNWS.

Sijpesteijn, P. J. 1987. *Customs duties in Graeco-Roman Egypt. Studia amstelodamensia ad epigraphicam ius antiquum et papyrologicam pertinentia* 17. Zutphen: Terra.

Sim, Soek-Fang. 2005. "Authoritarianism: East Asian," in *The new dictionary of the history of ideas*, vol. 1, ed. Maryanne Cline Horowitz, 175–78. Detroit: Charles Scribner's Sons. (Electronic resource.)

Simpson, R. S. 1996. *Demotic grammar in the Ptolemaic sacerdotal decrees*. Oxford: Griffith Institute.

Smith, Stuart T. 1995. *Askut in Nubia: The economics and ideology of Egyptian imperialism in the second millennium BC*. London: Kegan Paul International.

Smith, W. Stevenson. 1998. *The art and architecture of ancient Egypt*, 3rd rev ed., ed. William Kelly Simpson. New Haven: Yale University Press.

Spiegelberg, Wilhelm. 1908. *Demotische Papyrus von der Insel Elephantine*, vol. 1, *Demotische Studien* 2. Leipzig: J. C . Hinrichs.

———. 1914. *Die sogenannte demotische chronik des pap. 215 der Bibliothèque nationale zu Paris nebst den auf der rückseite des papyrus stehenden texten*. Leipzig: J. C. Hinrichs.

Springborg, Patricia. 1992. *Western republicanism and the oriental prince*. Austin: University of Texas Press.

Stadler, Martin Andreas. 2004. Rechtskodex von Hermupolis (P. Cairo JE 89127–30 + 89137–43). In *Texte aus der Umwelt des alten Testaments*, Neue Folge, vol. 1: *Texte zum Rechts- und Wirtschaftsleben*, ed. Bernd Janowski and Gernot Wilhelm, 185–207. Gütersloh: Gütersloher Verlagshaus.

Stanwick, Paul Edmund. 2002. *Portraits of the Ptolemies: Greek Kings as Egyptian Pharaohs*. Austin: University of Texas Press.

Stephens, Susan A. 2003. *Seeing Double: Intercultural poetics in Ptolemaic Alexandria*. Berkeley: University of California Press.

Stoneman, Richard. 1991. *The Greek Alexander romance*. London: Penguin Books.

Stroud, Ronald S. 1998. *The Athenian Grain-Tax Law of 374/3 B.C. Hesperia Supplement* 29. Athens: American School of Classical Studies.

Strudwick, Nigel. 1985. *The administration of Egypt in the Old Kingdom: The highest titles and their holders*. London: KPI.

Swedberg, Richard. 2003. *Principles of economic sociology*. Princeton: Princeton University Press.

Taagepera, Rein. 1978. Size and duration of empires: Growth-decline curves, 3000 to 600 B.C. *Social Science Research* 7:180–96.

————. 1979. Size and duration of empires: growth-decline curves, 600 BC–600 AD. *Social Science History* 3 3/4:115–38.

Tait, John. 1991. P. Carlsberg 236: Another fragment of a demotic legal manual. In *The Carlsberg papyri*, vol. 1: *Demotic texts from the collection*, ed. P. J. Frandsen, 93–101. Copenhagen: CNI Publications.

Tarn, W. W. and G. T. Griffith. 1952. *Hellenistic Civilisation, 3rd* ed. London: Edward Arnold.

Taubenschlag, Raphael. 1955. *The law of Greco-Roman Egypt in the light of the papyri, 332 B.C.–640 A.D.* 2nd ed, revised and enlarged. Warsaw: Panstwowe Wydawnictwo Naukowe.

Thiers, Christophe. 1999. Ptolémée Philadelphe et les prêtres de Saïs. La stèle Codex Ursinianus, fol. 6 ro + Naples 1034 + Louvre C. 123. *BIFAO* 99: 423–45.

————. 2007. *Ptolémée Philadelphe et les prêtres d'Atoum de Tjékou: Nouvelle édition commentée de la "stele de Pithom" (CGC 22183)*, Orientalia *Monspeliensia* 17. Montpellier: Université Paul Valéry-Montpellier III.

Thissen, Heinz-Joseph. 1966. *Studien zum Raphiadekret*. Beiträge zur klassichen Philologie 27. Meisenheim: Hain..

————. 1977. Zur Familie des Strategen Monkores. *ZPE* 27:181–89

————. 1980. Chronologie der frühdemotischen Papyri. *Enchoria* 10:122–25.

Thomas, J. David. 1975. *The epistrategos in Ptolemaic and Roman Egypt*, Part 1: *The Ptolemaic epistrategos, Papyrologica Coloniensia* 6. Opladen: Westdeutscherverlag.

Thompson, Dorothy B. 1973. *Ptolemaic oinochoai and portraits in faience; Aspects of the ruler-cult.* Oxford: Clarendon Press.

Thompson, Dorothy J. 1983. Nile grain transport under the Ptolemies. In *Trade in the ancient economy*, ed. P. Garnsey, K. Hopkins, and C. R. Whittaker, 64–75. Berkeley: University of California Press.

————. 1984. "Agriculture" *in* Hellenistic science: Its application in peace and war. In *CAH*, 2nd ed., vol. 7/1, 363–70. Cambridge: Cambridge University Press.

————. 1988. *Memphis under the Ptolemies*. Princeton: Princeton University Press.

————. 1994. Literacy and power in Ptolemaic Egypt. In *Literacy and power in the ancient world*, ed. Alan K. Bowman and Greg Woolf, 67–83. Cambridge: Cambridge University Press.

————. 1997a. The infrastructure of splendour: Census and taxes in Ptolemaic Egypt. In *Hellenistic constructs: Essays in culture, history and historiography*, ed. Paul Cartledge, Peter Garnsey, and Erich Gruen, 242–57. Berkeley: University of California Press.

————. 1997b. Policing the Ptolemaic countryside. In *Akten des 21. Internationalen Papyrologenkongresses, Berlin, 13.–19. 8. 1995*. Band II: *Archiv für Papyrusforschung und verwandte Gebiete*, Beihefte 3, ed. B. Kramer, 961–66. Stuttgart: Teubner.

————. 1999a. Irrigation and drainage in the early Ptolemaic Fayyum. In *Agriculture in Egypt: From pharaonic to modern times*, ed. Alan K. Bowman and Eugene Rogan, 107–22. Oxford: Oxford University Press.

Thompson, Dorothy J. 1999b. New and old in the Ptolemaic Fayyum. In *Agriculture in Egypt: From pharaonic to modern times*, ed. Alan K. Bowman and Eugene Rogan, 123–38. Oxford: Oxford University Press.

———. (2000a). A Ptolemaic *apomoira* account. In *Papyri in honorem Johannis Bingen octogenarii (P. Bingen)*, *Studia Varia Bruxellensia ad orbem Graeco-Latinum pertinentia 5*, ed. Henri Melaerts, 177–84. Leuven: Peeters.

———. 2000b. Philadelphus'procession: Dynastic power in a Mediterranean context. In *Politics, administration and society in the Hellenistic and Roman world, Proceedings of the international colloquium, Bertinoro 19–24 July 1997*, ed. Leon Mooren, 365–88. *Studia Hellenistica 36*.

———. 2001a. Hellenistic Hellenes: The case of Ptolemaic Egypt. In *Ancient perceptions of Greek ethnicity*, ed. Irad Malkin, 301–22. Cambridge, MA: Harvard University Press.

———. 2001b. *Ethnê*, taxes and administrative geography in early Ptolemaic Egypt. In *Atti del XXII Congresso internazionale di Papirologia*, vol. 2, ed. Isabella Andorlini et al., 1255–63. Florence: Istituto papirologica G. Vitelli.

———. 2008. Economic reforms in the mid-reign of Ptolemy Philadelphus II. In *Ptolemy Philadelphus and his world*, ed. Paul McKechnie and Philippe Guillaume, *Mnemosyne* Supplement 300. Leiden: E. J. Brill.

Thompson, Herbert. 1934. *A family archive from Siut from papyri in the British Museum*. Oxford: Oxford University Press.

Tietze, Christian, Eva R. Lange, and Klaus Halloff. 2005. Ein neues Exemplar des Kanopus-Dekrets aus Bubastis. *Archiv für Papyrusforschung* 51:1–30.

Tilly, Charles. 1981. *As sociology meets history*. New York: Academic Press.

———. 1985. War making and state making as organized crime. In *Bringing the state back in*, ed. Peter B. Evans, Dietrich Rueschemeyer, and Theda Skocpol, 169–91. Cambridge: Cambridge University Press.

———. 1990. *Coercion, capital, and European states, AD 990–1990*. Cambridge, MA: Harvard University Press.

Tobin, Vincent A. 2003. The tale of the eloquent peasant. In *The literature of ancient Egypt: An anthology of stories, instructions, stelae, autobiographies, and poetry*, 3rd ed., ed. William Kelly Simpson, 25–44. New Haven: Yale University Press.

Trigger, Bruce. 2003. *Understanding early civilizations*. Cambridge: Cambridge University Press.

Trigger, Bruce, B. J. Kemp, D. O'Connor and A. B. Lloyd. 1983. *Ancient Egypt. A social history*. Cambridge: Cambridge University Press.

Tsetskhladze, G. R., ed. 2006. *Greek colonization: An account of Greek colonies and other settlements overseas*, vol. 1, 25–44. Leiden: E. J. Brill.

Tuplin, Christopher. 1987. The administration of the Achaemenid empire. In *Coinage and administration in the Athenian and Persian empires: The ninth Oxford symposium on coinage and monetary history*. BAR int. series 343, 109–66. Oxford: Oxford University Press.

Turchin, Peter. 2003. *Historical dynamics: Why states rise and fall*. Princeton: Princeton University Press.

Turner, E.G. 1966. The "hanging" of a brewer. In *Essays in honor of C. Bradford Welles, American Studies in Papyrology* 1, 79–86. New Haven: American Society of Papyrologists.

———. 1974. A commander-in-chief's order from Saqqâra. *JEA* 60:239–42.

———. (1984). Ptolemaic Egypt. In *CAH*, vol. 7/1, 2nd ed., 118–74. Cambridge: Cambridge University Press.

Uebel, Fritz. 1968. *Die Kleruchen Ägyptens unter den ersten sechs Ptolemäern*, Abhandlungen der Deutschen Akademie der Wissenschaften zu Berlin, Klasse für Sprachen, Literatur und Kunst 3. Berlin.

Valbelle, Dominique. 1998. *Histoire de l'État pharaonique*. Paris: Presse universitaire de France.

Van 't-Dack, Edmond and Hans Hauben. 1978. L'apport egyptien à l'armée navale lagide. In *Das ptolemäischen Ägypten*, ed. H. Maehler and V. M. Strocka, 59–93. Mainz: Philipp von Zabern.

van de Mieroop, Marc 1997. *The ancient Mesopotamian city*. Oxford: Oxford University Press.

———. 2005. The Invention of Interest. In *The origins of value: The financial innovations that created modern capital markets*, ed. W. N. Goetzmann and K. Geert Rouwenhorst, 17–30. Oxford: Oxford University Press.

van den Boorn, G.P.F. 1988. *The duties of the vizier: Civil administration in the early New Kingdom*. London: Kegan Paul International.

van der Kooij, Arie. 2007. The Septuagint of the Pentateuch and Ptolemaic rule. In *The Pentateuch as Torah: New models for understanding its promulgation and acceptance*, ed. Gary N. Knoppers and Bernard M. Levinson, 289–300. Winona Lake, IN: Eisenbrauns.

van der Spek, Robartus J. 1995. Land ownership in Babylonian cuneiform documents. In *Legal documents of the Hellenistic world: Papers from a seminar*, ed. Markham J. Geller and Herwig Maehler, 173–245. London: Warburg Institute.

Vandier, Jacques. 1961. *Le papyrus Jumilhac*. Paris: Centre national de la recherche scientifique.

Vandorpe, Katelijn. 1994. Museum archaeology or how to reconstruct Pathyris archives. In *Acta Demotica, Acts of the Fifth International Conference for Demotists, Pisa, 4th–8th September 1993: Egitto e Vicino Oriente* 17, 289–300. Pisa: Giardini Editori e Stampatori.

———. 1995. City of many a gate, harbour for many a rebel. In *Hundred-gated Thebes*, ed. S. P. Vleeming, 203–39. Leiden: E. J. Brill.

———. 1996. Seals in and on the papyri of Greco-Roman and Byzantine Egypt. In *Archives et Sceaux du monde hellénestique, Torino, Villa Gualino 13–16 Gennaio 1993*, ed. Marie-Françoise Boussac and Antonio Invernizzi, *Bulletin de Correspondance hellénique*, Supplement 29, 231–91.

———. 1998. Interest in Ptolemaic loans of seed-corn from the "House of Hathor" (Pathyris). In *Egyptian religion, the last thousand years: Studies dedicated to the memory of Jan Quaegebeur. Orientalia Lovaniensia Analecta* 84–85, 1459–68. Louvain: Peeters.

———. 2000a. The Ptolemaic epigraphe or harvest tax (*shemu*). *AfP* 46/2: 169–232.

Vandorpe, Katelijn. 2000b. Paying taxes to the thesauroi of the Pathyrites in a century of rebellion (186–88 B.C.). *Politics, administration and society in the Hellenistic and Roman world, Proceedings of the international colloquium, Bertinoro 19–24 July 1997*, ed. Leon Mooren. *Studia Hellenistica* 36:405–36.

———. 2000c. Two agoranomic loans with demotic summary. In *Papyri in honorem Johannis Bingen Octogenarii (P. Bingen)*, Studi Varia Bruxellensia ad orbem Graeco-Latinum Pertinentia 5, ed. Henri Malaerts. Louvain: Peeters.

———. 2002. *The bilingual family archive of Dryton, his wife Apollonia and their daughter Senmouthis, Collectanea Hellenistica*, vol. 4. Brussels: Koninklijke Academie voor Wetenschappen, Letteren en Schone Kunsten van België.

———. 2004. A Greek register from Pathyris' notarial office: Loans and sales from the Pathyrite and Latopolite nomes. *ZPE* 150:161–86.

———. 2005. Agriculture, temples and tax law in Ptolemaic Egypt. *CRIPEL* 25, 165–71.

Vandorpe, Katelijn and Willy Clarysse. 2008. Egyptian bankers and bank receipts in Hellenistic and early Roman Egypt. In *Pistoi dia tèn technèn—Bankers, loans and archives in the ancient world: Studies in honour of Raymond Bogaert*, ed. Koenraad Verboven, Katelijn Vandoorpe, and Véronique Chankowski, 153–68. *Studia Hellenistica* 44.

Vandorpe, Katelijn and Willy Clarysse, eds. 2003. *Edfu. An Egyptian provincial capital in the Ptolemaic period*. Brussels: Koninklijke Vlaamse Academie van Belgïe voor Wetenschappen en Kunsten.

van Minnen, Peter. 2007. Review of Pfeiffer 2004 in *Gnomon* 79:709–13.

———. 2001. Dietary hellenization or ecological transformation? Beer, wine and oil in later Roman Egypt. In *Atti del XXII Congresso internazionale di Papirologia, Firenze, 23–29 agosto 1998*, vol. 2, ed. Isabella Andorlini et al., 1265–80. Florence: Istituto papirologica G. Vitelli.

Vasunia, Phiroze. 2001. *The Gift of the Nile: Hellenizing Egypt from Aeschylus to Alexander*. Berkeley: University of California Press.

Veïsse, Anne-Emmanuelle. 2004. *Les "Revoltes égyptiennes": Recherches sur les Troubles intérieurs en Égypte du regne de Ptolémée III Éuergete à la Conquête romaine, Studia Hellenistica* 41.

Venticinque, Philip F. 2006. What's in a name? Greek, Egyptian and biblical traditions in the *Cambyses Romance. BASP* 43:139–58.

Verbrugghe, G. P. and J. M. Wickersham. 1996. *Berossos and Manetho*. Ann Arbor: University of Michigan Press.

Vergote, Joseph. 1959. *Joseph en Égypte: Génèse Chap. 37–50 à la lumière des Études égyptologique récentes*. Louvain: Publications univérsitaires.

Verhoogt, Arthur. 1998. *Menches, Komogrammateus of Kerkeosiris: The doings and dealings of a village scribe in the late Ptolemaic period (120–110 B.C.)*. PLBat 29. Leiden: E. J. Brill.

Verner, Miroslav. 1989. La Tombe d'Oudjahorresnet et le Cimetière saïto-perse d'Abousir. *BIFAO* 89:283–90, pls. 36–39.

Vittmann, Günther. 1998. *Der demotische Papyrus Rylands 9 (ÄAT 38)*. Wiesbaden: Otto Harrassowitz.

———. 2003. *Ägypten und die Fremden im ersten vorchristlichen Jahrtausend*. Mainz: Philipp von Zabern.

Vleeming, Sven P. 1981. La phase initiale du démotique ancien. *CdE* 56:31–48.
———. 1983. Two unrecognized Greek concepts in Demotic P. BM 10597. *CdE* 58:97–99.
———. 1989. Strijd om het erfdeel van Tefhapi. In *Familiearchieven uit het land van Pharao*, ed. P. W. Pestman, 30–45. Zutphen: Terra.
———. 1991. *The gooseherds of Hou (Pap. Hou): A dossier relating to various agricultural affairs from provincial Egypt of the early fifth century* BC. Louvain: Peeters.
———. 1993. *Papyrus Reinhardt. An Egyptian land list from the tenth century* B.C., Hieratische Papyri aus den Staatliche Museen zu Berlin-Preussischer Kulturbesitz 2. Berlin: Academie Verlag.
———. 2001. *Some coins of Artaxerxes and other short texts in the demotic script found on various objects and gathered from many publication*s. Louvain: Peeters.
Vogt, J. 1971. Kleomenes von Naukratis: Herr von Ägypten. *Chiron* 1:153–57.
von Reden, Sitta. 1997. Money and coinage in Ptolemaic Egypt: Some preliminary remarks. In *Akten des 21. Internationalen Papyrologenkongresses Berlin, 13.– 19.8.1995*, ed. Bärbel Kramer et al., 1003–08. Stuttgart: Teubner.
———. 2001. The politics of monetization in third-century BC Egypt. In *Money and its uses in the ancient Greek world*. ed. Andrew Meadows and Kirsty Shipton, 65–76. Oxford: Oxford University Press.
———. 2002. Money in the ancient economy: A survey of recent research. *Klio* 84:141–74.
———. 2006. The ancient economy and Ptolemaic Egypt," in *Ancient economies, modern methodologies: Archaeology, comparative history, models, and institutions*, ed. Peter F. Bang, Mamoru Ikeguchi, and Harmut G. Ziche, 161–77. Bari: Edipuglia.
———. 2007. *Money in Ptolemaic Egypt: From the Macedonian conquest to the end of the third century* BC. Cambridge: Cambridge University Press.
Walbank, F. W. 1970. *A historical commentary on Polybius*, 3 vols. Oxford: Oxford University Press. Special edition for Sandpiper Books, 1999.
———. 1979. Egypt in Polybius. In *Glimpses of ancient Egypt: Studies in Honour of H. W. Fairman*, 180–89. Warminster: Aris and Phillips. Reprinted in Frank W. Walbank, *Polybius, Rome and the Hellenistic world: Essays and reflections*, 53–69. Cambridge: Cambridge University Press, 2002.
———. 1984. Monarchies and monarchic ideas. In *CAH*, 2nd ed., vol. 7, 62– 100. Cambridge: Cambridge University Press.
———. 1991–92. The Hellenistic world: New trends and directions. *Scripta Classica Israelica* 11:90–113.
———. 1993. Response. In *Images and ideologies: Self-definition in the Hellenistic world*, ed. A. Bulloch et. al., 116–24. Berkeley: University of California Press.
———. 1996. Two Hellenistic processions: A matter of self-definition. *Scripta Classica Israelica* 15:119–30. Reprinted in Frank W. Walbank, *Polybius, Rome and the Hellenistic world: Essays and reflections*, 79–90. Cambridge: Cambridge University Press, 2002.

Walker, Susan and Peter Higgs. 2001. *Cleopatra of Egypt: From history to myth.* Princeton: Princeton University Press.

Wångstedt, Sten V. 1954. *Ausgewählte demotische ostraka aus Sammlung des Victoria-museums zu Uppsala und der staatlichen Papyrussammlung zu Berlin.* Uppsala: Almqvist and Wiksells.

Warburton, David. 1997. *State and economy in ancient Egypt: Fiscal vocabulary of the New Kingdom.* Orbis Biblicus et Orientalis 151. Fribourg: University Press.

———. 2000. Before the IMF: The economic implications of unintentional structural adjustment in ancient Egypt. *JESHO* 43/2:65–131.

Watts, James W., ed. 2001. *Persia and Torah: The theory of imperial authorization of the Pentateuch.* Atlanta: Society of Biblical Literature.

Weber, Max [1909] 1998. *The agrarian sociology of ancient civilizations*, trans. R. I. Frank. London: Verso.

———. 1978. *Economy and society*, ed. Guenther Roth and Claus Wittich. Berkeley: University of California Press.

Welles, C. B. 1949. The Ptolemaic administration in Egypt. *JJP* 3:21–47.

Wes, M. A. 1990. *Michael Rostovtzeff, historian in exile: Russian roots in an American context*, Historia Einzelschriften 65. Stuttgart: F. Steiner.

Westbrook, Raymond. 1994. What is the Covenant Code? In *Theory and Method in Biblical and Cuneiform Law: Revision, Interpolation, and Development, Journal for the Study of the Old Testament*, Supplement Series 181, ed. Bernard Levinson, 15–36. Sheffield: Sheffield Academic Press.

Westermann, William Linn. 1938. The Ptolemies and the welfare of their subjects. *AHR* 43/2:270–87.

Whelan, Frederick G. 2001. Oriental despotism: Anquetil-du Perron's response to Montesquieu. *History of Political Thought* 22/4:619–47.

Wilcken, Ulrich. 1912. Allgemeine historische Grundzüge. In L. Mitteis and U. Wilcken, *Grundzüge und Chrestomathie der Papyruskunde*, 2 vols., 1–91. Hildesheim: Georg Olms Verlagsbuchhandlung.

———. 1921. Alexander der Grosse und die hellenistische Wirtschaft. *Schmollers Jahrbuch für Gesetzgebung, Verwaltung und Volkswirtschaft im Deutschen Reiche* 45:349–420.

———. 1935. *Urkunden der Ptolemäerzeit (Ältere Funde)*, Band 2. 1, Lieferung: Papyri aus Oberägypten. Berlin: De Gruyter.

Wilfong, Terry. 1998. The non-Muslim communities: Christian communities. In *The Cambridge History of Egypt*, vol. 1: Islamic Egypt, 640–1517, ed. Carl F. Petry, 175–97. Cambridge: Cambridge University Press.

Wilkinson, Endymion. 2000. *Chinese history: A manual*, revised and enlarged, Harvard-Yenching Institute Monograph Series 52. Cambridge: Harvard University Asia Center.

Wilkinson, Toby A. H. 2001. *Early dynastic Egypt.* London: Routledge.

Will, Edouard. 1985. Pour une 'anthropologie coloniale' du monde hellénistque. In *The craft of the ancient historian*, ed. John W. Eadie and Josiah Ober, 273–301. Lanham: University Press of America.

Williamson, Oliver E. 1983. Credible commitments: Using hostages to support exchange. *American Economic Review* 73/4:519–40.

Wilson, Andrew. 2002. Machines, power and the ancient economy. *JRS* 92:1–32.

Winnicki, Jan Krzysztof. 1978. *Ptolemäerarmee in Thebais. Archiwum Filologiczne* 38. Wroclaw: Polska Akademia Nauk.

———. 1994. Carrying off and bringing home the statues of the gods: On an aspect of the religious policy of the Ptolemies towards the Egyptians. *JJP* 24:149–90.

———. 2001. Die letzen Ereignisse des vierten syrischen Krieges: Eine neudeutung des Raphiadekrets. *JJP* 31:133–45.

Winter, F. E. 1984. Hellenistic science: Its application in peace and war. *CAH*, 2nd ed., vol. 7.1, 371–83. Cambridge: Cambridge University Press.

Wipszycka, Ewa. 1961. The *Doreā* of Apollonios the Dioiketes in the Memphite Nome. *Klio* 39:153–90.

Wirth, Gerhard. 2000. Hellas und Ägypten: Rezeption und Auseinandersetzung im 5.bzw. 4. Jht. v. Chr. In *Ägypten und der östliche Mittelmeerraum im 1. Jahrtausend v. Chr.*, ed. Manfred Görg and Günther Hölbl, *Ägypten und Altes Testament* 44, 281–319. Wiesbaden: Otto Harrassowitz.

Wittfogel, Karl. 1957. *Oriental despotism: A comparative study of total power.* New Haven: Yale University Press.

Wolff, Hans Julius. 1960. Plurality of laws in Ptolemaic Egypt. *Revue internationale des Droits de L'antiquité* 3:191–223.

———. 1962. *Das Justizwesen der Ptolemäer, Münchener Beiträge zur Papyrusforschung und antiken Rechtsgeschichte* 44. Munich:Beck. 2nd ed., 1971.

———. 1966. Law in Ptolemaic Egypt. *Essays in honor of C. Bradford Welles, American Studies in Papyrology* 1, 67–77. New Haven: American Society of Papyrologists.

———. 1978. *Das Recht der griechischen Papyri Ägyptens in der Zeit der Ptolemaeer und des Prinzipats*, vol. 1: *Bedingungen und Triebkräfte des Rechtsentwicklung*. Munich: Beck.

———. 2002. *Das Recht der griechischen Papyri Ägyptens in der Zeit der Ptolemaeer und des Prinzipats*, vol. 2: *Organisation und Kontrolle des privaten Rechtsverkehrs*. Munich: Beck.

Wong, R. Bin. (1997). *China transformed. Historical change and the limits of European experience.* Ithaca: Cornell University Press.

Yiftach-Firanko, Uri. 2008. Who killed the double document in Ptolemaic Egypt? *Archive für Papyrusforschung* 54/2: 203–18.

Yoyotte, Jean. 1969. Bakhthis: Religion égyptienne et culture grecque à Edfou. In *Religions en Égypte héllenistique et romaine, Bibliothèque des Centres d'étude supérieure spécialisés, Colloque de Strasbourg 16–18 mai 1967*, 127–141. Paris: Presses universitaires de France.

———. 1998. Pharaonica. In *Alexandria: The submerged royal quarters*, ed. Franck Goddio et al., 199–219. London: Periplus.

Zaghloul, el-H. 1994. Demotica from Qasr Ibrim: Marital problems and a love-affair in two messages written in a single letter from Ptolemaic Egypt (Papyrus Cairo JE 95205). *Bulletin of the Center for Papyrological Studies* 10:25–45.

Zauzich, Karl-Theodor. (1968). *Die ägyptische Schreibertradition in Aufbau: Sprache und Schrift der demotischen Kaufverträge aus ptolemäischer Zeit*, 2 vols., *Ägyptologische Abhandlungen* 19. Wiesbaden: Otto Harrassowitz.

———. 1991. Einleitung. In *Demotic Texts from the Collection: The Carlsberg Papyri*, vol. 1, ed. Paul John Frandsen, 1–11. Copenhagen: Museum Tusculanum Press.

———. 1999. "Zwei Orakelbitten aus Qasr Ibrim. *Enchoria* 25:178–82.

INDEX

INDEX OF SOURCES